As I Walked Out

Sabine Baring-Gould, 1834-1924
Photograph by W & D Downey (1893), Author's collection.

T0322373

As I Walked Out

Sabine Baring-Gould and the Search for the Folk Songs of Devon and Cornwall

Martin Graebe

Signal

Signal Books
Oxford

First published in 2017 by
Signal Books Limited
36 Minster Road
Oxford OX4 1LY
www.signalbooks.co.uk

A catalogue record for this book is available from the British Library

ISBN 978-1-909930-53-7 Paper

Cover Design: Tora Kelly
Production: Tora Kelly
Cover Images: Christine Molan,
Printed in India by Imprint Digital

For our grandchildren, Alfie, Eleiah, and Maya

Contents

Prologue

Dr Merriol Almond

Albert B Friedman, who according to his 2006 *New York Times* obituary helped to animate the renewed interest in traditional English and Scottish ballads, a great many years ago was my 'section man' in a freshman year college humanities course. Mr Friedman evidently held a low opinion of my great grandfather, Sabine Baring-Gould. In fact, when I first walked into his class, he greeted me with, 'Miss Baring-Gould, your grandfather was a lousy editor of ballads,' a remark I found daunting at that time.

Many years later when, after my father's death, I became responsible for Sabine Baring-Gould's family home, the Lewtrenchard estate, I met Martin Graebe who even then was able to assure me that my great grandfather was perhaps not quite as irresponsible a folksong collector as Mr Friedman had thought. I was relieved, and even more so later on when Martin told me about his discovery that Sabine had preserved his notes of the original, earthier folk song versions that Sabine had collected in the field. My understanding became that Sabine had altered then unacceptable texts not out of clerical prissiness but in order for them to be widely played and sung. Sabine had indeed respected the songs as he originally heard them and had taken care that the texts would eventually be available to future generations. Sabine, for his time, was fairly widely travelled and worldlier than, as a country clergyman, he has sometimes been believed to be.

I am extremely grateful to Martin Graebe, his wife Shan, and many others who have taken what is to me an extraordinary interest in the work and life of this unusual man. It has probably been easier at times for me to be aware of Sabine's shortcomings than his far greater strengths and virtues. We are very different people and Sabine I think would have been horrified to learn that his much loved family home would eventually become the responsibility of one of his American great granddaughters. Fortunately a number of extremely capable and interesting people have taken an interest in Sabine's work, studiously and laboriously deciphering his very difficult handwriting and researching the backgrounds for his writings. I think Professor Friedman's opinion of Sabine would at least be more nuanced if he had had the opportunity to read Martin Graebe's book.

My profound thanks to Martin and Shan and many others for their studies of the intellectual legacy of Sabine Baring-Gould. I hope you will enjoy Martin's book.

West Hartford, Connecticut
March 2017

Foreword

Steve Roud

In the small world of folk song scholarship, and the larger world of English music in general, we owe a great deal to the Victorian and Edwardian collectors who first recognised the value of traditional song and music, and who enthusiastically gathered what they could of what they were well aware was a rapidly dying art form. They defined the territory of folk song, mapped its terrain, and with their extensive manuscript collections and publications formed the bedrock of our discipline.

Sabine Baring-Gould was one of the very first, years before there was a movement to support and inspire him, which makes his achievement even more remarkable. Others had the benefit of his lectures and publications and followed his lead, but he was forced to invent the role of 'song collector' from scratch.

He spent countless hours in the field, in pubs and cottages, and amassed a huge collection of songs which was second only in size to that made later by Cecil Sharp, and was the only one to concentrate on Devon and Cornwall. Because he had a slightly wider definition of traditional song, and was a crucial decade or so earlier in the field, his work provides a more rounded picture of local repertoires than many of the other collectors. His antiquarian interests prompted him to devote considerable time, in his study and in the British Museum, to making a significant start at documenting the history and development of folk and popular song genres.

He combined the skills of the fieldworker and the scholar, and was definitely one of our key founding fathers.

We are only gradually getting to know our predecessors properly. Biographies of some of the major figures have appeared over the years, but most of these are concerned with those who were famous in other musical spheres, such as Ralph Vaughan Williams, George Butterworth and Percy Grainger. Useful as these books are, their subjects' folk song activities are usually treated superficially because the biographers lacked expertise in that area and, to be truthful, any real interest in it. Previous biographies of Baring-Gould have covered the broad sweep of his many other interests, without touching on his folk song collecting in any great detail.

This state of affairs is particularly regrettable because we know that many of them thought their 'folk song work' to be of national significance, and indeed both Baring-Gould and Vaughan Williams declared late in life that in their long careers it was saving the old songs of the people that was the achievement of which they were most proud.

Martin Graebe's work is therefore particularly welcome, in bringing Baring-Gould's folk song work centre stage and demonstrating how much it was part of his life and how it fitted into his countless other intellectual interests and enthusiasms.

The chapter on his musical collaborators, Frederick Bussell and Henry Fleetwood Sheppard, is also valuable in bringing two other important figures out of the shadows, and Martin demonstrates that Baring-Gould's writings show how fond he was of his 'old singing men and women', to a degree not found in the other collectors' notebooks. Despite his privileged social position as squire and parson, he never underestimated the contribution of the labouring people to the cultural life of rural England.

In the first decades of the twentieth century, the song and music of the people was much in the news, where it was seriously presented as having a significance well beyond its aesthetic qualities. It was widely seen as an essential element in a much-needed English Musical Renaissance, as a way to transform our education system and to reconnect the wider population with its traditional musical culture, and as making a significant contribution to the growing cultural nationalism in the run-up to the Great War.

As I Walked Out is not only a major contribution to the history of folk song studies, but illuminates an important strand in the wider cultural world of Victorian and Edwardian England and the part that Sabine Baring-Gould, the archetypal 'gentleman scholar', played in this world.

STEVE ROUD is a former local studies librarian who has written a number of books on English folklore and on folk song, including the *New Penguin Book of English Folk Songs* (2012), which he co-edited with Julia Bishop. He is the compiler of the Roud Folk Song Index, an online database containing the details of more than 200,000 songs, which is to be found on the website of the Vaughan Williams Memorial Library.

Introduction

Baring-Gould and Me (a Journey Towards Obsession)

I cannot remember exactly when I came across the name of Sabine Baring-Gould for the first time, though I know that it was attached to one of his hymns or carols. I would like to believe that it was on the sheet music of 'Gabriel's Message', his reworking of the lovely Basque carol which has been one of my favourites since I first sang it in the school choir. It may, though, have been one of his hymns: 'Now the Day is Over', 'Onward, Christian Soldiers' or 'Daily, Daily Sing the Praises'. It was not hard, then, to imagine what he looked like, even without seeing one of his sternly posed photographs. There was, of course, no question that it was a 'him', even with the rather strange forename. In the 1960s the prefix of 'Rev' made gender a certainty. When we did see photographs of the hymn-writers they were all black and white (and would have been even if shot with colour film). They were forbidding and undeserving of our interest when test pilots, racing drivers, footballers and pop stars demanded our attention.

It was not long, though, before the name came back to my notice. My school had a bright idea to deal with the problem of what to do with the older students who had finished their 'O' or 'A' level exams. We were sent off on 'Initiative Week'. With a couple of pounds in our pockets and a rucksack on our backs, we went out in pairs to complete a project of our choice somewhere in England. I had recently discovered Dartmoor while staying with my cousin at Princetown where her husband was then working at the prison. I persuaded my friend that a project on Dartmoor would be a really good idea and so we hitchhiked to Ivybridge and then walked, first to Princetown and then over to Buckfastleigh, stopping to look at old mine workings and prehistoric remains along the way. From there we headed into Plymouth and to the Central Library to do the research that would justify our trip. Baring-Gould came to our rescue and we shamelessly copied passages from his books on Devon and Dartmoor so that we could nonchalantly talk of our studies of stone rows, kistvaens and hut circles. I am not sure whether a school would nowadays be allowed so blatantly to expose its children to danger in order to save on teaching resources and catering costs. But the damage was done. I had been infected with Dartmooritis and this dangerous disease, which also affected Baring-Gould, was to determine the course of my career and my life.

As I was completing my studies at the National College of Food Technology I was faced with the reality that I needed a job. In the end it was a choice between doing quality control on cakes for Mr Kipling near Southampton or research and development for Ambrosia rice pudding based in Exeter. The prospect of being on Dartmoor's doorstep decided it and I thought I could afford a couple of pleasant years in Devon before getting a proper job. After all, how much research could there be to do on rice pudding? I stayed there twenty years. When the laboratory was moved to the factory site at Lifton, in West Devon, I also moved to live on Dartmoor's northern edge with a commute that took me twice a day past the majestic row of tors that stretches from Okehampton to Tavistock before driving up and along Lew Down, with Baring-Gould's parish of Lew Trenchard nestling into the slope below. I did not know then that I was also driving past the doors of cottages that had once been the homes to some of the men and women who sang their songs for him.

I had been introduced to folk songs at school and developed that interest further while at college so that when I arrived in Devon I started to visit the folk song clubs. It was not long before the name of Baring-Gould cropped up again, this time as the principal collector of songs in Devon and Cornwall. His name was not universally blessed, since the orthodox view was that he had changed the songs too much, leaving out the naughty bits (though that did not seem to stop people singing them). As part of my induction into Devonshire life I bought a number of Baring-Gould's books about the county and invested in the first of my copies of his *Songs of the West*. I also made visits to see the manuscript copies of the unaltered songs that he had given to the Plymouth Library. Within a few years I had acquired a reputation for knowing something about Baring-Gould and was asked to do some workshops and talks about his song collection. And so it began.

The moment at which my interest was transformed to near-obsession can be determined to within a few minutes. In 1989 I was asked by Paul Wilson and Marilyn Tucker of Wren Music to join them in a show to mark the centenary of the first publication of *Songs of the West* which was put on as part of the Okehampton Summer Festival. Apart from singing, my role was to construct a narrative based on Baring-Gould's writing, to link the show together and to impersonate him by reading some of the quotations. The show worked well and over the next two years we performed it around Devon with enough success to convince us that we should make a recording of it. We chose to do this as a live performance in the library at Killerton House, near Exeter, where the greater part of Baring-Gould's collection of books was then housed. We did two shows so that we could extract the best of each for the final version.

During the break between the two performances we were entertained to a meal by Denise Melhuish who manages the house for the National Trust. Before we started the second show, she showed us some of the books which visitors were not normally allowed to handle. My heart started beating faster when she took out one of three large, handwritten volumes of songs which I recognised to be similar to the manuscript books of songs that Baring-Gould had given to Plymouth Library. Being quite familiar by then with the Plymouth manuscripts, I also realised that this was a much bigger collection. I will write more about those manuscripts later in the book, but that was the moment, at about 6:30 on the evening of 22 March 1992, when the course of my life changed and I started down the path that has led to me writing this book.

I started to visit Killerton House to work with the manuscripts, aiming to catalogue them and to understand what Baring-Gould had done. On one of those later visits Denise surprised me again when she asked, 'Did I tell you about the boxes in the basement?' These turned out to be 36 large boxes that contained, among some general detritus from Baring-Gould's collection, a number of notebooks (including more folk songs), albums, letters, printers' proofs and other papers. These papers were transferred to the Devon Record Office (now the Devon Heritage Centre) in Exeter, where they have since been examined by me and by other scholars of Baring-Gould and his work, and have helped considerably in increasing our understanding of him. Two projects carried out with Wren Music and the English Folk Dance and Song Society have made Baring-Gould's folk song manuscripts freely accessible online to anyone who wishes to consult them.

We cannot pinpoint the date and time of the pricking of Baring-Gould's interest in the old and the odd with the same degree of accuracy, but we can get within a few weeks. In October 1843 his father took him to Mannheim, chosen so that the boy could attend an English school run by a Mr Lovell, while the family wintered in the town. One of the texts that he had to study was a book of general mythology in which he discovered the stories of the Northern Gods and heroes. He says: 'The Gods of Asgard laid hold of my imagination at once; classical mythology little interested me. Thus originated my devotion to Scandinavia, never to leave me.' He was nine years old at the time and this reading choice was to influence the course of his life over the next eighty years. We shall see how his childhood interest developed into the quest of an antiquarian and philologist, discovering ancient beliefs, tales, songs and artefacts and passing them on through his writing to a wider public.

After his death in January 1924, just short of his ninetieth birthday, Baring-Gould sank from public view and history formed a generally unfavourable impression of him as a man who wrote too much and imperfectly. As a folk song collector he was demonised as a bowdleriser. But some of his novels like *Mehalah* and *In the Roar of the Sea* have never been out of print. Likewise his *Book of Werewolves* and *Curiosities of Olden Times* have sold steadily, the former being an important prop for the industry that has grown up around the cult of vampirism and lycanthropy. The bibliography of Baring-Gould's works lists more than 1,200 books and articles. These publications reveal his magpie mind at work on an astonishing range of topics from complex questions of theology, through topography and biography to the mundane, such as 'Ovens and Stoves' and 'My Umbrella'.

In his own opinion, however, it was his work on the traditional songs of Devon and Cornwall on which he placed the highest value. He wrote: 'To this day I consider that the recovery of our West-Country melodies has been the principal achievement of my life.' Baring-Gould was the first of the large-scale collectors of folk song in England. Over two decades, working with his colleagues, Frederick Bussell and Henry Fleetwood Sheppard, and with contributions from many others, he compiled a collection of approaching two thousand songs, though it will never now be possible to give the number with precision. The songs that he noted down in Devon and Cornwall are a unique record of what the ordinary people of the two counties were singing at that time – and of what had been sung by their parents and grandparents.

There have been a number of biographies written about Baring-Gould, to support his own incomplete reminiscences, but even that by his grandson, Bickford Dickinson, failed to get through the barriers that this private man used to hide his own thoughts and feelings. The discovery of the 'Killerton Hoard' has given researchers and writers a considerable amount of new material to work with. One of the most important items in the collection was a diary, which Baring-Gould kept between 1880 and 1899. Like many diarists, he was initially very enthusiastic, but his entries became more intermittent as time passed and indeed the diary ends abruptly in the middle of a letter he was writing. It is particularly frustrating that there is no mention of folk song collecting at all. The diary has been transcribed and studied extensively by Dr Ronald Wawman, and his book, *Never Completely Submerged*, which includes his transcription of the 1880 Diary-Notebook as well as extensive annotations and additional information, has proved an indispensable resource when trying to piece together the time-line of Baring-Gould's life. Wawman's medical training and experience as a psychiatrist has enabled him to draw conclusions that might have passed others by. As well as his book, a website of the same title contains his transcriptions of a number of letters and texts with his helpful interpretations, which are of enormous value to those trying to understand Baring-Gould's life and work.

Since the emergence of the Killerton material a number of other manuscripts and family letters have been made public. This new material means that we are better able to draw conclusions about Baring-Gould's private beliefs as well as extending our knowledge of his life and work. A number of new studies have emerged as a result, but there is still much to do.

This book is not intended to be a complete biography of this extraordinary man. Indeed, writing such a thing would require familiarity with so many specialised areas of knowledge that the man or woman who succeeds in writing it will necessarily be an (almost) equally extraordinary person. While I have included some biographical information to provide the necessary context (and in doing so have included some new material arising from my own research) the main thrust of the book is to look in some depth at his work on folklore and traditional song.

The song collection was, in reality, a huge collaborative project. It involved hundreds of people and Baring-Gould operated at the centre of a network, driving the project forward over more than twenty years. It follows that this is a book in which names are important and in which you will find several: the singers, the friends, neighbours and colleagues, the people who sent him songs and stories. A name is a hook upon which a memory can be hung – that is why we put the names of our dead on gravestones and on war memorials. Memories of some of the singers and the ordinary people who played their part in ensuring that the songs were recorded for our future enjoyment might have been lost altogether if Baring-Gould had not recorded their names. For some, the name becomes a key that, through the study of public records and contemporary newspapers, unlocks some of the detail of their lives. He thought it important that they should be remembered and recognised. So do I. One of the greatest pleasures of this part of my research has been contacting and talking to descendants of the singers and of some of the other people who played a part in the story of Baring-Gould's song collection.

Of almost equal importance are the places associated with Baring-Gould. The first among these places is, of course, Lew Trenchard and his home for the greater part of his life, Lew House. In the 1970s, when I was working nearby, the house was, as it has been for much of the time since Baring-Gould's death, a hotel. His granddaughter Cecily Briggs and her family were then running what is now the Lewtrenchard Manor Hotel. It was, it must be said (but affectionately), a rather ramshackle operation at that time. More than once I saw the gardener working outside as I drove up and then, miraculously, I discovered his twin serving my drinks and sandwiches in his waiter's uniform. Jim was a remarkable quick-change artist. It was at this time that I met Baring-Gould's great-granddaughter, Merriol Almond, who is now responsible for the Baring-Gould estate and makes regular visits from her home in America to oversee its management. I still enjoy visiting Lew Trenchard and, it must be said, the hotel is now much more luxurious and efficiently organised. While I cannot, as Baring-Gould could, call that lovely valley my home, it is a place for peaceful recuperation.

But other places are important as well. Baring-Gould himself believed that it was necessary to spend time in a place that he was writing about to study its history, meet its people and to get a feeling for it. This ability to recreate that sense of a place was one of the skills that strengthened his novels and stories and made much of his non-fiction lively and readable. Like many other biographers I have found that understanding often comes through the feet as well as through the eyes and ears. To tell his story I have found it helpful to walk in his footsteps, so I have visited the places where he lived in England as well as the locations for key life events and the settings for his books. I have followed much of the route that he took for his journey in Iceland, though in a large 4 x 4 vehicle rather than on a pony. I have also travelled in Europe, often with one of his books in hand, finding the places that he wrote about and witnessing the changes that have taken place. And, of course, I have looked for the places in Devon and Cornwall where he met his singers, though many of the old inns have closed or have become places to eat rather than to enjoy a few songs with friends round a good fire with a glass or two of beer.

I have not read everything that Baring-Gould wrote, though over the years I have read a lot of it. Many of his books are easy to find, as they have been repeatedly re-published. Some others are much harder to get hold of. I have been fortunate in that the internet has made it possible to read many of his books on-line. It is also possible to find many of his magazine articles in the databases of journals available on the internet.

At the time of his death in 1924 Baring-Gould's reputation was high and he was still held in great affection by the reading public, though it had been some years since he had published any of the fiction that brought him large numbers of readers. His work on folk song was also highly regarded and his fellow song collectors spoke of him warmly. But over the next few years the most influential of them died: Cecil Sharp a few months after Baring-Gould in 1924, Frank Kidson in 1926, and Lucy Broadwood in 1929. They left a void, which was filled by new leaders with a new agenda and approach. In the run-up to the Second World War attitudes to the Victorian and Edwardian folk song collectors were starting to change. After the war, as a new, leftward-leaning folk song revival gathered pace there was less regard for the vicars and middle-class ladies and gentlemen who had noted down the songs of the working classes and, it was said, appropriated them for their own purposes. Baring-Gould has come in for more than his share of criticism, perhaps because he was more open than other collectors about his editing practices or perhaps, simply, because he had a posh name.

In recent years some of the definitions and theories that have guided our understanding of folk song have been challenged as the evidence of history and of social context has been looked at more carefully. This evidence, together with the additional material that has come to light, creates an opportunity to look afresh at Sabine Baring-Gould as a man, as a collector of folklore and folk song, and as the remarkable Victorian polymath that he undoubtedly was.

Helpful Information

The name, Sabine

The pronunciation of Baring-Gould's forename causes a lot of difficulty and I hear it pronounced in many different ways. The forename 'Sabine' is still used within the Baring-Gould family and his great-granddaughter, Merriol Almond, has assured me that the name was (and is) pronounced 'say bin'. He took that name from his distinguished great-uncle, General Sir Edward Sabine (1788–1883), whose sister, Diana Amelia, had married Baring-Gould's grandfather, William. Sir Edward fought the Americans in the War of 1812 before becoming an arctic explorer and a leading figure in the Royal Society and its scientific work, specialising in geomagnetism. As well as his great nephew, and a number of namesakes in subsequent generations, he has three species of bird and a crater on the Moon named after him.

Baring-Gould's Memory

It is important to say, at this early stage, that Baring-Gould was extraordinarily bad with numbers and dates. Sabine himself recognised this difficulty, which is why, in 1871, he wrote to his father saying that he was having trouble with dates – including his own age – and asking him for a list of the key dates in his life, so that he could write them up in a family bible. This useful list of dates has survived as a copy and is reproduced in Ron Wawman's book *Never Completely Submerged*. This inadequacy on Baring-Gould's part has been a constant problem in establishing the sequence of events and has frequently caused some bad language to pass my lips. Where Baring-Gould's errors have required it, I have noted the occurrence and made the appropriate correction. Lest anyone doubts that Baring-Gould's lapses could be extreme, let me give an example. His *A Book of Fairy Tales* was published in October 1894 and he gave his fourteen-year-old daughter, Barbara, a copy for Christmas. The inscription reads: 'Barbara Baring-Gould with much love from her father, Xmas 1893'.

He certainly had a remarkable memory, stored with millions of facts, but it was the memory of a magpie, not a well-ordered mind. This is a reason for the inconsistency in some of his anecdotes, but here there is another factor – his penchant for storytelling. His half-brother, Arthur, summed this up by saying, in his unpublished memoir, 'I don't think that Sabine ever told a story just as it happened, but must needs colour it up a little.'

Pre-Decimal Currency in the UK

In places I have quoted prices or other financial information. Most readers born before the late 1960s will have some memory of pre-decimal currency in the United Kingdom. As a reminder for them (and a brief introduction to younger readers) the main units (and their symbols) were the Pound (£), the Shilling (s) and the Penny (d). There were twenty shillings in the pound and twelve pence in the shilling (so 240 pence in the pound). Other commonly used coins were the Half-Crown (2s 6d) and the Florin (2s). You will also encounter the Guinea (£1 1s), which was a unit of pricing used in high-class businesses. Some of Baring-Gould's fees were paid to him in guineas.

Names and Their Spellings in the Book

As a rule I have tried to use the spellings and names of places that Baring-Gould used himself. These often differ from the name given in both modern and Victorian sources. Where it is impossible to be certain, I've gone for 'best guess'.

Baring-Gould did not always get people's names right. I have adopted, where appropriate, the name by which they appear in the census, newspapers or other public records. Where a person's name appears in a direct quote from Baring-Gould it is given as quoted. Otherwise, when referring to that person, the name will be given in its 'official' form, having noted the difference in the text. A few specific examples are given below.

Place Names

Lew Trenchard – A difficult choice. Baring-Gould himself wrote 'Lew Trenchard' in his books and at the head of his letters, so I have chosen to use this spelling. Ordnance Survey maps from his time give 'Lewtrenchard', as do modern maps. Baring-Gould would often abbreviate the name to 'Lew'.

Lew Down – Baring-Gould gives the name of both the village and the ridge on which it is situated as 'Lew Down'. Both Victorian and modern maps give it as 'Lewdown'.

Lew House – Though now known as 'Lewtrenchard Manor Hotel' the house was known as 'Lew House' by Baring-Gould and appears as such on Victorian maps.

Widecombe-in-the-Moor – The town appears on both Victorian and modern maps as Widecombe-in-the-Moor. This was usually abbreviated to Widecombe.

Widdicombe Fair (the song) – Baring-Gould demonstrates his inconsistency by giving the title of the song as both Widdicombe Fair and

Widdecombe Fair in different places in all versions of *Songs of the West*. In his *Further Reminiscences* he names it Widecombe Fair, and this is modern usage for the fair itself. The majority of references to the song however are to Widdicombe Fair.

People

Baring-Gould – Baring-Gould was not consistent in the use of the hyphen in his name. The hyphenated form is that which he used 'officially' and which I have used throughout the book.

Woodridge, John – One of Baring-Gould's principal singers, whom he consistently calls 'Woodrich'. His name appears as 'Woodridge' in the census and in the court report. It is also the spelling used by his descendants,

1: Early Life (1834–64)

When I was a boy, the pretty milkmaids with their glittering cans went into the field or to the stable to drain the cows, and sang ballads as they pulled with two hands as though ringing a pair of bells. Now, not a milkmaid exists. The men have to do the milking whilst the maids are strumming on pianos.[1]

Father and Son – The Wandering Years – Schooling – Further Education – The Runaway – Through Frost and Fire

Father and Son

There is no clear report of the accident in Madras in 1830 that dislocated Lieutenant Edward Baring-Gould's hip. His son tells us that he was driving in his dog-cart with a friend, after a good dinner in the regimental mess, when the vehicle overturned and his friend landed on top of him, though another account puts it down to a simple riding accident. This is typical of the diversity of accounts that we must deal with when looking at the life of that son, Sabine Baring-Gould, and we will encounter this difficulty many times as we travel together through this book.

Fig. 1.1 – Edward BaringGould in his cavalry uniform, from *Early Reminiscences*.

---

1   Sabine Baring-Gould, *Early Reminiscences* (London: John Lane The Bodley Head, 1923), p. 327.

The medical attention received by Edward Baring-Gould in Madras was poor and he was left with a permanent limp. As a result, he chose to leave India and the cavalry regiment of the East India Company in which he had been serving to return to England and to the family home, Lew House, in the parish of Lew Trenchard, on the north-west corner of Dartmoor. Here his father, William Baring-Gould, persuaded him to agree to sell the family's estates in South Devon. Such a sale required the permission of the son because of an entail intended to protect the estate from being split up. William was a handsome man (known as 'The Devonshire Adonis') and was renowned for his sweet temper, but he was permanently impoverished by his penchant for 'get-rich-quick' schemes. Edward agreed to his father's proposal and the money raised by the sale of the land was shared between father and son, helping the one to settle his debts and relieving the other from the necessity of having to return to military life or, indeed, from ever having to earn his living again.

For a time Edward Baring-Gould wandered, travelling to Europe and to the United States of America. He was, like his father, a handsome man, six feet tall and fair-haired. When he was courting his future wife, Sophia Charlotte Bond, her sisters gave him the nickname of 'The Silver Poplar'. The couple married in 1832 and settled into a house in Exeter. Their first child, whom they christened Sabine, was born there on 28 January 1834.[2] His unusual first name was given as a mark of respect to General Sir Edward Sabine, who was Sophia's uncle. Sir Edward had fought in the Americas before becoming a polar explorer and a president of the Royal Society. He was to prove a strong influence on the child, since he aroused his interest in science and encouraged him to take a scientific approach to his antiquarian studies.

The Wandering Years

Shortly after the son and prospective heir to the Baring-Gould estate was born the family moved to Bratton Clovelly, a few miles north of Lew Trenchard, to be close to his grandparents. If you walk eastwards out of the village you will cross a little stream, at which point a large house called 'Eversfield' can be seen on a rise to your left.[3] This is where the family set up their home.

2　Baring-Gould described his birthplace as 'a corner house in Dix's Field', but the current consensus is that he was actually born a few yards away at 1 Chichester Place. See Hazel Harvey, 'The House where Sabine was born?', *Sabine Baring-Gould Appreciation Society Newsletter,* 27 (June 1998), p. 8.

3　In September 2012 Eversfield, with its nine bedrooms, four reception rooms, four bathrooms, stables, a cottage and other extensive outbuildings, was offered for sale at an asking price of £1.7 million.

The Baring-Goulds engaged a young local woman, Ann Bickle, to act as nurse to Sabine. We know that she was married with a baby of her own and we can assume that she was, in fact, a wet nurse. Sabine's mother, Sophia, in common with many women of her class, had no wish to divert her energy into child-raising or to risk physical change by nursing a child. For Ann, like many young women of her time and class, the opportunity to be paid a reasonable wage and to be fed well so that she could feed the son and heir of a well-to-do family was some compensation for the pain of leaving her own child in the care of her husband and family.

There was a stream running through the garden of the house and a little wooden bridge that led to the village. One day, while Ann was crossing the bridge, carrying the baby, it broke and she fell into the stream. Reacting quickly, she lifted the child above her and protected him from the stones and water, though she herself was badly bruised and shaken. Sophia comforted the crying child and thanked the injured girl profusely for protecting him. The family were profoundly grateful to Ann for having, as they saw it, saved Sabine's life and she remained in their employ for three more years, before returning to live permanently with her husband and son in nearby Thrushelton.

In later years, Baring-Gould and his siblings would visit her at her husband's farm, where she would tell them stories. He describes the pleasure he took in drinking milk from her special mug, in the bottom of which a china frog was revealed as the milk was drained. Ann Bickle was an important influence on Baring-Gould's future development and interests, not just because of the time that she spent with him, nor even because she saved his life, but because of the fact that she sang to him and through the impact that her songs had on him. When he was collecting folk songs in middle age he received a number of songs sent in by ladies and gentlemen who recalled the nursery rhymes and children's songs that their nurses had sung to them. Like them, Baring-Gould remembered some of Ann Bickle's songs and reconstructed a few of them. One of these was 'My Ladye's Coach', a ballad that tells the story of the murderous Lady Howard who rides in her coach constructed with the bones of her four dead husbands. She travels at midnight from Tavistock to Okehampton to try to pluck every blade of grass from the Castle mound to atone for her wickedness.

My ladye hath a sable coach
And horses two and four
My ladye hath a black blood hound
That runneth on before

My ladye's coach hath nodding plumes
The driver hath no head
My ladye is an ashen white
As one that long was dead

She offers lifts to travellers along the way, but you would be foolish to accept. A strange song, perhaps, to sing to a young child and it clearly made an impression on the boy. He published it in his first song collection, *Songs of the West*, acknowledging that he got it from Ann Bickle.[4]

The Baring-Goulds' second child, Margaret, was born at Eversfield in March 1835 and then the third, William, in October 1836. But Edward Baring-Gould was getting restless. For a man used to an active military life the constraints of country living were proving irksome. He could not find in the countryside men who shared his interests and attitudes. So, in July 1837, the family boarded a steamer headed for Bordeaux on the first of the series of European journeys that would occupy most of Sabine Baring-Gould's childhood. After some weeks in Bayonne they moved on to spend the winter in Pau and then the spring in Montpellier.

The family stayed in the South of France until July 1839, when they were called home because of the illness of Admiral Bond, Sophia's father. By the time they got home he had rallied, but he finally succumbed the following October. The family spent another dreary winter in Bratton Clovelly before leasing The Castle at Bude, a fine house created by the Cornish inventor Sir Goldsworthy Gurney. The delights of the seaside soon paled, however and in the autumn they left England again, this time meandering for nearly four years through Germany, Switzerland, Italy and Austria.

Edward Baring-Gould was a firm disciplinarian and imposed strict rules on his children. Baring-Gould describes, for example, how his father would search the family coach before they set off on another leg of their journey and remove any collections of small objects that his son had made and hidden beneath the cushions.[5] His system for raising children included the belief that imagination was unhealthy for the childish mind, and young Sabine was not permitted to read fairy stories, which his father thought particularly unsuitable.

---

4 'My Ladye's Coach' was song number 30 in the early editions of *Songs of the West*. It was omitted from the 1905 edition. The antique spelling was dropped in later manuscript entries.

5 This procedure is described by Baring-Gould in his novel, *The Pennycomequicks*, 3 vols (London: Spencer Blackett and Hallam, 1889), I, pp. 249–51.

Schooling

In the winter of 1843, the family settled in Mannheim, specifically to allow Sabine, now nearly ten years old, to attend Dr Henry Lovell's English school, which had been set up there in 1836 for the sons of English gentlemen resident in the city. Here he was given books to read that opened new horizons to him. In old age he wrote:

> Never can I forget the delight afforded me by Simrock's 'Rheinsagen'. To the present day I see before my eyes Charlemagne looking dreamily into the waters into which the ring of Fastrada had been cast; and the Lorelei on her rock luring boats over to destruction. That book, read whilst I was but a child, impressed my whole life with delight in historical and legendary lore.[6]

The next stage of this story is predictable. Although his father controlled his reading at home, the boy went willingly to school so that he could explore the new world he had discovered, reading the forbidden books in their original German or French.

In his teenage years libraries would become his refuge, and when they were abroad he found several such as the one attached to the English church in Pau. It was here that he discovered Samuel Laing's translation of the *Heimskringla*: 'that wonderful chronicle of the Kings of Norway' which 'gave me an ineradicable craving to know Icelandic and to travel to Scandinavia'. He admitted, though, that his greatest enjoyment was gained from the medieval heroic romances that he discovered. He filled his head with tales of knight errantry, ghost stories, romances, love adventures and tales of all sorts.[7] He also discovered the fairy tales of the French aristocratic writers and the household tales of the Grimm brothers. His reading provided him with a basis for his style, a stock of plots and the love of a good story that would make him one of England's most popular authors in later years.

In the autumn of 1844 the family settled in London and, at the age of ten, Baring-Gould was sent to King's College School, which was then situated in a damp basement in Somerset House. In the following year his parents moved to Warwick, to enjoy the company of friends they had

---

6   Sabine Baring-Gould, *Early Reminiscences*, p. 105. The book referred to is a collection made by Karl Simrock of poems based on legends of the Rhineland. Fastrada was the wife of Charlemagne and possessed a magical ring that filled the heart of the beholder with love for the possessor. After her death, the ring was cast into the Rhine and Charlemagne came to revere its resting place in the river at Aachen as much as he had loved his wife.

7   Sabine Baring-Gould, *Early Reminiscences*, p. 252.

made in Switzerland, leaving him as a boarder at the school until, in the winter of 1845–46 he was taken ill with the bronchitis that was to be a problem for the rest of his life. He was removed to Warwick, where he was put into the grammar school as a day-boy. Then, in October 1846, his grandfather died and Edward and Sophia left immediately for Lew Trenchard to make the necessary arrangements and for Edward to take charge of the Lew Trenchard Estate. The children were left at Warwick, in the care of a governess.

The following year Sabine and his brother William caught whooping cough and had to be removed from school. It was thought that his lungs had been further damaged and, on the advice of a prominent London physician, Edward decided that despite the poor condition that the estate had been left in by his father there was no great urgency to deal with the situation, and that a winter in Pau might cure his son's illness. A tutor was engaged and the family set out for France in September 1847. They had not chosen the best time to travel in France, however, and although they avoided most of the action of the 1848 Revolution, they found themselves caught up in the 'June Days Uprising' as they made their way homeward. They were frequently taken for aristocrats and were forced to stand and cry *Vive la République!* before they were allowed to continue their journey.

In October 1849, after a year at Lew Trenchard, the state of Sabine's lungs once more gave the excuse for a journey to Pau, with a new tutor, the governess, a groom and a carriage and pair.[8] They stayed for a year at Pau where a third son, Edward Drake Baring-Gould, was born in May 1850. It was while the family were staying at Pau that Sabine, at the age of sixteen, discovered the remains of a Roman villa near the river at Gan. He led an excavation of the villa and made some beautifully coloured drawings of the mosaic floors that he uncovered. These drawings have survived among his papers. Sabine's father sent his son's notes and drawings to London and an account of his work was published in the *Illustrated London News* (See Plate 2).[9]

For a while the dig became a tourist attraction but, in the end, the remains were taken under the care of the local authorities who, Baring-Gould tells us, failed to protect them from souvenir hunters and from the

---

8   Baring-Gould's tutor for this journey was William Elliott Hadow, who, in 1851, became a curate in Tavistock. He later moved to Gloucestershire and was for many years the vicar of South Cerney. His son, Sir William Henry Hadow was a noted musician and educator and his daughter, Grace, a leading Suffragist.

9   'Discovery of a Roman Villa', *Illustrated London News*, 15 June 1850, pp. 430 and 432.

winter rains. Nothing can be seen of the remains today, as the site is now beneath a housing estate. This work sparked an interest in archaeology that re-emerged in later years when he carried out important investigations on Dartmoor and elsewhere.

The family spent the winter of 1850–51 in Bayonne. When a ship from Devonshire docked there, Edward Baring-Gould invited the captain to dinner. The family enjoyed his company, his rich Devonshire accent and some good old songs, including 'The Bay of Biscay' and 'Give me the Punch Ladle'. Edward contributed to the singing as well with an old hunting song, 'A Southerly Wind and a Cloudy Sky'. Sabine carried out another archaeological investigation at Cambo, a few miles from Bayonne, where he found the remains of an ancient camp. His findings were set out in a letter to Sir Henry Ellis and presented, by Sir Henry, at a meeting of the Society of Antiquaries before being published in their journal.[10]

Edward Baring-Gould took an interest in local culture and it is reported that while the family was staying in Bayonne he commissioned a local schoolmaster to make a collection of Basque dance tunes. His son recalled this on hearing Bizet's *Carmen*, many years later, but I have not yet found a copy of this collection.[11]

Further Education

That winter had been bad for farming in Devon and brought to a head the problems with the estate that Edward had been trying to ignore. The family returned to England in May 1851 and, because Lew House had been let, rented temporary accommodation in Tavistock. Dartmoor was on the doorstep and now, at the age of seventeen, Sabine was able to explore it on his pony, looking at many of the prehistoric remains on the moor and sketching them. This was the beginning of a love affair which was to last throughout his life, and he would return to Dartmoor whenever possible for physical and spiritual refreshment.

It was on one of these journeys that he had an experience that, although he did not recognise it at the time, would be of great significance in later years. He had been out for several days, staying at small inns, one of which was the Oxenham Arms in South Zeal, on the north-eastern edge of the moor. He gave an account of this visit in an article that he wrote for the *English Illustrated Magazine* in 1892.

---

10 Sabine Baring Gould, 'Account of the Remains of an Ancient Camp near Bayonne', *Archaeologia*. 34 (January 1852), pp. 399–402.
11 Ian Bradley, *The Daily Telegraph Book of Carols* (London: Continuum, 2006), p. 71. Dr Bradley was not able to recall for me where he discovered this information.

Fig. 1.2 – Sabine Baring-Gould aged about Seventeen (Courtesy of Merriol Almond and Devon Heritage Centre).

That day happened to have been pay day at a mine on the edge of the moor, and the miners had come to spend their money at the tavern. The room in which they caroused was the old hall of the mansion. The great fire-place had logs and peat burning in it, not that a fire was needed in summer, but, because this room served also as kitchen. The rafters and old timber of roof and walls were black with smoke. One candle with long wick smoked and guttered near the fire. At the table and in the high-backed settle sat the men, smoking, talking, drinking. Conspicuous among them was one man with a high forehead, partly bald, who with upturned eyes sang ballads. I learned that he was given free entertainment at the inn, on condition that he sang as long as the tavern was open, for the amusement of the guests. He seemed to be inexhaustible in his store of songs and ballads; with the utmost readiness, whenever called on, he sang, and skilfully varied the character of his pieces – to grave succeeded gay, to a ballad a lyric. At the time I listened, amused, till I was tired, and then went to bed, leaving him singing.[12]

---

12 Sabine Baring-Gould, 'Among the Western Song Men', *English Illustrated Magazine*, 9 (1892), pp. 468–77.

Thirty-five years later he visited the Oxenham Arms again, hoping to hear more songs. He would not be disappointed.

It was at this time that Baring-Gould formed three purposes for his life. These were:

1. The moral and spiritual improvement of Lew Trenchard parish. At that time the manganese mining in the village had resulted in overcrowding, with up to three families in a cottage that would have been comfortable for two people. 'The morality was very bad indeed and of spirituality there was none.'
2. The restoration of the parish church of St Peter. His grandfather had stripped the church and replaced the old carved oak furniture with wooden pews painted mustard yellow. Baring-Gould had found and hidden away some of the old carved bench ends and fragments of the screen and intended to use these as a model for his restoration.
3. The renovation and reconstruction of Lew House. The house, at that time, was an authentically old, but architecturally uninteresting rectangular box, which had been allowed to fall into a state of disrepair.

The next stage of his education was imminent and he was expected to go to Cambridge in the following year. But Voltaire, Rousseau, Schiller and Goethe were of no help in following his father's plan that he should read mathematics so that he could become an engineer. To prepare him for this, he was sent to live with the mathematician, Rev. Harvey Goodwin, at Cambridge. Goodwin rapidly discovered that there was no hope of his pupil acquiring the necessary mathematical skill. Indeed, he could barely handle basic arithmetic and, in later life, would get one of his children or a kitchen maid to help with the household accounts. Nevertheless, in the autumn of 1852, he entered Clare Hall (now Clare College) as planned.

There were large gaps in his education, apart from mathematics. He had only a little Greek and his Latin was not strong. He had not yet studied the classics. These deficiencies meant that he needed to work harder than his contemporaries. The fact that he had not had a public school education also hampered him when it came to making friends. He found many of his fellow students crude in their thoughts and behaviour. They, in turn, thought him something of a prig and an oddity. He began to take a much more serious interest in religious matters, and it was in this sphere that he discovered his friends. They formed a Society of the Holy Cross, meeting for prayer and discussion. His preference was for the ritual of the Anglo-Catholic movement, though he never considered turning to Rome, as some of his friends in the society would later do.

He also started to write for publication. His first book, *The Path of the Just: Tales of Holy Men and Children* was published in 1854. He wrote nine articles for the *Churchman's Companion*. One of these, 'Northern Mythology', is the first indication of his interest in the Icelandic sagas. This article was more concerned with the moral and spiritual content of the sagas than in the stories and the mythology that were to occupy him a few years later. Academically speaking, he bumped along the bottom of his course, graduating in 1857 with a pass degree – and was satisfied to have achieved that. But then he faced a serious disagreement with his father.

The Runaway

Edward Baring-Gould now accepted that his son did not have the makings of an engineer. Sabine himself had set his heart on entering the Church, but this was not something that his father was going to permit. It was not acceptable that the eldest son of a good family should become a priest. The alternative was to become a teacher, and Edward's brother-in-law, Frederick Bond, who was headmaster of Marlborough Grammar School, was prepared to take him on. But Baring-Gould would not agree to go to a school that was not committed to strong religious teaching. So, at the age of 23, he ran away from home.

Like so many runaways before him his destination was London though it was not streets paved with gold that were the attraction, but ritual and incense. St Barnabas, Pimlico, was set in the centre of what was then an area of slums. Consecrated in 1850, it was the first church designed from the outset for worship in the Anglo-Catholic fashion, and so had been richly furnished and decorated. There was much public concern about 'Popery in Pimlico' when it was opened and this had not died away by the time Baring-Gould arrived there to offer himself as a teacher to the choir school. The vicar at St Barnabas was James Skinner but, because of his illness, the day to day running of the church fell to his curate, Charles Fuge Lowder, an influential figure in the growth of the Anglo-Catholic movement. Lowder had started a mission to the slums of the East End of London and was also taking services at St George's-in-the-East when the rioting over ritualism took place there a few years later.

Baring-Gould took up residence in the Church House but did not cut off contact with his family completely, since he occasionally visited his great-uncle, General Sir Edward Sabine. The general ensured that the family knew that Sabine was alive and well, but he could not reassure them that he was not becoming dangerously infected with religious extremism. After a few months Baring-Gould ran out of money and was forced to write home for funds. Edward Baring-Gould refused to send any money and ordered his son to return home at once. Faced with an ignominious return to Lew Trenchard, Sabine consulted Father Lowder, who found him a position as a master with the Woodard group of schools. These had been founded by Nathaniel Woodard, who had recognised the need for schools that would give a sound Anglican education to the children of middle-class families.

Fig. 1.3 – The Church House, St Barnabas, Pimlico. (Author's photo).

Baring-Gould was sent first to Lancing College, near Shoreham in Sussex, where it was rapidly discovered that his knowledge of classics was inadequate to teach at the required level. He was transferred after only a few days to a sister foundation, St John's College, Hurstpierpoint, also in Sussex. Founded in 1849, Hurstpierpoint was the third of Woodard's schools and, like the others, its religious life reflected the values of the high church Oxford Movement, without being too ritualistic. The regime at Hurstpierpoint was less demanding than Lancing College and, Baring-Gould tells us, he spent eight very happy years there, teaching Latin, French, German, music, drawing and chemistry. While his father still had some concerns, and the disagreements between him and his son were far from over, the arrangement was acceptable enough to require no further bullying – for the time being at least. And Baring-Gould now had a modest income of his own: £25 per year, later raised to £40, 'and was pretty hard worked for that payment'.

The time he spent at Hurstpierpoint was important to Baring-Gould's development in many ways. He was free to broaden his religious thinking and, perhaps more importantly, to form the kind of friendships that were missing when he was a child. Indeed, as one learns of the practical jokes, the storytelling and the other amusements that had now became part of his life, it is tempting to think that he was enjoying some of the school life he did not have as a child. It was while he was at Hurstpierpoint that some of the stories that cling to him start to emerge, often to be presented as evidence of his eccentricity. One of the most frequently quoted is that of the pet bat that he had while at the school. The creature had fallen down the chimney of his room and he had given it a home in a woollen sock, nailed beside the fireplace, from where it emerged every lunch-time to receive its daily feed of milk. Sometimes it crawled onto his shoulder and refused to be dislodged, so that it had to go with him to the classroom, much to the amusement of the boys, who called it 'Baring-Gould's familiar'. The end came when a housemaid trod on it while she was cleaning Baring-Gould's room.

He was at this time a devotee of Ruskin and this was demonstrated in his dress. He wore knee breeches and stockings, velvet coats with braid frogging and coloured ties to match the ecclesiastical season. But his contributions to school life were more substantial. He encouraged the boys to take an interest in Sussex flora, fauna and geology. He wrote a number of stories for the school magazine, the *Hurst Johnian*, some of which, including 'Master Sacristan Eberhart', 'The Fireman' (a rather strange piece of science fiction) and 'The Dead Trumpeter of Hurst Castle', were republished later in his life. He was also interested in decorative arts and designed a number of pieces of furniture and ironwork for the school library. He created some murals of religious subjects to decorate his room at the school, which can still be seen *in situ*. After 150 years they are rather indistinct, but the colours remain bright. Baring-Gould saw them when he revisited the school in 1894 to deliver a sermon and was heard to mutter, 'Crude, crude!'

He also helped out by providing technical assistance for the school plays. For a performance of *Macbeth* he created a cauldron onstage, with a number of fireworks that were to be set off during the three witches scene to create magical effects. Baring-Gould was stationed, wearing his dinner suit, inside the cauldron to light the fireworks at the appropriate moments. One of the fireworks, however, was upset by the movement of the actors and fell onto the stage, whereupon one of the witches threw it back into the cauldron, forgetting that it was inhabited. Baring-Gould was not seriously hurt but his dinner suit and underclothes were reduced to a kind of lace. He did not act in the plays himself, claiming that he could not remember a speech of more than a few lines. He did, though, take part in some of the farces that were put on. One of his former pupils later recalled with delight Baring-Gould's performance as a certain 'Annie Babbecombe', wearing a wig of long curls under a broad-brimmed sun hat, a pink silk dress, short petticoat, white stockings and sandals.[13]

Because he had never had the opportunity to play team sports when he was a boy, Baring-Gould was not able to take the boys for games. Instead, he took some of those not engaged in sport for walks on half-holidays. He had become deeply interested in the Icelandic sagas and had taught himself to read them in Icelandic with the aid of a German-Icelandic dictionary. He had begun to translate *The Saga of Grettir the Strong* into English and told the story to the boys as they walked, aiming to produce a new episode each week. The stories must have made a strong impression on the boys as, thirty years later, he met one of his old pupils who reminded him of them and said how much he would like his own children to be able to read them. This prompted Baring-Gould to re-write and publish them as *Grettir the Outlaw*.[14] In similar vein he created *The Icelander's Sword* from the series of stories that he had written for the *Hurst Johnian* in 1858 which were based on another saga, and originally called *Öræfa-dal: An Icelandic Tale*.[15]

---

13 Martin Williams, 'At Hurstpierpoint', *SBGAS Newsletter*, 2 (February 1990), p. 13.

14 Sabine Baring-Gould, *Grettir the Outlaw* (London: Blackie and Son, 1890).

15 Sabine Baring-Gould, *The Icelander's Sword, or, The Story of Öraefa-Dal* (London: Methuen, 1894).

Through Frost and Fire

In 1862 he obtained leave from the school to make a journey to Iceland to see the places where the sagas were set. He intended to travel on horseback through Iceland's frozen deserts, making sketches and recording his impressions of the people and the places. This was, without any doubt, an original and potentially hazardous exploration. At that time few English people had visited the country and none had made the sort of extensive journey that Baring-Gould had in mind. Much of his planning is described in letters to his mother that survive in his papers. He says, for example:

> I take with me all that is necessary, by poncho I meant a waterproof one, and I shall have waterproof stockings for crossing rivers and a life belt in case of accidents. … I have got such a snug little tent with a hammock slung in it, just 7ft long by 5ft wide and nearly 6ft high, with a bit of waterproof over the top to let the rain run off. It all fits up with a neat case of tarpauling [sic] which will counterpoise my trunk on the horse's back. … The whole village here is in excitement about my expedition, the trades-people having received from me such extraordinary orders. I have just got today a knife and fork which shut up into one and go into the pocket easily. Genl Sabine provided me with opera glasses and compass.[16]

He included a little drawing of himself in his travelling costume, with his tent.

After discovering that he could not get a ship to the north of Iceland he planned a journey starting and finishing in Reykjavik which took him north through Thingvellir, and Kalmanstunga to Arnavatn. He would then strike across to Akureyri and Myvatn before the most difficult part of the journey, a great loop starting in a south-easterly direction then turning west to run along the edge of Vatna Jökull. He then planned to head northwards through the Sprengisandur desert back to Akureyri. It would be the first time, he said, that an Englishman had visited the Vatna Jökull glacier. He was planning to leave in early June and return in late September.

---

16 Exeter, Devon Heritage Centre, Baring-Gould manuscripts, 5203M, Box 25, Letter of Sabine Baring-Gould to his mother, 3 May 1862 [actually 3 June]. A full transcription of this set of letters can be read in Martin Graebe, 'Sabine Baring-Gould's Iceland Letters', *Transactions of the Sabine Baring-Gould Appreciation Society*, 16 (2016), pp. 17–43.

Fig. 1.4 – Illustration from letter of Sabine Baring-Gould to his mother, 3 June 1862 (Merriol Almond and Devon Heritage Centre).

Baring-Gould sailed on the steam ship *Arcturus* from Grangemouth and found himself in the company of a trio of young British men whom he regarded as ne'er-do-wells, 'rich, and reckless with their money'. There was also an American journalist, J. Ross Browne of *Harper's Magazine*, who was writing a series of articles about his travels in Scandinavia. In the article that he subsequently wrote for the magazine, Browne described the antics of the 'Jolly Bloods' in his humorous style.

> My English friends were so well provided with funds and equipments that they found it impossible to get ready. They had patent tents, sheets, bedsteads, mattresses, and medicine boxes. They had guns, too, in handsome gun-cases; and compasses, and chronometers, and pocket editions of the poets. They had portable kitchens packed in tin boxes, which they emptied out but never could get in again, comprising a general assortment of pots, pans, kettles, skillets, frying-pans, knives and forks, and pepper-castors. They had demijohns of brandy and kegs of Port wine; baskets of bottled porter and a dozen of Champagne; vinegar by the gallon and French mustard in patent pots; likewise, collodium for healing bruises, and mosquito-nets for keeping out snakes. They had improved oil-lamps to assist the daylight which prevails in this

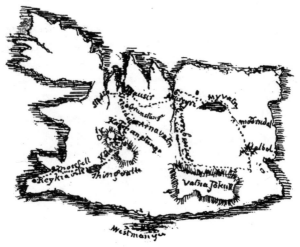

Fig. 1.5 – Map illustrating Baring-Gould's proposed route, from a letter to his mother, written in Iceland, 28 June 1862. (Merriol Almond and Devon Heritage Centre).

latitude during the twenty four hours; and shaving apparatus and nail-brushes, and cold cream for cracked lips, and dentifrice for the teeth, and patent preparations for the removal of dandruff from the hair; likewise, lint and splints for mending broken legs. One of them carried a theodolite for drawing inaccessible mountains within a reasonable distance; another a photographic apparatus for taking likenesses of the natives and securing facsimiles of the wild beasts; while a third was provided with a brass thief-defender for running under doors and keeping them shut against persons of evil character. They had bags, boxes and bales of crackers, preserved meats, vegetables, and pickles; jellies and sweet-cake; concentrated coffee, and a small apparatus for the manufacture of ice-cream. In addition to all these, they had patent overcoats and undercoats, patent hats and patent boots, gum-elastic bed-covers, and portable gutta-percha floors for tents; ropes, cords. Horse-shoes, bits, saddles and bridles, bags of oats, fancy packs for horses, and locomotive pegs for hanging guns on; besides many other articles commonly deemed useful in foreign countries by gentlemen of the British Islands who go abroad to rough it.[17]

---

17 Browne's articles were compiled into one volume: J. Ross Browne, *The Land of Thor* (New York: Harper and Brother, 1867). This passage is on pp. 445–46.

Browne included Baring-Gould with the group, although he described him as 'a quiet, scholastic-looking person, well versed in Icelandic literature'. Browne produced a number of sketches of the 'Dandy Tourists' and Baring-Gould is recognisable in some of them. One shows him on board the *Arcturus*, dressed in the travelling costume of knickerbockers and a 'Scottish hat' that he had described to his mother in another of his letters.

Baring-Gould had intended to travel on his own with an Icelandic guide, but his fellow countrymen prevailed upon him to go with them. This disrupted his plans more than a little and he was glad when, after several days of chaotic and slow travel, he was finally able to leave them behind. He followed his planned route for several more days, finally reaching Lake Myvatn. Here disappointing news awaited him. Because of the poor summer there was insufficient grass round the edge of Vatna Jökull for the horses to eat, and it was not going to be possible to go that way. Baring-Gould says:

> It was a bitter disappointment for me to have to postpone the execution of my scheme for another and more propitious summer, but it would have been insanity to have persisted in it; no guide would have accompanied me, and I should in all probability have lost my life with that of my ponies.[18]

He returned by a different route, finding further locations that were associated with the sagas. He rediscovered his travelling companions and together they went to Geysir where they spent three days conducting experiments in natural physics and observing the geysers. Baring-Gould was fascinated to see both Strokkur and the Great Geysir in action and when he got home he did a number of practical experiments and developed a theory of how geysers worked.[19]

They then returned to Reykjavik. Baring-Gould had been in the wilderness for forty days and forty nights. He recorded that he was sorry to leave Iceland but that the parting would have been more trying if he had not been confidant that he would return in the future. In fact, he never did go back.

They sold the horses at auction, getting back a quarter of what had been paid for them. Baring-Gould kept his favourite Icelandic pony, which

---

18 Sabine Baring-Gould, *Iceland, Its Scenes and Sagas* (London: Smith, Elder & Co., 1863), pp. 222-23.
19 He outlines his theory in Devon Heritage Centre, Baring-Gould Papers, 5203M, Box 2, Letter of Sabine Baring-Gould to William Baring-Gould (his brother), 19 November 1862.

A DANDY TOURIST.

Fig. 1.6 – Drawing of Baring-Gould by J. Ross Browne from *The Land of Thor*.

he had named 'Bottlebrush', and paid for its passage home to England. It grew fat and lazy on the rich Sussex pasture and was much loved by the boys of the school who took the little pony for unauthorised rides.

Shortly after his return he wrote a letter to his friend, Joseph Fowler, in which he told him about the progress he was making with identifying his specimens and stating his intention to return to Iceland the following year to make another attempt on Vatna Jökull. He also reported that he had sent sample chapters, based on his journal, to a publisher.[20] The account of his journey was published in July 1863 as *Iceland, Its Scenes and Sagas*. This was a large book, and only the third that he had written, yet it speaks with authority. It is important to recognise, though, that it is an entertainment as well as a documentary. While the itinerary and the scenery are recorded faithfully, there is some liberty taken with the people and events, such as his treatment of his guide and the introduction of 'the Yankee' as a travelling companion in place of one of the British men. It is constructed as a frame within which Baring-Gould tells the story of the travellers, breaking off at times to tell them tales from the sagas, and particularly that of Grettir the Strong, over the campfire at night.

It is a lavish production with 447 pages, including a lengthy introduction that gives a concise history of Iceland and outlines its economics, geography and volcanic activity. There are also five appendices covering the ornithology of Iceland, advice to sportsmen, a list of Icelandic plants and a catalogue of the published sagas. The final appendix gives an account of his expenses for the trip, which amounted to £100 16 shillings – equivalent to over £6,000 in today's money. We know that he borrowed much of this from his parents and from an aunt. The book includes a number of engraved plates (four of which are in colour) and illustrations, based on the drawings Baring-Gould made during the trip. There is also a large, fold-out map. Well-preserved copies of the book now fetch four-figure sums. We know from an entry in Baring-Gould's diary made in January 1885 that, as was the case with many of his early works, he made no profit from the book, although he managed to sell a number of articles about Iceland and his travels to various magazines over the next few years. On 12 March 1864 he exhibited his sketches of Iceland at a *soirée* at the Royal Society, in London.

He had acquired three manuscript volumes of Icelandic sagas during his journey and he gave these to the Printed Books Department of the

---

20 Letter of Sabine Baring-Gould to J. T. Fowler, Hurstpierpoint, 25 September 1862 (author's collection).

British Museum, the first of several generous gifts by him to public libraries. His studies of the sagas and his translations of them into English were a pioneering effort, as we shall see in a later chapter. Had he continued along this path, he might have become recognised as the foremost of the English saga scholars. In December 1863, however, Baring-Gould's mother died and on her deathbed persuaded his father to withdraw his objections to his entering the Church. At nearly thirty years of age the course of his life changed completely.

2: A Vicar by Accident (1864-94)

I live in my books, and for my books. You see, in a sense, I am vicar by accident, by which I mean that it has been the custom for three hundred years for the eldest son in our family to succeed to this manor; but my writings are my life's work.[1]

The Mission – Finding Love – A Parish of his Own – Married Life – Ten Years on the Mud – Inheritance – An Appeal to Gladstone – Problems with Tenants – Home at Last

The Mission

On Whit Monday, 16 May 1864, Sabine Baring-Gould stepped off the train at Horbury, in the West Riding of Yorkshire, for the first time. He had been ordained in Ripon only the previous day and he was to be a curate at the Parish Church of St Peter's. There were no cabs, and enquiries revealed that there was not a bus either. He shouldered his black cloth bag; a strange piece of luggage that he had devised to be slung over the back of a horse when he was travelling in Iceland, and which the boys at Hurstpierpoint had christened 'Gould's Black Slug'. As he was walking up Quarry Hill he came upon a procession marching with a band. Having been told that it was a school festival he left his bag at a shop for collection later and joined in. They marched up into the town to the strains of 'See the Conquering Hero Comes', but then, to his surprise, passed both church and vicarage and marched onwards. Further enquiries then established that the group was from one of the Methodist churches so, rather sheepishly, he dropped out, collected his bag and made his way to the vicarage. His earlier march-past had not gone unnoticed and was the cause of amusement for the vicar and other curates for some time afterwards.

Such was the arrival in Yorkshire of Sabine Baring-Gould. Not, perhaps, an auspicious start, but he achieved a great deal while he was working in Horbury.

Though on her deathbed his mother had persuaded Edward Baring-Gould not to stand in the way of his son's entering the Church, he owed his

---

1   J. Dunk, 'A Chat with Mr Baring-Gould', *The Methodist Recorder*, 17 February 1898.

new life to a happy coincidence. He had sought to be ordained while still teaching at Hurstpierpoint, but the Bishop of Chichester had rejected his application to do so. Then his friend Joseph Fowler had taken on the role of school chaplain at Hurstpierpoint instead of going to Horbury where he had been offered the position of curate. He knew that the curacy was still vacant, and suggested that Baring-Gould should go to Horbury in his place. He had a successful interview in London with the Bishop of Ripon, Robert Bickersteth, which he remembered chiefly for the bishop's efforts to remove the remnants of his breakfast egg from his black silk apron. He then underwent an examination at Ripon before his ordination as deacon on Whit Sunday 1864. He later recalled that the sermon preached by the bishop that day asserted that everything stated in the bible was true – no matter what science might say.

His father had allowed his ordination, but there was a price to be paid. The terms of the entail on the Lew Trenchard estate did not specify that the estate should necessarily go to the eldest son when the father died. Edward Baring-Gould had made it clear that if Sabine chose to enter the Church the estate would go to his younger brother, William. Such was Baring-Gould's determination to lead a clerical life that he accepted these terms.

The vicar of Horbury was John Sharp, who was unmarried and a strong high churchman in the Tractarian mode. Baring-Gould did not consider him a great preacher but admired his skills as a parish visitor and his commitment to his congregation. The village lay at the heart of the woollen industry and Foster's Mill had been a focus for a notorious attack by Luddites in 1812. It now boasted several mills and was still growing, its population at that time being about 3,500. It was a very different environment from that he had been used to, and Baring-Gould quickly discovered that the people were unlike the folk of Devonshire or Sussex. On his first parish visit he came into the kitchen of a house and found a little girl seated and playing with a knife. The child was startled by his entrance, and fell down onto the floor. He told the mother that she should have strapped the girl into the chair, saying, 'The poor child might have fallen on the knife and transfixed itself.' The mother replied, 'Eh! So she might, but she wouldn't ha' done it again.' He says, 'That was the way in which a Yorkshire woman taught me to mind my own business.' They remained good friends, and when he married she presented the couple with a nutmeg-grater. Baring-Gould came in time to understand the Horbury people better and to be very fond of them.

At first John Sharp allowed his new curate to work alongside his colleagues in the parish. This included visiting the newly established House of Mercy, where thirty beds were provided for 'fallen women' from the streets of London and other big cities. But the main task he was given was to set up a branch of the church in Horbury Bridge among the mill-workers, colliers and boat people of this rowdy part of the town. John Sharp must have realised that this was an appropriate challenge for his new curate who, thirty years old, may have been new to the Church but had honed his edge as a teacher for eight years while just managing to stay on the right side of authority himself.

The district was certainly tough. Crowds of men would meet on the bridge every Sunday morning with their dogs to arrange dogfights and races. Fighting in the ring was often an attraction – not always confined to men. There were four pubs in the area and drunks were a common sight on a Sunday. Baring-Gould threw himself into his new task with enormous energy, renting a three-room cottage to use as a chapel and schoolroom. The upstairs room, just fourteen by twelve feet, was used as a chapel and the schoolroom downstairs was twelve foot square. He began to offer a night school on four evenings each week, two nights for boys and two for girls, teaching them reading, writing and some basic arithmetic. Given his admitted failure in dealing with numbers, the thought of Baring-Gould teaching arithmetic is perhaps rather disturbing. It is a relief to find that he had several helpers in the community, including nuns from the House of Mercy. It is to be hoped that they also oversaw the savings bank that he organised for the villagers.

He held a Sunday school for the younger children in the afternoon before presiding at the evening service at 6.30. These services became so popular that the congregation first filled the stairs, and then overflowed into the schoolroom below. This had a curious effect on the hymn singing as the tune rolled down the stairs, into the room below and then back through the gaps in the floorboards.

The mission was a great success, and the youngsters of 'The Brig' filled the room, leaving Baring-Gould with just enough space to stand on a box placed on the hearthstone, with the cross on the mantle-piece. The young people of Horbury Brig were keen to learn and enthusiastic about the gentle brand of Christianity that he brought to them. In 1864 the number of scholars was about seventy. When Baring-Gould left Horbury in 1866, the number had increased to one hundred and fifty. There was a little trouble from the clientele of the Horse and Jockey public house just across the street, but a friendly giant by the name of Scholey, known as

'Old Nut', provided a personalised Neighbourhood Watch scheme. The sight of him cracking walnuts with his bare hands was enough to cause the young toughs to cross to the other side of the street. Baring-Gould exacted literary vengeance on the Horse and Jockey by having it washed away by a flood in his novel *Through Flood and Flame*.[2]

He recruited his choir in an equally unconventional manner. A group of boys had got into the habit of gathering outside the cottage and throwing mud at the windows. Baring-Gould went out of the back door and ran round to the front to seize the ringleader, who was then pressed into service as a chorister. His method seems to have worked, and some of his friends joined him, though the boys' habit of eating toffee or oranges during the service proved hard to break.

After he had cleared up he was sometimes too tired to walk back up the hill to his bed in the vicarage, so he would curl up in his coat on one of the benches, to be woken early in the morning by the clatter of the clogs on the street outside as the mill-girls made their way to the factories. That little cottage-chapel was later combined with the corner shop and is now a private dwelling. There is a blue plaque on the outside to mark its history.

Given the success of his cottage mission, Baring-Gould began seeking funds to build a new chapel and schoolroom on a nearby plot of land that he had bought, not far from his cottage mission. He had withdrawn £200 from his savings to cover the costs of the purchase. He wrote several letters to the *Church Times*, appealing for funds. The cost of the building was to be £100, and he had at that time raised £30 towards it. He made a number of suggestions of ways in which the readers could help, including the opportunity to buy quality hand-made worsted stockings knitted by his young pupils. Having put in money of his own he also borrowed more from his relatives, but he was successful in raising sufficient funds, and the cornerstone was laid in September 1865. The completed building was opened, free of debt, in January 1866. That building is now part of the local school. A new church was completed shortly after he left the parish. It has a finely carved rood screen, which was installed as a memorial to Baring-Gould by grateful parishioners.

As you drive into the town nowadays you are greeted with a stone monument that proclaims that you are entering 'Horbury Bridge, Home of *Onward, Christian Soldiers*'. When he was older, Baring-Gould's memories of writing his best-known hymn were, as with so many things, a little confused. Though he said that the hymn had been hastily written for the

---

2   Sabine Baring-Gould, *Through Flood and Flame* (London: Bentley, 1868).

procession of the children from Horbury Bridge to the mother church on Whitsunday 1865, it had in fact been published in the *Church Times* in October 1864. There is also some doubt about the tune to which it was originally sung. The setting of the hymn to a theme taken from Haydn's Symphony No. 15 in D by John Bacchus Dykes, and known as 'St Alban', is often given as the 'original' tune, but that tune was not published until 1868. This does not really matter since 'Onward, Christian Soldiers' is now firmly wedded to the tune 'St Gertrude', composed for it in 1871 by Arthur Sullivan.

Finding Love

Apart from the success of the hymn, the procession had an even greater impact on Baring-Gould's life. It was a big event in Horbury with up to seven hundred people taking part. A hundred of the children from Horbury Bridge were to march up to the mother church to join in the main event and all would be wearing their best clothes. Sabine heard that one of his young assistants was not going to be taking part in the procession, so he went round to her house to find out why. Her mother said that it was because she had nothing to wear. Sabine's answer was, 'What more does she want; she has a nice bonnet and looks well in it.'

That girl was Grace Taylor, who had been born on 27 March 1850 at Bank Hey Bottom, near Ripponden. The family had moved to Horbury where her father, Joseph, worked at Poppleton's Mill. By the age of fourteen Grace was herself working in the mill, and when Baring-Gould visited her at Whitsun 1865 she was just fifteen years old. The Baring-Gould family collection includes a picture of Grace wearing the red headscarf that was her customary workwear (Plate 3). Despite the difference in their ages – Baring-Gould was then 31 years old – they fell in love.

By 1866 Baring-Gould was settled into his clerical life, established in his position in Horbury, and in love. But the lingering difficulties of the relationship with his father now came back to disturb his equilibrium. His father demanded that he visit him at Lew Trenchard for talks on family matters. Edward had remarried the previous year, and Sabine's stepmother was Lavinia Maitland, a widow with two small children, who, as Lavinia Snow, had travelled to Pau with the family in 1848. Sabine's brother William (Willy) was there and Baring-Gould was upset by his brother's behaviour towards him and assumed that it had to do with his father's plans for the inheritance of the estate. In fact, Willy was displaying the early signs of mental illness that would develop over the next few years. Baring-Gould left earlier than planned, vowing to himself that he would not become Rector of Lew Trenchard if his brother were the squire. When he got back to Horbury he started to think about his future. His first step was to propose to Grace, who accepted, even though she knew that her intended was seriously considering becoming a missionary abroad. Two possible assignments, one in British Columbia and the other in Honolulu, fell through and he gave up the thought of missionary work when he was offered a parish of his own.

His engagement to Grace had set tongues in Horbury wagging, particularly among the middle-class mothers with unmarried daughters who had seen Baring-Gould as a potential son-in-law. His vicar, John Sharp, approved of the relationship, and arranged for Grace to stay with some female relatives of his, where she learned the finer points of Victorian etiquette and some of the skills of managing a middle-class household. We can get an idea of their courtship and a picture of life in Horbury at that time from Baring-Gould's early novel *Through Flood and Flame*, which tells the story of a mill owner's son who falls in love with one of the mill girls. In later life Baring-Gould had some regrets about writing this story and he was grateful that it went out of print. He did, though, use the setting and some of the incidents from the book in a later novel, *The Pennycomequicks*, which he recommended to his readers as a (fictionalised) description of Horbury at the time.

A Parish of his Own

Sabine left Horbury at the end of 1866 after an eventful two and a half years. He had been offered the perpetual curacy of the Parish of Dalton, near Thirsk, known to the locals as 'Dalton i' t' Muck' because of the mud that replaced the roads in the winter months. In 1870 the *Imperial Gazetteer of England and Wales* describes Dalton as

> A township in Topcliffe parish, N. R. [i.e. North Riding] Yorkshire; on the Great North of England railway, 4½ Miles S of Thirsk. Acres, 1,247. Real property, £1,709, Pop., 307. Houses, 77. There are chapels for Wesleyans and Primitive Methodists.[3]

Baring-Gould was now in a very different situation. The community was staid and agricultural, and his new patroness, The Viscountess Downe, daughter of Richard Bagot, the Bishop of Bath and Wells, was hard to please. The parish of Dalton had only recently been separated from that

---

3   John Marius Wilson, *Imperial Gazetteer of England and Wales* (Edinburgh: A. Fullarton and Co., 1870), p. 537.

of Topcliffe and there was not yet a proper church. Services were held in a converted barn, reached across open fields. Baring-Gould wrote:

> The rage of the winds down Swaledale in the autumn and winter was indescribable, and often I had to get to the little temporary chapel, clinging to the railings of the adjoining field, and struggling on yard after yard against the blasts of the icy gale.[4]

Viscountess Downe was, Baring-Gould tells us, a very beautiful woman, and very religious, but she was a very hands-on patroness. She chose the hymns, monitored the length of the sermons and took a dictatorial interest in every aspect of parish life, though she was genuinely concerned for the people on her estates and made sure that help was given to those who were sick or in need.

While Baring-Gould was living in Dalton a new church, dedicated to St John the Evangelist, was in the course of construction. It had been designed by the famous church architect William Butterfield, who had designed other churches for Viscount Downe (notably Baldersby St James) as well as much of the secular building in the villages on the estate. The church was created in an Arts and Crafts style and though its stone facing is unprepossessing Butterfield has executed the interior walls in patterned brick and stone with contrasting gothic timbers. William Morris, Ford Madox Brown and Edward Burne-Jones designed the stained glass windows. The building has since been given a grade II listing as a Building of Special Architectural or Historic Interest.

Married Life

Baring-Gould found that without the activity of the mission and with little to occupy his time apart from dinner with the countess at Baldersby Park or with other local worthies he had little to do and so devoted more of his time to writing. Things looked up considerably when he married Grace on 24 May 1868. It was a very small ceremony with none of their parents present – and only one of Grace's sisters. John Sharp was not able to take the service because he was convalescing in Italy, so the curate, Alfred Davies, married them. They honeymooned in Switzerland where they undertook a number of long hikes across the mountains to their next destination. The honeymoon also provided Baring-Gould with the material for a series of magazine articles on the European churches that he and Grace had visited.

---

4   Sabine Baring-Gould, *Early Reminiscences*, p. 19.

When they got back to Yorkshire Grace took on the responsibility for the household at Dalton. Sabine was not well versed in household affairs and was of little help to her. On one occasion she asked him while he was in Thirsk to go to the butcher's for meat. He had no idea of what to buy and Grace was alarmed when later that day the butcher's man delivered a forty-pound round of beef. It took them weeks to finish and they were heartily sick of it by the time they invited the choir in to polish it off. There were other excitements as well. One evening, Grace was in the bedroom when the window was shattered by a gunshot. It emerged that their maid, a pretty girl, had rejected the young man who was responsible, and she was the intended target. Luckily Grace, who was expecting their second child, was unharmed. The young man ran away and was never seen again.

When not engaged in parish work or disrupting Grace's running of the household, Baring-Gould continued with his writing. It was to prove both his downfall and his salvation. When he dedicated his book *The Silver Store*, a collection of medieval poems, to the countess, he did not anticipate that she might find the inclusion of some verses about domineering women to be a problem.[5] Relations grew frosty and when Sabine sought an extension to his house to accommodate his growing family – the first three of the fifteen children that he and Grace were going to have – his request was not granted.

Ten Years on the Mud

In 1859 Charles Darwin had published *On the Origin of Species*. Darwin's theories sparked an idea in Baring-Gould's mind that he should look at the way in which human beliefs had evolved. The outcome was *The Origin and Development of Religious Belief*, published in two volumes in 1869–70.[6] For a while it looked as if he had made an even bigger mistake with this book than with *The Silver Store*, since it stirred up a good deal of critical comment. Luckily, Prime Minister William Gladstone admired the book and arranged for Baring-Gould to be offered the Crown living of East Mersea. In March 1871 Baring-Gould left Yorkshire for Essex. In the preface to his book *Yorkshire Oddities, Incidents and Strange Events* he says, 'I look back with great pleasure to the kindness and hospitality I met with in Yorkshire, where I spent some of the happiest years of my life.'[7]

---

5 Sabine Baring-Gould, *The Silver Store, Collected from Medieval, Christian and Jewish Mines* (London: Longmans, 1868).
6 Sabine Baring-Gould, *The Origin and Development of Religious Belief* (London: Rivingtons, 1869–70).
7 Sabine Baring-Gould, *Yorkshire Oddities, Incidents and Strange Events* (London: John Hodges, 1874), p. v.

East Mersea is the lesser of the two parishes on Mersea Island, which lies at the confluence of the Rivers Colne and Blackwater. The island is joined to the mainland by a causeway, which is flooded at each high tide. In 1871 the population of the island was just under a thousand, with two-thirds of the people living in West Mersea. East Mersea was then an isolated spot and the easiest way for the inhabitants to get to the shops was to take the little ferry to Brightlingsea and then the train to Colchester. They made their living by farming, by shooting fowl in the surrounding marshes, or by collecting winkles from the mud flats for sale in London. The atmosphere was damp and unhealthy and Baring-Gould describes how in the autumn the mosquitoes were so numerous in the trees that they looked as if they were on fire and smoking. An illustration of another aspect of the unhealthy dampness is given in one of Baring-Gould's anecdotes about his time on Mersea. His children were troubled by obstinate sores and joint pains, for which the local doctor could not find a cure. Baring-Gould says:

> I had papered some of my rooms with highly aesthetic wall coverings by a certain well-known artist-poet who had a business in wallpapers. I passed my hand over the wall, and found that the colouring material came off on my hand. At once I drove into the nearest town and submitted the paper to an analyst. He told me that it was charged with sulphuret of arsenic, common orpiment, and that as the glue employed for holding the paint had lost all power, this arsenical dust floated freely in the air. I at once sent my children away, and they had not been from home a week before they began to recover. Of course all the wall-papers were removed.[8]

When the weather was good there were opportunities for the family to enjoy themselves. Grace enjoyed swimming in one of the inlets near the Rectory and on one occasion when she was swimming with a friend this caused some local excitement when they were reported as mermaids. Otherwise Grace quietly and efficiently managed the household, though the ten years at East Mersea added a further five children to her workload.

Inheritance
Baring-Gould's father died in May 1872, and Sabine was named as the heir to the Lew Trenchard estate. Given the past exchanges with his father

---

8   Sabine Baring-Gould, *A Book of the West, Vol. II. Cornwall* (London: Methuen, 1899), pp. 110–11.

this may seem a little surprising, but Edward had come to accept that Sabine's brother William was seriously ill and unlikely to recover. While Baring-Gould had seen that Willy's behaviour was increasingly erratic he had not at that stage recognised that this was a result of serious mental illness. Baring-Gould's father had told him the previous July that he was minded to leave the estate to him, provided that he agreed to an entail that prevented him from selling the estate, preserving it intact for his heir. The agreement was not, though, finalised until Baring-Gould and Grace visited Lew House eleven days before Edward died.

With his father's death Baring-Gould assumed responsibility for Willy, for his younger brother Edward Drake, and his sister Margaret, as well as for the Lew Trenchard estate. Willy's behaviour became increasingly unstable and deluded until, in 1874, he attacked his brother with a knife, demanding money, before breaking down. Baring-Gould had him committed to an asylum at Witham in Essex, where his condition continued to deteriorate. He died there in 1880. The cause of death was recorded as 'General Paralysis of the Insane', a description used at that time for the result of a syphilitic infection of the brain.[9] It is not perhaps surprising that Baring-Gould does not reveal the true nature of his brother's illness in his autobiography, or even in his diary, putting it down to the stress of his work as an engineer. Neither does he mention that he had taken on responsibility for Willy's illegitimate daughter who died in childhood.

Baring-Gould scarcely mentions his siblings at all in his public writing. In fact, none of them had happy lives, though details are hard to find. In 1857 his sister Margaret made what Baring-Gould considered to be an unfortunate marriage to Theodore Marsh, the Rector of Cawston, Norfolk. While we do not know the details, it appears that she left him for another man at some point in the late 1870s, but that this relationship did not last. Around 1881 she was for a time confined as a penitent at St James Infirmary in Fulham, London. There is a suspicion that she had become an alcoholic. After leaving there she went to Essex, living in a home with other vulnerable women near Colchester, where she died in 1903.

We know even less about the younger brother, Edward Drake Baring-Gould, who had pursued a career in civil engineering. Baring-Gould says that his health was broken after two bouts of yellow fever while he was

---

9   This information comes from Dr Ronald Wawman, a former army psychiatrist, and tireless researcher into the detail of Baring-Gould's life. See his book based on Baring-Gould's 1880 Diary, *Never Completely Submerged, The story of the Squarson of Lewtrenchard as revealed by 'The Diary of Sabine Baring-Gould'* (Guildford: Grosvenor House Publishing, 2009), pp. 255–56.

working in Brazil and two days in an open boat after being shipwrecked in the Pacific. What he does not disclose in Edward's case is that alcohol was also a factor in his problems, which had, in 1880, required Sabine to liaise with the British Consul in Hawaii to get his brother out of debt and keep him out of jail. Edward remained on the Pacific and died in Seattle at the age of 36 in August 1887. The full story has yet to be discovered.

Sabine Baring-Gould was in Belgium when the news of his father's death reached him, and he returned to Lew Trenchard to make the necessary arrangements. As the squire, he had the right to appoint the rector of the parish, and intended to take the position himself. He chose not to do so at once, however, as he did not wish to displace his uncle Charles, who was then Rector of Lew Trenchard. As a result, he did not resign from the living at East Mersea immediately, though he frequently asked his friend, James Gatrill, to cover for him while he absented himself to deal with estate matters – or simply to make another long European visit. Gatrill had succeeded Baring-Gould as curate in charge of the mission at Horbury Bridge and later followed him as Vicar of East Mersea.

An Appeal to Gladstone
Soon after he moved to East Mersea Baring-Gould was offered the job of writing a new edition of *Lives of the Saints*, a mammoth project that was to dominate his life until the publication of the final volume in 1877.[10] Though the isolation of East Mersea may have made it easier to focus on the task, he found it difficult to get access to the books that he needed for reference. In 1873 he wrote to the man who had given him the job, Prime Minister William Gladstone:

> I venture to ask if you would take me into consideration when you dispose of the vacant canonry at Westminster. I ask because my literary work necessitates my being near the libraries, as many of the books I am obliged to consult are not producable by me. I have not been idle since you so kindly presented me to this living, for in the two years I have written ten volumes ... besides editing a quarterly review of Ecclesiastical Art "The Sacristy".
>
> My 'Lives of the Saints' will occupy me two or three years more and will be, I really think, a useful contribution to Ecclesiastical history and biography. In addition I have been collecting for two other works I have in view, a History of the Hussite wars in Bohemia and a History of Anabaptism. I have now to make at

10 Sabine Baring-Gould, *Lives of the Saints*, 15 vols (London: J. Hodges, 1872–77).

times a journey to London merely to verify a quotation and this takes up time and is expensive; I am twelve miles from a railway and with high tides cut off from the mainland occasionally.

I can promise that preferment will not make me idle, for I only seek it to enable me to get more among books and use my pen more nimbly.[11]

On the reverse of the letter is an exchange of messages between Gladstone and his secretary that confirm that Baring-Gould's name was put forward for the canonry, though he was not successful. Gladstone also agrees with his secretary's suggestion that Baring-Gould should be thanked for his gift of the two volumes of *Legendary Lives of Old Testament Characters* and that he should be offered £50 towards the cost of buying more books.[12]

Though Baring-Gould chose not to engage too closely in politics, Gladstone was a politician with whom he was broadly in sympathy, and 'The Grand Old Man' recognised Baring-Gould's qualities while being realistic enough to understand that to give Baring-Gould preferment in the Church would be to set the cat among the pigeons. Baring-Gould continued to send Gladstone copies of his books, and received appropriate acknowledgement from him. When Bulgaria rose against Turkish rule in 1876, Disraeli, who was then prime minister, sided with the Ottoman Empire in what was then called 'The Eastern Question'. Stung by reports of massacres by Turkish troops in Bulgaria and by Disraeli's attitude in Parliament, Baring-Gould sent Gladstone a poem, 'The Turk and the Tory', which was severely critical of Disraeli.[13]

The Turk and the Tory

By Allah the Turk with his blade and brand
Is ruthlessly thinning a people down
Red rapine and murder race hand in hand
Through hamlet and village and town
And the fleet of old England is keeping the ring
That the Turk unmolested may have his fling

---

11 London, British Library, British Library Manuscripts, Additional MS 44485, f. 84, Letter of Sabine Baring-Gould to W. E. Gladstone, 15 March 1873.

12 The correct title was Sabine Baring-Gould, *Legends of Old Testament Characters from the Talmud and Other Sources* (London: Macmillan, 1871).

13 London, British Library, British Library Manuscripts, Additional MS 44485, f. 238, Letter of Sabine Baring-Gould to W. E. Gladstone, 23 September 1876.

Wild women are leaping and shriek in flame
Their babes beheaded and spiked by score
Weak maidens are outraged and dead in shame
The ravening Turk is yelling for more
And the premier of England has laughter and jeers
For woman's dishonour and widow's tears

The heart of the Turk is turned to stone
The life of the harmless is sifted chaff
The rust of their gold must have gnawed at the bone
When human misery wakens a laugh
And quivering zeal to re-rivet the chain
On the victim who's writhing in wrath and pain

The blood that has dripped from the wild beast's maw
On the scutcheon of England has left a smear
The red-spattered tiger is dubbed bashaw
The laughing hyena is crowned a peer
But the blood of our brothers cries out to God
For the Turk a gallows. The Tory a rod

O lion of Britain awake, arise!
With bristling mane and a wrathful roar
Bid liberty dawn on those Eastern skies
And tyranny trample and blight no more
To the bats and the owls with the Tory and Turk
The lying excuse and the fiendish work

Baring-Gould appended a note to a manuscript version of the poem in Composition Notebook 1 saying, 'After the Bulgarian atrocities D'Israeli in the House had the indecency to make them the subject of a joke. The English fleet was used to watch against Russian interference'. He identifies Disraeli as the 'Laughing Hyena' of his poem.

If Baring-Gould had known, when he was asked to write *Lives of the Saints*, how demanding a task it would prove to be, he might have turned down the opportunity. He accepted the job, however, and the result proved to be a classic book that has become a staple of English vicarage bookshelves to this day. The effort of producing 3,600 discrete biographies in fifteen volumes brought him close to nervous collapse. The publisher, John Hodges of London, became bankrupt, and the book was placed on the Roman Catholic Church's blacklist. Though Baring-Gould was not too dismayed by the last of these outcomes, the difficulties of his publisher meant that though he completed the project he never received full payment for it. For all its many faults, *Lives of the Saints* has proved one of the most enduring of Baring-Gould's works. Even though the number of people who have read every one of the biographies it contains is probably small, it has lasted as a valuable reference for clergymen, historians and archaeologists, as well as the general public.[14]

Problems with Tenants

The tenants of Lew House proved to be unsuitable, and Baring-Gould was called down in 1876 to resolve the problem. The husband was a weakling who had allowed his wife to fill the house with young men who 'drank, gambled and flirted with her'. They were given notice to quit, but the husband died in the last week of their tenancy. When Baring-Gould and his family came to the house they discovered that their former tenants' servants had stolen several items from the house, including a drawer-full of uncut opals. As if this were not enough to deal with he also had to resolve the scandal of the innkeeper of the Blue Lion in Lew Down having seduced the wife of the saddler. These, the excitements of village life, were to be his to deal with for the next fifty years. Though not yet resident at Lew Trenchard, he also started the alterations to the church and to the house that would occupy much of the same period.

With the tenants gone, the family joined Baring-Gould at Lew House for an extended visit, but this was marred by the illness of their two-year-old daughter, Beatrice Gracieuse, who had whooping cough. She had seemed to be on the mend but she died, suddenly, in her mother's arms. She was the only one of their children to die in childhood, quite an achievement in Victorian times. The memorial that Baring-Gould placed in the chancel of Lew Trenchard Church, sculpted by Gustav Knittel of Freiburg, shows her sleeping figure (based on her sister, Veronica) with a representation of her favourite cup lying on its side, as if the last drops of her life were spilling out from it.

Baring-Gould did not enjoy his time in Essex. The tides that cut him off from the mainland destroyed any chance of regular contact with those who shared his interests. He continued with his writing, mostly theological articles and books, but he also wrote a few articles based on things he had observed during his travels. As far as I can discover he collected no folk

---

14 For a more complete explanation of Baring-Gould's work on *The Lives of the Saints* see Martin Graebe, 'Foreword', in Sabine Baring-Gould, *Ecclesiastica Celtica*, (Bristol: Imagier, 2014), pp. ix–xv.

songs while he was living in East Mersea, but he did record a few fragments of folklore heard on the island. In 1879 he published *Germany, Past and Present*, which was not well received by reviewers. He did not take this rejection well and channelled his discontent into the most successful of his novels, *Mehalah: A Story of the Salt Marshes*, published anonymously in 1880.[15] This gritty tale of love and murder in the Essex marshes was likened by Swinburne to *Wuthering Heights* and it was, in contrast to *Germany*, very well received by the critics and went rapidly through many editions. Gladstone was reported to have said that *Mehalah* was one of his favourite modern novels and that he placed it 'very high for force and originality'.[16] Several of the characters were based on people whom he had met on Mersea and the picture he painted was not a flattering one. His authorship of the book became an open secret and there were those on the island who were not happy with him.

Home at Last

In July 1880 Baring-Gould left East Mersea for the final time. The move to Lew House became complicated by the sudden death of the most recent tenant, Colonel Cooper, on the day before he was due to leave. A flurry of telegrams secured temporary accommodation with Uncle Charles at the Rectory but the party that left Essex was incomplete as ten-year-old Margaret Baring-Gould had been left at East Mersea in the care of her governess because she was unwell. The resemblance of these events to the problems experienced with the tenant that Colonel Cooper had replaced in 1876 was reinforced when they discovered that Cooper's cook had taken much of the equipment from the kitchen.

Baring-Gould had already carried out some much-needed work on the house, which was in a poor state. Within a few days of moving in he demolished the semi-derelict west wing and started to build what is now the main stairway. For more than twenty years his family was to endure a succession of renovations and the necessary scaffolding. The summer was spent entertaining family and visitors, who included William Lukis, the Rector of Wath in North Yorkshire and a respected antiquarian. He and Baring-Gould spent several days together exploring the pre-historic remains on Dartmoor. The children also enjoyed an idyllic summer and there were tears when the stay at Lew Trenchard came to an end in

---

15 Sabine Baring-Gould, *Mehalah, A Story of the Salt Marshes* (London: Smith, Elder and Co., 1880).
16 'Mr Gladstone's Home Life', *Leeds Mercury*, 17 December 1891, p. 7, quoting an article published in *The Young Man*.

October 1880. Though he had borrowed money to finance the move and the repairs to the estate, the farm incomes that provided his main source of finance had dropped alarmingly. A disastrous harvest in 1879 coincided with the arrival of cheap grain from North America following the end of the Civil War. The total destruction of the sheep on his farms as a result of liver-rot was met with a flood of frozen lamb from abroad at unmatchable prices. His farmers were unable to pay their rents. Faced with extreme financial problems he packed the family up and, like his father before him, took them to Europe, letting the house for five years and hoping that this would generate a modest profit. He could not know that Devonshire agriculture would not fully recover in his lifetime.[17]

In February 1881 his uncle, Charles Baring-Gould, died. Sabine was in Germany at the time and could only make a brief visit to see to his uncle's affairs. He was heavily engaged in translating a play based on Wilhemine von Hillern's book *Die Geirwally* (The Vulture Maiden) into English for the London stage. This venture took an unfortunate turn when he discovered that Frau von Hillern was an untrustworthy business partner. He was unwise enough to say so in a letter to her, and under German law it was possible for her to sue him for libel. Baring-Gould counterattacked by threatening to take her to court for failing to comply with their contract. In the end he settled for a fifth of what he was owed to disentangle himself from von Hillern and he returned to England.

At the end of June he had written from Freiburg to the Bishop of Exeter, presenting himself at last to the family living of Lew Trenchard. This was followed by another brief visit, this time to meet with the bishop to formalise his appointment. The family arrived back in England in October, though without four precious items. Three of them were the eldest children who had been left behind so that they could go to school in Mannheim – the first evidence of Baring-Gould's policy of 'tough love'. The fourth item was the perambulator, which had been put off the train by mistake. They did not have time to wait for it, so Sabine gave it to one of the men in the Strasburg luggage office who had a large family – a gesture that earned him handshakes all round and an invitation to return to see the man's family.

Once back in Lew Trenchard the family moved into the Rectory since Lew House was still occupied by tenants. Without access to the house,

---

17 For a detailed analysis of the difficulties Baring-Gould faced in managing the Lew Trenchard estate see the article by Anthony Gibson, 'Farming in Sabine Baring-Gould's Time', *Transactions of the Sabine Baring-Gould Appreciation Society*, 14 (2014), pp. 4–13.

Baring-Gould focused on improvements to the church, the estate and the gardens. It was at this time that the quarry in front of the house was filled with water as an ornamental lake, complete with boathouse where a rowing boat was kept for the use of the adults only. Nonetheless, the children were often found floating in old baths or on crude rafts, despite being unable to swim. Today, the boathouse has fallen into the lake and the quarry is closed off for safety reasons.

While the children played there was much for him to do since, as he wrote many years later, 'everything – farms, cottages, Lew House – were in rack and ruin, and the property was so burdened with annuities, that I had to write night and day to make money to put things to rights'.[18] But he had little choice about what he produced, since it was fiction, and novels in particular, that were required rather than the serious books that he wanted to write. He came to hate this task and recorded in his diary:

> I protest that I write novels with anger and heat because they take me off my proper course of study, history, especially ecclesiastical, and mythology which is my favourite study. I write only because I can not build and restore this house, I can not live on the estate, without supplementing my income from my pen. When I have finished a novel, I regard it with loathing and bitterness against it, as having engaged my time and thought which might have been better employed. If the novel could do any good it would be other, but the novel is now read only to kill time. I have said my say on novel readers in "Richard Cable." I will add that I hate lending any of my novels except to special friends who I believe can appreciate them, and that if I see a young lady reading one of them, I leave the room, the sight irritates me beyond endurance.[19]

Now, in his fifties, he could sense that his responsibilities to family and estate were pulling him away from the things that he really wanted to do, and that time was slipping away.

Finally, on 1 October 1885, he returned to Lew Trenchard after having conducted the marriage ceremony for his cousin, Alexander Baring, in Paris. The family had moved into Lew House in his absence, under Grace's calm direction. He asked the coachman to drop him at the gates

---

18 Letter of Baring-Gould to Gladys Dawe, 17 December 1920, quoted in 'Correspondence with Gladys Dawe', *SBGAS Newsletter*, 9 (June 1992), pp. 7–9.
19 Devon Heritage Centre, Sabine Baring-Gould Papers, 5203 M, Box 25, 1880 Diary, 24 August 1886.

and walked up to the house through the garden, slipping in unnoticed to say a quick prayer at the threshold that God would now allow him to make this 'the last change until the great one of all'. His prayer was granted and he was to live for another 38 years in the beauty and tranquillity of Lew Trenchard, with his beloved Dartmoor near at hand.

3: Seeking the Old and the Odd

*Beneath the surface of his genuinely spiritual nature, and often in conflict
with it, lay strange depths that drew him to those dark byways that underlie
all folklore.*[1]

*Pixies – Studying the Sagas – Werewolves and Weirdness – Yorkshire Songs and
Folklore – Folklore of the Northern Counties – Curiosities – White Witches – Folklore
and Personal Belief*

Pixies

Traveling with the family from Carcassonne to Montpelier in 1837 Sabine
Baring-Gould, then three years old, sat proudly on the box at the front of
the carriage with his father. After a while, he was surprised to see a number
of tiny figures, dressed in brown and with red caps who were running
beside the horses and jumping onto them. When he asked his father about
them he was put into the back of the calash, under the shade of its canopy.
He wrote:

> I still saw the little creatures for a while, but gradually they became
> fewer and finally disappeared altogether. The vision was due to the
> sun on my head, but why the sun should conjure up such a vision
> is to me inexplicable. I cannot recall that my nurse at Bratton had
> ever spoken to me of, and described, the Pixies.[2]

This was his first encounter with the inexplicable, though its significance
would not occur to him until much later in life as he started to collect
instances of popular beliefs and superstitions.

While his religious beliefs were of the greatest importance to him he
started when he was at Hurstpierpoint to widen his interests to include
archaeology and folklore as well as ecclesiastical history. He helped to
create a museum at the school so that the pupils could be introduced to
ancient objects and fossils. He also started to look in more depth at the
Norse sagas, particularly those of Iceland. This passion for the old and
the odd stayed with him throughout his life, as did the desire to share his
discoveries with others. When you open one of Baring-Gould's books

---

1   Bickford H. C. Dickinson, *Sabine Baring-Gould* (Newton Abbot: David and
    Charles, 1970), p. 40.
2   Sabine Baring-Gould, *Early Reminiscences*, p. 19.

you cannot read far without finding examples of folklore, of songs, or of tales. They are an essential part of the tool kit for his storytelling. In his novels they are often a device that he uses to give depth to his characters. Fragments of folklore add interest to the description of places that he describes in his travelogues.

It has been said of Baring-Gould that his interests were too broad, and that he dabbled in too many different ponds to be regarded as a serious student of any one discipline. Writers such as the respected American folklorist Richard Dorson have downplayed his contribution, describing him as a popularist and a marginal figure who 'flirted with folklore'.[3] Baring-Gould was never a member of the Folklore Society and is not regarded as a 'scientific folklorist', though he was writing on folklore for many years before the Society was formed in 1878.[4] It is difficult to understand why his achievements as a folklorist are so undervalued, even if one only looks at his published books and articles. When the material he has left in manuscript form is taken into account it becomes clear that he deserves a better opinion. His popular writing on folklore was underpinned by serious scholarship, some of which was without parallel in his time.

Studying the Sagas

Baring-Gould's studies of the Icelandic sagas while he was at Hurstpierpoint, for example, were a much more extensive and serious effort than he has generally been given credit for. To the outside world the output of these studies might appear non-specialist: the book of his visit to Iceland, two books for boys based on stories from the sagas and a number of magazine articles about Iceland, based on his travels. *Iceland, Its Scenes and Sagas* is a mixture of excellent factual description with a semi-fictionalised account of his travels, larded with stories based on the sagas. The articles are journalistic in character, calculated to entertain as much as to inform, and in the style of the day they are somewhat scornful of the lives of foreigners while describing natural wonders rather extravagantly.

A glance at his library, as it survives at the present time, and at his manuscripts reveals the wider extent of his studies of the sagas and of

---

3   Richard Dorson, *The British Folklorists: A History* (London: Routledge and Kegan Paul, 1968), pp. 295–96.
4   Baring-Gould first used the term 'folk lore' in an article, 'Devonshire Household Tales', *Notes and Queries*, 8 (29 July 1865), 82–84.

the translations that he made.[5] Andrew Wawn, formerly Professor of Anglo-Icelandic Literature at the University of Leeds, has written that his achievement as a saga translator 'dwarfs that of the Grimm brothers or any British old northernist of his day'.[6] Baring-Gould's library includes a large number of the primary works required for the philological study of Icelandic saga literature in its original language. Many of these were bought through a Leipzig bookseller, whose catalogues are in Baring-Gould's library and which contain his 'wish list'. The books are well used, and many have his notes penciled into them.

There are several printed copies of sagas which Baring-Gould has had rebound with interleaved blank pages on which to write notes and translations of passages in minute, but perfectly legible handwriting (a great contrast to his scribble in later years). There are also a number of notebooks containing complete translations of sagas. There is no question but that Baring-Gould could have been the leading saga scholar of his generation, if not beyond. Why was that promise never fulfilled?

The answer lies in the diary entry for 21 February 1864 where he writes, 'I have been obliged wholly to give up my Icelandic studies: I cannot bear to read those dear Sagas now, when I know that my hopes of ever revisiting Iceland are over.'[7] Clearly he believed that his decision to take holy orders meant that he ought to focus completely on his religious duties and reading and that there would be no place for this kind of secular research. His sagas, notes and translations were packed away and he expected never to return to them or to similar work ever again. His assessment was, happily, over-pessimistic. He was over-dramatising. Despite never returning to Iceland, and although he never achieved his full potential as a saga scholar, he continued to take a keen interest in Iceland. He wrote further articles about the country and made more translations, such as that of the *Laxdaela Saga*, completed in the 1890s. And throughout his literary career there are many examples of anecdotes and footnotes based on these early studies.

---

5   The residue of the collection of books that belonged to the Baring-Gould family, and to which Sabine Baring-Gould was the major contributor, is split between two locations. Most are now in the Heritage Collection of the University of Exeter Library. A number of books also remain at Lew House, his former home in Devon. More will be written about this in Chapter 12.

6   Andrew Wawn, 'The Grimms, The Kirk-Grims, and Sabine Baring-Gould', in *Constructing Nations, Reconstructing Myth: Essays in honour of T. A. Shippey* ed. Andrew Wawn (Turnhout: Brepols, 2007).

7   Devon Heritage Centre, Sabine Baring-Gould Papers, 5203 M, Box 25, *1862 Diary Notebook*, 21 February 1864.

Werewolves and Weirdness

When he arrived in Horbury, Baring-Gould had a great deal to occupy him, particularly the task of setting up his new mission at Horbury Bridge. Yet he still found time for the reading and research for one of his most enduring works, *The Book of Werewolves*.[8] The book opens with a description of a personal experience in France. Having been out late examining an archaeological site at Vienne, Baring-Gould found that night was falling and he tried to persuade the local priest to get one of the villagers to accompany him back to his lodging. They refused because of the *loup garou* that terrorised the *marais*, or marsh, which he would have to cross in the darkness. No one would accompany him, even in pairs. Unable to keep his family waiting Baring-Gould elected to return alone, so confirming the impression of the French priest that all Englishmen were mad. He did take the precaution of arming himself with a stout stick but he was not required to use it and arrived safely at his lodging without having sighted anything alarming. This (non) event took place in 1850, when he was just sixteen years old.

The Book of Werewolves is one of the first modern studies of the folklore surrounding the werewolf. Baring-Gould says in his introductory chapter that his purpose is to outline the descriptions of werewolves in classical literature, in the Norse myths and in medieval legend and then to give some more recent examples. It was a great opportunity for him to demonstrate how widely he had read, but it also shows how the topics he was reading about differed from the classical studies undertaken by his contemporaries. Greek and Roman sources are dealt with quickly, and Baring-Gould rushes on to his beloved Norse texts, pulling out myths of transformation and tales of bad behaviour. He said that the clear Norse stream made it easier to fish for the early origins of lycanthropy than in the muddy river of medieval texts.

Further on in the book the tales are of later European monsters; not supernatural beings but psychotic humans of the sort described by Webster in *The Duchess of Malfi*.

> In those that are possess'd with 't there o'erflows
> Such melancholy humour they imagine
> Themselves to be transformed into wolves;
> Steal forth to church-yards in the dead of night,

---

8   Sabine Baring-Gould, *The Book of Werewolves* (London: Smith, Elder & Co., 1865).

And dig dead bodies up: as two nights since
One met the duke 'bout midnight in a lane
Behind Saint Mark's church, with the leg of a man
Upon his shoulder; and he howl'd fearfully;
Said he was a wolf, only the difference
Was, a wolf's skin was hairy on the outside,
His on the inside.[9]

You sense that Baring-Gould does not personally believe in the things that he describes, but that he relishes the exploration and the telling of the tales. It is a sensational book. At times it feels closer to a collection of horror stories than a serious study. But it is a book that has fascinated its readers for 150 years. It has been one of the foundation stones of the modern obsession with werewolves and vampires, retelling tales that have horrified people down the years. We know that Bram Stoker consulted it when he was writing *Dracula* and that he was looking forward to Baring-Gould writing on vampires – which he never did.[10]

Yorkshire Songs and Folklore
In the little cottage schoolroom at Horbury Bridge he was facing a very different audience from the middle-class schoolboys of Hurstpierpoint, but they also wanted to hear his stories once their lessons were over. The younger children would sit on Baring-Gould's coat tails until he obliged them – which he always did willingly – starting in the proper manner with 'Once upon a time…' and then making it up as he went along. Others of his former pupils recalled him telling them about Iceland: its geysers, scenery and other wonderful things. Baring-Gould was also learning from them and in his *Diary Notebook, 1862–1868*, he recorded a number of stories, songs and riddles given to him by his young pupils. One of these was the Christmas carol which Baring-Gould reported in Richard Chope's book, *Carols for Use in Church*, was 'taken down from the children at Horbury Bridge.'

---

9   John Webster, *The Tragedy of the Duchess of Malfi*, Originally published London, 1623, Act V, Scene 2. I am grateful to Dr Vic Gammon for drawing my attention to this passage.

10 Joan Passey, a PhD student at Exeter University, told me about an interview with Stoker published in the July 1897 issue of *The British Weekly*, in which he says. 'I also learned something from Mr Baring-Gould's 'Were-Wolves.' Mr. Gould has promised a book on vampires, but I do not know whether he has made any progress with it.' His research notes for *Dracula* are also said to refer to *The Book of Werewolves*.

I was teaching carols to a party of mill-girls in the West Riding of Yorkshire, some ten years ago, and amongst them that by Dr. Gauntlett, 'Saint Joseph was a-walking', when they burst out with "Nay! We know one a deal better nor yond;" and, lifting up their voices, they sang, to a curious old strain:

Sant Joseph was an old man
And an old man was he
He married sweet Mary
And a virgin was she. (etc.)[11]

No tune for the Horbury version of 'Cherry Tree Carol' has survived among Baring-Gould's papers, though the carol has been found many times by other collectors. In his introduction to Chope's book Baring-Gould lingers over this carol to demonstrate his knowledge as historian, philologist and folklorist. He shows possible connections with the Coventry mystery plays, the Finnish epic *Kalevala* and with an incident in the *Popol Vuh*, a collection of ancient Guatemalan mythology, as well as mentioning other sources for the tale on which the carol is based.

In July 1865 Baring-Gould contributed the first of a series of three articles to the antiquarian journal *Notes and Queries* with the title 'Devonshire Household Tales'. The introduction to these five tales anticipates his calls to action on folk song 25 years later:

It is of great importance that the household tales of England should be collected, as they have been collected in France, in Germany, in Russia, in Greece, in Scotland &c. ... Our antiquarian collectors of folk-lore have hitherto searched for legends, superstitions and charms; let them diligently seek out the household tale and I am sure they will find them still existing. I am now removed from my native county of Devonshire, where I know these tales may be picked up, and I have but a few which I was able to collect. Seeing before me no prospect of being able to continue my search for them I contribute what I have to 'N&Q' in hopes of setting others on the scent.[12]

---

11 'Introduction' by Sabine Baring-Gould to Richard Chope, *Carols for use in Church* (London: William Clowes and Sons, 1875) pp. iii–xv.
12 Sabine Baring-Gould, 'Devonshire Household Tales', *Notes and Queries*, 8 (29 July 1865), pp. 82–84.

In using the descriptor 'household tales' he was following the example of the Grimm brothers who described their stories as *Hausmärchen*. These were not always stories that were suitable for children (which the Grimms differentiated as *Kindermärchen*).

Having tried to encourage others, Baring-Gould now continued his own search for tales and folklore in Yorkshire. He contributed two articles on Yorkshire riddles to *Notes and Queries* remarking that they had 'been all orally collected in an outlying manufacturing hamlet in the West Riding; many of them from people who are unable to read, or at all events, unable to read with any comfort'.[13] There are 51 of these riddles recorded in his *1862 Diary Notebook*, which also includes three Yorkshire tales for which he records the names of the young people who told them to him.

One such tale is that of the 'Golden Ball' which, he notes, was told to him by a fourteen-year-old mill-girl, Sarah Ann Hirst. Her story was presented as a *cante-fable*, bringing song and story together. Baring-Gould included this story in the appendix, 'Household Tales', which he contributed to William Henderson's book, *The Folk Lore of the Northern Counties*.[14] He reports that he expanded and improved it, enclosing his additions in brackets. This, he says, he was able to do after hearing another version from a second, unnamed informant whose version included elements which resembled the Grimms' tale of 'Fearless John'.[15] He drew some parallels with a children's game, 'Mary Brown', and with a Swedish story, 'Fair Gundela'. He did not make a link, as he surely would have done in later years, with the ballad 'The Maid Freed from the Gallows'. The American ballad scholar, Francis Child, later included the Horbury *cante-fable* among the variants of this ballad in his *English and Scottish Popular Ballads*. For his 'Version H' of ballad number 95 he took the ballad part of the text from Sarah Ann Hirst's *cante-fable* from Henderson's book, and imposed a conjectural nine-verse structure on it. He also quoted parts of the tale from the original in Henderson in a note to this version.[16]

---

13 Sabine Baring-Gould, 'Yorkshire Household Riddles', *Notes and Queries*, 8 (21 October 1865), p. 325.

14 William Henderson, *Notes on the Folk Lore of the Northern Counties of England and the Borders. With an Appendix on Household Stories by S. Baring-Gould* (London: Longmans, Green and Co., 1866), pp. 333–36.

15 '*Märchen von einem, der auszog, das Fürchten zu lernen* (The Story of the Youth Who Went Forth to Learn What Fear Was)', Jacob Grimm, Wilhelm Grimm: *Kinder- und Haus-Märchen. Gesammelt durch die Brüder Grimm*, (Berlin, Realschulbuchhandlung, 1812/1815).

16 Francis J. Child, Mark F. Heiman, Laura Saxton Heiman (eds), *The English and Scottish Popular Ballads, Corrected Second Edition, Volume 2* (Minnesota: Loomis House Press, 2002), pp. 430–48.

The *Diary Notebook, 1862–1868* also contains the words of the first English secular folk song that Baring-Gould noted and published. This was 'The Jovial Reckless Boy' which appeared in *Notes and Queries* in 1865.[17] Baring-Gould said that he had obtained the song from some mill girls.

> I am a jovial reckless boy
> And by my trade I go
> I trudge the world all over
> And get my living so. (etc)

Baring-Gould later realised that this should have been 'The Jovial Heckler's Lad'. Frank Kidson included another version of this song in his 'Traditional Tunes' and he wrote:

> In the days of handloom weaving, a "Heckler," or "Hackler," was a man who heckled flax to make it ready for the distaff or spinning wheel. It was a labour which required some degree of exertion and skill, and therefore a heckler would, to ply his trade, travel from village to village to heckle the flax which many house-holders who had suitable land would grow themselves. ... The hecklers were famous for wearing a fancy linen apron with an ornamental fringe hanging from it.[18]

Baring-Gould later wrote:

> The other day, in 1896, I was back in Horbury, and I went to see old friends I had not seen for thirty years and more. One of these my first singers came running to see me when "'t mill loosed" at noon. "Eh, lass!" said I, "dost' remember singing to me the 'Jovial Heckler's Boy'? She laughed, and her eyes danced as she said, "Aye — but if thou'lt stay a bit I sing thee a score more."[19]

'The Jovial Reckless Boy' and 'The Cherry Tree Carol' were not the only songs that he collected while he was in Yorkshire. Elsewhere he claims that in 1867 he took down a version of 'The Spanish Lady' from a workman on a train between Leeds and Thirsk, though there is no version of this song

---

17 Sabine Baring-Gould, 'Yorkshire Ballad', *Notes and Queries*, 9 (10 January 1866), p. 57.
18 Frank Kidson, 'The Roving Heckler Lad', *Traditional Tunes: A Collection of Ballad Airs* (Oxford: Chas. Taphouse, 1891), pp. 146–47.
19 Sabine Baring-Gould, 'Introductory Essay on English Folk Music', *English Minstrelsie*, VII, p. ix.

in his manuscript collection that was noted in Yorkshire. He did not collect any more songs, as far as we know, until 1888, when his great project in Devon and Cornwall commenced. His work on folklore continued, however, and his next project was one of his most significant contributions to English folklore.

Folklore of the Northern Counties

When the carpet manufacturer, William Henderson, became president of the Durham Athenaeum in 1861 he chose to talk about the folklore of the North-East for his presidential address. He later showed the text of his lecture to the author Charlotte Yonge, who was also the editor of *The Monthly Packet*, a Christian magazine for the young middle class. She asked him to turn his lecture into an article for the magazine and it was this that formed the nucleus of a book published in 1866, *Notes on the Folk Lore of the Northern Counties of England and the Borders* (usually known as *Folk Lore of the Northern Counties*), the first of the regional studies of folklore made in Victorian times.

Henderson had acquired a manuscript of notes of Border customs, legends and superstitions that had been compiled by Thomas Wilkie, at the request of Sir Walter Scott, for a project that was never carried forward. This provided a large part of the material for the book. A number of correspondents contributed, including Baring-Gould, who gave Henderson a number of anecdotes and footnotes. He also wrote an appendix of household tales that earned him a place on the title page of the first edition

Henderson stated that he wished to share the credit for writing the book with a collaborator who wished to be known only by her initials, S. W. In the second edition of the book the identity of this mystery woman is revealed to be 'my relative, Miss Susanna Warren'. She was his aunt, although she was a year younger than him, and for a period in the 1860s she lived with Henderson in Durham before returning to the house at Hennock in Devon that she shared with four of her sisters, all of them unmarried. Susanna Warren was a writer and produced a number of books and tracts for the Society for Promoting Christian Knowledge (SPCK), under the initials 'S. W'.

It seems likely that it was Susanna Warren, rather than Henderson himself, who brought Baring-Gould into the project. This can be deduced from a set of four letters to her written by Baring-Gould from Horbury between 26 July and 27 November 1865, which came up for auction in

1996.[20] The letters themselves went to a private buyer and it has not proved possible to gain access to them, but the description from the auction catalogue gives a good indication of the content.

In the first letter in the sequence Baring-Gould gave his permission for the use of his account of the 'Wild Huntsman' from *Iceland, Its Scenes and Sagas* which Henderson's book quotes in full, but he added, 'I have any amount of material concerning the wild huntsman and his dogs and could fill a volume'. He was given the opportunity to read the manuscript of the book, and when he returned it he said that 'the amount of matter and the valuable nature of it has delighted me'. He was so impressed that he promised to send Susanna Warren a number of notes on 'sundry superstitions and customs gathered in various parts of England'. He also suggested that the book should include an appendix of household tales based on his collection made in Devonshire and Yorkshire adding that 'the household tales of England are especially valuable as they have not yet been collected, and a flood of French tales such as Puss in Boots, Cinderella etc. have taken their place'.

Baring-Gould's riposte to the French flood of fairy tales did not appear for nearly thirty years, but his offer of a collection of household tales was taken up. The appendix included sixteen tales, five of which had previously appeared in *Notes and Queries*.

Baring-Gould's appendix also contained another product of his spare evenings at Horbury. This was his list of 'Story Radicals' – an attempt to classify folk tales by content and plot, an early example of the application of a scientific approach to folklore. Baring-Gould was not the first to attempt this, since his system was a development of that devised by the Austrian, Johann von Hahn, and first described in an appendix to his *Griechische und Albanesische Märchen* (Greek and Albanian Tales).[21] Von Hahn's book was published in 1864 and Baring-Gould must have laid his hands on it soon after publication in order to develop his own system so quickly.

Baring-Gould's system breaks stories down into a series of elements that allow folk tales to be compared and similar plots from different sources identified. The classification is based on Class, Section and Root so, for

---

20 The auction details were included in an article, David Shacklock, 'The Susannah [sic] Warren Correspondence', *Sabine Baring-Gould Appreciation Society Newsletter*, 20 (February 1996), pp. 4–5. I approached the auctioneers to ask for access to the letters from the buyer but, though passed on, my request was refused.

21 Johann von Hahn, *Griechische und Albanesische Märchen* (Leipzig: Wilhelm Engelmann, 1864).

example, the story of Cinderella, which is widely spread throughout the world, is classified as follows:

Group I – Family Stories
  Class III – Relating to Brothers and Sisters
    Section II. – Three Sisters.
      A. Cinderella root.
        1. The youngest of three sisters is employed as kitchen-maid.
        3. The eldest sisters go to a ball. By supernatural means the youngest obtains a gorgeous dress, and goes as well.
        3. This happens [three times] thrice. The last time she leaves her slipper.
        4. The Prince, by means of the slipper, discovers her and marries her.[22]

Baring-Gould's original work on his 'List of Story Radicals' is contained in a small notebook titled *Dictionary of Household Mythology* that is among his papers in the Devon History Centre.[23] Baring-Gould continued to work on the list after its publication in 1866 and a number of new sections and roots were added. The notebook also contains his notes on a number of foreign sources of folklore that he had read, mostly in German. This demonstrates that Baring-Gould read widely for the projects that he was engaged in. He used the London Library and the British Museum Library regularly, but also bought books, new and second-hand, even when money was short. Many of his books have survived in the Baring-Gould family library, which will be described in Chapter 12, and the examination of this collection enables us to get a good idea of Baring-Gould's sources. There are a large number of books in German about folklore published in Leipzig, the centre for publication of folklore in Germany (and for Europe at that time), as well as folklore books from France and Britain. There are many books about folk song and street literature and, as mentioned earlier, a good collection of books about Iceland. This is a scholar's library, and an important aid to Baring-Gould's writing.

One of the books is a copy of the second edition of William Henderson's *Folklore of the Northern Counties*, which was published by the Folklore Society in 1879, shortly after its foundation. Baring-Gould's contribution was reduced. His name was removed from the title page and

---

22 William Henderson, *Folklore of the Northern Counties*, pp. 304–05.
23 Exeter, Devon Heritage Centre, Sabine Baring-Gould Papers, 5203 M, Box 24. 'A Dictionary of Household Tales'.

many of the footnotes that he had supplied were omitted. The 'Appendix on Household Stories' disappeared, as did the list of 'Story Radicals'. One cannot help but wonder what Baring-Gould made of this, and it would not be surprising if he felt a little hurt by the dramatic surgery that had reduced his contribution to the book so greatly. Inside the book is a letter from Henderson, commending it to him because it was 'fully one third larger than its predecessor' and thanking him for 'the very valuable assistance you have rendered to both editions'.

There was a great deal of discussion about tale classification within the Folklore Society in its early years, and the Society launched a trial of Baring-Gould's system, together with that of von Hahn and a third devised by Alfred Nutt, founding editor of the Society's journal. The committee who were conducting the trial reported in June 1882 that the results were not conclusive and that further work was needed. They did not believe that any of the systems met all of their requirements. They did, though, feel that Baring-Gould's system had 'the merit of detailing the characteristic elements of a large number of typical stories' and when, in 1890, the Society published *The Handbook of Folklore*, edited by its director, George Laurence Gomme, it included an appendix with Baring-Gould's list of roots and the story elements in folk tales but without the classification.

A system of classification with which many modern folklorists are familiar is the result of painstaking work by the Finn Antti Aarne, who published his *Verzeichnis der Märchentypen* (*The Types of Folk Tale*) in 1910. Aarne's system was subsequently taken up and developed further by the American Stith Thompson, who published his *Motif-Index of Folk-Literature* in six volumes between 1955 and 1958. Other folklorists have been influenced by the work of Vladimir Propp and his *Morphology of the Folktale* (1928), which focuses on narrative structure. At present folk tales are more likely to be looked at as social history, particularly through feminist critique and through psychoanalytical approaches, with the result that the sort of classification that Baring-Gould attempted has become much less used.[24]

It is tempting to draw a comparison between Baring-Gould's unregarded work on the classification of folk tales and that of the Rev. Edward Casaubon on his doomed 'Key to All Mythologies' in George Eliot's novel, *Middlemarch* (1871–72). Baring-Gould is not the model for Casaubon (though his project could have inspired Casaubon's, and the

---

24 I am grateful to Dr Deborah Thacker for trying to explain this to me and to Dr Vic Gammon for reminding me that she had done so.

timing is right, if Eliot had been aware of Henderson's book).[25] One of the characters, Will Ladislaw, says, '... the Germans have taken the lead in historical enquiries, and they laugh at results which are got by groping about in the woods with a pocket compass while they have made good roads .... If Mr Casaubon had read German he would have saved himself a great deal of trouble'. But this is, of course, precisely the advantage that Baring-Gould had over many contemporary English folklorists, since he was able to read German fluently and had access to the newest texts out of Leipzig.

Curiosities

In one of Baring-Gould's letters to Susanna Warren he told her that he had 'just started work on the Curiosities of Popular Superstitions', in respect of which he mentions divination, men with tails, pig faced women, toads living in the stomach, salamanders, etc. This is a book format that he was to use many times over the coming years; collections of essays describing the old and the odd things that he had come across in his wide reading.

The book he was describing was the popular and enduring *Curious Myths of the Middle Ages* (1866). The twelve topics covered included two of those mentioned: divination and tailed men. He also takes the opportunity to demolish some popular legends, stating: 'It is one of the painful duties of the antiquarian to dispel many a popular belief, and to probe the groundlessness of many a historical statement.' So he tackles the stories of 'William Tell', which he shows to be derived from a twelfth-century Finnish text, before showing that the tale of 'The Dog Gelert' could be related to a story in Sanskrit, found in the Indian collection of animal fables, the *Panchatantra*, from the third century BC.[26] A second series of *Curious Myths* was published in 1868 in which he examined and explained the stories of St George, St Ursula and her Eleven Thousand Virgins and the Pied Piper of Hamelin, among other legends. In 1869 the two series were combined in one volume with some new appendices expanding on material in the first series and dealing with some other topics in shorter essays. *Curious Myths of the Middle Ages* was a very successful book. It was published in the United States in 1867, the first of Baring-Gould's books to

---

25 It is generally accepted that Casaubon is a conflation of people that Eliot knew and of some public figures
26 Benfey, T. *Pantschatantra, fünf Bücher indischer Fabeln, Märchen und Erzaählungen*, 2 vols (Leipzig: F. U. Brodhaus, 1859). Baring-Gould was wrong about the source of the story. It had been put about by the landlord of the Royal Goat Hotel in Beddgelert to help attract tourists.

cross the Atlantic. Like *The Book of Werewolves* it has been reprinted almost continuously since its first publication. The otherwise dismissive Richard Dorson described it as 'an alert round-up', which 'everyone' quoted. It continues to be regularly cited in academic folklore studies.

He followed *Curious Myths* with another collection, *Curiosities of Olden Times*, published in 1869 and revised in 1895 with additional material. *Curiosities* contains less folklore than its predecessor, but does contain a chapter on 'Ghosts in Court' and a fascinating description of a 'Mysterious Vale' which starts by describing a passage in *Grettir's Saga*, where the hero discovers an idyllic valley, Thorir's Dale, entirely surrounded by glacial mountains. Grettir settled here for the winter, but eventually became bored by his private paradise, and returned to the outside world, having erected a holed stone to direct others towards the entrance to the valley. Baring-Gould wrote that his intention to search for this valley in 1862 was frustrated when he was not been able to continue his planned journey because of the lack of good grass that year.

The year of 1869 saw an alteration in the course of Baring-Gould's studies and writing as he re-set his compass towards heaven. With *Curiosities* finished, his writing became focused almost exclusively on ecclesiastical topics, starting with the publication of the first part of *The Origin and Development of Religious Belief*. Between 1871 and 1873 he was the editor of *The Sacristy, a Quarterly Review of Ecclesiastical Art and Literature* published by John Hodges, who was also the publisher of *Lives of the Saints*. He wrote some articles for the magazine himself, as did his friend and later collaborator, Henry Fleetwood Sheppard, whose contributions included 'Noels and Carols of French Flanders'. An advertisement for the magazine quoted the *Weekly Register* as saying, 'Such a contribution to the folk-lore of Europe cannot but be welcomed by all antiquarians.' Unfortunately not enough of them welcomed it and the journal ceased publication in 1873 as a consequence of Hodges' financial difficulties.

Baring-Gould maintained a steady trickle of articles about folklore throughout his life and after he moved to Lew Trenchard in 1881 focused on West Country and, particularly, Dartmoor lore, tales and dialect. His discoveries were shared in a number of pieces that he contributed to the *Transactions of the Devonshire Association* and in magazine articles.

Another use that he made of such material was to enliven his articles, stories and novels with anecdotes and little bits of folklore that he had picked up. In his novel *Mrs Curgenven* (1893) he introduced a 'witch ladder' as a plot device to deal with an offending lawyer. It was made of woollen thread, with bunches of feathers knotted into it, each representing an ill wish.

And when gran'mother hey' done the ladder her'll tie a stone to the end and sink it i' Dosmare Pool, and ivery ill wish ull find a way, one after the other, to the j'ints and bones, and head and limbs, o' Lawyer Physic. See if they don't.[27]

Sir Edward B. Tylor, Reader in Anthropology at Oxford University, had obtained such a witch ladder from the cottage of a reputed witch in Somerset and showed it at a meeting of the British Association in 1887. It is now in Oxford's Pitt-Rivers Museum. In 1893, when the novel was published, he wrote to Baring-Gould asking where he had got the idea for his story and was told that the release of the ill wishes as the object decayed was the author's own invention. Baring-Gould subsequently asked the local 'wise woman', Mary Ann Voaden, whether she had ever seen anything like the witch ladder and she said that it was 'nothing but a string set with feathers to frighten birds from a line of peas'. It seems likely that Baring-Gould took the idea from contemporary newspaper reports of Tylor's find and built his own ideas around it. In the context of writing a novel, rather than an academic article, this seems fair enough.[28]

His last major work on folklore, *A Book of Folklore*, was published by Collins in 1913. This, like many folklore collections, is an omnium-gatherum of anecdotes and information garnered from his extensive reading over many years. There is a lot of interesting material in it, but one senses that he had no clear plan for the book and it does not live up to its promise.

White Witches

An aspect of the supernatural in which Baring-Gould took a particular interest was that of witchcraft, something he encountered a number of times in his parish and elsewhere in Devon and Cornwall. He met several people whom he described as white witches, such as 'Old Snow' from Tiverton, and one of his Cornish singers, Adam Laundry, who was known to heal wounds and 'strike' tumours. In his novel *Arminell*, a key character is Patience Kite, who is a recognisable pen-portrait of a real woman, Mary Ann (or Marianne) Voaden whom I referred to above.[29] Baring-Gould

---

27 Sabine Baring-Gould, *Mrs Curgenven of Curgenven* (London: Methuen, 1893).
28 I am grateful to Ollie Angus Douglas of the Museum of English Rural Life for drawing my attention to the work of Chris Wingfield on the story of the 'witch's ladder'. Wingfield's article will be of interest to those who wish to explore the topic further: Chris Wingfield, 'A Case Re-opened: The Science and Folklore of a Witch's Ladder', *Journal of Material Culture*, 15 (2010), pp. 1–21.
29 Sabine Baring-Gould, *Arminell: A Social Romance* (London: Methuen, 1890).

described her in several non-fictional accounts as his local 'white witch'. The woman in the book saves the heroine, Arminell, when she is trapped on a ledge and invites her into her cottage (and even offers to wipe a chair for her). The cottage is described as follows:

> The chimney threatened to fall; it was gnawed into on the south-west side like a bit of mice-eaten cheese. The thatch was rotten, the rafters were exposed and decayed. The walls, bulged out by the thrust of the bedroom floor-joists, were full of rents and out of the perpendicular. The place looked so ruinous, so unsafe, that Arminell hesitated to enter.

A photograph of Mary Ann Voaden's cottage shows that this is, if anything, an understated description.

Fig. 3.1 and 3.2 – Mary Ann Voaden and her cottage from *Devonshire Characters and Strange Events*.

Mary Ann Voaden was born in 1823, probably in the same cottage in Bratton Clovelly, seven miles north of Lew Trenchard. Baring-Gould knew her well as her cottage was on one of the routes that he used regularly. He said that she must have been a handsome woman in her day. She had a lifetime lease on her cottage and although local farmers had offered repairs she had refused all help. Over time, as the cottage roof fell in, she moved downstairs. When the flooring failed she moved into a corner where her only piece of furniture was an old bacon box. No-one knew how she managed to live but certainly she exacted some tributes from local folk with mild threats. Baring-Gould wrote:

Sometimes she would meet a child coming from school, and stay it, and fixing her wild dark eye on it, say, "My dear, I knawed a child jist like you—same age, red rosy cheeks, and curlin' black hair. And that child shrivelled up, shrumped like an apple as is picked in the third quarter of the moon. The cheeks grew white, the hair went out of curl, and she jist died right on end and away." Before the day was out, a chicken or a basket of eggs as a present from the mother of that child was sure to arrive.[30]

Baring-Gould maintained that she was a God-fearing woman who would have no truck with the Devil, but that she had the gift of healing. He published some of the charms that she gave him and reports that she had the gift of staunching blood, even at a distance. The village postman would bring her handkerchiefs that had been dipped in the owner's blood to be blessed. In 1901, shortly after *Arminell* was written, a fire destroyed what was left of the cottage and all of Marianne's possessions. She was forced to leave the ruin of her cottage and go into the workhouse in Okehampton, where she died a year later.

Baring-Gould also wrote about another Marianne – Mary Ann Perkin, who had lived since her marriage to John Perkin in 1840 in one of the cottages at Lew Quarry. John farmed the land south of the quarry. He died in 1877 and his widow farmed the land for several more years, remaining in the cottage until her death in 1904. He emphasised that she was not a witch, but that she had good knowledge of herbs and their healing properties. His daughter, Joan, recalled meeting her as a child and being given a glass of her homemade metheglin.[31]

Folklore and Personal Belief

It is perhaps appropriate at this point to say a little about Baring-Gould's personal beliefs and to consider how he reconciled his strong religious convictions with his observations of the beliefs of the people around him in the supernatural, the magical and the un-Christian.

In one of his letters written to Susanna Warren in 1865, Baring-Gould describes a 'curious painting of a Pixy frolic we have, at Lew Trenchard,

---

30 Sabine Baring-Gould, *Devonshire Characters and Strange Events* (London: John Lane 1908), pp. 73–79.
31 Devon Heritage Centre, Baring-Gould Papers, M5203M, Joan Priestly, 'Memoir Notes' manuscript c. 1956. In her manuscript she refers to Mrs Perkin as 'The Lew Witch' and has attached some of the stories Baring-Gould had told about Mary Ann Voaden to her. Metheglin is an alcoholic drink based on honey.

date William & Mary, I fancy. Very quaint indeed.' A detailed description
of the painting was included in Henderson's book and it is clear that it was
a work of great imagination, with the faery court floating in a boat made
from a pumpkin surrounded by pixy musicians and with various goblins
and others floating around them in eggshells.[32] This painting is no longer
at Lew Trenchard and it is likely that it was disposed of in the 1970s, when
most of the paintings that were not family portraits were sold to help meet
the cost of death duties on the estate. Its loss is a pity, since I have been
told that a pictorial representation of fairy-folk of this age is very rare. It
was clearly very prominent in Baring-Gould's mind, and one cannot help
but speculate what effect seeing a painting of this sort might have had
upon him as a child, and the extent to which it might have influenced his
interests and beliefs. Had he, without recalling it, seen this picture before
his vision of pixies on the road to Montpelier, for example?

Writing in 1922 Baring-Gould recalled:

> There was an incredible amount of superstition among the people
> in the days when I was a child, and I heard such stories of ghosts,
> spectral flames, pixies and goblins, that it took me a good many
> years to clear my head of them. It is really wonderful how that
> all this superstition has been dissipated in recent years. I am not,
> however, quite sure that it is wholly gone; only not mentioned.[33]

Among his papers is a proof for a newspaper article written by him,
'Personal Experiences of the Occult'. In it he states:

> I must premise that I have no faith whatsoever in the supernatural
> character or appearances that are 'occult' because inexplicable.
> I have had no occasion to see anything that in any way could
> be regarded as an apparition. Perhaps ghosts know that I am
> extremely short sighted, and would have to put on my spectacles
> to do them the justice they would demand.[34]

He goes on to admit that while he has not actually seen such things, he
has heard sounds that he could not explain, though that did not mean
that there was no explanation for them. He quotes examples of a personal

---

32 William Henderson, *Folklore of the Northern Counties*, pp. 239–40.
33 Sabine Baring-Gould, *Early Reminiscences*, p. 142.
34 Devon Heritage Centre, Baring-Gould Papers, M5203M, Box 33, Sabine
    Baring-Gould, 'Personal Experiences of the Occult', undated, unattributed,
    newspaper cutting (printer's proof?).

experience of telepathy, such as when he wanted to tell his sister Margaret something, but did not know where she was.

> The second morning after this I got a letter from her, saying – "What do you want to say to me? You came to my bedside last night and said, 'Margaret, write, I have something urgent to say' – what is it?" Now, in the meantime, in revolving the matter in my head, I had arrived at a conclusion not to say anything about it to my sister. So I replied that I had nothing to say, but that she must not trust to dreams. Of course, it was a coincidence, and nothing more.

As with the pixies that he saw as a child he tells the story, appearing to hover on the edge of belief before drawing back from the brink and seeking a rational explanation.

He emphasises that he has seen nothing in the way of a ghost – but gives several examples of things that he has heard: a sinister laugh at midnight, the rustle of a gown behind his chair while sitting with a friend, the strange sounds, like a coffin being carried downstairs, that he and his wife heard before the death of his daughter, Beatrice.

> When little Beatrice was ill, cutting teeth and with whooping cough, I did not think that the nurse-girl was sufficiently alert to attend to her, and so advised my wife to go into the bedroom, and sleep with Beatrice. I was then in the room above the drawing-room. I was awoke about the middle of the night by my wife, who came in and said: "I cannot sleep. I hear people tramping, carrying something down the stairs." I sat up and argued with her. It was a windy night, and the noise might be caused by the gale. As I was speaking there sounded three heavy strokes as if made by a clenched fist against the partition between the bedroom and the dressing-room. "It is only the starting of the timber," said I, and I induced my wife to go back to her bed. Next day, so little did we think that Beatrice was in a serious condition, that we went off to make a call in Launceston. On our return I was sitting in the drawing room, and my wife fetched the child, who was dressed, and took her down into the library. I heard a cry, and ran in, and found that the child had died on her mother's knees. Her coffin was carried down the staircase, as my wife had heard on the night before her death.[35]

---

35 Sabine Baring-Gould, *Early Reminiscences*, p. 159.

He also recorded with remarkable equanimity the unimaginably insensitive suggestion by his coachman's wife that Beatrice would not have died if she had been able to tie a bag containing special herbs round the child's neck.

In his story for boys, *Grettir the Outlaw*, Baring-Gould described how Grettir struggled manfully, if rather bad-temperedly, against other men, against nature and against the supernatural until finally he was killed in his retreat on the Icelandic island of Drangey. The rational Baring-Gould

ILLUGI DEFENDS THE DYING GRETTIR.

Fig. 3.3 – The Death of Grettir. Illustration by M. Zeno Diemer from *Grettir the Outlaw*, 1890.

explains that this was not due to witchcraft as the saga suggests but to the weakness resulting from a lack of vitamin C in his diet! 'The condition of the wound was due to the scorbutic condition of his blood, through a lack of green food.'[36] But then, a few pages later, the romantic Baring-Gould recalled that Grettir's head was supposed to have been carried to the mainland and presented to Asdis, his mother, who buried it in the garden of her home at Bjarg, and so:

> I obtained leave to dig there, and I examined the spot, but found only a great stone under the turf, and this we had not the appliances to move. And perhaps it was as well; for if Grettir's head be there, it were better that it should rest undisturbed.

Visitors can still see the mound in the home field where Grettir's head lies, and on the glacier-scarred hill overlooking the farm there is a fine memorial – not to Grettir but to Asdis, his remarkable mother. But Baring-Gould had sufficient belief that the head was there that he invested time (and money – he paid the farmer one Icelandic dollar) to search for it.

Folklore and superstition are, like religion, founded on people's beliefs and, indeed, the borders between the two are sometimes paper thin, as Baring-Gould discovered when he was working on his *Lives of the Saints*. He was tolerant of the views of his people and showed a strong interest in them as a result of his lifelong interest in the old and the odd. Mary Ann Voaden had no problem in reconciling her craft as a white witch with her religious principles, so perhaps we should expect the same of Baring-Gould. I believe that he remained contentedly uncommitted on these issues. He knew that many of these beliefs were irrational, but he recognised that they were of value because they made good stories, and because they were important to the people who believed them. At some level, perhaps, he hoped that some of these supernatural phenomena were actually real.

One of the specific criticisms that Richard Dorson made of Baring-Gould's 'flirtation with folklore' was that he 'engaged in little or no fieldwork'.[37] This seems overcritical given that Baring-Gould invested money, time and effort in a ground-breaking trip to Iceland, that his work as a parish priest gave him endless opportunities to engage with

---

36 Sabine Baring-Gould, *Grettir the Outlaw* (London: Blackie and Son, 1890), p. 373.
37 Dorson, *British Folklorists* p. 296. He goes on to praise the later fieldwork that Baring-Gould carried out on folk song.

ordinary people and learn about their beliefs, and that, if he wanted to ask about aspects of white witchcraft, he could walk from his house and ask a practitioner. Unlike many folklorists he did not need to make special expeditions from the city to conduct his fieldwork because the field was, literally, just yards from his door. But there is some justification for Dorson's comments, since Baring-Gould's fieldwork was not demonstrably systematic and theory-driven. His greatest strength was in his study of the literature: both the medieval writings and the contemporary texts coming out of Germany.

Certainly he was a 'popularist'. That was his mission and he was very good at it. *The Book of Werewolves* demonstrated his ability to give an account of a serious subject in a readable manner. In later years his status as a popular writer gave him opportunities to reach a wider public that most contemporary folklorists could only dream of, though his inclination to embellish the facts for the sake of the story sometimes devalues a well-made observation. But his work was founded on sound scholarship that, in the 1860s in particular, put him ahead in the game. This may not make him a great folklorist or anthropologist, and to some extent this was his choice. As Andrew Wawn puts it, his agenda was 'faith, folk, and family – or, ultimately, the Kingdom of God and the County of Devon'.[38]

---

38 Wawn, 'The Grimms, The Kirk-grims and Sabine Baring-Gould', p. 225.

4: The Search for Songs

Those who would hear the folk-music of our English peasantry must go amongst them, must gain their confidence, and must show them that their own hearts warm to one of the ancient melodies that are dear to the labourer in the fields. But it will be lost labour if they go to some of the prigs turned out by our Board Schools.[1]

Dinner at Mount Tavy – Daniel Radford – The Challenge – Keeping a Record – Beginning the Collection – An Appeal to the Public – James Parsons – A Change of Strategy

Dinner at Mount Tavy

Baring-Gould's quest for the folk songs of Devon and Cornwall began at a dinner at Mount Tavy, the house near Tavistock that belonged to his friend, Daniel Radford. The men present were reminiscing about the songs that they had heard when they were young, particularly the old hunting songs. They found that they could remember a few of them like 'Arscott of Tetcott', a local hunting song, or the ever-popular 'Widdicombe Fair'. But there were other old songs like 'Green Broom' or 'The Oxen Ploughing' of which they could remember only a few fragments of words and tune. Baring-Gould told them how he had ridden around Dartmoor as a teenager and heard the old men singing in the inns where he stayed overnight. He might have mentioned his having found songs among the mill-workers in Horbury Bridge as well. He later recalled that it was Radford who turned to him at this point and suggested that he might make a project of finding and writing down these old songs.

Daniel Radford

Daniel Radford was born in 1828 in Plymouth. His father, William, was a veteran of the Peninsular War against Napoleon and had married Elizabeth Lock who owned a baker's shop in Plymouth. They had six daughters and two sons. As their sons grew older she set up a drapery business and put the older boy, George, in charge of it. It was intended that Daniel should

---

1   Sabine Baring-Gould, 'Introductory Essay on English Folk Music', in Sabine Baring-Gould, Henry Fleetwood Sheppard, Frederick Bussell, and W. H. Hopkinson, *English Minstrelsie*, 8 vols (Edinburgh: T. C. and E. C. Jack, 1895–97), VII, p. i.

join him, but following his marriage to Louisa Vooght Daniel decided to go into the coal business with his father-in-law in London. William Vooght had been a mariner before he turned to the coal trade and had a good understanding of coastal shipping. As the population of London grew, so did the demand for Welsh coal and their company prospered. Radford became a rich man, known for his liberal charity.

Tragedy struck in 1868 when his wife and his eldest son, just seventeen years old, died in a short space of time. Radford was then living in Exeter, but in 1871 he began to build a house on fifty acres of land that he had bought at Lydford, which included Lydford Gorge.[2] He married Emily Allen, 22 years his junior, in 1872. At first the Radfords used their new house as a summer home, living there from June to November so that Daniel could fish the local rivers. He was an enthusiastic fisherman, though Baring-Gould wrote, rather mischievously, that he never caught anything but trees. The house was extended to accommodate three more children and Radford acquired more land in the district. He ultimately owned nearly two thousand acres, the farming of which he took very seriously. He provided a great deal of practical help to the local community including the provision of a water supply and a library in Lydford as well as building a new aisle for the parish church. He also cut new paths around Lydford Gorge to allow public access.

Fig. 4.1 – Mount Tavy c. 1916.

2   Bridge House and Lydford Gorge are now owned by the National Trust, having been donated by the Radford family in 1943.

Over the years Bridge House became the Radfords' main residence but in 1886, as his growing family demanded still more space, Radford bought Mount Tavy on the outskirts of Tavistock. He spent several thousand pounds extending and renovating the house, employing up to eighty workmen on the task. In the same year he became the first county councillor for Tavistock. He was a pillar of Tavistock society and continued his charitable work, which included daily visits to the local Hospital, the construction of which he had been a key supporter. He was also a pioneer of affordable housing for working people in Exeter (where he built 200 such houses) and elsewhere in Devon. He died on 3 January 1900 and was buried in Lydford churchyard, where a large boulder taken from his favourite fishing spot in the river Lyd marks his grave.[3]

Baring-Gould's diary gives us some idea of when the two men met (or rather it identifies the first date on which they failed to meet) and his initial feelings about him. He recorded on 22 July 1880 that he wished to take some friends to visit Lydford Gorge and so called at Bridge House to ask for permission. Radford was out fishing but Baring-Gould met his wife, Emily. He described the meeting and explained that he had some reservations about Radford, based on information from other friends.

> When I was a boy the ravine [i.e. Lydford Gorge] could not be explored. A few years ago a Mr Radford, a London coal merchant, a relation/cousin of Radford the linen-draper at Plymouth, bought a bit of land above it, along with the ravine itself, built a house there, 1875, and established himself there. He cut walks about the ravine and made it accessible. After some hesitation the Hamlyns called and invited Mr and Mrs Radford to [lunch. They came but he was so coarse and vulgar that they have dropped them again. He was himself so offensive with his bad manners that no one else in the neighbourhood ventured to call after the experience of the Hamlyns].[4] We shall want to go to the ravine, and take friends to see it so have called. Mr Radford

---

3 In constructing this biography I have referred to Radford's obituary in the *Tavistock Gazette*, 5 January 1900, that in the *Transactions of the Devonshire Association*, Vol. 32 (1900), p. 43, and to Barbara Weeks, *The Book of Lydford*, (Tiverton: Halsgrove, 2004).

4 Devon Heritage Centre, Baring-Gould Papers, 1880 Diary-Notebook, 22 July 1880. This passage in the diary was heavily scored out but Ron Wawman was able to reconstruct it after examining the manuscript under ultraviolet light. Baring-Gould must have regretted making these remarks about a man who later became a good friend.

was [fortunately] out fishing. Mrs Radford, his second wife, is a very sweet looking and pleasant person. She is said to be gradually licking her bear into shape.

When Baring-Gould met Radford he found him genial and enjoyed his company. They became good friends. Both men became Justices of the Peace and both were members of the Devonshire Association. On Radford's death in 1900, Baring-Gould described him as '... one of the noblest and kindest of men, and one of the most modest ... Not without deep feeling can I pen these lines to commemorate one of the best men whom it has been my happiness to know.'[5] Baring-Gould dedicated his first published collection of folk songs, *Songs of the West*, to Radford, 'at whose hospitable table this collection was first mooted'. In the revised edition of 1905 Baring-Gould said about Radford that he was:

> An enthusiastic lover of all that pertained to his county. He knew that a number of traditional songs and ballads floated about. And he saw clearly that unless these were at once collected, they would be lost irretrievably, and he pressed upon me the advisability of making a collection, and of setting about it at once. ... Mr Radford was one for whom I entertained the deepest affection. Inspired by his high character; and I knew that what he judged to be advisable should be undertaken in no perfunctory way.[6]

The Challenge

Baring-Gould is characteristically inconsistent about the date of the dinner at Mount Tavy, and there has been some doubt, as a result, about the year in which he started to collect folk songs in Devon and Cornwall. There is a gap in the entries in his diary from October 1886 to September 1888, so we have no help from that source.[7] In the 'Introductory Essay on English Song' included in volume 7 of *English Minstrelsie* (1897) he gives the year that he commenced collecting as 1887 and a few of the songs in his manuscript collection do have this year against them. In a letter to fellow song collector Lucy Broadwood, written on 21 January 1900, he tells her

5   Sabine Baring-Gould, *A Book of Dartmoor* (London: Methuen and Co., 1900), p 132.
6   Sabine Baring-Gould, *Songs of the West* (1905), p. xii.
7   There is hardly any mention of folk songs or of his journeys in search of them in the 1880 Diary-Notebook.

that he began his collection in May 1888.[8] This is also the year that he gives in the note on the title page of his 'Fair Copy' song manuscript, dated 1892, and which he quotes in *Further Reminiscences* written in 1925. Baring-Gould's entry in the Family Bible, where he habitually recorded key events in his life says against the year 1888, 'Began collecting folk songs and music of Devon and Cornwall. Began in May.' We know, however, that Baring-Gould often added these entries some time after the event. The nearest we have to a contemporaneous record is a newspaper report of a talk that he gave at the Royal Albert Memorial Museum, Exeter, on 21 January 1889 where it is reported that: 'This autumn it occurred to him that it would be worth while to see if there really was anything in the old music and ballads of our county.'[9] Then, in the *Tavistock Gazette* for 8 February 1889, a very full account was given of a lecture-concert given by him three days earlier at Tavistock Town Hall, chaired by Daniel Radford. Baring-Gould is reported as saying that:

> One evening during last autumn he was dining with his friend the chairman of that gathering, at Mount Tavy, and after the ladies had left the room, the conversation happened to turn on the old songs and ballads of Devon, and some one mentioned 'Tom Pearce's Old Mare', and another 'Arscott of Tetcott'. He (the speaker) said he knew the words of the latter, but he had never been able to get hold of the tune. He asked those in the room if they were able to furnish him with a tune, but no one could. Then Mr. Radford said he thought it was a great pity these old songs should not be collected and preserved. That initiated the whole thing.

These accounts from January 1889 are strong evidence that Baring-Gould started collecting songs in the early autumn of 1888, and are the closest in time to the event. It is possible that the suggestion that he should do so was made, as he says, in May, but that a period of several weeks elapsed before he actually started the work of collecting seriously. Assigning a date of 1887 to some of the songs was a slip of the kind to which he was prone. Baring-Gould's account of how he decided that he would take up Radford's suggestion also varies. In his *Further Reminiscences* he reports that:

---

8 Woking, Surrey History Centre, Lucy Broadwood Correspondence and Papers, Letter of Sabine Baring-Gould to Lucy Broadwood, 21 January 1900, 2185/LEB/1/299a.

9 'Devonshire Songs and Ballads', *Exeter Flying Post*, 21 January 1889, p. 2.

I shall not forget my walk back next day from Mount Tavy to Lew. My mind was in a ferment. I considered that I was on the outstart of a great and important work; and to this day I consider that the recovery of our West-country melodies has been the principal achievement of my life.[10]

Here he has painted a memorable picture of his walk home from Tavistock to Lew Trenchard. It is a distance of nearly ten miles, which would have left him a lot of time to think about the prospective project, and he was certainly more than capable of such a walk. It may, though, be another of his embellishments since in the earlier account in *English Minstrelsie* he says simply, 'As I drove home I considered...' The walk makes the better story.

The seed provided by Radford fell on well-prepared soil. What is clear from the various descriptions of the event, however, is that it was not a decision instantly taken in the dining room at Mount Tavy. It was not until the journey home (whether on foot or by carriage) that Baring-Gould made his mind up to accept the challenge.

The fruits of Baring-Gould's collecting were to be published in, *Songs of the West,* the production of which will be described later in this book. Baring-Gould was not the first to publish a collection of folk songs in England, and not even the first to do so by listening to the people who sang the songs, but he was the first of the large-scale collectors of songs. When he began his project there was no recognised process for collecting songs and no clear agreement as to how they should be presented to the public. These were things that he had to work out for himself. Later collectors (and several others) have criticised him for his methods and actions, but he had no one to advise him as he settled to the task he had set himself. His approach changed as he went along. Initially, as he described in a letter to Francis Child, the American authority on ballads, he was interested primarily in the tunes he was hearing. He assumed that the song texts were all derived from printed sources, particularly broadsides and songsters, and so readily available. Later he came to understand that the words of the songs were also characteristic and valuable.[11]

---

10 Sabine Baring-Gould, *Further Reminiscences, 1864–1894* (London: John Lane The Bodley Head, 1925), p. 184.

11 Cambridge (MA), Houghton Library, Harvard University, Baring-Gould Manuscript: Ballads and Songs collected by the Rev. S. Baring-Gould, chiefly in Devonshire, and sent by him to Professor F. J. Child, MS Eng 863, Letter of Sabine Baring-Gould to Francis Child, 23 August 1890. Appendix item 5.

Keeping a Record

Baring-Gould realised that the audience he wanted to reach was unused to hearing songs of this kind. He hoped to change that situation and, in modern terms, to create a market for his product by presenting the songs in an appealing form and giving them a context that the audience would understand and accept. His method for doing this was to present extensive notes about the songs in his book, to write explanatory articles for the press and to deliver a programme of lectures and concerts that would introduce the songs to a wider public.

He wanted people to sing the songs, not just to study them, and to do this successfully some compromises were needed if he was to appeal to the musical tastes of the time. A piano accompaniment was essential, and some of the modal tunes were strange to ears accustomed to conventional scales. Some of the songs that he wanted to use were incomplete and he needed to fill them out, either by taking verses from elsewhere or by writing new words himself. Sometimes the subject matter of the song with a good tune was, in the circumstances, impossible to use and so he used it for a song that he had written himself.

He realised that he was likely to be criticised for the way he edited the songs for publication and so committed himself within the first few months to compiling a complete record of the songs that he collected in their original form. In December 1888 he wrote in an article in *The Western Antiquary*:

> A few of these original songs need altering from their coarseness, and some of the melodies have been taken down in two or more variations. I propose to put a MS. copy of all the songs and ballads, with their various readings, exactly as taken down from the mouths of the people; one in the Library of the Institution at Exeter, the other in the Plymouth Library, for reference in time to come, as in five years or so, these will be the only records of the songs of the men of the West.[12]

The Devon and Exeter Institution never did receive its copy of Baring-Gould's song manuscripts but he kept his promise to give a set to the Plymouth Library. In 1910 he delivered a hand-written copy of 220 songs with the original words and tunes for most of the songs that he had included in *Songs of the West* and *A Garland of Country Song*. This became

---

12 Sabine Baring-Gould, 'Folk Songs and Melodies of the West', *The Western Antiquary'*, 8 (December), pp. 105–06.

known as the 'Fair Copy'. In 1914 he gave the library the thirteen surviving notebooks of tunes as taken down by him and by his colleagues in the field. These became known, collectively, as the 'Rough Copy'. Some writers such as James Reeves and Gordon Hitchcock examined these manuscripts and wrote about Baring-Gould's collection. The well-known singer Cyril Tawney, who lived in Plymouth for many years, probably spent more time working with these manuscripts than anyone else. He recorded a number of songs taken from them, which subsequently entered the repertoire of other singers, particularly in the South West.

Rev. Francis Nicolle, a great fan of Baring-Gould and a collector of all sorts of Baring-Gouldiana, had in his collection the earliest of Baring-Gould's folk song notebooks to have survived. This was among the large collection of material he bequeathed to Plymouth Library when he died in 1955, now known as 'Working Notebook 1'. Then, in 1992, further manuscripts and notebooks were discovered amongst Baring-Gould's books and papers, creating the opportunity for a re-evaluation of his collection and its importance. We will come back to look at the story of his folk song manuscripts in more detail in Chapter 12.

His records were not as detailed in the early stages of the project as they were to become later on and his manuscripts give us limited help in understanding what he did and the sequence of events.[13] But we do have some anecdotal accounts from Baring-Gould as well as letters to him from informants as well as correspondence from him to newspapers that clarify the picture.

Beginning the Collection

In the account of the Tavistock talk in January 1889 Baring-Gould remarks that those who had been at the dinner at Mount Tavy were asked to start the ball rolling by writing down all the old songs that they could remember. The first of the diners to send a contribution was William Collier, a Plymouth wine merchant who lived near Sampford Spiney, on the western edge of Dartmoor. He wrote to Baring-Gould on 15 September 1888 with words and tune for 'Tom Pearse, Tom Pearse', the first of many versions of 'Widdicombe Fair' and the first song in Baring-Gould's earliest surviving notebook, Working Notebook 1. It was Collier's song that Baring-Gould chose to publish in *Songs of the West*. As a result it has become the best known and most frequently played version of the song. It is the regimental march

---

13 They can also mislead with contradictory dates and descriptions. After several years of study I have pieced together what I believe to be the most likely sequence of events.

of the Devonshire and Dorset Regiment and has become the unofficial anthem of Devonshire.

Another early contributor was the instigator of the project, Daniel Radford, who sent Baring-Gould a version of what he called the 'Zummersetshire Zong'. Radford's original handwritten text of this song is the second item in the same notebook, and Radford has rendered the song in an approximation to dialect.

> Moy veyther died oi can't tell ee heaow
> 'E left me zix horses to vollow the pleaowgh
> chorus Wimmee Wimmee Wobble O
>   Jiggee Jiggee Stobble O
>   Little Boys a wobble O
>   Lived under the gloam

Baring-Gould recorded this and other variants of the song that he heard later as 'The Foolish Boy'. It is a song that has subsequently been collected from a number of singers in Britain and North America. Radford provided a tune, which is also pasted into the notebook. The covering letter has not survived, but Baring-Gould recorded that Radford wrote: 'I heard this, words and tune more than forty years ago from an old ploughman.'

An Appeal to the Public

But he found that most of the songs that the farmers and landowners were singing were old favourites by Hook, Dibdin and the like, or other composed songs published in the early nineteenth century. From his experience of listening to the pub singers of his teenage travels, Baring-Gould knew that there were older and, to him, more interesting songs to be found. A change of strategy was needed and for the next phase of his search he decided to write to some of the local newspapers, seeking memories of songs from the West of England from their readers. His letter to the *Western Morning News* ran as follows:

> Sir,
> Will you kindly allow me to use your columns to appeal to any of your readers who know words and tunes of old West-country songs to send them to me, as I am collecting such.
>
> Scotland, Ireland, Wales have their collections of songs and melodies, why not our West-country also? Such exist, and require

only to be collected before they disappear. Perhaps some reader may be able to supply me with the air to the Cornish song of 'The Sweet Nightingale'. Mr. R. Bell printed the words in his 'Ballads and Songs of the Peasantry', 1857, and says: "We heard it first in Germany, at Marienberg, on the Moselle. The singers were four Cornish miners, who were at that time, 1854, employed at some local mines near the town of Zell. The leader, a 'captain', John Stocker, said the song was an established favourite with the miners of Cornwall and Devon, and was always sung on the pay-days. The tune is simple and original". Mr. Bell gives the words, but, unfortunately, not the melody.

Another song he gives is a Somersetshire hunting song –
  "There's no pleasure can compare
  Wi' the hunting o' the hare,
  In the morning, in the morning,
  In fine and pleasant weather."
 – but also without the tune.

So also with "The Jolly Waggoner", once very popular in the West of England. So also with the Cornish song "As Tom was a walking", and the Cornish midsummer bonfire song "The Bonny Month of June", and the Devon version of the "Barley-mow". Now, any help that can be given towards the recovery of our West-country melodies, as well as words, will be most thankfully received by –

  Yours truly,
    S. Baring-Gould.

Lew Trenchard, North Devon.
September 28th, 1888.

The significance of this letter for a public figure like Baring-Gould was that he was now committed to the project. His readers, of whom there were thousands, would be contributing and following his progress.

 The response was, he tells us, a deluge of versions of 'Widdicombe Fair', confirming its popularity with the people of Devon. He did, though, receive a number of other songs including the prize that he had sought – a tune for 'The Sweet Nightingale'. This was sent to him by Edward

Stevens of St Ives, who said that the tune had 'run in his head any time these eight and thirty years'. Stevens was the first of many such informants who contributed to Baring-Gould's song collection over the next few years. Baring-Gould later heard the same tune sung by other Cornish singers, but it is Stevens' version, published in *Songs of the West*, that has become the 'standard' version of a song that is still widely sung in Cornwall and in folk clubs throughout England.

One of the most interesting and important songs that he received at this time was sent to him by Mrs Anne Gibbons, then living in Boscastle. This was a version of the old ballad 'Cold Blows the Wind', also known as 'The Unquiet Grave', one of the 'ballads of tradition' that interested the American scholar, Francis J. Child. Like a number of Baring-Gould's informants, Mrs Gibbons had heard the song from a maidservant, Elizabeth Doidge, when she was a child in Calstock. She only remembered eight verses of the ballad and though she knew the tune, was not, at the time, able to put it on paper for Baring-Gould. The tune is not in Baring-Gould's manuscripts, but he writes in the notes to 'Childe the Hunter' issued with the fourth part of *Songs of the West* that he had set the words of that ballad to Mrs Gibbons' tune, so she must have provided it at a later date.

There is a second letter in which, apart from confirming some details about Elizabeth Doidge, she gently chides Baring-Gould for having forgotten that she was the widow of an old friend, George Buckmaster Gibbons, who had been Rector of Werrington, a few miles north of Launceston. The letter was addressed from Davidstow Vicarage, where she was staying with her daughter Alice, whose husband was another cleric, John Ponsford Cann. Baring-Gould knew his father, Ponsford Cann, who had been Rector of Stowford parish, which adjoined Lew Trenchard, and then of nearby Virginstow, where John was for a while his curate. I include this detail to illustrate how the network of family and church linked Baring-Gould to many of the people who assisted him with songs. We will meet the Canns again in a later chapter, and see how this network continued to extend.

Anne Gibbons' second letter is dated 4 December and we can safely assume that this is 1888, since Baring-Gould used the words supplied by Mrs Gibbons in an article in *Notes and Queries* in the following month in which he asks for further information about the song.[14] 'Cold Blows the Wind, Sweet-Heart' was published in the first part of *Songs of the West* shortly afterwards.

---

14 Sabine Baring-Gould, 'Ballads and Songs of the West of England', *Notes and Queries*, 7 (19 January 1889), p. 44.

Writing to the newspapers produced some useful results since a number of people from Devon and Cornwall sent Baring-Gould songs. There were also contributions from other parts of England as other newspapers reported his quest, then seen as unusual and intriguing. Such contributions were to form a significant part of the collection but he was not happy with the rate of progress. His appeal had come up with versions of some of the songs that he had specifically asked for, but little more. Those who were responding to his requests were mostly middle-class men and women who knew a few songs; some of them learnt as children, others heard from servants. While he found many of these interesting he had begun to realise that he was not hearing the songs being sung, only seeing their reflection on paper.

The people who were sending him the songs were not singers of the sort he had heard in his teenage travels, the pub singers with large repertoires of old songs that had been handed down through their families and could entertain the public bar for an evening. This gave him a new challenge – how to find them.

Some of the letters he had received gave him a few leads. A Plymouth dentist, Charles Spence Bate, told him about some old singers he had met in South Brent, and John Prickman, a solicitor whom Baring-Gould knew in Okehampton, referred to an old farmer that he knew in Belstone. These suggestions were tucked away to be followed up later, but it is not surprising that Baring-Gould searched his own village first. He soon discovered that there were men nearby who had large stores of songs in their heads, and good reputations as singers. A number of likely men from around the district were invited to come to Lew House to sing their songs. Some came from the parishes around Lew Trenchard, often after they had finished their day's work. Some walked from as far away as Lydford or Bridestowe, each a distance of four miles.

James Parsons

One evening in the late autumn of 1888 James Parsons walked from his house on Lew Down to meet Baring-Gould at Lew House. He later admitted to having been very nervous about the invitation to sing his old songs for the Squire of Lew Trenchard. He was, though, used to singing for an audience, as he had been singing in public houses and at village revels since he was a boy in North Devon. His father, John Parsons, had been a singer as well. In fact, he was such a prolific singer that he was known as 'The Singing Machine' because of his seemingly inexhaustible repertoire of the old favourites of his country audience. As a young man

James had learnt a large number of his father's songs, though he modestly said that he knew only a part of his stock. Nonetheless, since his father's death he had inherited his title and acquired a good reputation as a singer.

He was taken through to the hall where the squire greeted him. Because of the geography of Lew Down, Parsons' house was actually in the neighbouring parish of Marystow and so, though he had seen Baring-Gould out and about in the village, they had not met before. He was offered a seat in the old oak settle (see Plate 7) by the fire, while the squire sat down in an armchair on the other side of the hearth. There was a little table beside the settle with a glass on it and the butler brought in a jug of hot, spiced wine and filled the glass before leaving the two men alone.

After a few friendly questions about his family, and his work, the conversation turned to song and it was made clear to him that Baring-Gould was genuinely interested in his old tunes. Before long he was asked to sing one of his songs and, turning up his eyes and crossing his hands on his chest, James launched into one of his favourites – perhaps 'By Chance It Was'.

> 'Twas there by chance I met my love
> It did me much surprise.
> Down by a myrtle shady grove
> Just as the sun did rise.
> The birds they sang right gloriously
> And pleasant was the air
> And there was none but she and I
> Among the lilies fair.

The song continues with the young lovers walking out to see her flock of sheep (perhaps a metaphor for some love-making) and on the way he asks her to wait another four years until he has completed his apprenticeship, since an apprentice was not allowed to marry. She replies that it is too long to wait and despite his reassurance that the time will pass quickly, she says that it would be a waste of years and of her beauty. The song ends without our knowing whether she did or did not wait and whether or not true love will triumph.

Baring-Gould was keen to discover the origins of the songs that he heard and this was one of the earliest that he studied. On one of his visits to the British Museum Library he discovered a version of the song in a printed garland, *The Court of Apollo*, from about 1770, where it is called 'Lover and Shepherdess'. Garlands were one of the forms of cheap printed literature sold on the streets of cities and at markets or fairs in the countryside and which contained a small number of songs printed as a booklet. The songs in this collection were described as having been 'Sung this season at Ranelagh, Vauxhall, Sadler's Wells, the Theatres and in the most polite company'. The song appeared again with minor differences on a broadside printed in 1791 by the London printer, John Evans, who called it 'The Lover and Shepherdess, or, True Lovers Meeting'. We do not know the name of the writer nor do we know the tune that it was originally sung to. It may well be that the song was written specially for a singer in one of the pleasure gardens, or it may have been included in a stage show earlier in the eighteenth century. Even with all the resources available to modern scholars, no version earlier than that in *The Court of Apollo* has been found

A century later a Devonshire hedger was still singing the song. It is unlikely that James Parsons could have heard the song sung in its original version. His father was not born until 1797 so was equally unlikely to have heard it – it could be that his grandfather, who was also accounted a singer of some quality, had heard a performance of it and learned it, or that the grandfather or a friend got hold of the broadside and began to sing the song to a tune he already knew.

James Parsons was born in 1831 in the parish of Black Torrington, in North Devon where his father was labouring at Fraunches, a farm about two miles south-west of Black Torrington village. Though there is some inconsistency in his age as recorded by the census takers over the years, the census was never as far out as Baring-Gould who, writing about him in his book *Old Country Life* in 1889, described him as 'a very infirm man, over seventy, asthmatic and failing'. Parsons was only three years older than Baring-Gould himself. The latter seems to have been a poor judge of age and overstated the ages of several of the men that he recorded songs from, a fault that he shared with several other folk song collectors.[15]

Ten years later the census found both John and James Parsons eight miles further south at Gradners, a farm in the parish of Thrushelton, which is next to that of Lew Trenchard. James was then recorded on the census form as a visitor and his occupation is given as agricultural labourer, like his father. Ten years on again and James was listed as living separately at Gradners as a married man, and his wife, Jane, had borne the first three of the eleven children they were to have together. When Parsons and Baring-Gould met in 1888 the family had moved to a house in that part of Lew

---

15 Ralph Vaughan Williams, for example.

Down known as Holster Yard, half a mile west of Lew Down village in the parish of Marystow.[16] By this time Parsons was renowned for his skills as a hedger and thatcher and was often asked to work on other farms and estates in the area.

On one occasion he was sent by the farmer he worked for to look after a small farm he had bought at Sourton, a village on the northern edge of Dartmoor, and lying about seven miles to the east of Lew Down. In the evenings he would go to a local pub and was usually asked to sing, in return for which he would be bought drinks. He told Baring-Gould about an occasion when he was given a challenge:

> I'd been singing there one evening till I got a bit fresh, and I thought 'twere time for me to be off. So I stood up to go, and then one chap he said to me, 'Got to the end o' your songs old man?' 'Not I,' said I, 'not by a long ways; but I reckon it be time for me to be going.'
>
> 'Looky here, Jim,' said he. 'I' give you a quart of ale for every fresh song you sing us tonight.' Well, your honour, I sat down again, and I zinged on – I zinged sixteen fresh songs, and that chap had to pay for sixteen quarts.'[17]

Baring-Gould was doubtful about the claim, but another man who worked for him, John Voysey, had been present that evening and was able to confirm the story. As Baring-Gould noted, to be feeling 'fresh' and then to consume a further sixteen quarts and still walk home demonstrated a remarkable capacity for alcohol. But Parsons admitted that it had taken its toll. 'I hadn't come to the end o' my songs,' he said, 'only I were that fuddled I couldn't remember no more.'[18]

When James' father, John, was alive he and his wife Ann, together with James and Jane Parsons, used to sing together in harmony at village feasts and other occasions. They would also walk into Lew Down village on Saturday evenings and sing at the crossroads to entertain the villagers, often going on for several hours.[19] This is an interesting

---

16 Parts of Lew Down lie in four different parishes.
17 Sabine Baring-Gould, *Old Country Life* (London: Methuen, 1889), p. 271.
18 Sabine Baring-Gould, *Old Country Life*, Chapter 11 'The Village Bard', p. 270. This story, like many of Baring-Gould's anecdotes, is given with variations in different places.
19 Surrey History Centre, Lucy Broadwood Correspondence and papers, Letter of Sabine Baring-Gould to Lucy Broadwood, 21 January 1900, 2185/ LEB/1/299a.

reference to harmony singing by traditional singers. Because Baring-Gould and his colleagues, like the other folk song collectors, were noting melodies, and because they usually dealt with singers as individuals, they did not make a record of any harmony singing that they heard. He reported a few occasions where they heard songs sung in parts, such as his visit to Mawgan in Pydar, where he heard a Mr S. James sing 'While Pensive I Thought' in harmony with Mary Gilbert and Joseph Dyer. The harmonies were not noted in any of these instances, only the melody.

In respect of harmony, then, Parsons is an exception. Baring-Gould wrote:

> It must be borne well in mind that to the rustic singer, melody is everything. It was so in the days before Elizabeth. The people then did not want harmony: to them harmony is a modern invention and need.[20]

But Parsons was also a master of melody with a strong preference for modal tunes 'of an early and archaic character'.

Baring-Gould tells us that Parsons soon got over his nervousness about coming to his house and enjoyed his musical evenings with him. Their meetings continued to follow a similar pattern with the two men sitting by the great fireplace in the hall of Lew House. There is a photograph of the hall taken in 1895 which shows the settle in which the singers sat in its place by the fire.[21]

As Parsons sang Baring-Gould would write down the words and then the tune, sometimes getting up to play it over on the piano; sometimes singing the song back to Parsons to make sure that he had got it right. As Parsons grew in confidence he took charge. Baring-Gould wrote: 'He is most particular that I should have all the turns right.'

> 'You mun give thickey (that) a bit stronger,' he says – and by stronger he means take a tone or a semitone higher. He will not allow the smallest deviation from what he has to impart.[22]

---

20 Sabine Baring-Gould, 'Introduction', *Songs of the West* (1905), p. ix.
21 I wrote this passage on a cold December evening in front of a crackling log fire in the hall at Lew House. At the time that same old oak settle was just to my right, no more than six feet from its original position. It has since moved into the porch, where hotel guests can sit and change their shoes after a muddy walk around the Lew Valley.
22 Sabine Baring-Gould, *Further Reminiscences*, pp. 197–98.

Fig. 4.2 – The hall at Lew House, c. 1895.

It is not possible to say with any certainty how many times Parsons and Baring-Gould met since in the early days Baring-Gould did not record dates.[23] From those that we do know we can establish that he collected songs from Parsons on at least ten occasions. Again, we cannot be certain how many items he actually collected from him. The manuscripts record 89 of his songs, though Baring-Gould says in the obituary that he wrote for Parsons that he collected about 200 songs from him.

Of the 110 songs in the first version of *Songs of the West*, twenty had been sung to Baring-Gould by James Parsons. This is an impressive tally, but Baring-Gould regarded him as special for reasons other than the sheer volume of material that he knew. He liked to believe that Parsons was one of those singers who were descended from a long line of old bards and that his ancestors, particularly his father, had passed on a number of unusual and rare songs from earlier times. While his repertoire contained many songs that were well represented in later collections, he also had a number of songs that have not been found anywhere else. Several of these can be identified as versions of songs written in the eighteenth century, often for the London stage or for performance in the pleasure gardens.

---

23 In the Personal Copy manuscript, for example, he gives a date of December 1887 for collecting 'The Mower'. In a letter to Francis Child written in about 1890, the date is given as September 1888.

In later years Parsons' health gave increasing cause for concern. Asthma and bronchitis limited his singing. Then in November 1897 an accident with an axe, when he cut into his knee while sharpening 'spears' for attaching thatch, was expected to lead to his end and Baring-Gould visited him in his home to collect a few last songs. As it turned out the village doctor was over-pessimistic and Parsons lived for another two years. The spell in bed eased his asthma and enabled him to sing those 'few last songs', for which Baring-Gould gave him money to support him while he was out of work.

James Parsons died on 6 January 1900 at the age of seventy. A few days later, on 11 January, the *Western Morning News* carried a long obituary for him written by Baring-Gould. In it he described him as '... the principal old singer, from whom were obtained the ballads and melodies published in *Songs of the West*', and acknowledged his capability as a musician.[24] For a labouring man to be remembered in this way is unusual but his name was well known to those who read Baring-Gould's books and heard him speak.

There is a poignant coincidence in that the day Parsons died was the day that Baring-Gould's good friend Daniel Radford was buried, having passed away three days earlier. The man who fired the starting gun for the great collecting project was less than a year older than the singer whom Baring-Gould had come to regard as the archetype of country singers.

A Change of Strategy

Parsons had been a very fortunate discovery and Baring-Gould was lucky enough to find another outstanding singer, John Woodridge, who also lived on Lew Down. Both men became regular visitors to Lew House. Woodridge was a younger man and met Cecil Sharp at Lew House 25 years later. Baring-Gould now knew that such men could be found but needed to find a way to reach them. He was also aware that he had not as yet met many woman singers.

There were other difficulties, illustrated by his experience in meeting a singer whom he thought might know 'The Oxen Ploughing', a song he was particularly anxious to complete. Adam Laundry was then 77 years old and lived at North Hill in Cornwall.

---

24 Sabine Baring-Gould, 'Death of a Devonshire Singing Man, A Graceful Tribute', *Western Morning News*, 11 January, 1900. This obituary was pasted into the front of the Fair Copy manuscript. An image of it can be viewed in the Vaughan Williams Memorial Library Digital Collection, <http://vwml.org/record/SBG/3/1/4> [Accessed 22 Jan 2017].

I found him cutting ferns in a field. I asked him if he knew "The Oxen Ploughing." He did. So I sat on a heap of cut fern and he on another and he sang it, and I after him, till I had got it by heart. All the way home, a drive of eighteen miles, I continued singing it till I reached Lew, and was able to note it down with the aid of my piano.[25]

It should be emphasised that there is no evidence that this was the way in which Baring-Gould regularly collected songs, though it is a practice that he has been criticised for.

Noting down the tunes from the singers was a difficult and time-consuming process with many complicating factors. Many of the singers were past their best singing days, and missing teeth coupled with strong regional accents made mishearing a virtual certainty. Singers would naturally vary what they were singing, both words and tune. The memory of the tune sung previously might influence that of the next song. Decoration would differ between verses, making it difficult to decide what the 'real tune' was. And the words might be different when repeated, either immediately or on a later visit, as the singer fought to recover the memory of what he or she had sung a long time ago. Accuracy of pitching was an issue, though compounded by the unfamiliarity of the scales and decorative styles of the singers. The timing of the songs was often irregular. Baring-Gould wrote:

> I must, however, note here the remarkable tenacity with which old English peasant singers cling to the natural system and reject the artificial. They now sing strictly according to the sense of the words, and entirely ignore time, so that in taking down one of their airs it is often not possible to say in what time it is, whether in common or in triple measure.[26]

And:

> As a matter of fact, the peasant singer knows no time; he sings as suits the sense of his words and according to the character of his ballad. This makes it a difficult matter to note down his melodies correctly; and indeed it is not possible to do them justice apart from the words.[27]

---

25 Sabine Baring-Gould, *Further Reminiscences*, p. 204.
26 Sabine Baring-Gould, 'An Historical Sketch of English National Song', *English Minstrelsie*, I, p. x.
27 Sabine Baring-Gould, 'Introductory Essay on English Folk Music', *English Minstrelsie*, VII, p. xi.

He admitted that he was not a good enough musician to handle these difficulties and that a change of strategy was required. He wrote:

> When I had made a resolve to collect the folk-music of the West of England, my difficulty was how to get it noted down. The singing of our peasant song-men is very peculiar, with wonderful twirls, and they love a great range of notes, often rising to falsetto. Now I myself can note a melody if I can bring my singer to a piano; but I cannot write – or, as he would say, prick down – the air without this assistance. I might, perhaps, induce an old minstrel to come to my house, but the majority of singers were not to be lured from their own houses any further than the tavern, and in neither was there a piano. Moreover, a singer was uncomfortable in a strange house, nervous and shy. It was essential to put him completely at his ease. So I was obliged to turn to a skilled musician, and I at once wrote to my friend, the Rev. Henry Fleetwood Sheppard, Rector of Thurnscoe, in Yorkshire, to come to my aid.[28]

Since he lived in Yorkshire, Sheppard could not visit regularly. Luckily, further help was available a short distance from his house in the form of one of the most unusual characters in the history of the folk song movement – Frederick William Bussell.

---

28 Sabine Baring-Gould, 'Introductory Essay on English Folk Music', *English Minstrelsie*, VII, p. v.

5: The Collaborators

*I shall always have a pride in, and look back with pleasure to the days when
we 'went a'gypsying' and collecting material, and when from time to time you
led my weary old limbs long tramps of 6 or 8 miles, so beguiling the way
with springy Dartmoor turf and springy Dartmoor air, and from our springy
companionship that I knew neither fatigue nor satiety.[1]*

Frederick Bussell – Henry Fleetwood Sheppard

Frederick Bussell

*He was of enormous advantage to me in collecting the folk airs of Devon, and
was ever good natured, obliging, and ready to help in the matter.[2]*

If you stand on the terrace in front of Lew House and look to the south,
your view is of a wooded hill separated from the garden by a paddock. In
winter, when the trees have fewer leaves on them, you can see as you get
closer that there is a lake in front of that hill. When Baring-Gould first
came to Lew Trenchard the trees had not grown to conceal the quarry
rubble, ripped out to extract the limestone that lay beneath – one of his
grandfather's ventures. Faced with this eyesore, Baring-Gould set out to
landscape the quarry and the spoil heap, known as 'The Ramps', which
lay behind it. He diverted the stream that ran from the 'Holy Well' behind
the house through the garden to fill the quarry with water. He also planted
a number of ornamental trees, most of which failed to grow, and laid out
a walk along the top of the spoil heap. A boathouse was built at the water's
edge and visitors could enjoy gentle voyages on the calm water. The folk
song collector Lucy Broadwood undertook such a voyage in the company
of Baring-Gould's daughter Daisy, and referred to the lake as 'Arminell's
Pool'.[3] (Arminell was the heroine of a novel of the same name written by
Baring-Gould in 1899 and the lake plays a central role in the early part of
the book.[4])

---

1   Devon Heritage Centre, Sabine Baring-Gould Papers, 5203/M, Box 25, Letter
    of Henry Fleetwood Sheppard to Sabine Baring-Gould, 3 December 1897, in
    Baring-Gould's 1880 Diary-Notebook.
2   Sabine Baring-Gould, *Further Reminiscences*, p. 135.
3   Surrey History Centre, Lucy Broadwood Correspondence and Papers, Diary,
    6782/9, 6 September 1893.
4   Sabine Baring-Gould, *Arminell: a Social Romance* (London: Methuen, 1889).

Baring-Gould built a cottage on the south-western corner of the spoil heap, which had the advantage of the view down the valley that the mound of waste excludes from Lew House, though trees have now grown up around it.[5] At the time he started to collect folk songs the tenant was Mary Jane Bussell, the widow of Frederick Bussell, the former Rector of Great Marlow, who lived there with her daughter, Mary Frances. Her son, also named Frederick, was in the early stages of what was to be a distinguished academic career at the University of Oxford. The young don usually came to stay with his mother during college vacations and it was on one of these visits that Baring-Gould, knowing that he was a capable musician, persuaded him to act as one of his musical amanuenses. Bussell accepted the assignment with good humour and, one senses, some enthusiasm.

Frederick William Bussell was born on 23 April 1863 at Cadmore End, in Buckinghamshire. His father had died suddenly in November of the previous year and his mother had moved from Marlow to the neighbouring parish. It was a difficult time for her, as her father, a retired naval captain who had been wounded several times in the Napoleonic Wars, died the following year. Her difficulties were eased by a fund raised by the parishioners of Marlow in memory of their well-liked vicar to support her and her children. With this support she was able to send her boy to Charterhouse school, from where he went on to Magdalen College, Oxford and gained his first degree in 1886. To the surprise of his friends he then accepted an offer of a fellowship at Brasenose College. When Baring-Gould congratulated him on his success Bussell said: 'Either the fellows of Magdalen or those of Brasenose have made a great mistake.' He gained an impressive selection of first class degrees in Classics, Theology and Music as well as winning a number of other academic honours. The most prestigious of these came to him in 1905 when he was selected to present the Bampton Lectures for the year, for which he chose the topic of 'Christian Theology and Social Progress'.[6] He also held a number of other roles, such as that of Almoner of Christ's Hospital, on behalf of the University of Oxford.

---

5   The cottage has, at different times, been called 'The Ramps' or 'Ramps Cottage'. It was also known to the Bussells and to Baring-Gould as 'Rampenstein' and appears as such on the contemporary Ordnance Survey map. Baring-Gould was amused to discover that on one occasion Bussell and his mother travelled abroad as Baroness Rampenstein and the Baron Frederick William von Rampenstein.

6   Frederick Bussell, *Christian Theology and Social Progress: The Bampton Lectures for 1905* (London: Methuen & Co., 1907).

Bussell was a close friend of the essayist and art critic Walter Pater from 1891 until the latter's death in 1894 and became a guardian of his memory. Pater was a leader in the Aesthetic Movement and was surrounded by a number of young men, including Oscar Wilde, who admired his ideas and aspired to live free from dogma, 'to burn always with this hard, gem-like flame'. The two men regularly walked and dined together and attended church and chapel services. They were both sketched by William Rothenstein for the book *Oxford Characters* and Pater wrote the short essay on Bussell that accompanied his portrait.[7]

MR. F. W. BUSSELL
FELLOW OF B.N.C., B.D., AND MUS BAC.

Is as young as he looks here. He was early distinguished in the University, and has already preached some remarkable sermons in Saint Mary's pulpit. His friends love him; and he is popular with the undergraduates whom he instructs. His versatility is considerable; but he is above all a student, with something like genius for classical literature, especially for the early Christian theology and late Pagan philosophy of the imperial age, which he reads as other people read the newspapers. His expression after some hours of such reading is here recorded with remarkable fineness. He is capable of much.

WALTER PATER

Fig. 5.1 – Frederick Bussell, Portrait by William Rothenstein.

---

7   William Rothenstein, *Oxford Characters: Twenty-Four Lithographs* (London: John Lane, 1896).

Bussell was ordained an Anglican deacon in 1891 and priest in 1892, at which time he took on the role of chaplain to Brasenose College. In 1896 he became the vice-principal of the college and he gained his doctorate in Divinity in 1897. He was serious about religion in the way of his time, and within the scope of his own intellectual approach. It gave him, however, the opportunity to indulge in a hobby that was possibly unique, and certainly of doubtful morality. That hobby was the purchase and sale of perpetual curacies and donative livings. His 'collection' at its peak numbered twenty livings in different parts of the country. Apart from the requirement that he should hold a minimum number of services in the churches for which he had assumed responsibility, there were some unusual duties and privileges that delighted him. For one living he was required to attend the investiture of the Prince of Wales and to present him with a horse and a manservant. The prince graciously returned the small golden horse that Bussell gave him as well as the ancient gardener and general factotum who accompanied it.[8] His hobby could also be profitable. He bought the Manor of Exbourne, with its living, for £4,000 and sold it a few years later for £6,200, having had great fun being a squire in the meantime. He was also the official ale taster for the town of Hatherleigh.

This activity was a mild form of simony, which, though not a civil crime, is an offence against Canon Law, and some of the bishops did not approve of his activities. The University authorities were not happy with him either and he was suspended from the college for a while and he chose to spend his exile in Ostend. He was forgiven, but decided to sell off most of the livings he owned, retaining only North Tuddenham in Norfolk where he lived for some time, and his first purchase, Shelland, Suffolk, which he kept until 1938.

Bussell was a fast thinker, with a wide range of knowledge. He taught classics, philosophy, theology and history and was a memorable, rather than a popular teacher. He was not one to suffer fools gladly, and favoured the brightest of his students, with whom he developed an intellectual rapport. His lectures were sparsely attended and, on one occasion, when his lecture room was next to a popular maths teacher he stood outside and diverted the students into his own room and then lectured to them on Byzantine history. Most were too polite to leave. One of the students to whom he was tutor was the author John Buchan. He recorded in his autobiography that he enjoyed surprising Bussell by including in his essays quotes from

---

8   'Busselliana', *The Brazen Nose*, 9 (May 1951), p. 176.

Nietzsche, 'which were a little startling to a clerk in holy orders'.[9]

Bussell was a prolific writer, though never a widely read one. His books are clearly written and vigorous. There is one theme that runs through many of them and that is his dislike and distrust of democracy. In our own times few people would think it worth railing against the status quo as he did. In the introduction to his 1905 Bampton Lecture series, for example, he writes:

> I find in the mouth of every one a vague word, 'democracy,' a term (whether as fact or hope or movement) to which I have hitherto repeatedly failed to attach a clear and precise meaning. I see personal liberty everywhere threatened, personal value everywhere denied; and men set aside as an old wives' fable the Gospel-teaching of the worth of souls.[10]

His arguments were developed and alternatives to democracy proposed in his book *A New Government for the British Empire* in 1912.[11] This is not the place to examine those arguments but it is worth saying that some of the problems he saw, such as the yah-boo nature of bipartisan politics, or the concentration of real power in 'a brief dictatorship of one or two able and determined men, who will be as much detested by half the nation as they are popular with the other', have some resonance a century after they were written. His suggested remedies include devolution of power to regional assemblies, accompanied by the abolition of the House of Commons. A non-partisan House of Lords with members chosen from the Empire would direct the affairs of Empire and there would be an increased role for the monarchy. It is an interesting read but in places difficult to reconcile with twenty-first-century political thought and culture.

As vice-principal, Bussell ruled Brasenose autocratically, taking all decisions about disciplinary matters himself. When he first took on the role there were doubts as to whether he could handle the student body, which had become very unruly, with drunkenness and disobedience of the rules commonplace. Things had for a time got so out of hand that one of his predecessors had been placed on a bonfire by drunken students on 5 November and was only saved by the intervention of the porters. As it turned out Bussell's wit, sense of humour and ability to know when to turn

---

9   John Buchan, *Memory Hold-the-Door* (London: Hodder and Stoughton, 1940).
10   Frederick Bussell, *Christian Theology and Social Progress*, pp. vii–viii.
11   Frederick Bussell, *A New Government for the British Empire* (London: Longmans, Green and Co., 1912).

a blind eye helped him to succeed where those before him had failed. He never dined out of the college in the evenings, regarding it as his duty to be there to forestall any trouble. Though he retired early each night, he required the college porters to provide him with a list of any malefactors in the morning. Another element in his disciplinary policy was to suppress bad behaviour on the part of small groups or individuals, but to be tolerant of excesses during functions involving the whole college.

In September 1905, at the age 42, he married Mary Dibdin, daughter of a prominent lawyer and a descendant of the famous writer of sea songs. Like Baring-Gould, Bussell had chosen to marry a woman half his age. According to John Buchan, the marriage came as a complete surprise to everyone at Brasenose. They never had any children – indeed, it is hard to imagine Bussell as a father.

Bussell resigned as vice-principal in 1913 though he continued as a fellow of the college until he reached pensionable age in 1917, at which time he left Oxford and became Rector of Northolt, Middlesex, then still a village. Here he immersed himself in parish work and became a popular priest. Sadly, he found that his outgoings exceeded the church's income and in 1925 he gave up the struggle and resigned the living, having sold his property to the college in exchange for a lifetime annuity for himself and his wife. He retired to Worthing, where he died on 29 February 1944. Mary Bussell lived on in Worthing until she died there in 1977 at the age of 92. Apart from simony, his interests outside of his academic studies were few. His entry in the 1935 edition of *Who's Who* says of his recreations: 'none, is interested in the question of housing'. While he was at Oxford he wrote and enjoyed music, having studied harmony, and had gained his BMus in 1892. He told Baring-Gould:

> A good melody affords me no pleasure. What I love is a fugue or intricate piece of harmony; it gives me as much gratification as working out a mathematical problem does a mathematician.[12]

Though there are a number of serious compositions to his credit, he wrote several lighter pieces for university occasions and for dramatic performances and made arrangements of some folk songs. He composed the music for an 1897 production of Aristophanes' *The Knights* in which he used the tunes of old English songs for the choruses. He sang as an alto, not then a fashionable way of singing other than in cathedral choirs. With audiences that did not know him, this provoked some amusement and Baring-Gould tells us that 'at

---

12 Sabine Baring-Gould, *Further Reminiscences*, pp. 135–37.

a concert the audience was convulsed with laughter, and his mother would look about her with glances of fury at those who dared to feel amusement at Freddy's squawks'. To those who knew him better, he was much in demand, particularly for his party piece, 'Dinah Doe', a blackface minstrel song from the 1850s, the words of which could not be quoted let alone sung nowadays, but which were much enjoyed in their time. The curious reader may choose to search for it on the internet.[13]

Another description of Bussell's singing was given by the folk song collector, Anne Gilchrist, who wrote:

> Oddly enough, the first time I ever heard a folk-song sung in public was at a Brasenose college concert in Eights Week, nearly fifty years ago. It was sung by F. W. Bussell, a fellow of the college and one of Baring-Gould's collaborators in collecting the songs shortly afterwards published as 'Songs of the West.' Mr (afterwards Dr.) Bussell was already a Personality in his deacon days.[14] I recall his monocle, knee-breeches and yellow kid gloves. As a male alto he sat among the contraltos at vocal concerts, but on this occasion he sang – to the delight of the undergraduates – from a music stand placed in front of him on the platform, his selections being 'Dinah Doe' and a 'Chimney Sweeper's Song' which he had noted from a Devonshire miller and arranged himself. Though not exactly a folk-song in the sense of being of folk origin, it was a quaint eighteenth-century ditty which pleased his audience as something new and strange, and on the recommendation of a friend I acquired a copy of 'Songs of the West' (1895) in which it is No. 20.[15]

It will have become obvious to the reader that Bussell was, to say the least, an unusual character. Baring-Gould tells several stories about Bussell, and after his death *The Brazen Nose*, the Brasenose College magazine, carried a number of anecdotes about his peculiarities. In both cases it is clear that these are given as amusing memories of a man who was respected despite his oddities, rather than remembered for them.

---

13 'Dinah Doe', words by Silas Sexton Steele, composed and sung by Anthony F. Winnemore, 1850s.
14 Gilchrist's description of Bussell as 'Deacon' places the concert in 1891 or 1892. Bussell was ordained deacon in 1891 and to the priesthood the following year.
15 Anne Gilchrist, 'Let Us Remember', *English Dance and Song*, vol. 6, No. 4 (April-May 1942), pp. 62–63. Bussell and Baring-Gould had heard John Helmore sing 'The Chimney Sweep' at South Brent in 1888. It was a favourite of Bussell's.

First, there is the manner of his dress. Baring-Gould describes him as a dandy, wearing dressy ties and having a hot-house flower to match sent down from London every day. On another occasion he describes the attire Bussell considered appropriate for a stroll on the moor.

> I shall never forget the shrieks and cries for help he [Bussell] emitted at Trewartha Marsh on the Bodmin moors, where he came to see the excavations I was making in a very ancient settlement. Incautiously he had trodden upon a quaking bog, which began to eat him up, beginning at his boots and ankles and proceeding to his knees, when my workmen and I succeeded in extricating him. From his waist to his knees his trousers were of a delicate lavender hue; below, black as peat.[16]

This is supported by reports in the *Brazen Nose* of his wearing loud check suits. The portrait by William Rothenstein in *Oxford Characters* (Fig. 5.1) shows us Bussell as a young man with a waxed moustache and in a relaxed pose. He also adopted a monocle. A photograph of him in middle age shows a plumper man wearing the same high collar and white bow tie, glaring sternly with straight lips and jutting chin: the image of a vice-principal. He went to bed at ten each night, rose early and never took any exercise. Once it was necessary for him to be vaccinated when there was a smallpox scare and for some days afterwards he had himself wheeled in a bath chair by a junior porter lest the strain should prove too much for him, while his pupils walked beside him, reading their essays aloud.

Bussell travelled with Baring-Gould on song collecting expeditions that took them to the further corners of Dartmoor and down into Cornwall. John Betjeman pointed affectionately to the incongruity of the clergyman and the young dandy driving up to a country cottage to ask the inhabitants if they knew any old songs.[17] In practice, it was an amiable partnership that worked very well as they travelled together through the West Country, staying at country inns to listen to the old men singing their songs in the bar of an evening. Baring-Gould wrote: 'Mr. Bussell was remarkable for the extreme accuracy with which he noted every twist and flourish of the singer. Nothing escaped him.'[18]

---

16 Sabine Baring-Gould, *Further Reminiscences*, p. 136.
17 John Betjeman, 'Sabine Baring-Gould' (Radio talk, 21 September 1945), in *Trains and Buttered Toast*, ed. Stephen Games (London: John Murray, 2006), pp. 189–95.
18 Sabine Baring-Gould, 'Introductory Essay on English Folk Music', *English Minstrelsie*, VII, pp. vii–ix.

In his Preface to the first edition of *Songs of the West* he expressed his thanks to Bussell for 'his unflagging good humour and readiness to go with me anywhere and in any weather after a song-man'.[19] Only once do we hear a hint of a grumble from Bussell and a sign of that good humour failing:

> We made a journey through Cornwall song-collecting. After some rough experience in very country inns we reached Fowey. 'Come,' said my companion, 'let us now taste the sweets of civilisation, and go to the Fowey Hotel.' 'Very well,' said I with a sigh. 'But no songs there.' 'No, but we shall have the electric light.'[20]

Their collecting sessions did not always go quite to plan:

> One wild and stormy day, Mr Bussell and I visited Huccaby to interview old Sally Satterley, who knew a number of songs. Her father was a notable singer and his old daughter, now a grandmother, remembered some of his songs. But old Sally could not sit down and sing. We found that the sole way in which we could extract the ballads from her was by following her about as she did her usual work. Accordingly we went after her when she fed the pigs, or got sticks from the firewood rick or filled a pail from the spring, pencil and notebook in hand, dotting down words and melody. Finally she did sit to peel some potatoes, when Mr Bussell, with a manuscript music-book in hand, seated himself on the copper. This position he maintained as she sang the ballad of 'Lord Thomas and the Fair Eleanor', till her daughter applied fire under the cauldron and Mr Bussell was forced to skip from his perch.[21]

Baring-Gould does suggest that he felt somewhat constrained by one aspect of his partnership with Bussell, and that is the question of recording sexually explicit songs. He told the American ballad scholar Francis Child that one of the reasons that he did not take down such material was that: 'I had a scruple about it especially when Mr Bussell, a young Oxford man, was with me helping to note the melodies.'[22]

19 Sabine Baring-Gould, 'Preface', *Songs of the West* (1891), Part 4, p. xii.
20 Sabine Baring-Gould, 'Introductory Essay on English Folk Music', *English Minstrelsie*, VII, p. viii.
21 Sabine Baring-Gould, *A Book of Dartmoor*, London: Methuen, 1900, p. 201.
22 Cambridge (MA), Houghton Library, Harvard University, Baring-Gould Manuscript, Ballads and Songs collected by the Rev. S. Baring-Gould, chiefly in Devonshire, and sent by him to Professor F. J. Child, MS Eng 863, Letter from Baring-Gould to Francis Child, 23 August 1890, Appendix Item 5.

Bussell noted the greater proportion of the tunes for the songs in the collection. Over 300 of the 850 songs in the 'Personal Copy' manuscript that were collected in the field are attributed to him and there are more than that in the collection as a whole. Bussell's field notebooks are among those that Baring-Gould gave to Plymouth Library in February 1914, and which are now known collectively as the 'Rough Copy'. The first volume contains the only surviving letter from Bussell to Baring-Gould, apologising for not having sent on one of the books in which he had been inking over his pencilled notation to make it clearer. In Bussell's notebooks there are little jokes: song titles given in Greek or French, attempts to record the singers' dialect, and so on. There are also several examples of his arrangements of songs.

In the first edition of *Songs of the West*, 26 of the 110 songs had arrangements by Bussell, and in two cases he provided two settings. Baring-Gould explains this as being a consequence of Henry Fleetwood Sheppard's role as musical editor:

> Mr. Sheppard entertained a very strong objection to arranging any song he had not himself 'pricked down' from the lips of the singers, and as Mr. Bussell had noted down hundreds as well, these, for the most part, had to be laid on one side. Mr. Sheppard was, doubtless, right in his assertion, that unless he had himself heard the song sung, he could not catch its special character, and so render it justly.[23]

Sheppard himself recognised the difficulty in his own notes on the music in *Songs of the West* and referred to the contribution made by Frederick Bussel: 'whose valuable help and great kindness I gratefully acknowledge, and to whose excellent taste and musician-like writing the following pages bear too infrequent testimony'. Bussell was not involved in the production of *A Garland of Country Song* in 1895, but rejoined Baring-Gould and Sheppard in editing the eight-volume *English Minstrelsie* in the same year.

When the revised edition of *Songs of the West* was published in 1905, Cecil Sharp was brought in as musical editor to replace Henry Fleetwood Sheppard, who had died in 1901. This was an opportunity to redress the balance and recognise Bussell's contribution more fully. The opportunity was not taken. In the new edition with 121 songs, just five of Bussell's arrangements were retained. He was irate and wrote to Methuen, demanding that his name be removed from the title page. George Webster

---

23 Sabine Baring-Gould, 'Introduction', *Songs of the West* (1905), p. xi.

of Methuen wrote in turn to Baring-Gould, asking him to pacify the wronged arranger saying, 'I have explained that all alterations were made at your suggestion, and under your supervision'.[24] It appears that he succeeded, since Bussell's name remained in place.

In the manuscript memoir that he wrote, and which is now in the archive at Brasenose College, Bussell summed up the years he spent collecting songs with Baring-Gould in a single sentence:

> We had very pleasant times together, collecting songs all over Devon and Cornwall, the credit of which was annexed by a Mr Cecil Sharpe [sic] who rearranged them to very tame settings indeed.

Henry Fleetwood Sheppard

A remarkably kind and genial spirit, always ready to help, and always wise in judgment.[25]

In the 'Introductory Essay on English Folk-Music' that opens the seventh volume of Baring-Gould's *English Minstrelsie* there is a grainy photograph of the Rev. Henry Fleetwood Sheppard, MA, Rector of Thurnscoe in the West Riding of Yorkshire, the other man who joined Baring-Gould in his quest for West Country song. The photograph shows us an elderly man – he was then in his seventies – with receding hair and a white, neatly trimmed beard. That beard conceals his mouth but there is just a hint of a smile. It is the eyes that draw your attention: bright, intelligent and quizzical. Sheppard's papers were destroyed by his wife and daughter after his death, so we have only a fragmentary picture of his life outside of the work that he did with Baring-Gould. We know from what was published and from the letters that he wrote to Baring-Gould that he could be witty and that he had strong opinions on music. We also know from those letters, when taken together with those that Baring-Gould wrote to Lucy Broadwood, that he could be difficult and rather obstinate.

Henry Fleetwood Sheppard was born in London on 5 February 1824. After he graduated from Trinity Hall, Cambridge, he was made deacon in 1856 and ordained a priest in the following year. His first post was as a curate at Marton in Cheshire until in 1858 he became the Vicar of St

---

24 Devon Heritage Centre, Sabine Baring-Gould Papers, Letter of George Webster to Sabine Baring-Gould, 13 October 1905, 5203 M, Box 33.
25 Sabine Baring-Gould, 'In Memoriam, The Reverend H. Fleetwood Sheppard', *The Church Times,* 10 January 1902, p. 53.

Fig. 5.2 – Henry Fleetwood Sheppard. From *English Minstrelsie.*

Thomas, Kilnhurst, in Yorkshire. Kilnhurst was the centre of a developing coalfield and had been experiencing rapid population growth as new mines were opened. What had formerly been a small village within the parish of Swinton had grown rapidly and it was seen as a rough place where both Church and law were under-represented. It was decided to build a new parish church and Sheppard was its first parson. He spent nine years there ministering to this rowdy congregation and the records of the ceremonies he performed show that he met a wide range of people from colliers and factory workers to the local gentry. His wife, Eliza Mary, bore two children, Mary and Henry, while they were living in Kilnhurst. Henry studied medicine and emigrated to Calgary. Mary shared her father's musical interests and was later to perform in some of the concerts of folk songs that Baring-Gould organised. She never married.

Sheppard held his post at Kilnhurst for nine years before moving a few miles north to St Helen's Parish Church, Thurnscoe in 1868 as rector. Here he stayed until he retired more than thirty years later. When he first came to the parish the population of Thurnscoe was, according to Baring-

Gould, just 180 people and it was a largely agricultural community. This smaller congregation would have allowed him more time to spend on his music, without detriment to the care he gave to his parishioners.

Sheppard was a skilled musician and a driving force behind the formation in 1863 of the Doncaster Choral Union of which he became the precentor, a position he was to hold for over twenty years. The object of the organisation was to improve the singing in the churches of the deanery, though implicit in this was the movement towards 'High Church' principles of worship. The Choral Union held a festival in Doncaster Parish Church every year at which the member choirs came together. The day's events, which involved several hundred choristers and clergymen, were centred on two services, one in the morning and one in the afternoon, separated by a communal lunch in a local hall.[26] The music for the services was selected and arranged by Sheppard, who intoned the prayers during the services. It became the practice for the music to be provided to the choirs as a booklet, which was published by Novello some months before the festival so that they had plenty of time to learn and rehearse.

The Doncaster Choral Union included both surpliced and unsurpliced choirs, and the festival services, which featured plain-song and Gregorian chant, contained ritualistic elements that were, at the time, controversial and were criticised by Anglican conservatives. *The Leeds Mercury* carried a letter in 1870 deploring the 'Romanising Tendencies of the Church of England'.[27] The letter-writer, Richard Morris, took the festival organisers to task for including the Roman Catholic hymn 'Faith of our Fathers' in the service, even though the lines that offended most:

Faith of our fathers! Mary's prayers
Shall win our country back to thee;

had been modified by replacing 'Mary's' with 'Ceaseless'. The chief sinner in the letter-writer's view, however, was the Archbishop of York, who preached at the morning service, and who had declined to forbid the singing of the hymn when approached by a delegation from the Doncaster congregation. The writer recommended that 'If choral unions are to be used by ritualistic clergymen as means of propagating Romanism, the sooner they are discouraged by Protestants the better.'

---

26 The 1870 festival, for example, brought together close to 600 choristers and fifty clergymen, according to the report in the *Sheffield and Rotherham Independent*, 11 June 1870, p. 10.
27 'Romanising Tendencies of the Church of England', *The Leeds Mercury*, 16 June 1870, p. 7.

Even the interest in plain-song, which seems innocuous enough in the present day, attracted criticism because it was perceived to be Anglo-Catholic in its character. The writer of the report on the 1874 meeting of the Plain-Song Union in the *Bradford Observer* asked:

> Why all the labour and experience of hundreds of years in the perfecting of the science of music should be ignored, and the discarded barbarities of square headed notes, diamonds and a four-line stave, and the monotony of unison chanting, be revived we know not; we suppose that the devotees of plain-song are anxious to copy the monks of old as closely in their music as in other respects. If this be their aim, they are to be complimented on the success with which the beautiful service of the Church of England was yesterday metamorphosed into a travestie on the High Mass as performed in the cathedrals on the Continent.[28]

John Sharp, the Vicar of Horbury for whom Baring-Gould acted as curate, was the president of the West Yorkshire Plain-Song Union, which had its first festival in Horbury in 1867. Sheppard was also the precentor for this organisation and it is likely that he and Baring-Gould met at Horbury when Sheppard visited John Sharp in connection with the formation of the Union.

The majority of Sheppard's compositions were church music, though there are a few lighter pieces. It is particularly interesting, given the later work he did with Baring-Gould, that he made some arrangements of folk songs as early as 1877, when Novello published a small booklet called *Three English Rustic Songs for Harvest Homes*.[29] The songs included were 'The Useful Plough', 'The Farmer's Boy' and 'The New-Mown Hay' and they were described as being 'old words set to new music'. There is a copy of the publication among Baring-Gould's books, though only the first and third songs are now present.

The explanation for the absence of 'The Farmer's Boy' may be that Baring-Gould had not replaced it in its cover after using it for a performance of the song in a village concert. He described this event in his book *Old Country Life*:

---

28 'West Yorkshire Plain-Song Union', *The Bradford Observer*, 10 June 1874, p. 4.
29 Henry Fleetwood Sheppard, *Three English Rustic Songs for Harvest Homes* (London: Novello, Ewer & Co., 1877).

At a village concert, I sang an old ballad, 'The Sun was Set behind the Hill', set by a friend to a melody he had composed for it. A very old labourer who was present began to grumble. 'He's gotten the words right, but he's not got the right tune. He should zing 'un right or not at all,' and he got up and left the room in disdain.[30]

When he formed his intention to collect folk songs Baring-Gould recognised that as well as helping him to collect tunes Sheppard's knowledge of musical history would be of value in understanding the background to the songs he was hearing. Sheppard travelled to Lew Trenchard in the autumn of 1888, where he took down tunes from James Parsons, whom Baring-Gould had invited to Lew House for the purpose. Shortly afterwards he visited again and heard John Woodridge sing at Lew Trenchard, before going with Baring-Gould on a second visit to South Brent, which he had previously visited in Bussell's company, where they heard more songs from John Helmore and Robert Hard.

Baring-Gould was already making plans for publishing the songs and asked Sheppard for his help. His intentions were announced in a letter published in the *Western Morning News* on 7 December 1888 in which he wrote that Sheppard was to undertake the arrangements for the proposed book, *Songs of the West*.[31] The first advertisement for that book was in the same issue of the newspaper. Sheppard's role was to be that of musical editor and, *de facto*, chief arranger. He also provided Baring-Gould with some leads to material of interest. It was he, for example, who suggested in a letter to Baring-Gould in June 1889 that he look at Davies Gilbert's collection of Cornish carols, of which he had been able to borrow a copy in Yorkshire.[32] In July the following year he wrote that he had laid his hands on the three volumes of the *Universal Songster* and had been combing through its five thousand songs.[33] He had found many that he recognised from his youth, though he says that there were 'only 2 or 3 that bear upon our subject'.

Like Bussell, he went out on overnight trips with Baring-Gould who described some of them, such as a visit to Holne in May 1890.

---

30 Sabine Baring-Gould, *Old Country Life*, p. 266.
31 Sabine Baring-Gould, 'Folk Songs and Melodies of the West', *The Western Antiquary*, 8 (December), pp. 105–06.
32 Plymouth, Plymouth Central Library, Working Notebook 1, Letter of Henry Fleetwood Sheppard to Sabine Baring-Gould, 4 June 1889, loose in notebook.
33 Devon Heritage Centre, Sabine Baring-Gould Papers, 5203 M, Box 36, Letter of Henry Fleetwood Sheppard to Sabine Baring-Gould, 7 July 1890.

Mr. Sheppard and I put up for a week at Holne, near Ashburton, song collecting. We got together a number of singers, and gave them a supper. Then they sang each a song in turn; most of these were rubbish, many modern, published songs, and just as one old fellow began a strain in the Dorian mode, in came the village constable to order all out, because the public-house must be closed. However, we had pretty well discovered which were the singers who had the real good stuff in them, and these we invited to warble to us on the following evenings; and from them we collected some excellent airs.[34]

Most of the song collecting that Sheppard did was in the early days of the project. It is hard to get an accurate picture of what happened because Baring-Gould did not at first record the details of the collection of each song and, where he did record dates, he sometimes got them wrong. The fact that few of Sheppard's field notes have survived also make it hard to follow the course of his collecting, or to judge his treatment of the tunes he noted. We know that he collected fewer songs than Bussell, as we can only identify 138 songs noted by him from 31 different singers between 1888 and 1895. Nonetheless, three quarters of the songs published in *Songs of the West* had been collected by him.

He also acted as musical editor for two other collections that Baring-Gould published in the 1890s: *A Garland of Country Song*, and *English Minstrelsie*, and he strongly influenced the construction of these books. For these and for *Songs of the West* it was Sheppard who created the majority of the arrangements.[35] His piano accompaniments were complex and more than one contemporary reviewer considered them beyond the capability of the average drawing room pianist. Lucy Broadwood disliked Sheppard's arrangements intensely, but Baring-Gould remained convinced of their worth saying, in a letter to Cecil Sharp, 'I have always loved Mr Sheppard's settings of the Devonshire songs in the original edition ... there was a radiance of poetry about his arrangements.'[36]

---

34 Sabine Baring-Gould, 'Introductory Essay on English Folk Music', *English Minstrelsie*, VII, p. vii.

35 For *A Garland of Country Song*, he was the sole arranger.

36 Broadwood's dislike of Sheppard's accompaniments is evident from the diary entry after her visit to hear Baring-Gould talk at the Royal Institution on 11 May 1894. 'Bad singing – was irritated afresh by Revd H. Fleetwood Sheppard's accompt's.' Surrey History Centre, Lucy Broadwood Papers, 6782/10, 11 May 1894. Baring-Gould's preference for Sheppard's settings: London, Vaughan Williams Memorial Library, Cecil Sharp Correspondence, Letter of Sabine Baring-Gould to Cecil Sharp, 7 January 1917.

In 1891 Sheppard provided an essay, 'On the Melodies of Songs of the West', which appeared in the pre-1905 editions of the book. In it he made a number of observations that are perceptive and of significance, even now. He understood that untaught composers are quite capable of producing melodies, writing, 'Melody is not a progressive art, nor is any scientific knowledge of music necessary for the production of tunes both striking and touching.' This made it quite conceivable that the melodies they had found were the compositions of local people. He suggested that this was true of early hymns, even if the tunes sometimes seemed strange to more experienced ears. He described the preference of the old singers for singing in modal keys and for using the flattened seventh. He also justified his approach to accompaniment, arguing that while ballads may carry the listener along by the power of the story, a shorter, romantic song might be tedious without an accompaniment to add interest.

He cites 'The Bell Ringing' as a characteristic song with:

> …an indolent easy grace […] which is in keeping with the words and charmingly suggestive. The sunny valleys, the breezy downs, the sweet bell-music swelling and sinking on the soft autumn air, the old folk creeping out of their chimney-nooks to listen, and all employment in the little town suspended in the popular excitement at the contest for a hat laced with gold. All this, told in a few words and illustrated by a few notes, quite calls up a picture of life, and stamps the number as a genuine folk song.[37]

He goes on to comment on the morality of the song, and of folk song more generally:

> The narrator is unhappily slightly intoxicated, but no one thinks the worse of him: stern morality on that or any other score will in vain be looked for in Songs of the West. This very easy morality is perhaps one reason why the younger generation of singers takes no care, nor shows any readiness to hand down the songs which delighted our forefathers. Public opinions will not now tolerate the coarse humour, and coarser sentiment of the seventeenth and eighteenth centuries; and, although we may lament the loss of the tunes, the singers who eschew these songs are more to be praised for their good ethical sense than blamed for their bad musical taste.

---

37 Henry Fleetwood Sheppard, 'On the Melodies of Songs of the West', *Songs of the West* (1891) Part 4, pp. xliv–xlvii.

This passage indicates that Sheppard agreed with Baring-Gould's editing of coarse material for *Songs of the West*.

It is clear from the few surviving letters that the working relationship between the two men was at times difficult and that Baring-Gould came close to despair over Sheppard's attitude, though it is possible that his own rather cavalier approach may not have helped. The tone of Sheppard's letters often shows an edginess that barely concealed a deeper unhappiness.

By 1894 it appears that Sheppard was losing interest in folk song. Baring-Gould wrote to Lucy Broadwood on 27 January: 'I fear we shall never get Mr Sheppard to note down any more folk melodies. He says that his interest is gone in them as soon as he has published his arrangements. In fact I do not think he ever really entered into them from an archaeological point of view; he was interested but never zealous'.[38] A few days later he wrote again, complaining:

> I have over and over sent him tunes that were provided to me by correspondents, or which I had taken down, & have begged him to bar or tell me something about them, & he does neither, but absorbs the lot into his box of material. Thus he has many things I have been unable to use. In my volume are many words of songs without tunes, waiting for him to bar, & as he never did this, the songs remain without their airs.[39]

Then, in August, Baring-Gould told her, that Sheppard had written, saying 'Don't worry me with any more musical finds, I have done with the whole thing'.[40]

The two men were working on *A Garland of Country Song* at the time and this may explain the delays in publishing that book, though Sheppard was presumably happy enough arranging the songs they had already chosen. Then another project arose which seems to have rekindled Sheppard's interest. Baring-Gould invited him to join the team working on the mammoth song collection *English Minstrelsie*. Sheppard threw himself

---

38 London, Vaughan Williams Memorial Library, Lucy Broadwood Manuscripts, Letter of Sabine Baring-Gould to Lucy Broadwood, 27 January 1894, LEB/4/9 27. The letter is undated but it reports the death of Baring-Gould's butler, which happened on this day.

39 VWML, Lucy Broadwood Manuscripts, Letter to Lucy Broadwood, 1 February 1894, LEB/4/20.

40 Surrey History Centre, Lucy Broadwood Correspondence and Papers, Letter of Sabine Baring-Gould to Lucy Broadwood, 6 August 1894, 2185/LEB/1/275a.

back into arranging songs, though this time he shared the responsibility for arranging the material that Baring-Gould chose with Frederick Bussell and W. H. Hopkinson.[41] Bussell, Sheppard and Hopkinson subsequently took on another multi-volume project, *British Minstrelsie*, a selection of songs from the four countries of the British Isles, though this did not involve Baring-Gould.

Sheppard visited Lew Trenchard in August 1895 and went with Baring-Gould for what was their last song collecting trip together. They visited Sam Fone, from whom they noted ten songs.

Though Sheppard had escaped the hurly-burly, industrial and coal mining culture of Kilnhurst for the rural peace of Thurnscoe in 1868, it did not last. There had been small surface workings for coal when he arrived but the opening of the Hickleton Main Colliery in 1892 and the discovery of the Barnsley Seam led the population to grow from 180 to 3,366 by 1898. This proved too much work for Sheppard who wrote to Baring-Gould in 1897: 'This place is getting quite beyond me. The curate that I had did at least as much harm as good & I don't seem likely to find the right man.'[42] He left Thurnscoe in February 1899 and moved with his wife and daughter to Oxford, where he hoped to find the companionship of books and lively minds as well as some good music. Sadly, his retirement was not a long one as he died of a stroke at his home in Oxford on 27 December 1901. He was then in his 78th year. His former parishes were represented at the funeral in St Margaret's Church, but the villagers of Thurnscoe held their own memorial service the same afternoon, where they were joined by some of those from Kilnhurst who remembered him. The church was draped in black and his obituary writer described the music as 'very impressive'.

His wife and daughter burned his papers after his death, including most of his rough notes and his work on the songs. There were also several notes of song texts and tunes collected by his colleagues that were not returned. We also know that he had retained many of the original manuscripts of tunes sent to Baring-Gould by post and these too were lost.

For this reason, the only record we have of which songs he collected is where Baring-Gould has named him in his manuscripts. This gives us about 140 titles that can definitely be attributed to Sheppard – less than half of the number that can be assigned to Bussell on the same basis.

---

41 Hopkinson was an Edinburgh-based organist and composer.
42 Devon Heritage Centre, Baring-Gould Papers, 5203/M, Box 25, Letter of Henry Fleetwood Sheppard to Sabine Baring-Gould, 13 Dec 1897, in Baring-Gould's 1880 Diary-Notebook.

The absence of field notes makes it hard to judge how well Sheppard transcribed the tunes he collected into the versions that he submitted for publication. Bussell was readily available when he was at Lew Trenchard for his vacations and enthusiastically joined Baring-Gould on his song collecting expeditions. Sheppard lived further away, but from a distance he worked closely with Baring-Gould to select and prepare material for publication. He also had a strong influence on the style and content of *Songs of the West*. It is this that is the greatest strength of his contribution.

The wheel of Fortune has turned again and the village of Thurnscoe has declined greatly since the pit closed in 1988. Shops are boarded up and many public buildings have been closed, some demolished. The pithead area has been cleared and landscaped to provide industrial units and a public park. St Helen's Church, where Sheppard served for so many years, is now a sad sight from the outside. The tower, which is the oldest part of the church, is cracking with age and the settlement caused by the mines that run through the area. The church is normally kept locked, but we were fortunate when we visited to find one of the church wardens in the parish hall over the road. She let us into the church and proudly showed us the warm, beating heart that lies behind the bleak walls. The interior is well kept and attractive and it is not long before one finds traces of Henry Fleetwood Sheppard. The choir stalls and the wooden pulpit were both provided early in the twentieth century as memorials to him. The most touching memorial, though, is the carved inscription on the vestry wall. It was Sheppard himself who had the stone with the first part of the inscription, let into the wall before he left the parish: 'Pray for the peace of Henry Fleetwood Sheppard, thirty years rector of this church 1868–1898.' In his farewell speech to his parishioners he suggested that 'When he was dead and gone, if any known friend liked to place upon that stone "Went to rest," on such a date, he would be glad.'[43] His invitation was taken up and the inscription was completed with the words: 'who went to rest December 27th 1901 aged 77 years'. Baring-Gould says that a long-serving member of Sheppard's choir cut these words. The obituary concluded by observing that this fully described 'the characteristics and originality of the deceased, who was frank, real and genuine in all things ... he had not a single enemy.'

Frederick Bussell and Henry Fleetwood Sheppard were very different in age and in their attitude to life. Each was, in his own way, something of a rebel. They were both very capable musicians and it is unlikely that the project would have succeeded without their involvement. Baring-

---

43 'Obituary', *Mexborough and Swinton Times*, 3 January 1902, p. 8.

Gould was consistently complimentary about their skill in noting down the tunes from the singers in the field. Each was also a competent arranger, though Bussell had less opportunity to demonstrate this in *Songs of the West*. There were occasions when the three men got together and the broader 'project team' also included Bussell's sister, who was the accompanist for the majority of the concerts that Baring-Gould organised, and Sheppard's daughter, who sang in some of the early concerts. The quotation from Sheppard that heads this chapter and that from Bussell that ends the first section suggests that they actually had a very pleasant time together.

As I Walked Out

6: Sweet Nightingales

I reckon the days is departed, when folks would have listened to me
And I feels like as one broken-hearted, a-thinking o' what used to be
And I don't know as much be amended, than was in them merry old times
When wi' pipes and good ale folks attended, to me and my purty old rhymes
To me and my purty old rhymes.[1]

Who Were the Singers? − Where Were They to be Found? − Two Bridges − South Brent − Robert Hard − John Helmore− John Woodridge − Harry Westaway − Sally Satterley − Samuel Fone − South Zeal − The Singing Birds

Baring-Gould's manuscript notes and books of songs name the men and women who sang for him, often recording details about them and their lives that are not included in his songbooks. Most of them had just one or two songs, but some more accomplished singers could sing fifty songs immediately (if imperfectly) and, with time for recollection, a hundred more. These were the stars in Baring-Gould's folk firmament; men like James Parsons, 'The Singing Machine', for whom Baring-Gould had the highest regard.

This book is centred on a collection of songs, but much of its content is about the people who were involved in the making of that collection. None were more important than the singers themselves − a view which Baring-Gould held, and which I wholeheartedly endorse. That is why I have, from an early stage in my research into the collection, listed the singers as I came across them, together with what Baring-Gould wrote about them. I have then worked with this information, confirming the details that Baring-Gould gave and trying to find out more.[2] This has required searches of census and other public records, as well as contemporary newspapers.[3] In some cases I have had the good fortune to make contact with descendants of the singers, and to hear more about their relatives from them.

---

1   'The Old Singing Man', song text by Baring-Gould to the tune of 'The Little Girl Down the Row' that he collected from Will Huggins, and in whose memory he wrote these words.
2   It will be no longer be a surprise to the reader when I say that not all of the information that Baring-Gould recorded was complete or accurate.
3   I must acknowledge my debt to the late Dr Christopher Bearman who collaborated with me on this work in its early stages and whose skills in retrieving this information were remarkable, given that this was a time before it was available on the internet, and that he was working solely with hard-copy documents.

Who Were the Singers?

There is much to be discovered beyond their names. We can, for example, establish the occupations of many of the singers in Baring-Gould's notes or from studying the census. In Appendix D I have listed the 189 singers named by Baring-Gould and tabulated their locations and occupations. Of the 183 singers whose location is known 137 (74%) lived in Devon and 46 (25%) in Cornwall. As might be expected, given the region in which he collected, 44 (28%) of the 154 whose occupations can be ascertained were agricultural labourers or farmers.[4] Otherwise, the work that people did reflected the economy of the region at the time.

The remainder of the singers included general labourers, tradesmen, craftsmen, and skilled agricultural workers as well as a handful of professional men or those who lived on their own means, who qualify because they sang traditional songs for him.

Women were not well represented as they formed only 19% of the singers, something Baring-Gould was well aware of and regretted. Of these, the majority worked within the home.

This information does not tell the whole story. It was an age when there was no formal provision for old age other than parish relief or the workhouse and many of the farm labourers were in their sixties and seventies and beyond. Some would have been treated well by their employers and allowed to remain in their cottages even when 'retired' due to ill health. Matthew Baker, for example, was a 74-year-old agricultural labourer notionally employed on Baring-Gould's estate but who was unable to work on a regular basis. He continued to live in one of the estate cottages on Lew Down until his death in 1894, and his wife Betsy was allowed to stay there until she died the following year.

Richard Mortimore, a retired stonemason who lived in Princetown on Dartmoor, was less fortunate. He was partly bed-ridden but was up and dressed when Baring-Gould and Bussell called on him in 1890, and heard some songs from him. They went back a few weeks later, hoping to hear more, but were met by his wife who refused to let them see him, saying, 'You ought to have been ashamed to get an old man like that to sing worldly songs. At his age he shouldn't sing nought but psalms and hymns.' While we might not approve of Elizabeth Mortimore's attitude to her

---

4   The description 'farmer' includes both small tenant farmers and those who owned and farmed a larger acreage, employing several hands.

husband's singing, it was not uncommon among the spouses of singers.[5]
And the situation that the Mortimores faced was a difficult one, as Baring-
Gould went on to describe:

> The case of the old fellow was one in which the cruelty that may
> occur in the working of our English poor laws was made evident.
> He lived in a mean cottage of his own, and because his own, the
> Guardians were unable to allow him anything. If his wife went out
> charring, he was left in bed, so crippled that he was unable to turn
> himself; if she remained at home, they were absolutely penniless.
> He was urged to sell his house, and go into the Union. 'No, let
> me starve and die under my own roof,' he replied, and starve he
> would have, had it not been for the charity of his neighbours. One
> can understand the clinging of this old sick man to his house, in
> which he had lived for so many years, and his inability to endure
> the wrench of parting with it, and being turned out of it. It was
> surely barbarity to punish him, by denial of a pittance, for this
> very natural feeling.[6]

Where Were They to be Found?

Once he had recruited the two musicians who were to help him, Baring-
Gould had more options available. Getting the singers to come to him was
one possibility and local singers like John Woodridge and James Parsons
would be invited to Lew House after their day's work to meet with him,
and whichever of his colleagues was with him at the time, to sing and chat.

Baring-Gould could be quite determined in his quest:

> There was, I heard, an old man in the cold clay district north of
> Broadbury Down, in the parish of Halwell, in North Devon, who
> was reputed to be a singer. It was for me a drive of nearly seventeen
> miles; however, I went after him, driving over a moor strewn with
> tumuli, found him in a field weeding turnips, and at once began on
> the topic of old songs. I soon learned from him the names of several

---

5   In her essay 'On the collecting of English Folk Song' (*Proceedings of the Musical
     Association*, 31st Session (1904–5), pp. 89–109) Lucy Broadwood describes
     meeting Patience Vaisey, a gardener's wife, at Adwell in Oxfordshire, who sang
     nineteen songs for her including 'My Bonnie, Bonnie Boy'. Her husband,
     who was eight years younger than she was, did not approve of her singing the old
     songs, exclaiming, 'Don't teach them that rubbish; teach them Hymns Ancient
     and Modern!'
6   Sabine Baring-Gould, Note to 'Spring and Winter' in *English Minstrelsie*, II, p. iv.

that he sung, and got from him a promise to come and stay with me
for a few days, so soon as Mr. Sheppard arrived. Accordingly, old
Luxton — that was his name — came, and he gave us a number of
delightful songs, some of exquisite delicacy.[7]

One can imagine the surprise of Roger Luxton's neighbours when a
carriage, driven by a liveried coachman, whisked him away for a couple
of days. We can be certain, though, that the old singer would have been
treated well, not least by the long-serving coachman, Charlie Dustan, then
only twenty years old but already known as 'a bit of a lad'.[8]

But Baring-Gould now also had the option, when his colleagues were
available, of travelling out to meet singers in their homes, in the pubs where
they met to sing, and even occasionally by the roadside. Most of those
journeys were made in a carriage or dog-cart, usually driven by Charlie
Dustan. For longer journeys Baring-Gould would use the train, since there
were a number of lines then operating in Devon, though some of the lines
into Cornwall were still under construction.

Many of these journeys were day-trips, visiting singers whom Baring-
Gould had heard about in the locality. For others he would stay overnight
in a pub where he knew singers were going to be present.

Two Bridges

One of the first of these excursions was the visit he made with Frederick
Bussell to the Saracen's Head Inn at Two Bridges on 7/8 January 1890.
He described how he

> was sitting in winter in an inn kitchen on Dartmoor, in the
> settle, beside a huge fire of heaped-up and glowing peat. Several
> moormen were present, having their ale, talking over politics, the
> weather, the condition of the turf harvest the preceding season,
> the cattle, and the horses that ran wild on the moor.[9]

---

7   Sabine Baring-Gould, 'Introductory Essay on English Folk Music', *English
    Minstrelsie*, VII, p. vii.
8   Charles Dustan served the Baring-Gould family for fifty years as coachman
    and then as a gardener. He was welcomed into the kitchen of any house his
    employer visited and was said to have 'a wonderful way with cider'. One of
    Baring-Gould's daughters reported that he once drove them to a local dance
    but that, on the way home, her sister had to take the reins because he had
    drunk a little too much. Her father was not told.
9   Sabine Baring-Gould, 'Ploughing Oxen', *Chambers's Journal*, 16 February 1895,
    pp. 81–82.

One of the songs they heard that night was 'The Bell Ringing', which was sung by a farmer, William Kerswell, and which is now a favourite with West Country folk singers of today.

> One day in October, neither drunken nor sober,
> O'er Broadbury Down I was taking my way.
> When I heard of some ringing, some dancing & singing
> I ought to remember that Jubilee Day.
>> 'Twas in Ashwater town
>> The bells they did soun'
>> They rang for a belt and a hat laced with gold
>> But the men of North Lew,
>> Rang so steady and true
>> That never were better in Devon I hold.

In his note to the song, which is No. 82 in *Songs of the West*, Baring-Gould remarks, 'When sung by the old farmer over a great fire in the kitchen, his clear, robust voice imitating the bells, produced an indescribable charm.'[10] A bell ringer who has heard the song told me that the metre of the tune is that of a well-known ringing peel.[11]

'The Bell Ringing', which had clearly delighted Baring-Gould, was one of more than thirty songs collected on that trip. They had begun collecting in Princetown with the three songs noted from Richard Mortimore, whose condition I described above. They then went on to the Saracen's Head Inn where they heard songs from several other men including the farmer William Kerswell, Richard Gregory (a water bailiff), James Mortimore (another farmer), William Setters (a labourer) and Harry Smith, the landlady's son, who was also a farmer. The following morning Baring-Gould and Bussell drove over to Huccaby to meet the landlord of the Forest Inn, Richard Cleave. Just one song resulted from this side-trip – 'The Dragoon's Ride' about which Bussell wrote above his notation in the Rough Copy manuscript:

> This tune is a very memorable one to us. It is the sole spoils of a long drive in the stormiest of Dartmoor weather from Two B[ridges] to Huccaby B[ridge]. We value the Dragon's ride particularly highly.[12]

---

10 For some reason this evocative sentence was dropped from the note in the 1905 edition of *Songs of the West*.

11 Don Roberts told me that the tune is based on a famous peal, '60 on thirds'. It is rung at every Devonshire Ringers competition. Personal communication.

12 Plymouth Central Library, Baring-Gould Collection, 'Dragon's Ride (R. Cleave)', Rough Copy manuscript, Vol 2, p. 24.

They returned to the Saracen's Head for another night and heard more songs. Bussell has made a note of some dialogue between two of the men, the first of whom said of the previous evening, 'I had music in my head all night', to which one of his friends unkindly replied, 'I dare say, if anybody had taken your head as a tambourine, he'd have got some music out of it.' The difficulty that the collectors faced in noting tunes is reflected in Baring-Gould's comment in the Personal Copy manuscript that 'W. Setters is a most uncertain singer; he rarely sings two verses alike.' Nevertheless, they obtained ten songs from him.

South Brent

One of those who responded to Baring-Gould's newspaper appeal in September 1888 was Charles Spence Bate (1819–89), who invited him to stay with him at South Brent so that he could meet some of the singers who lived there.

Spence Bate had recently retired from his practice as a dentist in Plymouth and was living at his holiday home, Rock House, just outside the village of South Brent. He had been one of the leading dentists in the city, and his patients included many prominent members of society in South West Devon. He had written a number of academic papers and books about dentistry but he needed something more to satisfy his vigorous intellect. His great passion was marine biology and he had become recognised as a leading authority on some genera of crustaceae, with five species named after him. He had corresponded with Charles Darwin about their mutual interest in barnacles and he authored that part of the report of the *Challenger* expedition of 1873–76 that dealt with the *Crustacea Macrura*. This report took him ten years to write and involved the study of about 2,000 specimens. He was an active member of the Plymouth Institution as well as a number of other learned societies, including the Devonshire Association, of which he was a founder and for a time its secretary and president. He was also one of the early archaeologists of Dartmoor with a number of publications to his credit, although the accuracy of his deductions left a little to be desired. He concluded, for example, that Grimspound was a Viking settlement: something Baring-Gould later challenged.

You might have expected that Baring-Gould would have known Spence Bate through the Devonshire Association or another connection, but it appears not, as Baring-Gould recorded that:

A gentleman at South Brent wrote to me — quite a stranger — to say that there were a miller and a stonebreaker near him who were reputed to be song-men. Would I visit him and see what I could get?[13]

The old miller was John Helmore who owned Lydia Mill, just across the River Avon from Rock House. The stonebreaker was Robert Hard, who lived in the village.

Fig 6.1 – Rock House, South Brent. Lydia Mill in the background, over the bridge. (Author's photo).

So Baring-Gould travelled down to South Brent, taking Frederick Bussell with him. His account of the visit continued:

My host who had invited me, had invited neighbours to dinner to meet me; and after dinner the entire party adjourned to the roomy,

---

13 Sabine Baring-Gould, 'Introductory Essay on English Folk Music', *English Minstrelsie*, VII, p. iv.

warm, and pleasant kitchen, where we found the miller and the stonebreaker, and the wife of the former in an old white mob-cap. They were seated by the fire, with a table before them on which stood grog. The servants of the house sat along one side of the kitchen, the guests on the other. The old fellows sang some times in parts with great effect, the old woman striking in with a curious faux bourdon. When they ceased singing we applauded; then came a lull, during which the roar of the river Avon, that leaps and brawls through a cleft of rocks, and thunders over a cascade hard by, filled the kitchen, like the murmur of an angry sea.

This is one of those rare reports of traditional performers singing in harmony together, as well as Caroline Helmore adding her *faux bourdon*, but there is no notation of the harmonies. The two men returned separately the next day to allow the collectors to hear more of their songs. The records of the songs collected at this time were not as good as they were to become later and we do not have a clear picture of what was sung on that first visit. We do know, though, that Baring-Gould returned to South Brent on other occasions, taking either Bussell or Sheppard with him and they also met other singers from the village.

The accounts that Baring-Gould gives of his visits to South Brent are subject to the usual variation and retelling of the story. In his *Further Reminiscences*, published after his death more than thirty years after the event, we have a different picture of that first 'concert' in Spence Bate's house.

After dinner we adjourned to the kitchen, where was a roaring fire, and the old men were set up with jugs and tankards of ale. But some neighbouring gentlemen and ladies, notably the latter, had been invited to be present at the performance. ... I was not at all sure that the words of the ballads would in all cases be fit for ladies' ears. And so it proved. For after the singing of "The Mole-Catcher" by John Helmore, the aged miller, there ensued a rapid dissolution of the company. I inserted the song in the last edition of Songs of the West, but to very much chastened words.[14]

It is a nice story – and may be true, though the only version of 'The Molecatcher' in Baring-Gould's collection came from another South Brent singer, J. Hoskins. Though this was not included in the early editions of *Songs of the West* it was introduced in the 1905 edition. Baring-Gould's note read:

---

14 Sabine Baring-Gould, *Further Reminiscences*, pp. 189–90.

In the British Museum is an early Garland, and in the list of contents on the cover is 'The Mole Catcher' but the song has been torn out, probably for the same reason that prevented me from taking it down. All I copied was the beginning of the song. I have supplemented this with fresh words.

The source that he refers to is in the British Library collection and is called *Daniel Cooper's Garland*. The cover lists 'The Farmer and the Mole-Catcher' on its cover, but the centre section of the garland that would have contained the song (pages 3 to 6) is, indeed, missing.

Robert Hard

Robert Hard was born at Diptford, near South Brent, in 1813 and worked as a farm labourer for most of his life. He had been widowed twice, and his three wives gave him ten children – the youngest of whom was born when he was seventy years old. Baring-Gould met him when he was 75 and described him as having 'sharply-chiselled features – he must have been a handsome man in his youth, bright eyes, a gentle, courteous manner, and a marvellous store of old words and tunes in his head.' He went on to say that Hard '… has a charming old wife; and he and the old woman sing together in parts their quaint ancient ballads'. This remark would have referred to his third wife, Ann, who was then 45 years old and who, like Caroline Helmore, joined in with her husband in some form of harmony. A newspaper obituary for Robert Hard reported that he was a member of the church choir for over forty years, and so would have been accustomed to harmony singing in that context.[15]

A life of farm-work had left Hard unable to walk without sticks and he was living on £4 a year from the parish, for which he was expected to break stones for road repairs. When Baring-Gould visited South Brent to give a lecture-concert in January 1889 he arranged that part of the proceeds should go to the old men from whom he had collected songs. Robert Hard was sent £5 – more than his whole annual dole – but when the authorities found out they threatened to stop his relief money. Luckily, and probably due to Baring-Gould's intervention, the threat was not carried out.

In 1892 Baring-Gould heard that Hard's health was deteriorating and so, on 8 November, he took the early train down to South Brent to meet with him again. Charles Spence Bate had died in the summer of 1889 and so Baring-Gould asked the Vicar of South Brent, William Speare Cole, to

---

15 Obituary notice for Robert Hard, *Bath Chronicle and Weekly Gazette*, 8 December 1892, p. 6.

Fig. 6.2 – Robert Hard, from *Further Reminiscences.*

let him use his living room and his piano, and he and Hard spent the whole day together, from 9:30 in the morning to 6:30 at night, with only a break for lunch. The 'Rough Copy' manuscript contains a sequence of 21 songs, in Baring-Gould's hand, noted down that day.[16]

16 Plymouth Central Library, Baring-Gould Collection, Rough Copy manuscript, Vol. 14, pp. 28–31. Some have been copied more neatly into Vol. 11, pp. 23–24.

Less than a month later, Hard fell while walking home from his day's stone breaking and was stranded out at night in winter weather. Though Baring-Gould reported him as having been found 'frozen on a heap of stones by the roadside', he really died at home a few days later. Hard's name was widely known through Baring-Gould's books and concerts, and newspapers around the south-western region ran obituaries for him. He was said to 'sing a good song and make good company almost at the last.'

Hard told Baring-Gould that his memory was failing, but he still managed to give him eighty distinct melodies, although only 51 of these are recorded in the song manuscripts. We can judge, from the songs that were collected from him, that Hard was a good singer, with an ear for a good tune. Some of his songs were slightly risqué, such as 'A Frigate Well Manned', in which the frigate is a metaphor for a well turned out young woman who was, as my grandmother might have said, 'no better than she ought to be'. The original version of this song is 'The Pinnace Rigg'd with Silken Sail', which is mentioned in John Fletcher's play *Monsieur Robert*, published in 1639. But Hard also had many of the songs that we regard as typical of country singers at the end of the nineteenth century, such as 'The Farmer's Boy', 'Cupid the Ploughboy', 'Greenland Whale Fishery' and 'The Lark in the Morning'. There were a few songs that Baring-Gould felt unable to record in full because they were too earthy, such as 'The Flailman' – Hard's take on the old favourite 'Rap-a-tap-tap', in which the flailman passes the time with a farmer's wife while her husband is at market. We can judge from the songs that he sang that Hard was used to performing as an entertainer and would indeed have been 'good company', as his obituary suggested.

John Helmore

The other principal singer Baring-Gould met in South Brent, John Helmore, was seventy years old when Baring-Gould made his first visit to the village, and his wife, Caroline, was three years younger. Helmore had been born in 1817 at Rewe to the north-west of Exeter and Caroline nearby in Exwick. They knew each other as children and married in 1843. Helmore learned the skills of a miller and the couple moved to Harbertonford until, in the 1860s, John Helmore bought Lydia Mill, a few miles away in South Brent. For many years they made a good living but by the time Baring-Gould and Helmore met the business was in decline. A new mill, powered by steam, had opened nearby and was taking custom away.

JOHN HELMORE, THE MILLER.

Fig. 6.3 – John Helmore, from *English Minstrelsie*.

Baring-Gould wrote an article, 'In the Sound of the Mill Wheel', in 1894 which appeared in several newspapers and which he later incorporated in his book *An Old English Home* in 1898. This article contains a dialogue between the author and the old miller who, though not named, is clearly John Helmore and 'Anne' is his wife Caroline. When asked if the new mill is spoiling his custom, the miller replies:

> It is killing of us old folks out. It isn't so much that we gets no grinding I mind, but it leaves me and my Anne with no means in our old age, and we don't like to go on to the childer, and we don't like to go into the work'us. There it is. We did reckon on being able honestly to get our bread for ourselves and ax nobody for nothing. But now this ere new mill wi' the steam ingens and the electric light – someone must pay for all that,

and who is that but the customers? I've no electric light here, water costs nothing. Coals costs twenty-one shillings a ton, and it takes a deal of coals to make the ingen march. Who pays for the coals? Who pays for the electric light? The customers get the flour at the same price as I send it out with none of them jangangles. How do they manage it? I reckon the corn is tampered with – there's white china-clay or something put with the flour. It can't be done otherwise. But I reckon folk like to say, "Our flour comed from that there mill worked wi' steam and lighted by electric light," and if they have those things, then, I say they can't have pure flour. So it must be I think, but folk say that I am an old stooped and don't understand nothing. All I can say is I can turn out wholesome flour, and never put nothing in but corn-grains, and turned out nothing but corn flour, wheat and oat and barley.[17]

John and Caroline Helmore celebrated their golden wedding in 1893, an event reported in the *Western Times* whose reporter wrote that, 'though his days of prosperity and labour are ebbing on, he is a jolly example of humanity, and when in company with him a few days since I found that he was still able to sing "The Miller and his Mill" and "Fare Thee Well" which are two of his favourite songs.' Baring-Gould made a point of visiting them on the day of their anniversary and reported in the same article:

I found them very happy. A son and a daughter had taken a holiday to see their parents and congratulate them. The parson's wife had sent in a plum pudding, the squire a bottle of old port. Several friends had remembered them – even the miller in the new style, who had electric light and steam power, had contributed a cake.

Caroline died the following year and after the mill had been sold Helmore moved to Ivybridge to live with his widowed sister-in-law. Baring-Gould reports him as having said: 'Us growed up together, and us did ever love one another; and now hers took, please God I be took soon too, for I want to be wi' her. Us till now have niver been apart, and I du feel queer and lone at present.'[18]

17 Sabine Baring-Gould, *An Old English Home* (London: Methuen & Co., 1898), pp. 179–80.
18 Sabine Baring-Gould, *Further Reminiscences*, p.190.

One of Helmore's songs was 'The Miller's Last Will' which was sung, perhaps, as a little joke at the expense of his own profession.

It's of a miller in Devonshire
He had three sons, as you shall hear.
He called for them one by one
Saying my glass is well nigh run.

He called for his eldest son,
Said unto him – my glass is run,
If I my mill to you should make
What toll do you intend to take?

The song tells of an old miller who asks his three sons in turn how they would operate the mill with a view to choosing which of them should inherit it. The youngest son wins by saying he would steal more of his customers' grain than his brothers – he would leave them only the sack. This reflects a common view of the miller who was often regarded as one of the more dishonest members of rural society. Along with the tailor and the weaver, they were trusted with hard-won product to turn into goods on behalf of the owner, and were sometimes suspected of abusing that trust. This is reflected in a number of traditional songs, and of the three, it is the tailor who is the most frequently satirised.

John Helmore was not as prolific a singer as his friend Robert Hard, and we know of just a dozen songs that he sang to Baring-Gould. He sang several songs that could be seen as staples of the repertoire of country singers of his time, such as 'Sweep, Chimney Sweep', 'The Spotted Cow', 'The Jolly Waggoner' and 'When Joan's Ale Was New'. Baring-Gould clearly had a lot of time for him and visited him in later years when opportunity allowed for purely social reasons. Henry Fleetwood Sheppard also kept in touch with him. In his obituary of Sheppard, Baring-Gould recorded that Helmore died in the Ivybridge workhouse just two weeks before his colleague, and that the last letter that Sheppard wrote to him was about the old miller.

John Woodridge

Another of the singers whom Baring-Gould considered to be among the best that he met was the man whose name he always gave as 'John Woodrich', though we know from a number of sources, including living family members, that his name was actually Woodridge. His nickname was

116

'Ginger Jack', and that was the name that Cecil Sharp knew him by when they met in Baring-Gould's company several years later.

John James Woodridge was born, one of fourteen children, in Bridgwater, Somerset, in 1847. At the age of four he was sent to live with his grandmother where he stayed for six years until she died. He returned to live with his father but ran away when he was fourteen and never returned, wandering round the country, picking up work and lodgings as he found them. In his twenties he was employed for a while as a blacksmith in Black Torrington before going to work for John Ellis at Wollacott Moor, then a lonely spot in Thrushelton parish but now in view of the holiday traffic speeding down the A30. While he was there he met Mary Walters at nearby Sprytown, whom he married in 1885, taking on responsibility for her three illegitimate children. The couple were to have another six children together.

Baring-Gould met him shortly after he met James Parsons and it is possible that Parsons told him about this younger man (Woodridge was then 41 years old) who lived at Down Park Cottages on Lew Down with his growing family. Woodridge was still working for John Ellis at Wollacott Moor, walking three miles to work every morning. He was not a skilled blacksmith; Baring-Gould wrote: 'He was really not fit for more at the forge than to blow the bellows, and that was work which he found monotonous.' Inevitably, he lost his job and went back to casual labouring, travelling in search of work.

For a while he worked as a navvy on the railway line that was built between Launceston and Wadebridge. After a number of absences from home, he pushed his luck too far and was arrested in April 1898 for deserting his wife and family. The long-suffering Mary had been forced to turn to the guardians of the Tavistock Union for relief when his disappearance for several weeks coincided with the birth of their sixth child. She had received no money from him for nearly ten weeks. The parish guardians paid out £1 12s 6d in relief for the family and then sought to recover the money through the court. Woodridge was discovered working on the new reservoir at Burrator and brought before the magistrates in Tavistock. He told the court that he had been out of work for a long time and that he had travelled all round the area, looking for work. He had secured the job on the new waterworks at Burrator just a fortnight earlier. Some of the guardian's money and the court's costs were recovered from him before he was discharged, having agreed to pay Mary ten shillings a week in future. Baring-Gould hints that on other occasions he had seen the inside of a jail.

His incarceration does not seem to have changed his ways overmuch, as three years later he was working in Plymouth and living in a working men's hostel there, while Mary and five of the children remained in Stowford, where she worked as a charwoman to support them. John Woodridge did eventually return to the parish, however, and the family settled into a cottage at Portgate. Mary Woodridge died of cancer in 1914 at the age of 57. John's youngest son, Alfred, came to live in the cottage with him and it was Alfred's wife, Eva, who was with John when he died of bronchitis on 2 March 1916.

John Woodridge was an exceptional singer and both his father and his grandmother had been singers. When he was living with his grandmother as a child he learned the songs that she and her women friends sang, such as 'Green Broom', a song that Cecil Sharp found in Bridgwater (and other places in the area) in 1907. The songs that Woodridge received from his father included 'The Hay Making Song' (said to have been the father's favourite) and 'Old Humphrey Hodge' (also known as 'Rock the Cradle, John'). There is also one song, 'I Can Let it Alone', which he said came from his mother. With these and others he earned his drink by singing in public houses and at other gatherings. But he continued to build his store. He was one of those people who could learn songs easily. Baring-Gould said that he could usually learn a tune by hearing it once, and that he would only have to hear a song twice to remember the words as well as the melody. While he was working as a navvy he was engaged in moving earth to create embankments and cuttings. Another navvy was a singer and as their paths crossed with their barrows one would try a song with the other. Baring-Gould encouraged him to do this. Woodridge acquired a number of the Irish songs in his repertoire from fellow navvies.

Baring-Gould met with John Woodridge a number of times, sometimes in the company of James Parsons. Baring-Gould talked at length with Woodridge about the songs and where he had obtained them. The singer's retentive memory helped in this respect as he could often quote the year, the place and the circumstances in which he heard a song. Of the song 'Richard Malvine', for example, Baring-Gould recorded that Woodridge told him that he had

> Heard this recited and sung in 1874 near Bideford by a very old man in a public house who, as he said and sang it, stood bent leaning on his staff that shook with him under the palsy of old age. This old man did not know all the verses, and recited where he had forgotten.[19]

Of another song, 'If I Had Two Ships on the Ocean', Woodridge recalled: 'This was sung by a woman – she was so drunk that she couldn't sing more

---

19 Devon Heritage Centre, Baring-Gould Papers, 5203M, Box 23, Working Notebook 2, p. 95.

than these two verses, and she sung 'em over and over – that there was no forgetting 'em.'[20]

When Cecil Sharp made a series of visits to Lew Trenchard between 1904 and 1907 to work with Baring-Gould, he met a number of singers and dancers, including John Woodridge. Sharp collected five songs from him in Baring-Gould's company on 12 September 1905: 'Little Mary, my Bride', 'Lad Randal', 'Cold Blows the Wind', 'The Rout is Out' and 'Searching for Lambs'.

The tune of the last mentioned of these, 'Searching for Lambs' (wrongly attributed to John Dingle in Baring-Gould's Personal Copy manuscript), has some similarities with the now well-known version that Sharp collected two years later from Mrs Sweet of Somerton, not far from Bridgwater, where Woodridge grew up. It is unfortunate that neither Sharp nor Baring-Gould wrote down the words that Woodridge sang.

John Woodridge was one of the first singers that Baring-Gould met, and there are 82 songs in the manuscripts that can be attributed to him. He was also one of the last to sing for the collection, since Baring-Gould visited him on New Year's Day 1912 when he was passing through Portgate. He was given a version of 'When Shall We Be Married' which Woodridge had heard from a girl in nearby Dippertown. Though Baring-Gould made a few entries of songs that had been sent to him in his manuscripts after this date, this was almost certainly the last occasion on which he collected a song himself. When Cecil Sharp was collecting songs in Cornwall in January 1912, he called in to see Baring-Gould on his way back through Devon and was given this song, which he transcribed into one of his 'Folk Words' notebooks (as No. 2237).

Harry Westaway

A friend of Baring-Gould's, John Dunning Prickman, an Okehampton solicitor, introduced Henry (Harry) Westaway to Baring-Gould in 1888 when the singer was 64. Harry farmed 100 acres at Priestacott Farm, near Belstone, where he and his wife, Elizabeth, raised twelve children – seven girls and five boys.

Prickman arranged a meeting between the two men in Okehampton. It was the first of several meetings, as Baring-Gould visited Harry on three more occasions and collected at least eighteen songs from him.

Baring-Gould tells a story that illustrates that singers were capable of self-censorship when they deemed it necessary. He wrote:

---

20 Devon Heritage Centre, Sabine Baring-Gould Papers, 5203M, Personal Copy MSS, Note to 'I had Three (Two) Ships', P2, 398 (391).

One day I was at Belstone visiting a famous singer, Harry Westaway, when he sang a ballad to us, but dropped one of the verses, whereupon his daughter, a tall, handsome girl of about eighteen, shouted from the kitchen: 'Fayther, you've left out someut,' and she struck up and sang a most – to say the least – indelicate verse.[21]

Clearly Harry was more concerned than his daughter about singing a smutty verse to a clergyman. Baring-Gould also remarked that Harry had '...stalwart sons, all notable singers', but goes on to observe that:

His sons sang none of their father's [songs]: they knew and appreciated only Christy Minstrel and Music Hall pieces; void of merit or interest to us. They despised, and did not care to learn, the old ballads and songs that had come down as an heirloom from their tuneful ancestors.[22]

Steve Roud has highlighted Victorian and Edwardian descriptions of singing, such as that given by Flora Thompson in her 1939 novel *Lark Rise*. These show that young and old men would often sing in the same pub sessions together so that while the young men were singing their own material they would hear the songs sung by their elders. Nevertheless, when some of these younger men were approached by song collectors later in the twentieth century they were able to recall some of these more traditional songs, though they would not have sung them in their younger days.[23]

There are only a few cases where a Victorian singer's family has been revisited in the next generation to hear whether any songs had survived in the family repertoire. In 1951 the folk song collector Peter Kennedy visited Belstone and met two of Harry Westaway's sons, Bill and Harry (Junior), and recorded a few songs from them. These certainly included some of the music hall songs that Baring-Gould deprecated, such as 'Down by the Old Watermill' and 'Where Did you Get That Hat', but they were also able to recall songs that their father had sung like (of course) 'Widdicombe Fair', 'The Jolly Goshawk' and 'Harry the Tailor', the last of these being another instance of the way that tailors were stereotypically treated in English folk song. The tailor goes to pay court to Dolly but she pushes him into the well, putting him off matrimony forever.

---

21 Sabine Baring-Gould, *Further Reminiscences*, pp.190–91. The daughter was probably Annie Westaway, born in 1870.
22 Sabine Baring-Gould, 'Preface', *Songs of the West* (1889), Part 1, p. ix.
23 Steve Roud, 'General Introduction' in *The New Penguin Book of Folk Songs*, ed. Steve Roud and Julia Bishop (London: Penguin, 2012).

In another interview with Peter Kennedy, Bill Westaway talked about his father's meeting with Baring-Gould in 1888.[24] He recalled that the old man was treated very well with both drink and a little money and he believed that Baring-Gould had deliberately got him drunk so that he could get the words of 'Widdicombe Fair'. Baring-Gould did not, in fact, include Westaway's words in his manuscripts, only the tune and chorus. The version that he published, and which went on to greater fame, was one sent to him by William Collier, the wine merchant from Plymouth.

While we do not have Harry Westaway's version, we know that the chorus was the same as that sung by his son and can assume that the verses were similar.

> Tom Pearce, Tom Pearce, lend me thy grey mare
>   Right-fol-lol-li-dol, diddle-i-do
> That I may ride out to Widdicombe Fair
>   With Will Lewer, Jan Brewer, Harry Hawkins, Hugh Davey,
>   Philly Wigpot, George Parsley, Dick Wilson
>   Tom Cobleigh and all, here is Uncle Tom Cobleigh and all.

Sally Satterley

So far this chapter has only considered the men whom Baring-Gould met, so it is time to meet a woman who as well as being an important source of songs was also something of a 'Dartmoor Character'. Baring-Gould did not believe that he had done a very good job of collecting songs from women. Though he was less successful than Cecil Sharp, who was very good at charming songs from the women he met, he is probably being overly critical of himself.

In an article that he wrote for *The Queen* magazine in 1894 Baring-Gould considered that:

> A woman is much more shy of singing before men, especially –
> "old-fashioned" songs, than is a man. She is humble-minded, as
> well as shy. She fears lest her songs, "silly trash they be," … should
> make her seem ridiculous in the eyes of a man! But she will open
> out to a fellow woman, and here it is that a lady can do so much
> more than is possible for a man.[25]

---

24 Peter Kennedy, *Folk Songs of Britain and Ireland* (London: Oak Publications, 1975), Note on 'Tom Pearce', p. 682.
25 Sabine Baring-Gould, 'The Collection of Folk Airs', *The Queen: The Lady's Newspaper*, 1 December 1894, p. 983.

He did, in fact, obtain over 100 songs from women singers. Often this was done in the company of the ladies who had found the women for him, such as Bertha Bidder of Stoke Fleming who introduced him to Mary Langworthy and other singers in the South Hams. But on other occasions he went with a male colleague.

Baring-Gould wrote a number of times about Sally Satterley who lived at Huccaby, in the middle of Dartmoor. Her house, Jolly Lane Cot, was said to be the last to have been built taking advantage of 'squatter's rights' on the moor. Her husband, Thomas, constructed it for his invalid parents who had been left homeless when they could no longer work. He waited for a day when all the local farmers had gone to Ashburton June Fair and, with a group of friends, assembled the materials that they had secretly accumulated so that by sunset the roof was thatched and the old couple were sitting by the hearth with the fire burning. This, according to old custom, should have been enough to secure them free tenancy of the property, but the landowners, the Duchy of Cornwall, were not happy with that arrangement. They relented sufficiently that the cottage was not demolished, but a modest rent was charged.[26] When the old people died Thomas and Sally moved into the cottage and she remained there until her death in 1901.

Fig. 6.4 – Jolly Lane Cot. Sally Satterley, her daughter Sarah Colwill and granddaughter Frances Mary Colwill are standing by the door. Photo by Robert Burnard, c, 1890 (Courtesy of The Dartmoor Trust Archive).

26 See, for example, Sabine Baring-Gould, *Further Reminiscences*, p. 203. Baring-Gould also told the story in a fictionalised form as 'Jolly Lane Cot' in *Dartmoor Idylls* (London: Methuen, 1896), pp. 201–13.

Sally Satterley was born on Dartmoor in 1815 and never left it. When she was a young woman her father was farming Peat Cott, a few miles to the south-east of Princetown, in the heart of the moor. One of her jobs was to take a pack-train loaded with peat to the markets in towns on the edge of the moor such as Ashburton and Horrabridge, where she sold it to the townsfolk. She married an agricultural labourer, Thomas Satterley, in 1841 and they moved to Jolly Lane Cot after the death of Thomas' parents. They had five daughters before Thomas died in 1868, leaving Sally to manage fifty acres of farmland which the couple had taken on. The eldest daughter, Sarah Jane, returned to live with her mother at Huccaby shortly afterwards with her husband, Robert Colwill, a miner.

Baring-Gould's accounts of his meetings with Sally Satterley are more than usually incomplete and inconsistent, but he probably met her for the first time in 1889. He also had problems with her name, calling her 'Mary Satcherley' in several accounts. At the time of their meeting her occupation was described as a monthly nurse. These were the women who looked after mothers in the weeks following the birth of their children. Some had a little basic training and certification by that time, but it is likely that Sally was relying on long experience. She also acted as midwife and boasted that 'Her'd never lost one in childbirth.' Even late in her life she would walk long distances across the moor to see those in her charge and often after her day's work was finished she would walk the eight miles to Ashburton to purchase necessary items before returning the same night. The noted writer on Dartmoor, William Crossing, said of her that:

> She was during the greater part of her life engaged in work usually performed by men. She was for some time employed in the mine at Eylesbarrow, drove pack-horses, could cut peat, was able to mow with a scythe, and [...] could nail a shoe to a horse's hoof as well as a blacksmith. She was probably the last of her kind.

As described in Chapter 5, Baring-Gould visited her with Frederick Bussell on 23 September 1890 and she continued with her housework while they followed her around, trying to note down her songs. They succeeded in getting a few songs from her on this and subsequent visits, though Bussell admitted to having difficulty with the tune of 'The Lady and the Prentice'. She sang it four or five times but she never sang two verses alike and she could not slow down to a pace at which he could write down the notes.

In 1891 Baring-Gould visited Sally with Henry Fleetwood Sheppard but felt that there were still songs to be recovered. He wrote:

Fig. 6.5 – Sally Satterley. Photo by Robert Burnard, c. 1890 (Courtesy of The Dartmoor Trust Archive).

'I turned to Mr. Sheppard and said, "We have not yet exhausted her store. You *must* go back, and don't let her go till she drives you away with the pitchfork," and like a zealous and conscientious collector, back he went.' Unfortunately, even Sheppard's zeal did not increase the total of songs collected from her and there are only eight of her songs in the collection. These included some fine ballads which came from her father, Peter Hannaford, a proficient song-man who, she told Baring-Gould, could sing old ballads without repeating himself for 36 hours on end.

When she died in April 1901 the *Tavistock Gazette* ran an obituary, suggesting that she 'had probably seen more winters than any other woman on Dartmoor'. The obituary concluded, 'With her death another of the links that bind us to the Dartmoor of the past is snapped.'

Samuel Fone

Another of Baring-Gould's favourite singers was Sam Fone, whom he met with at least fifteen times. It is possible to recognise from Fone's songs that he was an exceptional singer with a fine repertoire. Baring-Gould met him too late for his songs to be included in the first edition of *Songs of the West*, but some of them appeared in *A Garland of Country Song*.

Samuel John Wilkins Fone was born in Exeter in 1837, the son of Francis and Charlotte Fone. Francis was a baker, but he left the family home when Samuel was six years old and never returned. In 1851 the family was living in Plymouth where Sam was working as an errand boy, probably for his uncle's business, which was making the noted 'Fone's Captains Biscuits', a high quality ship's biscuit. He married Elizabeth Hopper in 1859, by which time he had become a mason, working in Devonport dockyard. When this work slackened he became a stoker on HMS *Indus*, the Plymouth guard ship. Although he was a naval rating, the role of the *Indus* did not require her to leave port and he lived ashore. We know that he also worked for a while as a navvy on the line that ran across Dartmoor and up to Princetown. Eventually he settled in Mary Tavy where he found steady employment working as a mason in the mines there. By that time the mines in the village had passed their heyday, when the Devon Friendship mine had been the most productive copper mine in the world, employing over 1,000 men. But there was still plenty of work for a mason as the mines extracted other profitable minerals such as arsenic. He and his wife Elizabeth had seven children, three of whom died as young children – two of them on the same day in 1878.

Baring-Gould met Sam Fone for the first time on 4 October 1892. On that occasion he recorded the words of only one song, 'The Drummer Boy', and it was not until March of the following year, at their fourth meeting, that Frederick Bussell noted the tune. By this time Baring-Gould and Bussell were more experienced in collecting, but had also learned the value of listening to the singers' stories, asking more about where they got the songs and about the singers themselves. We know, for example, that when Fone visited Baring-Gould he wore white trousers tied below the knee and a scarlet neckerchief. He was often referred to as 'old', though he was three years younger than Baring-Gould himself; an indication perhaps that the years had treated his appearance unkindly.

When he was a boy he used to fetch milk for an old widow every day. She had little money to spare so she paid for the pennyworth of milk that Sam brought her with a song. He identified two of these songs to Baring-Gould: a version of the 'Gypsy Laddie' and 'The Drowned Lovers', in which Baring-Gould found it necessary to alter one of the verses as he found it 'very gross'. This seems to have been unusual as Baring-Gould wrote: 'Unhappily we have found that some of the earliest and boldest airs are associated to very objectionable words. Fone is free largely from this sort of song but some wild and rugged moor men are very bad, yet the airs are splendid.'

Fone's family included several singers. His father's favourite song was 'Arthur le Bride'. His mother sang to him as well. Fone told Baring-Gould that one of the songs that she sang while doing the washing was 'Harmless Molly', a sweet song about a soldier going off to war and leaving his sweetheart behind, which was probably a survival from an eighteenth-century stage show. Another of her songs, by way of contrast, was 'Lady Isabella's Tragedy'. This is a long ballad which had been printed on seventeenth-century broadsides, and is a horror story about a wicked woman who orders her stepdaughter to be killed and cooked in a pie which is then given to her husband to eat. Luckily the kitchen boy speaks up and the stepmother is burnt at the stake, the cook is drowned in boiling lead and the kitchen boy is made heir to all the Lord's land.

Sam's younger sister, Charlotte, sang as well. When he was a boy he went up to London with her by carrier's cart, a journey of several days. Fone recalled that she sang 'Seventeen Come Sunday' over and over; not, as Baring-Gould wrote, 'quite such a song as you would expect from a child'. There were, of course, other sources and influences. Fone reported that he had, for a while, worked with a mason who sang while he worked. The man fell off a ladder and was killed, but by that time Fone had absorbed all of his songs. Like John Woodridge, he would also have had opportunities for learning songs while working as a navvy.

On one occasion Baring-Gould arranged for Sam to attend a concert of folk songs that he had organised in Tavistock. He writes:

> The other day, a concert of old west country songs was given at Tavistock by professionals in costume. Fone was present, at the back of the hall, and would sing out every song with which he was familiar, along with the performer, somewhat to the disconcertion of the artist, but to the amusement of the audience.[27]

He records with some amusement that Sam joined in all the choruses, perplexing an audience more used to the etiquette of the drawing room and concert hall.

Baring-Gould noted 124 songs from Samuel Fone, but it is unlikely that this was the sum of his repertoire, as he knew a number of other songs when prompted. In May 1894 he was ill and it was thought that he might die. Luckily he recovered, though he was bedridden for some time. Baring-Gould lent him a large volume of broadside ballads before he went off for one of his continental journeys, hoping that it would act as a refresher for his memory. When he got back he found that Fone had marked more than 130 songs that he knew. Baring-Gould believed that the men like Sam Fone and John Woodridge, who were slightly younger than the majority of his singers, knew more songs that were printed on broadsides. Another measure of his repertoire was reported to Baring-Gould by Elizabeth Fone, who told him that on a night that he had been unable to sleep he spent the hours of darkness singing the songs that he could remember. She counted seventy, a number verified by their daughter who was there at the time. This demonstrates, incidentally, that Fone could read, and could probably write as well since, unlike his wife, he signed his name to his marriage certificate.

---

27 Sabine Baring-Gould, 'Introductory Essay on English Folk Music', *English Minstrelsie*, Vol. 7, p. vi.

Samuel Fone's Songs

Arthur le Bride
As a Jolly Old Farmer
Barnet Races
Be Quick for I'm in Haste
Beggar, The
Bold Fisherman, The
Bold Trooper, The
Bonny Blue
  Handkerchief, The
Bonny Boy
Bonny Irish Boy
Brennan on the Moor
Brisk young miner, The
Buffalo, The
Capstan Song
Captain Ward the Pirate
Carrier Pigeon, The
Colin's Heart
Come All You Free
  Masons
Cottagers Daughter, The
Country Lad Am I, A
Cuckold's Song, The
Cupid's Garden
Damsel Possessed of
  Great Beauty
Death of Parker
Death of Queen Jane
Don't You Go a'
  Rushing
Drowned Lovers
Drummer Boy
Effects of Love
Fair Daphne
Farewell to Kingsbridge
Farmers Son So Sweet, A
Fisherman's Daughter,
  The
Flora, the Flower (or
  Lily) of the West
Flowers of Maiden Lane
Fox Hunt, The
Free and Easy
Frog and Mouse, The

Gallant Hussar
Gathering Flowers
Gilderoy
Gosford (Gosport) Beach
Grand Conversation
  Under the Rose
Grand Conversation
  With Napoleon
Great Boobie, The
Green Bushes
Greenland Whale
  Fishery, The
Ground For the Floor
Gypsy Countess, The
Hard Times in England
Harmless Molly
High Germany
Holland Smock
I Would That the Wars
  Were All Over
I'm a Man That's Done
  Wrong to My Parents
If I Had a Thousand a
  Year
In Bedfordshire Town
In the Days When I Was
  Hard Up
In the Snow
Indian Lass, The
Isle of France
Joe the Collier's Son
Jolly Boatswain, The
Jolly Boys that Follow the
  Plough
Jordan
Lady and 'Prentice, The
Lady in the West, A
Lady Isabella's Tragedy
Leave Me Alone
Little Girl Down the
  Lane (Row), The
Lost Lady Found, The
Lubin's Rural Cot
Maid of Chatham, The

Maiden Sweet in May, A
Masterpiece of Love
  Songs, The
Minnie Clyde
My Mother Did So
  Before Me
My Valentine
New Garden Fields
No, My Love, No!
North Country Maid
Old Miller, The (Miller's
  Last Will, The)
On the Dew So Pearly
One Night at 10 o' Clock
Own Bonny Mary
Pack of Cards
Poor Little Sweep
Poverty No Sin
Ramble Away
Richard of Taunton
  Deane
Rosa Bell
Rosemary Lane
Setting of the Sun, The
Springtime of the Year
Squire of Tamworth, The
Stow-away, The
Stranger from America,
  The
Stutter and Stammer
Sweet Susan
Sweet William
Sweet, Farewell
Three Pretty Maids
Trial of Willy Reily
Tyburn Hill
Undutiful Daughter, The
When First in London
When Joan's Ale Was
  New
Wrestling and Ringing
Yorkshire Boy, The
Young Roger of the Vale

Sam Fone's repertoire is very varied with some traditional ballads as well as the songs that we would consider typical folk songs. He also sang a number of sentimental songs from the later years of the nineteenth century. One of his favourites was 'The Grand Conversation of Napoleon', with its flowery language and distorted view of historical events – Baring-Gould described it as 'arrant nonsense'. He also sang some of the songs about poverty that appeared on broadsides around the 1860s, such as 'In the Days When I Was Hard Up':

> In the days when I was hard up,
> Not many years ago,
> I suffered that which only can
> The sons of misery know
> Relations, friends, companions
> They all turned up their nose
> And they rated me a vagabond
> For want of better clothes.

Another of the same kind is 'I'm a Man That's Done Wrong to My Parents', about which Fone told Baring-Gould a story that he passed on to Lucy Broadwood in one of his letters.

> He sang me, but broke down in the middle with a choke in his throat 'I'm a man that has wronged my parents' and told me a pathetic tale about it and about a navvy working with him on the line to Princetown. The fellow had been sent by his father to sell a cow in Plymouth, he did so, got £20 and – getting among some young scamps lost or squandered it. He was ashamed to go home, and years had passed – and he had knocked about with poor luck. One evening at the tavern Fone sang this song when 'Punch' as the young fellow as nicknamed burst into floods of tears, 'he cried like rain' and ran out. The line was being cut near his father's farm and he would look over the hedge or wall and see the old people there, but he would not make himself known till he had saved the cost of the cow and could say 'the rascal had turned out a man'. Fone told me he never after that could sing the song through without feeling inclined to cry and seeing the poor fellows face 'rained over with tears'.[28]

---

28 VWML, Lucy Etheldred Broadwood Manuscripts, Letter of Sabine Baring-Gould to Lucy Broadwood, c 22 July 1897, LEB/4/13.

At that time he was working on the eighth and final volume of *English Minstrelsie* and he decided to include this song in the book. This was despite the fact that Lucy Broadwood had already published a version, and that he was breaking the unwritten rule that collectors did not print versions of songs that others had already included in a book of songs. It would be some years before it was realised that this practice prevented the publication of many fine variants – some better than those published first – and it restricted the activities of the Folk Song Society in the first years of its existence.

Baring-Gould retold the story in his notes to the song when he printed it in *English Minstrelsie*.[29] It is an excellent illustration of the valuable time that he spent with several of his singers, drawing out memories and anecdotes that fill out our knowledge of them. In this case he shows us the emotional connection that Sam Fone had with this particular song and in the process engages our own emotions through his story. Very few song collectors could get that close to the singers they met.

This was the last song that Baring-Gould obtained from Fone, when he visited him on 16 July 1897. Fone had been in poor health after 1894 and though Baring-Gould visited him in his home a number of times after that, there are only a few songs collected from him and none after 1897. Samuel Fone died at his home on 6 May 1902 of pleurisy following a bout of pneumonia.

South Zeal

As already described, Baring-Gould rode out on Dartmoor when he was a teenager, and heard folk songs in the inns where he stayed overnight. One of those was the Oxenham Arms in South Zeal.

He went back to South Zeal in August 1894 and stayed at the same inn – this time intending to collect songs with Frederick Bussell. The evening did not go quite to plan, and yet it turned out well in the end.

> I spent an amusing evening [at the Oxenham Arms] a few winters ago. I had gone there with my friend Mr. Bussell collecting folksongs, for I remembered hearing many sung there when I was a boy some forty years before. I had worked the place for two or three days previously, visiting and 'yarning' with some of the old singers, till shyness was broken down and good fellowship established. Then I invited them to meet me at the "Oxenham Arms" in the evening.
>
> But when the evening arrived the inn was crowded with men.

---

29 Note from Sabine Baring-Gould, *English Minstrelsie* Volume 8, p xii. The song is on p. 114.

Fig. 6.6 – The Oxenham Arms (1892), South Zeal, Drawing by Louis Davis, from *English Minstrelsie.*

The women – wives and daughters – were dense in the passage, and outside boys stood on each others shoulders flattening their noses, so that they looked like dabs of putty, against the window panes. Evidently a grand concert was expected, and the old men rose to the occasion, and stood up in order and sang – but only modern songs – to suit the audience.

However, the ice was broken, and during the next few days we had them in separately to sup with us, and after supper and a glass, over a roaring fire, they sang lustily some of the old songs drawn up from the bottom-most depths of their memory. There were 'Lucky' Fewins, and old Charles Arscott, and lame Radmore, James Glanville, and Samuel Westaway, the cobbler.[30]

There were eighteen songs collected on 10 August – the day after the 'grand concert', including several not heard anywhere else. Bussell recorded the tunes of the songs sung at South Zeal in his rough notebook, and they appear as the first entries in Volume 1 of the Rough Copy manuscript.

The five men had all been born in South Tawton parish and had lived in South Zeal all their lives. The youngest was William (Lucky) Fewins, who at the time of Baring-Gould's visit lived in Ramsley, the hamlet to the south-east of the village. He was an agricultural labourer, aged sixty,

---

30 Sabine Baring-Gould, *A Book of the West: Devon* (London: Methuen, 1899), pp. 216–17.

living with his second wife Mary Ann and his unmarried daughter, Annie. John Radmore, a widowed agricultural labourer, was living on his own in Ramsley, aged 78. James Glanville was a widowed stonemason, aged 76 in 1894 and living in South Zeal village. He is listed in *Kelly's Directory* for 1893, as is Samuel Westaway, the boot maker. Westaway was 82 years old when he sang for Baring-Gould.

The fifth singer was Charles Arscott, a carpenter who lived two doors from Lucky Fewins in Ramsley. He had been widowed since the 1860s and had been looked after by his daughter until she married, after which he lived on his own. The 1901 census tells us that his granddaughter, Hetty, with her husband, John Hooper, a copper miner, and their baby son had moved in with him. In August 1904 he committed suicide at the age of 87. He had left his home at his usual time of seven o'clock to go to work at Dishcombe Farm but without shaving or having breakfast. The farmer's wife discovered him at eleven o'clock with his throat cut and his razor lying by him. The jury at his inquest delivered a verdict of 'suicide whilst of unsound mind'.

One of the songs that Arscott sang for Baring-Gould was 'The Winter of Life' – an unusual song dealing with old age and death. For some reason he would not allow its words to be noted down. Baring-Gould, however, remembered much of it and wrote up as much as he could recall in his Personal Copy manuscript in pencil, with the tune that Bussell had noted down from Arscott. Then, in March 1896, he visited South Zeal again and this time Arscott allowed him to make a note of the words. Baring-Gould has inked over the pencilled text with the correct words.

> I should like for to have in the winter of life
> A neat little cottage for me and my wife,
> With a barrel of ale & a snug little fire
> And food that's sufficient is all my desire.
> For I'm growing old, and my locks they are grey,
> No more shall I dance with the young and the gay,
> For time hath determined, the truth to unfold,
> I've a mark on my forehead to show I am old.

The Singing Birds

None of the singers I have described above could be said to have had an easy life. Concerns about survival in old age with poor health and low incomes are common to all of them. And yet these men and women were the carriers of precious songs, many of which spoke of a life of love and happiness.

In a letter to Lucy Broadwood, Baring-Gould told her about the misdeeds of the old fiddler, who he had set to collecting songs and tunes for him in South Devon.

> My poor old fiddler, Peter Isaacs of Stoke Fleming, has been in Exeter Gaol! Locked up because he slept in a barn and smoked there![31]

It was probably not a first offence, as there is a record of his having been cautioned the previous year, but in one of the most touching things that he says about his singers Baring-Gould added: 'The singing birds are not, I am sorry to say a very respectable lot – but I love them and I am sure they love me.'

This is a sentiment that needs to be reflected upon, since it is so revealing of Baring-Gould's attitude. His affection for many of his singers, particularly those 'star singers' whom he met more often, appears to have been genuine. When writing about them he refers to them as his friends on several occasions and he felt that this was reciprocated. He may have been overstating the nature of the relationship but it is evident that he, and they, enjoyed the warm companionship of a shared interest in song.

I have given several examples of the stories that Baring-Gould told about his singers and there are many others in his books, in his letters to friends and colleagues and in his manuscript notes. Baring-Gould told stories about people in his written work, some of them real, others imagined. Sometimes he combines an element of fiction with his underlying truths. When looking at his work on folk song we should count ourselves fortunate that he had this skill, which tells us more about the old singers than most of the later folk song collectors.

Frank Kidson stayed at Lew Trenchard in 1911 and wrote about his visit in the *Yorkshire Weekly Post*:

> There is a touching tenderness when he speaks of the old singers, and tells of such a one, perhaps now dead, from whom he had obtained a particular song. The old folk-songs of Devon have for him great sacredness, and it is pleasant to listen to his stories of his long rambles in search of them and of nights spent in lonely inns where he had gathered round the board those old men in whose memories they linger.[32]

---

31 VWML, Lucy Broadwood Manuscripts, Letter of Sabine Baring-Gould to Lucy Broadwood, 18 March, 1893, LEB/4/34.
32 Frank Kidson, 'The Rev. S. Baring-Gould at Home', *Yorkshire Weekly Post*, 16 September 1911, p. 15.

While this book is focused on a collection of songs, the people who contributed to the project are central to the story. And of the people who have been described, the singers are the most important. Accounts of the lives of ordinary working people are rare. While Baring-Gould's project was primarily about the songs that they sang, his genuine interest in them has made it possible to reconstruct the stories of some of the people who sang them and to recognise them as more than names on a page.

7: Collecting by Post

There is no time to be lost. Every winter with its storms sweeps away some of our old singers. The young know nothing; the middle-aged nothing. I sat over a fire with a Scottish shepherd one night and asked him to sing to me, and he gave me nothing but music-hall balderdash. But then he was a young man. Many of the oldest singers can no longer be heard in the public houses, they must be sought out in their humble homes.[1]

The Victorian Web – A Promising Lead – Bertha Bidder – Lady Edith Lethbridge – Sister Emma – The Rankin/Waring Family – William Crossing – Thomas Cayzer – Other Informants – Priscilla Wyatt-Edgell.

The Victorian Web

Baring-Gould may not have had access to the internet, but the 'Victorian Web' was astonishingly effective in exchanging information. Learned (and not-so-learned) societies with their associated magazines and journals enabled those who had a need to know, or knowledge to share, to get in contact with each other. The popular press spread the information further so that letters, such as those Baring-Gould wrote asking for information about songs, reached the wider public. And the means of transmitting that information was a very efficient postal system that used the railways to ensure that he could write a letter in the morning, receive a reply in the afternoon and, if necessary, send out additional information to reach a London desk by the evening post.

Baring-Gould's project relied on the musicians who worked with him and the many singers who gave him the songs. There was, though, another large group of people who were an active part of the project and contributed significantly to its success. More than 120 people sent him material through the post.[2] Most of these were people who never actually met Baring-Gould but were caught up by his vision and sent songs or information about singers whom they thought might be of interest. The majority were men, but more than a quarter were women, and although

---

1 Sabine Baring-Gould, 'English Folk Song', quoted in the report of the talk given at the Royal Institution on 11 May, 1894, *Notices of the Proceedings of the Meetings of the Members of the Royal Institution of Great Britain*, 14 (1893–95), pp. 286–88.
2 This figure is based on the Personal Copy manuscript, which records contributions from 123 informants.

they included gentlefolk there were also ordinary villagers who wrote to Baring-Gould with a song or a memory. Some of their contributions were small, a single song or suggestion, sometimes a single verse or even a thought shared. Others made a greater contribution and were encouraged by Baring-Gould to become collectors in their own right.

A Promising Lead

On 23 January 1893 Baring-Gould wrote to an unknown correspondent in Kingswear to thank him for telling him about an old singer called Pepperell, and to say that he would visit him in the following week.[3]

He wrote that since neither Henry Fleetwood Sheppard nor Frederick Bussell was available he would like to have access to a piano, although he hoped to persuade Miss Bidder, who lived at Stoke Fleming, to join him to note the tunes. A few days later he wrote to Lucy Broadwood saying: 'I am off early tomorrow morning to Dartmouth, where I hear of an old fellow who boasts he knows thousands of old songs.'[4] Baring-Gould met William Pepperell on 30 January at his home in Kingswear. He was seventy years old and still employed as a labourer, living with his wife Mary and his 27-year-old son, Phillip.

Baring-Gould must have been rather disappointed by his visit since there is only one song attributed to Pepperell in his collection, which he described as 'a badly remembered version of "The Sheffield Apprentice"' rather than the thousands promised. Luckily it was not a totally wasted journey, as he was able to meet another singer in Kingswear, Mary Knapman, from whom he obtained eight excellent songs. He described her as 'an old charwoman, a very respectable old thing, but I was informed in confidence that she swore 'outrageous wuss nor a man'. From Kingswear he went on to Stoke Fleming, where he stayed with Bertha Bidder.

Bertha Bidder

In May 1894 Baring-Gould wrote to Lucy Broadwood:

> I am thinking of writing an article for some Lady's magazine or paper to urge ladies to collect folk songs, and I should like to instance your energy and work. May I do so?[5]

---

3   Letter of Sabine Baring-Gould to an unknown correspondent in Kingswear, South Devon, 23 January 1893, Author's collection.
4   VWML, Lucy Broadwood Manuscripts, Letter of Sabine Baring-Gould to Lucy Broadwood, 29 January 1893, LEB/4/6.
5   Surrey History Centre, Lucy Broadwood Papers, Letter of Sabine Baring-Gould to Lucy Broadwood, 31 May 1894, 2185/LEB/1/21.

The resulting article, 'The Collection of Folk Airs', was published in *The Queen, The Lady's Newspaper* in December 1894. In it he tried to persuade the magazine's gentle readers to go out and collect folk songs, and he cited Broadwood as an example of a successful female collector. He also described another woman who had contributed songs to his collection:

> Last year a lady on the south coast of Devon, near Dartmouth, wrote to tell me that she believed there was at least one woman in the parish where she lived who remembered old songs – would I visit her and ascertain their value? Of course I went, and I was taken to a farmhouse, where this woman was then engaged washing. The farmer's wife very kindly said she could spare her for an hour, and then I got this singer – Mary Langworthy is her name – to tell me what songs she could recall, and to chant me a verse of each. I very soon satisfied myself that I had come upon a new vein of melody and of words. The songs Mary Langworthy knew she had acquired from her mother, long ago dead.[6]

The lady was Bertha Bidder of Stoke Fleming. She had trained at the Slade School of Arts in London, and was an accomplished amateur musician who played the violin to a level that enabled her to be a named performer in public concerts. After the death of her father, the renowned engineer George Bidder, she occupied much of her time with charitable work and became known locally as 'a friend of the poor'. She was also a supporter of local agricultural shows, giving, judging and presenting prizes in various classes.

Baring-Gould only noted a few scraps of songs and tunes himself on this visit. As he said in his *The Queen* article: '…it was a very difficult thing for me to open the lips of the old women who had been singing milkmaids and nurses. I found them very shy of giving up to me their treasures of old-world song.' Miss Bidder noted the rest of the words and music from the women he met that day and sent them on to him by post. He saw this as an important step forward as he was very conscious that up to that time he had not been so successful in collecting songs from women.

The singer whom Baring-Gould mentioned in his article, Mary Langworthy, was then aged 43. She lived with her husband, William, who was a gardener, a few miles west of the village of Stoke Fleming. They

---

6   Sabine Baring-Gould, 'The Collection of Folk Airs', *The Queen, The Lady's Newspaper*, 1 December 1894, p. 983.

later moved to the Green Dragon in the village when William became the publican. Baring-Gould told Francis Child in one of his letters that she

> ...was brought up by her grandmother on a farm in S. Devon, and her grandmother whilst butter-making used to sing ballads and songs and the woman, Mary Langworthy remembers many of them, and is quite keen on getting them taken down.

Nine of her songs are included in Baring-Gould's collection.[7]

He met two other women in Miss Bidder's company. Elizabeth Burgoyne, who lived in the picturesquely named Strawberry Valley just outside Stoke Fleming, sang 'Lonely Nancy, Sad Lamenting', while Betsy Chilcote provided two songs, 'Have You Seen My Moggy' (which does not refer to a missing feline) and 'Grandmother's Lessons'. Miss Bidder herself also contributed a tune for 'The Golden Vanity' that she had heard from her nurse. She later gave Lucy Broadwood a more complete set of words to the same tune, adding that they were heard from 'an old seaman's singing'.

Lucy Broadwood knew of Bertha Bidder's work with Baring-Gould and wrote to her in 1905, asking if she had songs that could be included in the *Journal of the Folk Song Society*. Bidder sent Broadwood two of Mary Langworthy's songs and her tune for 'All the Trees They Are So High' was published in the next issue.[8] It appeared with the note, 'Sung by a village-woman of Stoke Fleming', which was the way she was described on Miss Bidder's manuscript. Vaughan Williams and Lloyd selected the tune for inclusion in the *Penguin Book of English Folk Songs* because, as they said in their notes, 'The melody given is in the Phrygian mode, seldom met within English folk song.[9] Since only one verse was given in the Journal they compiled a text using versions from Sharp and Broadwood. Lloyd described it as 'one of the most curious, most beautiful and most widespread of British ballads' and, like many of the songs in that book, it has been much sung in the years since. Unfortunately, because of the lack of attribution in the *Journal of the Folk Song Society*, the woman who

---

7   Her songs were 'All the Trees They Are So High', 'The Green Bed', 'The Greenland Whale Fishery', 'The Cuckoo', 'Old Times and New', 'Too Many Lovers Will Puzzle a Maid', 'The Old Couple', 'The Old Maid's Song' ('Some at Eighteen') and 'Come All you Jolly Sailors'.

8   'The Trees They Do Grow High', *Journal of the Folk Song Society*, 2 (1905), p. 95.

9   Ralph Vaughan Williams, and A. L. Lloyd, *The Penguin Book of English Folk Songs* (Harmondsworth: Penguin Books, 1959), p. 99. For more about 'modes' in English folk song see Appendix A.

sang the tune remained anonymous until the correction was made in the second edition of the revised version published as *Classic English Folk Songs* in 2009.[10]

Miss Bidder also introduced Baring-Gould to Peter Isaacs, an itinerant leather-worker, formerly a shoemaker, who travelled around the farms in the district, repairing harnesses and saddles, and who carried his fiddle with him in a green baize bag under his arm – his only possession. Baring-Gould told Broadwood about him in a letter:

> I had a most interesting few days last week near Dartmouth. I made the acquaintance of a poor old ragged fiddler with white hair, a beautiful intelligent face, a man whose occupation is gone: he is somewhat of a dreamer and not a little given I fear to liquor, but a genuine musical enthusiast, and desperately poor. I have promised him 6d for every genuine old ballad air he can pick up for me and he is going round the country for that purpose.[11]

He appears to have earned just one shilling, since only two tunes are recorded as having been obtained from him – a version of 'General Wolfe' and 'Follow My Love', but Baring-Gould based a short story, 'Daniel Jacobs', on him, which was included in his book *Dartmoor Idylls*.[12] The description of his coming to a lady's garden to play his tunes is vivid and the inclusion of the song 'General Wolfe' in the story is sure confirmation of the 'borrowed' identity of Daniel Jacobs. Otherwise the story is a piece of fantasy.

Lady Edith Lethbridge

A later contributor to Baring-Gould's collection was Lady Lethbridge who in 1905 sent Baring-Gould several songs which he included in his manuscript collection. They were mostly children's songs and she told Baring-Gould that she had heard them from her parents and from her nurse when she was a child.

Lady Lethbridge was born Edith Seymour Waring in Lyme Regis in 1850 where her father, Henry Waring, was a solicitor and the Town Clerk. In 1862, when Edith was eleven, Henry Waring died and his

---

10 Ralph Vaughan Williams, A. L. Lloyd, and Malcolm Douglas (eds), *Classic English Folk Songs* (London: EFDSS, 2nd edition, 2009, p. 67). A brief biography of Mary Langworthy is included on p. 137.

11 VWML, Lucy Broadwood Manuscripts, Letter of Sabine Baring-Gould to Lucy Broadwood [probably week of 6 February 1893], LEB/4/39.

12 Sabine Baring-Gould, 'Daniel Jacobs', *Dartmoor Idylls*, pp. 51–67.

widow, Catherine Waring, née Rankin, moved with the younger children to Bristol, where she had been born. When she reached adulthood Edith worked as a governess in Bristol until she married George Bellett, who was an inspector of schools in Bengal and by whom she had two daughters. On their return from India the family lived in Brentford where George Bellett died in May 1898. The following year she married Sir Alfred Swaine Lethbridge, a doctor who had enjoyed a distinguished career in India as the Inspector General of Gaols in Bengal, and who had led operations to suppress banditry, for which services he had been knighted. He and Edith Bellett had met in India and renewed their acquaintance when Lethbridge retired to England in 1898.[13] The couple lived at Windhover in Hampshire until Sir Alfred's death in 1917 when Lady Lethbridge moved first to Surrey and then to Chalfont St Peter, where she died in 1933.

Lady Lethbridge sent several songs to Baring-Gould in 1905. They arrived too late to be considered for inclusion in the 1905 edition of *Songs of the West* but Baring-Gould and Cecil Sharp included three of them in *English Folk Songs for Schools*, published the following year.[14] Her original manuscripts have not survived among Baring-Gould's papers but he noted some of her comments about them when he transcribed twenty items into his Personal Copy manuscript. Most are described as having been learnt when she was a child, many from her mother, one from her nurse and one from her father. Baring-Gould mistakenly referred to her as having come from South Devon whereas her childhood home in Lyme Regis is just inside the Dorset border. We do not know for certain why Lady Lethbridge wrote to Baring-Gould but it is likely that the thought of passing her songs on to a major collector was prompted by the contacts that Lucy Broadwood and Ralph Vaughan Williams had with other family members, as described below.

---

13 There is a group photograph in the India Office Collection at the British Library [Ref 897/2(56)] taken in Darjeeling in June 1886 in which Alfred Lethbridge and Edith Bellett appear together.

14 The songs sent by Lady Lethbridge to Baring-Gould were versions of 'The Gipsy Countess', 'Deep in Love', 'Three Jovial Welshmen', 'The Cuckoo', 'If Roses be but Fading Flowers', 'Johnny Greyman', 'The Derby Ram', 'Giles Collins', 'Little Sir William', 'The Tailor and the Mouse', 'King Henry V and the King of France', 'Codlin Apple Tree', 'Purr-a-by', 'I Had Four Sisters', 'Robin a Thrush', 'Lord Thomas and Fair Eleanor', 'Gaffer Grey', 'Little Old Woman who Went to Market', 'The Maid and her Swain' and 'Christmas Mummers Tune'. The songs underlined were used in *English Folk Songs for Schools*.

Sister Emma

Four years later, in 1909, Cecil Sharp visited an Anglican nun, Sister Emma, at the Convent of St John the Baptist in Clewer, near Windsor, and collected a number of songs from her. Another researcher, Matthew Edwards, wrote to me to say that he had noticed that Sister Emma's repertoire included a song 'As She Was Keeping Her Flock', which was very similar to 'The Maid and Her Swain', which Lady Lethbridge had sent to Baring-Gould. After some work together we discovered that the two women were, in fact, sisters, and that Eleanor Emma Waring (Sister Emma) had been born twelve years before Edith. Further study showed that of the 25 songs that Sharp collected from Sister Emma very similar versions of eight of them had also been sent to Baring-Gould by Lady Lethbridge.

Cecil Sharp's visit to Sister Emma at Clewer took place on 27 February 1909, and he collected nineteen songs from her on that day. She sent him a further six by post on 13 March together with the following information which Sharp copied into his notebook:

> I must have been certainly not over six years of age when my old nurse sang several of them and my mother the others. My mother would have been then about 35 years of age, my nurse quite 45. My mother learnt them from her grandmother – my great grandmother, whom I remember at the time as over 90. She had no music written, nor had my mother. The only ones I have seen in print were 'We be soldiers three' and 'Here's a health to all those we love'. All the rest are traditional. My own age is 71. The calculations are quite too difficult for me! But may be of use to you.

Sister Emma died nine days later. Her great-grandmother, mentioned in the letter to Sharp, was Ann Rankin (née Cole), who was born in Newcastle in 1749 and died there in 1840. She had passed her songs on to her grandchildren including Catherine (Rankin) Waring, who in turn sang them for the Waring siblings. This explains why several of the songs that Sister Emma recalled originate from north-east England. In a pamphlet called *Peeps into an old Playground* Sister Emma recalled her childhood in Lyme Regis.[15] In this she mentions their nurse, Priscilla Tucker, from Shute in Devon, who was another source of songs for the family.

One of the songs that Sister Emma gave to Cecil Sharp is a version of the gory ballad 'Long Lankin', which has been recovered many times

---

15 S. E., *Peeps into an old Playground* (Lyme Regis: Dunster, 1865).

in northern England and in Scotland.[16] An article had been published in *Notes and Queries* in 1856 describing the ballad and giving a very full text of it that is close to that sung by Sister Emma to Cecil Sharp. The article is signed simply 'M.H.R', but it became obvious with the information to hand that the author was Sister Emma's uncle, Michael Rankin. He says that the ballad was '…derived from tradition from the nurse of an ancestor of mine who heard it sung nearly a century ago in Northumberland'. This ancestor from whom the song originated was, we can deduce, Ann (Cole) Rankin. She had been born in 1749, so if Sister Emma learnt it as a child in the nursery it would have been in the 1850s. This fits with the date given by her uncle, Michael Rankin. But the story does not end there.

The Rankin/Waring Family

Matthew Edwards then told me that one of Edith and Emma's brothers, Charles Waring, had corresponded with Lucy Broadwood in 1906 and 1907, and had sent her a number of songs that he remembered. He also told her of others that he knew, including 'Long Lankin'.[17] He confirmed that some of the songs came from his Devonshire nurse, 'Priscilla', and others from his parents, who, he says, were both enthusiastic musicians who performed the songs with fine piano accompaniments.

I had meanwhile discovered a letter written in April 1926 to Ralph Vaughan Williams by Mrs Nyanza Johnston of Evershot, in Dorset, which provided further evidence of the Rankin/Waring family's interest in song:

> I have heard that you are interested in collecting the old English Ballads. I know several that, perhaps may be new to you, and I wonder whether you would care to hear of them. I know words and music, but unfortunately cannot write the tunes out properly harmonised. My grandmother who was an old woman when she died in 1872 was a real musician, and she collected these old ballads, and taught them to my mother, who in her turn taught

---

16 Sister Emma's version of 'Long Lankin' was published by Ralph Vaughan Williams and A. L. Lloyd in the *Penguin Book of English Folk Songs* (Harmondsworth, Penguin Books, 1959), pp. 60–61.

17 VWML, Lucy Broadwood Manuscripts, Letter of Charles Waring to Lucy Broadwood, 25 June 1907 (LEB/5/401). The songs Charles Waring sent to Lucy Broadwood were 'Henry V', 'The Bonnie Bunch of Roses' and 'Rodney So Bold'. In his letter he mentions some other songs including 'Little Cabin Boy, 'Little Sir William', 'I Saw a Ship a' Sailing', 'King Henry My Son' and 'Long Lankin'.

us, hoping that they might not be altogether lost. Among others I know Long Lankin – evidently a Border ballad – Lord Lovell, Little Sir William, The Pretty Fair Maid, Johnnie Cook, and Giles Collins. Would it be possible to get these published in a volume to themselves? I know several others besides.[18]

Vaughan Williams visited Mrs Johnston on 31 July 1926 and noted the tunes of eleven songs from her, though not the words.[19] Nyanza Johnston's mother was Lucy Waring, another sister of Edith Lethbridge and Sister Emma, and so the primary source of her songs was her grandmother, Catherine (Rankin) Waring.

I have written about the Waring family and their songs at some length because the discovery of a family who shared their songs over five generations is quite extraordinary. We can state with certainty that the ballad of 'Long Lankin' was sung in the family for at least 175 years. The total number of songs in their combined repertoire is 42, though there is just one song that was collected from, or mentioned by, all five of the sources. That was 'Little Sir William', the family's version of the blood-libel story of Hugh of Lincoln.[20]

The earliest known source for many of the songs was Ann (Cole) Rankin, while another key figure is her granddaughter, Catherine (Rankin) Waring, who passed the songs on so successfully to her children. Catherine also shared her enthusiasm for the songs outside her family, as is illustrated by another strand to the story.

In 1902 Ralph Vaughan Williams embarked on a series of talks about folk song for the Oxford University Extension Unit, the adult education department of the university. In 1902 he gave a series of six lectures in Bournemouth.[21] For the fourth talk (14 November 1902) he invited Lucy Broadwood to illustrate the lecture with examples of songs. One unexpected outcome of the lecture series was that in December he met

18 London, British Library, Ralph Vaughan Williams Manuscript Collection, Letter of Mrs N. M. Johnston to R. Vaughan Williams, 22 April 1926, Loose sheets IV.
19 London, British Library, Ralph Vaughan Williams Manuscript Collection, Loose sheets IV 1–4. The songs for which Vaughan Williams noted the tunes were: 'The Pretty Fair Maid', 'Johnny Cook', 'Lady Ansabel (Lord Lovell)', 'Three Gypsies', 'Bonny Bunch of Roses', 'Robin-a-Thrush', 'Rodney', 'Can You Sew Cushions?', 'King of France' and 'Four Sisters'.
20 'Sir Hugh or the Jew's Daughter', Child 155.
21 This series of lectures is described by Michael Holyoake, 'Towards a folk song awakening: Vaughan Williams in Bournemouth, 1902', *Ralph Vaughan Williams Society Journal*, 46 (October 2009), pp. 9–15.

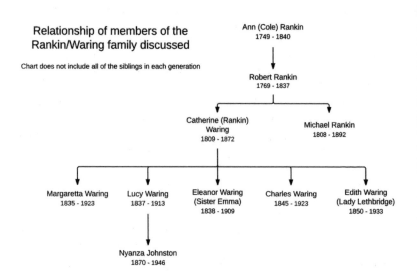

Fig. 7.1 – The Rankin/Waring Family Tree.

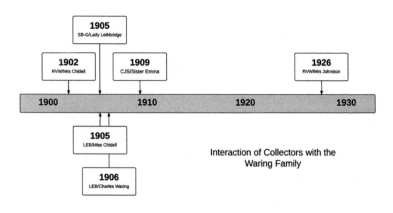

Fig. 7.2 – Interaction of collectors with the Waring family.

Mrs Katherine Chidell and noted the tunes of five folk songs from her, which he sent to Lucy Broadwood and which can be found among her papers.[22] Mrs Chidell told Vaughan Williams that she had learned these from a Mrs Waring.

Neither Vaughan Williams nor Broadwood followed up this matter until 1905, when Lucy Broadwood sent a card to Mrs Chidell. She received a reply from Adelaide Chidell, her daughter, who said that her mother had died in the autumn of 1904, but she told Broadwood that her mother had learned the songs from a Mrs Waring in Lyme Regis, whom we can identify as Catherine (Rankin) Waring.[23] Sometime later Adelaide Chidell sent Broadwood the words for four of her mother's songs ('Little Sir Hugh', 'Lord Ronald', 'Giles Collins' and 'Lord Thomas') as well as another notation of the 'Long Lankin' tune. Katherine Chidell's sister, Isabel Thrupp also wrote to Broadwood:

> I can tell you that we learnt all of them, – 'Lord Thomas & Fair Eleanor,' 'Giles Collins', – 'Little Sir William', 'Long Lankin', &c, – from Mrs. H. Waring, – of Lyme Regis (Dorset). I believe she was of Somersetshire, – but whether she got the ballads locally, I do not know. But she had several daughters with whom we used to sing many of the ballads, and other part songs.[24]

This, again, highlights the role played by Catherine Waring, inspiring a lasting interest in her family's traditional songs not only in her daughters, but in their friends as well.

The Rankin-Warings are clearly important as carriers of traditional songs, but they present us with the difficulty that as a prosperous middle-class family some would not consider them to be legitimate representatives of the folk song tradition. This is another consequence of the definitional dilemma that the same song might be considered traditional if it came from the mouth of a gypsy, but not if it was sung by a teacher.

This may be why Vaughan Williams did not make much of this little

---

22 VWML, Lucy Broadwood Manuscripts, Words of four songs, LEB/5/118 – 125. The songs that Mrs Chidell sang to Vaughan Williams were 'Little Sir William', 'Lord Ronald', 'Lord Thomas and Fair Elinor', 'Giles Collins' and 'Long Lankin'. She also sang him a version of 'The Lady and the Box', which her brother had heard in London in about 1842.

23 VWML, Lucy Broadwood Manuscripts, Letter of Adelaide Chiddell to Lucy Broadwood, 10 June 1905, LEB/5/124. The songs she sent later are LEB/5/121/1–3.

24 VWML, Lucy Broadwood Manuscripts, Letter of Isabel Thrupp to Lucy Broadwood, c. June 1905, LEB/5/125.

group of songs, though it predates by a year his encounter with the more authentically proletarian Charles Potiphar in an Essex garden in December 1903, when he heard him sing the beautiful 'Bushes and Briars'.[25] Yet, as we have seen among Baring-Gould's own friends, the 'old songs' were enjoyed by several middle-class men and women, particularly those brought up in the countryside. Many, but by no means all, of the people who sent songs to Baring-Gould were of this class and were passing on songs taught to them by nurses, heard in the fields at harvest time or sung by parents with a passion for old songs, like Catherine Waring.

William Crossing

There are two men who sent songs to Baring-Gould from collections that they made on Dartmoor in the middle of the nineteenth century. The first of these was the antiquarian and writer William Crossing, whose books about Dartmoor are still well known and much admired. He was born in Plymouth in 1847, the son of a grocer, and was introduced to the moor through family holidays at a cottage near Roborough. His mother was interested in the history, folklore and antiquities of the moor and her son followed her example, with Dartmoor becoming a life-long passion. He worked at his father's sailcloth mill in South Brent, from where he could walk out onto the southern part of the moor. He had written fiction and poetry since he was a schoolboy and, after the sail-making business failed he resolved to continue his exploration of Dartmoor and to write about his discoveries.

The first of his books was *The Ancient Crosses of Dartmoor*.[26] His rambles took him all over the moor and he would often stay out overnight, keeping company with the moor-men in isolated pubs. Around the peat fire he would tell of his day's journey in improvised verse and play tunes on an old tin whistle. In the 1890s he moved to the north-western edge of Dartmoor. By now he was badly affected by arthritis as a result of frequent soakings on Dartmoor, and was in financial difficulty. Baring-Gould was among those who contributed to a public subscription to help support him. Another benefactor, W. P. Collins, gave him the use of a house in Mary Tavy and employed him as a tutor for his children.

After the death of his wife in 1921 his situation became even more difficult and he had to resort first to the workhouse in Tavistock and then to a nursing home in Plymouth where he died in 1928. Not long before

---

25 This places Vaughan Williams ahead of Cecil Sharp in the timeline of Edwardian folk song collectors by several months.

26 William Crossing, *The Ancient Crosses of Dartmoor With a Description of their Surroundings* (Exeter: James Commin, 1887).

his death the woman who cleaned for him came across a pile of his papers that were mouse-eaten and could not, she thought, be of any value. The manuscript record of his life's work was consigned to the rubbish heap. What remains, however, are his books, which give us a remarkable picture of Dartmoor life as it was in the nineteenth century, as well as a detailed topography of the moor.

Baring-Gould's manuscripts contain six songs that were noted by Crossing from unnamed men on Dartmoor between 1857 and 1878 and sent to him from South Brent. Crossing seems to have been a competent musician since tunes have been provided for three of the songs. They are all light-hearted or romantic songs, such as he might well have heard sitting around the peat fire with old Dartmoor moor-men. And two of them were risqué.

The version of 'The Bold Dragoon' that Crossing sent was included Baring-Gould's manuscripts with no obvious mediation.[27]

In the dragoon's ride from out the North
He came up to a lady
And then she knew him by his horse
And she loved him very dearly
O dearly, O dearly.

She took the horse by the bridle rein
To lead him to the stable
She said, There's hay and corn for the horse
So let him eat whilst able.
O able, O able.

She said, there's cake and wine for you
There's corn and hay for horses.
There's bread and ale for the King's soldiers,
Aye and there's pretty lasses.
O lasses, aye, lasses.

She stepped upstairs, she made the bed,
She made it plum and easy.
And into bed she nimbly jumped
And said, Dragoon, I'm ready
O ready, O ready!

O he pulled off his armour bright
He cast it on the table.
And into bed he nimbly jumps
To kiss whilst he was able
O able, O able.

They spent the night till break of dawn
They saw the light full grieving.
O hark! I hear the trumpet sound,
Sweet maid! I must be leaving.
O leaving, O leaving!

I would the trumpet ne'er would call
So cruel does it grieve me
My heart, my very heart will break,
Because, dragoon, you leave me.
O leave me, O leave me!

Here's half a crown for Saturday night
Sheep's head and lungs for Sunday.
Here's bread and cheese for all the week,
And Devil a bit for Monday,
O Monday, O Monday!

---

27 Devon Heritage Centre, Baring-Gould Papers, Personal Copy MSS, 'The Bold Dragoon', P1, 141 (66).

Baring-Gould published 'The Bold Dragoon' in *Songs of the West* using Crossing's tune but rewrote the words. It is not one of his best efforts. The soldier arrives at the lady's house and puts on such a display of arrogance that when he has asked for the finest food she offers bacon, pease and mouldy cheese, and then dismisses him:

> Your distance keep, I esteem you cheap
> Tho' your wishes I've granted, partly
> But no kisses from me for a chimpanzee
> The lady responded tartly.
> Why, a rude dragoon is a mere Baboon
> And she boxed his ears full smartly
> Smartly, aye smartly

Baring-Gould also liked the tune of Crossing's version of 'Rosemary Lane', but wrote, 'The words are objectionable'. In *Songs of the West* he used the tune as a vehicle for his own story of 'The Blue Flame'. While it is regrettable that Baring-Gould needed to rewrite the songs – and particularly regrettable that he did so poorly with the 'Bold Dragoon', we can appreciate in both cases that he has left the words as originally collected in his manuscripts.

Crossing himself does not appear to have published any of the songs he collected. The transcripts of the words are in Baring-Gould's Working Notebook 2. There is also Crossing's original manuscript of 'Forty Long Miles'. The manuscript of 'The Lady and the Dragoon' was originally present but has been lost. None of the tune manuscripts appears to have survived among Baring-Gould's papers. We must assume that Crossing's cleaning woman destroyed anything he had retained. This is a great loss, since it is likely that Crossing had more songs and, given the quality of what Baring-Gould recorded in his manuscripts, there may have been some gems among them.

Thomas Cayzer

The other man who sent Baring-Gould songs that he had heard on Dartmoor was Thomas Stollery Cayzer, a retired headmaster who was then living in Cambridgeshire. His father had been a teacher and much of Cayzer's childhood was spent in Plymouth. He followed his father into the teaching profession and taught at Chudleigh Grammar School in Devon until he was offered the post of headmaster at Queen Elizabeth's Hospital School in Bristol in 1859. He left this post twenty years later in 1879 after some controversy about his teaching methods. He had married an Italian woman, (Nellie) Amata Ferrari, in 1877 when she was 25 and he was 48. The first of their four children was born in Bristol but after he left Bristol they lived for a while at Withycombe Raleigh in Devon and then at Ickleton, Cambridgeshire, before settling at Queen Camel in Somerset. Amata died at the age of forty, leaving Thomas to look after his children and his 91-year-old father who was living with them. Cayzer died in Bristol in 1907.

While he was teaching at Chudleigh Cayzer spent his leisure time on Dartmoor. Like Crossing, he enjoyed staying overnight in moorland inns and keeping company with the moor-men. He described such an occasion in a letter to Baring-Gould,

> The scene was a lonely one (I think Two Bridges, but it may have been Post Bridge). It had been raining all day. There was not a book in the house, nor musical instrument of any kind, except two hungry pigs and a baby that was being weaned. Towards nightfall there dropped in several miners and shepherds, and I well remember how the appearance of these Gentiles [sic] cheered us. We soon got up a glorious fire – such a fire as peat only can make, and drew the benches and settles round. By the friendly aid of sundry quarts of cyder I, before long, gained the confidence of the whole circle, and got a song from each in turn; and noted down two that were quite new to me: no easy matter, considering that they were performed in a strange mixture of double bass and falsetto. The action with which they accompanied the singing was extremely appropriate. They always sang standing.

Baring-Gould copied this passage into the record for 'Cup of Poison' in his Personal Copy manuscript.[28] This is a rare description of the way in which a pub singing session was conducted in the mid-nineteenth century. The singers stood to perform, employing a wide vocal range. The information that they used actions for emphasis (presumably with their arms) is not something that I have seen reported elsewhere. It is also interesting to note that it was Cayzer who initiated the session and gained the confidence of the singers – and provided the drink that fuelled the performance.

Three songs that Cayzer sent to Baring-Gould sometime in 1890 are recorded in the Personal Copy manuscript. 'Cup of Poison' is a version of the murder ballad 'Oxford City'. Baring-Gould liked the tune but thought

---

28 Devon Heritage Centre, Baring-Gould Papers, Personal Copy MSS, 'The Cup of Poison', P1, 144 (66). This song has been included as one of the examples in Appendix B.

the words unsuitable for publication in *Songs of the West* so he wrote a set of words, 'Trinity Sunday', to go with Cayzer's tune.

The tune of the 'May Day Carol' was collected on Dartmoor in 1850, but Cayzer does not seem to have had the words. He remembered having heard them sung at Melbourn, Cambridgeshire, when he lived there many years earlier and drove over to collect a set from an old man living there, which he then sent to Baring-Gould. Cayzer's tune for 'May-Day Carol' was used in *Songs of the West* but despite the trouble Cayzer had taken Baring-Gould used a set of words that he remembered having been sung by children in Lew Trenchard in the 1850s. Interestingly, Baring-Gould has chosen to use a more secular version than the moralising texts he obtained from others, including Cayzer.

The third song was 'As Johnny Walked Out' which Baring-Gould had included in the first part of *Songs of the West* in a version collected from James Parsons, and published before Cayzer contacted him.

The letters and manuscript that Cayzer sent to Baring-Gould have not survived, nor have Cayzer's papers been placed in any public record office, so we do not know if he collected any other songs. It is the fact that he made a note of these songs and their tunes at a time before folk song collecting began in earnest that makes his work of interest. The description of the singing session around the peat fire on Dartmoor is also of great value. Baring-Gould was fortunate to have encountered two men who had heard songs on Dartmoor at around the time that he, as a teenager, rode out on the moor and had some of the same experiences. This must have encouraged him greatly.

Other Informants

We know that a lot of Baring-Gould's correspondence was destroyed after his death. Local people have talked of cart-loads of paper having been carried to the quarry to be burned. Very few of the letters sent to Baring-Gould from fellow collectors and others associated with the project have survived. One of the exceptions is in the letters and manuscript notes of songs sent to him by members of the general public. He stuck a number of these into his notebooks or left them between the pages of his manuscripts.[29]

---

29 His favoured method of attaching the letters to a notebook page was to use the perforated edge strips from sheets of stamps: a useful economy and an indication of the large number of stamps that he got through. These have proved far more effective at holding letters etc. in his manuscripts than the acidic starch paste that he sometimes resorted to which has caused the paper to rot and to release the letter it held into the vagaries of the library and archive systems.

We are fortunate that some significant collections of letters sent to other colleagues, such as Lucy Broadwood, Cecil Sharp and Francis Child, have been saved. Some of those have been quoted in this chapter and they have also provided a great deal of information about the relationship between Baring-Gould and this other important part of his network.

There were 123 people who posted songs to Baring-Gould and they contributed 242 songs between them, though 84 of them sent him just one song. There is only a handful of super-informants, like the four described above, who might be considered 'collectors' in their own right.

The people who sent Baring-Gould songs came from all parts of society. The following table assigns the informants to categories of occupations based on census returns, newspaper searches and other information.[30]

Occupation	No of informants
Professional man	21
Clergyman	14
Unidentified women	13
Writer/Artist/Antiquarian	10
Farmer/Landowner	9
Unidentified (gender unknown)	9
Own means, older woman	8
Artisan/Dressmaker/Labourer etc.	7
Unidentified man	7
Armed forces	6
Clergyman's wife/daughter/relative	6
Musician	5
Younger unmarried women (dependent)	2
Servant/Gardener/Coachman	2
Own means, older man	2
Professional woman	1
Wife of professional man	1

Fig.7.3 – Baring-Gould's informants and their occupations (table)

30 My primary source has been the names given in the Personal Copy manuscript, but I have also added some names from other sources. I have described informants as 'unidentified' where there is insufficient evidence. The unidentified informants constitute 24% of the total, but I think it unlikely that complete identification would have changed the result dramatically.

The spread of occupations ranges widely and covers those of the majority of the population as a whole – from titled ladies to labourers. We should not read too much into this. Male, middle-class informants dominate the picture. The artisans, servants and labourers, and their wives, would have had more direct access to the songs, but they would not all have felt comfortable with writing to Baring-Gould.

Professional men and clergymen form 28% of the sample as a whole. Many of these would have known Baring-Gould in person or by reputation and would have seen value in helping him. At least 32 of the informants (26%) were women and most of these were the wives, daughters or widows of professional men or were living on their own means. Women form the larger part of the unidentified informants, since women are, for a number of reasons, harder to track in census data.

Baring-Gould preferred to use versions of songs that he and his colleagues collected themselves in *Songs of the West*, though a few of the items sent by informants (eight out of the 110 songs in the earlier editions) were used where they were the sole source or where the postal version enabled him to make a point.

There was one particular part of the 'Victorian Web' network that should be singled out for mention because of the help that it gave him, not only with song collecting but also in other fields of activity, and that was his fellow clergymen. Several vicars were among those who sent him songs that they recalled or pointed him towards a good singer. If he had a query about something in a distant location, then he would often contact the local vicar who might know the answer or could point him to the person in his parish who did. If Baring-Gould needed to visit a location, he might also be able to get a bed in the vicarage for the duration of his stay.

Priscilla Wyatt-Edgell

Another woman who sent songs to Baring-Gould was Priscilla Wyatt-Edgell. She is a significant figure, not only because of the songs that she sent to his collection, but also because of her contributions to folk song and dance more generally.

Lucy Priscilla Wyatt-Edgell was born in Westminster, London, in the spring of 1871. Her father was Lt. Colonel Arthur Wyatt-Edgell, formerly of the Royal Hussars. He was wealthy and well connected and in addition to his activities as a landowner and Justice of the Peace was a competent watercolourist and amateur geologist. He had also edited a collection of soldiers' songs, published in the year of his daughter's birth.[31] The family's home was Cowley Place to the north-west of Exeter, close to Upton Pyne and to Pynes, the seat of the Northcote family. Jacquetta Baring-Gould, Sabine's great-aunt, had married Sir Stafford Northcote (later Lord Iddesleigh) and Sabine stayed at Pynes a number of times, so it is likely that he had met the Wyatt-Edgell family. We know that Priscilla became friendly with Baring-Gould's daughters and that she had visited Lew Trenchard. She wrote to Sharp's biographer, Arthur Fox Strangways, describing her experience of visiting Lew House.

> It was a funny household at Lew. I loved going there. The house was lovely as you know. Mrs Baring-Gould always very kind and placid and they were an amusing family. I think he was a very kind squire. I have stayed there for one of his village dance evenings – and he walked about and talked to them all – and saw to it they all had cider afterwards. There is a plaster ceiling in the ball room at Lew – made by one of his Villagers who was ill and depressed and Mr. B. G. started him on this work to give him an interest and cheer him up – which he succeeded in doing; the man was an excellent workman and soon got keen on his job.[32]

The 21 songs she sent to Baring-Gould were heard from men and women who lived near Cowley Place. Most of the entries for the songs in his Personal Copy manuscript are dated and it appears that the majority were sent to him in 1902, with a few more added over the years. The tune for one song, 'The Hundred Haymakers', is in Wyatt-Edgell's own hand and pasted into the Personal Copy. An indication of the duration of their correspondence is that one song, a version of 'The Jolly Goss Hawk', is dated spring 1923. This was the last item that he entered into his manuscripts.

Several of the songs are noted as having been taken down from an old blind woman at Upton Pyne. In correspondence with Lucy Broadwood some years later Wyatt-Edgell identified her as Mary Blamey. Study of the census data shows her to have been a widow who was 66 in 1891, which is the date given to Broadwood for two songs taken from her. Her gravestone in Upton Pyne churchyard records that she died in 1894. In the manuscripts that she sent to Broadwood, Wyatt-Edgell gave the date of collection as 1891, so she would have been just twenty years old when she started to

---

31 Arthur Wyatt-Edgell, *A Collection of Soldiers' Songs with Music* (Exeter: Eland, 1871).
32 London, Vaughan Williams Memorial Library, Cecil Sharp Manuscripts, Letter of Priscilla Wyatt-Edgell to Arthur Fox Strangways, 18 Aug 1932, CJS1/12/21/9/7.

collect songs. We have no information in the various surviving letters that she wrote that tells us what led her to start collecting folk songs. It is likely that she knew the Baring-Gould family and had stayed at Lew House. If she had done so at any time from 1888 onwards she would certainly have heard about Sabine Baring-Gould's collecting project and might have been prompted to do some collecting herself. This is conjecture, but what is certain is that a large part of her life became dedicated to folk song.

In April 1907 she arranged, at Baring-Gould's request, for William Ford, the local blacksmith, to go to Lew Trenchard to teach country dances to some of the villagers in preparation for an event that was planned to take place a few weeks later (more will be said about this event in Chapter 13). Ford played the concertina for the dancers and demonstrated a number of the dances. Sharp was staying at Lew House and he noted Ford's steps, which were published in the first volume of his *Country Dance Book*.[33]

Wyatt-Edgell met Sharp for the first time a few months later in September 1907 when he cycled up the drive of Cowley House and asked to see 'Miss Priscilla'. He had been at Stafford Common, near Seaton in East Devon, to collect songs from the travellers, Rebecca Holland and Priscilla Cooper. Wyatt-Edgell later wrote, 'He said that never before had he met a Priscilla – and now he had come across two in one day.' They were to become good friends, and Sharp stayed at Cowley House on several occasions.

On his first stay, in January 1908, he went out with Wyatt-Edgell to collect songs from William and Eliza Beer at Budlake, near Killerton, not far from Cowley House. Killerton House was one of the estates owned by the Acland family and at this time home to Sir Charles Acland, his wife Gertrude and their niece, Cherry Hart-Davis.[34]

> Mr and Mrs Beer were exactly the sort of old couple you would expect to find in that sort of cottage. Mrs Beer had pink cheeks and blue eyes, and sang in a little voice, but quite in tune, and the words very distinct. Mr Sharp sat in the settle with Mrs Beer on one side of the hearth with his little manuscript book to take down her songs – Mr Beer sat in his elbow chair on the other side. Of course in five minutes Mr Sharp was friends with them both,

---

33 Cecil Sharp, *The Country Dance Book* (London: Novello, 1909).
34 Sylvia Charity (Cherry) Hart-Davis, was the daughter of the Rev. Richard Hart-Davis and his wife, Mary Lydia, daughter of Sir Thomas Acland. The Aclands had no children and she lived permanently with them at Killerton, describing herself as a 'substitute daughter'.

and perfectly at home – Mr Beer was not by way of singing, and would not have done it at all, if Mr Sharp had not made us feel so pleasant and homely.[35]

They then went to Killerton House for afternoon tea with Cherry Hart-Davis, who had collected songs around the village and had suggested that Sharp might visit the Beers.

Sharp stayed at Cowley Place again in July 1909 when he gave a lecture on folk song at a fete at Killerton, held to raise funds for the Devonshire Nursing Association. Earlier in the afternoon there was a display of Morris dancing by a group of young women trained by Wyatt-Edgell and of singing games by village children, under the guidance of Cherry Hart-Davis. Sharp made a note of seven children's songs and singing games while he was there. He also took the opportunity to meet with William Ford again and he collected another dance from him.

In 1923 Wyatt-Edgell met up with Sharp again while he was in Exeter. They had planned to visit Rewe, just outside Exeter, to meet an old man whom she had heard sing. Sharp was in the event too unwell to go out and the only songs that were noted that day were from Wyatt-Edgell herself. One was 'Poor Old Maids', which she remembered a Mrs Fursdon singing at Sidmouth when she was young. The other was 'The Grey Hawk', which she had heard from the man they had planned to visit that day. Sharp's manuscript does not identify the singer but she gave the song to Baring-Gould and he entered it into his Personal Copy manuscript as a version of 'The Jolly Goss Hawk'. Here the singer is identified as Mr Sprague.

Wyatt-Edgell also sent a number of the songs that she had collected around Cowley Place to Lucy Broadwood for possible inclusion in the *Journal of the Folk Song Society*, saying rather modestly: 'I am not very well up in folk songs, so I am not certain that they may not have been printed – but I have not found anyone who knew them.' Of the ten songs she sent three appeared in the *Journal* in 1910 – 'Henry Martin', 'Three Pretty Maidens Milking Did Go' and ''Twas on One April Morning'.[36]

On 27 September 1912 Lucy Broadwood went to stay with Sabine Baring-Gould at Lew House for a night while she was in Devon. Priscilla Wyatt-Edgell was also there that day and it was arranged that Broadwood would go to stay at Cowley Place a few days later. On the afternoon of 1

---

35 VWML, Cecil Sharp Correspondence, Letter of Priscilla Wyatt-Edgell to Annie Fursdon, undated, CJS/12/21/9/3.
36 'Songs from Devon', *Journal of the Folk Song Society*, 4 (December 1910), pp. 92–96.

October she was met at Exeter station by Miss Wyatt-Edgell who took her to Cowley Place. After meeting Wyatt-Edgell's mother and some friends over tea, the two women heard some folk songs from a local labourer.

The following day they spent some time singing and playing music before Elizabeth Parkin, the Wyatt-Edgell's gardener's daughter came to sing to them. On the Wednesday morning they drove into Exeter where, after some sightseeing, they hired a Phonograph. They visited Pynes to take tea with the Northcotes where an old gamekeeper sang for them and told some amusing Devonshire stories. The following day they set up the Phonograph at Cowley Place and Broadwood sang into it to test it before catching her train back to London. The plan was that Wyatt-Edgell would use the Phonograph to record some of her local singers and then send the recordings to Broadwood for transcription.

On 19 October Broadwood reported in her diary that she had started to note a 'Devon Phonograph-record from Miss Wyatt-Edgell's old singer'. This process continued over several days and on 31 October Wyatt-Edgell visited her at Carlisle Mansions to view the transcription of 'The Pretty Ploughboy', which had been sung by Richard Bryant of Cowley. This detailed transcription was printed over four pages in the 1913 volume of the *Journal of the Folk Song Society*.[37] It appears to be the only fruit of Wyatt-Edgell's experiment with Phonograph recording.

Priscilla Wyatt-Edgell died on 4 December 1934. The latter part of her life was blighted by severe arthritis – and yet one senses that she made the best of things, as is indicated by the rather quirky obituary that Arthur Fox Strangways wrote for the *Journal of the English Folk Dance and Song Society* in 1936.

Miss Wyatt-Edgell came of a good Devonshire family. She was a keen musician, and until she became a martyr to arthritis, played the violin with a reasonable number of wrong notes and a true feeling of the composer's intention. She had the keenest enjoyment of a bit of dialect, of the re-emergence of a Shakespearean word, of a funny turn of speech or a look on a face or trick of manner, and would search for these in first editions of herbals and county histories, and in her numerous acquaintances, high and low. She told a story well, and it is a pity her maiming disease made writing

---

37 '11 – The Pretty Ploughboy (Version B)', *Journal of the Folk-Song Society*, 4, (January 1913), 304–07. This issue was mainly given over to songs collected by George Butterworth and the transcription was appended to the tune he had collected in Sussex.

such a labour. She and Sharp were great friends; she usually had some find for him, or news of where to look for it, and he could disburthen himself of his aspiration and difficulties and get a sane and heartening view of them in return. In the presence of her ardent spirit one would forget the weak body that took pleasure in the dances in which she had never joined.[38]

If there is one thing that she deserves to be remembered for, it should be her discovery of "'Twas on One April Morning', one of the most beautiful songs in the English folk song canon. It was sung by Richard Bryant, a railway worker who lived near her at Cowley.

'Twas on one April morning, just as the sun was rising
'Twas on one April morning, I heard the small birds sing
They were singing Lovely Nancy for love it is a fancy
So sweet were the notes that I heard the small birds sing.

Young men are false and full of all deceiving
Young men are false and seldom do prove true
For they're roving and they're ranging and their minds are always
    changing
For they're thinking for to find out some pretty girl that's new.

O if I had but my own heart in keeping
O if I had but my own heart back again
Close in my bosom I would lock it up forever
And it should wander never so far from me again.

Why would you spend all your long time in courting?
Why would you spend all your long time in vain?
For I don't intend to marry, I'd rather longer tarry
So young man, don't you spend all your long time in vain.

It is now widely sung, having been popularised by Cyril Tawney and Tony Rose, and few realise that it is a rare song, having been heard once each in Devon and Somerset and twice in Cornwall. Sharp only noted the first verse of what is a version somewhat similar in words and tune to that collected by Wyatt-Edgell. Baring-Gould heard two versions in Cornwall.

---

38 A. H. Fox Strangways, 'Obituary: Lucy Priscilla Wyatt-Edgell', *Journal of the English Folk Dance and Song Society*, 3 (December 1936), 79.

The first is called 'The Complaining Maid' and it came from the old farmer, dock gate keeper and ex-smuggler, William Houghton, who lived in Charlestown, near St Austell. Though the tune is very different, the words have many of the same phrases as the Devonshire version and they are evidently related.[39] The other version that Baring-Gould heard was only a single verse, sung by Mary Gilbert when he visited the Falcon Inn, Mawgan-in-Pydar, in July 1891. This is nearly the same as the third verse of 'April Morning'.

> O that I had but my own true heart in keeping
> O if I had but my own true heart again
> So safe in my bosom I'd lock it up forever
> Never to wander so far from me in pain.

Miss Gilbert remembered only this fragment and Frederick Bussell was not able to note down the tune because she was so uncertain in her singing of it.

When Wyatt-Edgell's song was first published in the *Journal of the Folk Song Society*, Lucy Broadwood suggested that it was probably a theatre or ballad opera song from the eighteenth century. Broadwood also drew attention to precursors of the well-known 'Early One Morning' that had been noted by Chappell, who remarks: 'it is curious that scarcely any two copies agree beyond the second line, although the subject is always the same – a damsel's complaint for the loss of her lover'. That the song should have been found in this particular form only in the western counties is, in itself, curious. Perhaps one day a researcher looking through a collection of eighteenth-century playbooks will come across the true ancestor of this lovely little song.

---

39 Devon Heritage Centre, Baring-Gould Papers, Personal Copy MSS, 'The Complaining Maid', P2, 206 (222). This song has been included as one of the examples in Appendix B.

8: Friends and Rivals

Let us then hold in pious memory the names of Baring-Gould, Broadwood, Kidson and others, the strong men before Agamemnon without whose spade-work it is doubtful if Cecil Sharp would have had the incentive to initiate his great campaign.[1]

William Barrett − Lucy Broadwood − Marianne Mason − Frank Kidson − Cecil Sharp − George Gardiner −Ralph Vaughan Williams − Anne Gilchrist − Francis Child − Connections

When he began collecting folk songs, Baring-Gould found himself in a largely untilled field. Previous collections of folk songs had been mostly selected from printed sources and only a few, like Davis Gilbert, John Broadwood and Edward Rimbault, had obtained their songs directly from the singing of ordinary people. Each collected only a few songs in this way and there was as yet no established 'way of working' for the collection of traditional songs.

Baring-Gould contacted some of the people then alive who had already published collections of songs, seeking their advice. In later years, as more people began to take an interest in folk songs, some of these newer collectors reversed the flow, since he was now in a position to offer them the benefit of his experience. These included Cecil Sharp, who sought Baring-Gould's advice soon after he started his work in Somerset. Sharp and several others visited Lew Trenchard to talk with Baring-Gould, to look at his collection and, in some cases, to collect songs in his company. Those who visited all seem to have been charmed by the place, by their host and by his family.

William Barrett
The first of his fellow enthusiasts whom Baring-Gould contacted was William Alexander Barrett, who was the editor of the *Musical Times* as well as being the music critic of the *Morning Post*. Barrett had written down songs that he had heard as early as 1877 when on a sailing holiday a member of the yacht's crew sang a version of 'Undaunted Mary'. Though he lectured on traditional ballads in the early 1880s, he did not publish his

---

1   Ralph Vaughan Williams, 'Preface', *Journal of the English Folk Dance and Song Society*, 5 (1948), p. v.

own collection of English folk songs until 1891. He had used the columns of the *Musical Times* in April 1889 to ask for 'quaint traditional songs' to be sent to him.[2] In an article in the same journal he said that he was following the example of Baring-Gould and Andrew Lang in recording the songs 'before they disappear and are no more known'. His book, *English Folk Songs*, included songs from all over the country and from a wide range of sources.[3] Though he has not given detailed notes on the songs, he does include information about the singers and identifies the locations of some of them. His search was not confined to country areas, as he recorded some songs that he found in the streets of London.

We do not know exactly when he and Baring-Gould started to correspond with each other, but there are three letters written by Barrett among Baring-Gould's folk song manuscripts. The earliest is dated 11 November 1889 and, like the other two, is clearly a response to a request for information about some songs that Baring-Gould had found. Each of the letters is brief, fitting onto a single sheet of writing paper and very much to the point. Only the second, written in January 1890, includes any kind of small talk, as Barrett responds to Baring-Gould's having told him of his collecting plans: 'I hope you will be successful with your octogenarian Homer. My shepherd paid me a visit last night and gave me five new ditties all quaint and striking.'[4]

The two men met to discuss folk songs on at least one occasion. Baring-Gould wrote, in a note about the ballad 'The Death of Queen Jane':

> The late Dr. W. A. Barrett one day sang to me this ballad to an air that was of a very beautiful and skillful construction, taken down by him in Somersetshire, and, if my memory is correct, from a gipsy. I have had that ballad, but to a different air, from an old mason on the fringe of Dartmoor.[5]

Barrett was recognised as an authority on old songs and he provided Baring-Gould with guidance such as:

---

2   *Musical Times*, 1 April 1889, p. 234. 'Mr W. A. Barrett, 39, Angell Road, Brixton, London, asks us to make known that he will be glad to receive contributions of quaint traditional songs, words and music, which are popular in various places, for insertion in his forthcoming work on the subject.'
3   William Alexander Barrett, *English Folk Songs* (London: Novello, 1891).
4   Devon Heritage Centre, Baring-Gould Papers, Ref 5203 M, Box 36, Working Notebook 3, loose item, Letters of William Barrett to Sabine Baring-Gould, 11 November 1889 and 8 Jan 1890.
5   Sabine Baring-Gould, 'Introductory Essay on English Folk Song', *English Minstrelsie*, VII, p. xi.

'The Fly is on the Turmuts' is one of Clifton's songs written about 1869 I think. 'I'm Roger Rough the Ploughman' is a pirated version by H. Sidney (c. 1858) of "I likes a drop of good beer", written by W. T. Moncrieff about 1836 when William the Fourth was King.[6]

Baring-Gould did not always believe him. In a letter to Lucy Broadwood in December 1891 he asked:

Can you ascertain for me, most kindly, if "Roger Rough" by H. Sydney pub[lished] in 1858. Dr Barrett said it was, but I always found it necessary to verify these statements. I could not find that he was always right.[7]

Baring-Gould was right to be cautious, particularly in this instance. The song that begins 'I'm Roger Rough and a Ploughman' has a complicated history. In a note on the song in his Personal Copy manuscript Baring-Gould quotes Barrett's letter, but he adds:

Like most of Dr. Barrett's assertions it is inaccurate. 'Roger Ruff, the Ploughman' was written and composed by J. B. Geoghegan, pub. Cramer, Beale and Co., 201 Regent St, 1860.

He is perhaps being a little unfair to Barrett. There was an earlier version of the song, 'I likes a drop of good beer', which was probably that written by Moncrieff and which mentions '... Billy the King, who bated the tax on beer' but makes no mention of Roger Ruff, who was Joseph Geoghegan's invention two decades later.[8] Such are the difficulties of trying to establish the origin of songs.

Only a few weeks after the publication of *English Folk Songs*, Barrett collapsed at home and died before medical help could reach him. He was only 57 years old when he died and, had he lived longer he would certainly have been a significant figure in the study and collection of traditional

---

6   Devon Heritage Centre, Baring-Gould Papers, Ref 5203 M, Box 36, Working Notebook 3, loose item, Letter of William Barrett to Sabine Baring-Gould, 11 November 1889.

7   VWML, Lucy Broadwood Manuscripts, Letter of Sabine Baring-Gould to Lucy Broadwood, 15 December 1891, LEB/4/30.

8   Joseph B. Geoghegan wrote several songs that became popular in the music halls, some of which were based on existing songs. Many of these have later turned up in the repertoires of traditional singers and he has been a source of some confusion to folk song researchers.

song. A few copies of his book have survived but his reputation has been totally eclipsed by those who followed.

Lucy Broadwood

Lucy Etheldred Broadwood was one of the most important and influential of the folk song collectors that Baring-Gould came into contact with in the 1890s. Hers is a name that occurs frequently in this book and, in this chapter, her influence on the course of English folk song collection will become apparent.

Born in Scotland in 1858, she grew up in a musical family, whose business was making pianos. She was a competent musician who played the piano well and she was well regarded as a singer. The Broadwood family home was Lyne, near Rusper on the Surrey-Sussex border, and it was while he was living there that her uncle, the Rev. John Broadwood, had heard folk carols and songs and made a collection of them. These were printed for circulation within the family in 1847.[9] Despite its not having been available to the general public, it is considered a landmark collection. Though she was only six years old when her uncle died, there was continued family interest in folk song as Lucy's father, Henry Fowler Broadwood, also noted some songs that he had heard locally and sang them around the house. Lucy Broadwood was surrounded by folk songs throughout her life.

Alfred Hipkins was the Broadwood company's designer and technical advisor and an authority on early musical instruments. He became a mentor to Lucy Broadwood and introduced her to many aspects of music, and it was he who encouraged her in a letter written in 1884 to write down the old Sussex airs, fearing that '...in these days of rapid change, many good airs will be lost that should be preserved'.[10] So she began to take a greater interest in folk song and started to collect songs from people she came into contact with around Lyne. She also obtained a reading ticket for the British Museum, so that she could explore its collections of music books and printed ballads. With her cousin, Herbert Birch Reynardson, she decided to produce a book based on her uncle's songs, but with new

---

9 John Broadwood's collection is generally known as *Old English Songs*, since its full title is 117 words long. The musical arrangements were made by G. A. Dusart, who was under instructions from Broadwood to maintain the character of the song as originally heard. It was privately published in 1847, though it is sometimes assigned to 1843 as this, the date of collection, rather than publication, appears in the title.

10 Surrey History Centre, Lucy Broadwood Papers, Letter of Alfred Hipkins to Lucy Broadwood, 25 October 1884, SHC 2185/LEB/1, No. 3.

Fig. 8.1 – Lucy Broadwood, Memorial tablet in Rusper Church (Courtesy of Vaughan Williams Memorial Library).

accompaniments and with additional songs collected by her. This book of 25 songs was published in 1890.[11] Reynardson's is the only name on the title page, though Broadwood's contribution is noted in the introduction.

The greater part of Lucy Broadwood's papers are held with the collection of correspondence of the Broadwood family at the Surrey History Centre in Woking. These include her private correspondence and a wide range of other material. Of particular importance are her diaries, written regularly from October 1882 until the day before she died. The Vaughan Williams Memorial Library in London has the bulk of her notes and correspondence about folk song, as well as her folk song manuscripts.[12] Taken together, these provide an enormous amount of material that helps us understand the life and work of this extraordinary woman and how she influenced the fortunes of the revival of interest in folk song in Britain through three decades. In the present context it is of particular interest that her papers contain a number of letters written to her by Sabine

---

11 Herbert Birch Reynardson, *Sussex Songs: Popular Songs of Sussex* (London: Staley Lucas & Weber, 1890).
12 The sorting process was not fully effective and some important letters about folk song remain in the collection of the Surrey History Centre.

Baring-Gould. As well as communicating songs and tunes and sharing information about them, these letters tell us about some of his experiences in collecting songs. Interpretation of these letters is made more difficult by the fact that Baring-Gould did not always date his letters (and that, where he did, he sometimes got the date wrong). Her diaries refer to other letters and meetings between them.

Lucy Broadwood was aware of Baring-Gould as a writer before she knew of him as a folk song collector. Her diary entry for 2 July 1888 reports that she had read his novel, *Richard Cable*, over two days and enjoyed it. The first we know of their correspondence is an entry in her diary for 14 December 1889 where she records that she wrote to Baring-Gould. Three days later she writes 'Hd [heard] from Revd S. Baring-Gould abt [about] traditional songs of Celtic Cornwall and Devonshire – interesting letter'. The diary records a further exchange of letters over the next two weeks and then, on 25 April, she sent him a copy of *Sussex Songs*, which had just been published. She had an acknowledgement from one of his children, as Baring-Gould was on a long research trip, having left in January to spend time in Germany, Italy and Provence, and he did not return until the end of April. Twelve months passed before she wrote to him again, and from then onwards their exchanges became more regular. Though we only have Baring-Gould's side of the correspondence, the letters give us a lot of useful information about his collecting activities and demonstrate some of the issues that puzzled him.

The first of Baring-Gould's letters to Broadwood to survive was that written on 21 May 1891.[13] It has been given in full because it sets the tone for the correspondence that follows over subsequent years.

Lew Trenchard
N. Devon
May 21 / 91

Dear Miss Broadwood

I do not in the least think a German student air could have got among the singers among the people attached to "Adam & Eve", this is sung to the same melody in Yorkshire as here. Possibly Mendelsohn [sic] may have heard the air in England and jotted it down.

---

13 Surrey History Centre, Lucy Broadwood Correspondence and Papers, Letter of Sabine Baring-Gould to Lucy Broadwood, 21 May 1891, SHC 2185/ LEB/1/268.

I do hope the Folk Lore soc. will rise to my proposal. I think at present they are scared at the cost.

I have no great opinion of the words of many of our Folk Songs, I find that most of them (not all) are to be detected in Broadsides. Of these I have 5 thick vols. & I have gone through all the vols in the Brit. Mus. They are coarse, vulgar things & void of poetry, but I find that the traditional versions are almost invariably better than the Broadside versions.

I have your "Banks of the Lea" it is a Broadside of Fortey's.

> When first in this country a stranger
> Curiosity caused me to roam.
> Over Europe I resolved to be a ranger
> When I left Philadelphia my home

It consists of 6 double verses. It is unobjectionable; every stanza ends "On the green mossy banks of the Lea".

It is very kind of you to ask me to pay Lyne a visit, but I do not think I shall be able to get away. I shall however be much obliged if you will kindly sometimes help me at the Brit. Museum, & I will take the liberty of asking your aid occasionally

Yours truly
S. Baring Gould

P.S. Indeed I will take you at your word at once and ask you for chap. & verse about that tune in Mendelsohn's letters & a transcript. The matter is curious & must be gone into.

Do partake in the "Early English Musical Magazine" 100 Gt. Russell St. I like it & am sending to it full details of several of the ballads & all the variants of airs.

The second paragraph is intriguing. What is it that Baring-Gould was proposing to the Folklore Society? There are no further clues in this correspondence, or anywhere else in Baring-Gould's papers. Neither is there any mention of a proposal from Baring-Gould in the Minute Books of the Folklore Society.[14] As noted earlier, the Folklore Society had finally published part of Baring-Gould's work on 'Story Radicals' in the previous

14 I am grateful to Dr Caroline Oates for having arranged access to the Folklore Society's Minute Books and other papers that might have held the answer.

year as an appendix to its *Handbook of Folklore*. Did he have further work planned or was this a new proposal to do with folk song?

The short-lived journal *Early English Musical Magazine* ceased publication only a few weeks after Baring-Gould, who contributed a few articles to it, recommended that Broadwood should take out a subscription.

In further correspondence Baring-Gould gave Broadwood progress reports on his work throughout 1891 and 1892, sending a number of songs and tunes as well as information about the singers. For much of this period Broadwood was occupied with compiling a new song collection, *English County Songs*, in collaboration with her friend, J. A. (Alec) Fuller Maitland, a musicologist and journalist whose cousin, Evelyn, was married to Broadwood's brother, James. The expectation was that she would act as Fuller Maitland's assistant in gathering and arranging the songs, but it quickly became evident that her contribution more than matched his and that she deserved the status of co-author.

English County Songs, published on 1 July 1893, was another important contribution to the record of English traditional songs. Like other editors since, Broadwood found it necessary to make compromises to produce a book that included songs from every county and some nimble footwork was necessary.[15] Baring-Gould supplied two songs to represent Devonshire, 'The Green Bushes' and 'The Loyal Lover', each to a different tune than that with which it had appeared in his *Songs of the West*. Cornwall was represented by just one song, 'Adam and Eve', to a tune supposedly derived from the chime of Stratton church clock.[16] This is the tune that Baring-Gould commented on in his letter of 21 May 1891 (above).

Lucy Broadwood's father, Henry Fowler Broadwood, died a week after the publication of *English County Songs*. Baring-Gould wrote a note of condolence.[17] His letter included a list of songs that he had heard sung by Sam Fone, and of the songs intended for the first part of *A Garland of Country Song*. He noted that she had published some of the songs in *English*

---

15 The notion that songs 'belong' to particular counties, regions or, indeed, nations is undermined by the ease with which songs and people travel. To take just two examples from Broadwood's book, 'Robbie Tamson's Smiddie' was certainly collected in Northumberland, but most would regard it as a Scottish song. 'My bonnie, bonnie boy' is categorised as a Hampshire song, though collected in Oxfordshire, on the grounds that the singer, Mrs Patience Vaisey, had been born in Hampshire.

16 The chime of the present-day clock, installed in 1843, bears no resemblance to this tune.

17 VWML, Lucy Broadwood Manuscripts, Letter of Sabine Baring-Gould to Lucy Broadwood, Undated but mid-end July 1893, LEB/4/26.

County Songs. Although it was too late to take these out he also listed some of the songs intended for the second part and said that he might replace those that overlapped.[18]

In this letter he invited her to visit him at Lew Trenchard to hear one of the series of costume concerts that was being put on around the country, based on songs from his collection. The arrangements were concluded over the next few weeks and she arrived at Lew Trenchard on 4 September. Her diary recorded that she spent time with Baring-Gould, looking at his manuscript collection and having long talks with him before going with him on the evening of 5 September to the concert in Launceston, where 'two indifferent professional ladies sang, in costumes (poor)'.

After a day spent walking and boating on the lake near the house with Baring-Gould's daughters and their friends, she went out with him on 7 September 1893 to Dunterton, where they had tea with the vicar's wife, Alice Cann, before going to see Jane Jeffrey in a nearby cottage. Broadwood wrote a description of the visit:

> Mr Baring-Gould and I once drove twenty-four miles in Cornwall to hear an old, and reputedly valuable, songstress. When we arrived she put on all the airs of a capricious operatic favourite, and declared that she was not in voice enough to sing. It was only after singing to her myself, in elaborately croaking tones, that she deigned charily to exhibit her own.[19]

Baring-Gould had heard that Jane Jeffrey was a singer late in the previous year, but she had then had a stroke and had been unable to sing. By September she was able to give Baring-Gould and Broadwood a version of 'Cold Blows the Wind', for which Lucy Broadwood noted the tune, while Baring-Gould recorded the words. Broadwood later included this in her *English Traditional Songs and Carols*. Coincidentally, Alice Cann was the daughter of Anne Gibbons who, as reported in Chapter 4, had sent Baring-Gould her own version of 'Cold Blows the Wind' five years earlier.

Though her diary does not record it, there are two tunes on slips pasted into Baring-Gould's Personal Copy manuscript ('Green Gravel' and 'Nothing Else to Do') in Lucy Broadwood's hand and dated 7 September. These were taken down from Elizabeth and Louisa, the

---

18 *A Garland of Country Song* was in the event issued as one book of fifty songs rather than in two parts.

19 Lucy Broadwood, 'On the Collecting of English Folk Song', p. 99. Dunterton is, in fact, in Devon and it is not likely that their route took them into Cornwall.

daughters of Richard and Margaret Hamley, the tenants of Down House Farm, on the hill above Lew House. In a letter to the American ballad scholar Francis Child, written in June 1892, Baring-Gould wrote, 'Last Xmas at our choir supper and dance two strapping farmer's daughters stood up and sang right through "The Squire of Tamworth", to my great satisfaction'.[20] He had noted two songs from them in July of that year, so it is likely that he had suggested to Lucy Broadwood that there might be more to be heard.

Broadwood then left to spend ten days at Bude with friends before returning to spend two more nights at Lew Trenchard. A letter written by her at that time reported:

> I have just come from the Baring-Goulds where I had delightful talks and walks with the quaint and entertaining author, & his wife and 14 children [...] On the way back the Goulds bid me stay with them again, he & I capture old songs from old singers in the cottages and have great fun over it.[21]

On 20 September she travelled by coach to Holsworthy and then to Ashbury by train, where Baring-Gould collected her in his dog-cart. On their way back to Lew House, she records that he showed her the place where Mary Ann Voaden, the white witch whom we met in Chapter 3, lived in her decaying cottage.

The following morning Baring-Gould drove her over to see Mary Fletcher, a farmer's widow at Carley, near Lifton. They heard three songs from her: a version of 'The Outlandish Knight', which she had heard sung by an old haymaker at Egloskerry in Cornwall, 'Damon and Phyllis', an eighteenth-century art song, and 'Oh, What's the Matter Now', both of the latter two learned from her mother in about 1830. Mary Fletcher was, in fact, the sister of Margaret Hamley, whom Broadwood had met a few days earlier. Broadwood's notation of all of the tunes she had heard during her visit to Lew Trenchard can be found in her manuscripts, as well as Baring-Gould's notation of the words of some of the songs, which he sent on later. Lucy Broadwood left for home the following day.

---

20 Cambridge (MA), Houghton Library, Harvard University, Baring-Gould Manuscript, Ballads and Songs collected by the Rev. S. Baring-Gould, Chiefly in Devonshire, and sent by him to Professor F. J. Child, MS Eng 863. Postscript to letter of Sabine Baring-Gould to Francis Child, 5 June 1892.
21 Surrey History Centre, Broadwood Correspondence and Papers, *Book of letters maintained by Lord Farrer dated 1893*, Letter of Lucy Broadwood to Mr Farrer, 13 September 1893, SHC 2572/1/21.

Their correspondence continued with exchanges of information about songs and family events and there were some meetings in London when Baring-Gould was in town. The last surviving dated letter from Baring-Gould to Broadwood is that of 21 January 1900 when he said that he was 'most delighted to hear from you again' and answered a question about an apple song. He also told her of the deaths of James Parsons and Daniel Radford.

There was another occasion when Broadwood asked to visit Baring-Gould at short notice but he was unable to accommodate her. There is, in my own collection, an undated letter in which Baring-Gould responds to her request:

> I am so vexed – next week we could and would gladly have received you, but this week we have an overflow, 3 ladies & a gentleman, and the latter put out in a friend's house, and one of the ladies in the town.[22]

His regret is genuine, as there was an opportunity to take her out collecting songs in Ashbury, a village ten miles from Lew Trenchard.

> What makes it doubly provoking is that I have heard from Mrs Woollcombe of Ashbury of an old woman there who remembered the original Uncle Tom Cobleigh and can sing one of his old songs.

Baring-Gould never did make this visit and so we do not know what Tom Cobleigh's old song was.

Broadwood's diary records that she eventually made a second visit to Lew Trenchard in September 1912 and that she 'spent the afternoon talking and walking with Mr Baring-Gould and looking at his folk-song books'. As reported in the last chapter, Priscilla Wyatt Edgell was also staying at Lew House that day. After spending the following morning talking and reading she took the train back to Plymouth, where she had been staying.

Lucy Broadwood became one of the leading figures in the formation and early development of the Folk Song Society after its foundation in 1898, a body in which Baring-Gould never played a significant role. Correspondence between the two dropped off. Baring-Gould received very few mentions in the *Journal of the Folk Song Society* during Broadwood's time as its editor. He was no longer active in folk song collecting, and so they had little left to talk about. I do not believe either party would have

---

22 Letter of Sabine Baring-Gould to Lucy Broadwood, undated. (Author's collection).

regarded the other as a friend, though their interactions were cordial enough. Nevertheless, it is surprising that Baring-Gould's death is not recorded in her diary, though that of Cecil Sharp a few months later received the equivalent of an illuminated entry, despite her low opinion of him. She resigned as editor of the *Journal of the Folk Song Society* in 1924 but in her final issue she included obituary notices for Sharp and for Sir Charles Stanford who both died in that year, but did not record Baring-Gould's passing.[23] She was a complex woman, and totally committed to the causes she believed in. In the later years of his life, Baring-Gould could offer little, other than his reputation, to help her.

Marianne Mason

Marianne Harriet Mason was born in London in 1845, but spent much of her childhood at the home of her maternal grandfather, Colonel Joseph Mitford, who came from the aristocratic Northumbrian family of that name, and lived at Laugharne in Carmarthenshire. It was while living there that she heard her nurses sing some of the songs that she would later include in her book. She wrote:

> Our nurses had good voices and sang well naturally. Our donkey-boy sang with them when they walked beside the donkey which carried two of my brothers in a Spanish saddle, while I, being the eldest, sat on a pad strapped behind. Thus I learned Welsh folk songs, such as 'The Cutty Wren', 'Sally, and the Sailor', 'The Seeds of Love' and others, some of which I published in 'Nursery Rhymes and Country Songs' in 1877.[24]

Music was a great delight to her and she was accounted a good singer, though it was 'not done' for a young woman of her class to sing professionally, as she would have liked. Nevertheless, opportunities to sing in drawing room concerts and local events were grasped eagerly. Even this became impossible when, at the age of 32, she permanently damaged her voice by singing too much while she had an infection. In 1925 she wrote: 'It was, and still is, like losing half of oneself. To feel the song inside one, and to fail in bringing it out is like trying to run with a broken leg.' It was after losing her voice that she diverted her energy into compiling her collection of songs.

---

23 Broadwood's position on this could be seen as justified by the fact that Baring-Gould was no longer a member of the Society.

24 Nottingham, Nottinghamshire Archives, M. H. Mason, *A Pioneer Life*, Unpublished autobiography, typescript with additions and corrections by hand, DD716/51.

Fig. 8.2 – Marianne Mason (Photo courtesy of Nottinghamshire Archives, DD/716/58/3).

In her typescript autobiography, *A Pioneer Life*, Mason wrote: 'It was in 1887 that I first published my collection of *Nursery Rhymes and Country Songs*. I called it this because "Folksongs" did not seem to me to be proper English.' Her memory let her down seriously here, since the book was published a decade earlier, in 1877. In the brief preface to the first edition Mason explains that her intention was to rescue the songs from oblivion and that, although some well-known favourites were included, they had not been taken from other collections. All had been learned 'from persons to whom they had been handed down by oral tradition', among whom she included family members. The arrangements were all her own work and they were, she says, 'very simply arranged, the words being given, as far as possible as they were sung'.

The emphasis on nursery rhymes in the title ensured that most reviewers would place the book firmly in the genre of children's literature. This may not have been what Mason had originally hoped for since, of the 58 songs in the book, 24 can be considered as 'Country Songs' for grown-ups rather than children. Indeed, some of the songs might have been considered unsuitable for children, or even others of a certain temperament. Mason noted in *A Pioneer Life*: 'Some people told me that some of my ancient ditties were vulgar, and one Clergyman was much shocked at one which tells how the devil went off with the little tailor.'

The family moved to a new house, Morton, near Retford in Nottinghamshire, where Mason's main occupation became the welfare of needy children, particularly those 'boarded out' from the workhouse and placed in foster homes. Her work as the voluntary supervisor of the Poor Law Boarding-out Committees in Nottinghamshire came to the notice of the Local Government Board, and she was appointed Inspector of Boarded-out Children for England and Wales. This was the first appointment of a woman to a senior post in the civil service. She continued in this role for 25 years, travelling all over England to visit 300 or 400 children each year, often in isolated country locations or in the poorer parts of towns. She kept notes on each of the children she visited and stayed in contact with many of them into adulthood, often helping them to find work and housing in later life. She also found time to write about alpine plants, old furniture, the paranormal and the charming of warts.

When she retired in 1910 she went to stay with her brother, Edward, who had moved to South Africa. For two years she travelled throughout southern Africa, collecting and painting plants. She discovered three new varieties that now bear her name, including *crocosmia masoniorum*, the popular garden plant known as Montbretia. After the First World War she built a house near Cape Town which she named 'Morton' after the family home in Nottinghamshire and it was there that she died in 1932, aged 87.

An article about Mason published in *The Queen* in March 1890 credited her with 'a valuable service by arranging and adapting the old melodies for Mr Baring-Gould's *Songs of the West*'. This statement is not accurate, as she had no hand in the arrangements in Baring-Gould's book. It is probable that this mistake caused the two song collectors to introduce themselves to each other, and in 1892 Mason visited Baring-Gould at Lew Trenchard. She wrote in her memoir:

> I spent some delightful days with him and his family at Lew Trenchard when official work brought me near. Mr. Baring-Gould's singing of his 'Songs of the West', especially of 'The Three Drunken Maidens', was worth hearing.

She kept in touch with him and supplied him with thirteen songs that he included in his Personal Copy manuscript, as well as two tunes that she had heard as a child in Laugharne – 'The Saucy Sailor' and 'The Seeds of Love' – which are not in *Nursery Rhymes and Country Songs* and must have been given to Baring-Gould from a manuscript record.

She had known the Broadwood family for some years though she was at first closer to Lucy's sister, Bertha, who was nearer to her in age and with whom she shared interests in aspects of social work. It was Bertha who gave her a copy of John Broadwood's book and suggested that she should include some of her uncle's songs in her own publication. This she did, including six of the Sussex songs, with arrangements she composed herself. Lucy Broadwood recorded later visits by her to Lyne and she also returned the compliment by staying with the Masons at their home near Retford. During this visit Broadwood acquired some of the songs from Mason's book for use in *English County Songs*, for which she composed her own arrangements. In later years Marianne Mason's London home was in Vincent Square, a few minutes from Lucy Broadwood's apartment at Carlisle Mansions. Broadwood's diary records a number of occasions on which they visited each other after Mason returned from South Africa in 1912.

Mason published a new edition of *Nursery Rhymes and Country Songs* in 1908. In the preface she wrote: 'This may be said to have been the earliest serious attempt to collect what are now called "folk songs", with the old nursery rhymes and traditional tunes, and thus attempt to save them before they were entirely forgotten.' This may not have been the first oral collection of folk songs to be published but Mason's collection of traditional songs was certainly the first to be made by a woman in England – or, as far as I have been able to discover, anywhere in the world.

If Marianne Mason is now remembered at all, it is for her achievements as a botanist and as a social worker. Folk song was just one of a portfolio of interests and activities, and is covered in her entry in the *Oxford Dictionary of National Biography* in just twelve words. Though she played a relatively minor role in the Victorian folk song revival her achievements deserve to be better remembered.[25]

Frank Kidson

Frank Kidson was born in Leeds, the youngest of nine children. He described himself as having had only a limited education, which he supplemented with extensive reading. For a while he worked with his brother, Joseph, in his antiques business and acquired a good knowledge of paintings and ceramics. After a brief spell when he tried to establish himself as a painter he started to write on antiquarian topics. He later described himself as 'a journalist and a bit of an author'. He took a

---

25 For an extended study of Marianne Mason and her collection, see Martin Graebe, 'Old Songs and Sugar Mice: The Story of the Remarkable Miss Mason', *Folk Music Journal*, 10 (2014), pp. 449–77.

particular interest in the history of printed music and wrote a number of articles for various newspapers and magazines. To support his studies he acquired a collection of more than 9,000 books, which meant that he rarely had to go to London to consult libraries there.

Fig. 8.3 – Frank Kidson from *English Minstrelsie.*

His mother sang traditional songs and he had as a boy read the novels of Captain Marryat, in which fragments of traditional songs were introduced. His first publications on traditional song were in 1886, when he wrote a series of 32 articles on old songs for the *Leeds Mercury Supplement.* In 1890 he published, at his own expense, *Old English Country Dances, Gathered from Scarce Printed Collections and from Manuscripts. With Illustrative Notes and a Bibliography of English Country Dance Music.* This collection of tunes has a very full set of notes on the background to the tunes – in the case of 'Well May the Keel Row' running over four pages. An advertisement at the front of the book announced that Kidson was working on *A Collection of Ballad Tunes* 'Noted down from oral tradition, chiefly gathered in Yorkshire and the South of Scotland, and which, it is believed, will be now for the first time printed. Taken with their appropriate words from Broadsides and from Traditional Sources.' Potential subscribers were invited to apply to Kidson for an order form. This became *Traditional Tunes*, published in 1891, and is his most important book on folk song. Sabine Baring-Gould was a subscriber and his copy, signed by Kidson, was number 44 of a limited edition of 200 copies.

This collection, unlike most others published at the time, gave the tunes without accompaniments and with extensive notes on the origin of the songs. For some songs he reveals his source, but this information is often limited. It is perhaps this lack of information, together with the timing of the publication, that gave rise to some misunderstanding by Baring-Gould of Kidson's work. He shared these views with Lucy Broadwood and she prompted Kidson, in turn, to tell her what he thought of Baring-Gould's work. These exchanges can be followed in Broadwood's correspondence.

Lucy Broadwood's diary entry for 30 June 1891 records that her mentor, Alfred Hipkins, sent her a copy of *Traditional Tunes*, which she noted as being 'very interesting'.[26] It was not until January of the following year, though, that she wrote to Kidson. She received a reply two days later, with what she described as a 'book of old songs of his'. This was a copy of Kidson's *Old English Country Dances* (described above) which was inscribed 'Miss Lucy E. Broadwood with Frank Kidson's compliments, Jan 1892'. Another letter was sent on the following day, and they became regular correspondents. Some letters from Kidson to Broadwood are preserved in the Vaughan Williams Memorial Library and in the Surrey History Centre, but none of her letters to him have as yet been discovered.

Most of the letters that survive deal with questions about song and advice from Kidson on folk song research. A number of them, however, include thoughts on Baring-Gould and his collection. Broadwood had made a brief visit to Kidson at his home on 10 April 1893 and they talked about Baring-Gould and his collection since, in a letter dated 14 May 1893, Kidson wrote:

> You asked me my full opinion of Mr. Baring Gould's Songs of the West, but we had so little time that I think I failed to give you it. This is it:
>
> He is among a perfect treasury of old traditional song but I'm afraid his ear is not quick enough or his memory too defective to retain the <u>subtle</u> points in an air (<u>in note & in time</u>) that makes the air so beautiful & so removed from the common place, for unless great attention is paid to this, it is terribly easy to snip the corners off of an air. The airs that he thus gets imperfectly he sends to Mr. Shepherd who possibly seeing technical defects in the tune thus noted down again alters or <u>corrects</u>.

---

26 This copy is number 75 of the limited edition and is among Broadwood's papers in the Surrey History Centre.

Then, as they confess, they do not give different versions of the air as noted down but give what they imagine to be the correct form of it compiled from all the ones they have got.

This accounts for the character of the <u>airs</u> in <u>Songs of the West</u>.

Regarding the words, upon the plea of doggerel or coarseness they suppress even the <u>title</u> or first-few lines of a song & in place of it write songs totally out of keeping with the spirit of the original (Compare Robert Burns' handling of the old Scottish songs he collected for Johnson's Museum)…

To me I cannot in the least believe that a single song is there placed as it was sung to Baring Gould. The general spirit of the book being opposed to unadulterated Country Song, witness a couple of songs & airs composed by Shepherd & Gould being inserted in the body of the collection without comment until Part IV was published. Part IV was published some months after Baring Gould had for a [sic] copy of my Traditional Tunes. In it are several airs that I published but he seems to have been careful to keep all mention of my book out of his notes which was not the case with me. I have mentioned Songs of the West on every occasion where a ballad he published occurred in my book.[27]

Clearly, he was not a fan of Baring-Gould's book, and had serious reservations about his methods, and those of his collaborators. He continued:

From what you hinted he does not think much of my book because he has an impression that I have not gone among <u>the people</u> to collect my tunes. He is in this mistaken I have not sat at home & received tunes already noted down by post. People whose names I prefix with the title 'Mr' he would have spoken of as 'Old John So & So (very illiterate)'.

Lucy Broadwood had also asked Baring-Gould what he thought of Kidson's collection. He responded in a couple of letters that are unfortunately undated, though it can be assumed that they were connected with her having asked Kidson similar questions.

---

27 VWML, Lucy Broadwood Manuscripts, Letter of Frank Kidson to Lucy Broadwood, 14 May 1893, LEB/4/100.

I do not think much of Kidson's collection. If you examine it you will see he has taken down very few himself from the pot house singers, and Barrett told me he mistrusted his version, as taken by persons who did not understand the character of the music they noted for him.[28]

And

Mr. Kidson doesn't seem to have taken down the airs <u>himself</u> but to have had them sent him.[29]

Lucy Broadwood sent Kidson an account of her September 1893 visit to Lew Trenchard, which Kidson responded to on 14 October. Though there is no record in Baring-Gould's manuscripts, it seems from this letter that the two men had met in the intervening period since Kidson wrote:

I was glad to hear that you had had such a pleasant time at Mr Baring-Gould's. I can quite understand how delightful it must have been. He is certainly a singularly talented man. His novels, I think hold a very high place in the literature of today. The little I saw of him personally, gave me a very pleasant impression of his kindness. It is his treatment of the Songs of the West that has rather vexed me.[30]

There the matter rested for some time and there was certainly some correspondence between Baring-Gould and Kidson, though we do not have any letters from either side. Then, in September 1896, Broadwood sent him a cutting from the Anglican newspaper, *The Guardian*, that sparked the comment:

It is unfortunate that Mr. B Gould has got such reckless musical collaborators who don't seem to care two pins about the spirit of the tunes they harmonise & make no bones at any alteration they think fit. Whether Mr. Gould has any control over their vagaries or not I don't know.[31]

---

28 VWML, Lucy Broadwood Manuscripts, Letter of Sabine Baring-Gould to Lucy Broadwood, undated, LEB/4/2.
29 VWML, Lucy Broadwood Manuscripts, Letter of Sabine Baring-Gould to Lucy Broadwood, undated, LEB/4/33.
30 VWML, Lucy Broadwood Manuscripts, Letter of Frank Kidson to Lucy Broadwood, 14 October 1893, LEB/4/151.
31 VWML, Lucy Broadwood Manuscripts, Letter of Frank Kidson to Lucy Broadwood, 26 September 1896, LEB/4/86.

This touches on one of the fundamental differences of opinion between them. Baring-Gould believed that the songs would never be taken up by the public of the time if accompaniments were not provided. He had written to Lucy Broadwood in 1894 saying:

> I do not think it well to publish the airs alone. They then sink into a mere archaeological curiosity – no spell of renewed life is given them. This was the case with the Northumbrian Minstrelsie – now Drs. Reay & Stokoe have republished with accompaniments. Kidson's will remain death struck until some musician takes them in hand.[32]

Kidson was ambivalent on the question. In his letter of 14 October 1893, already referred to, he sympathised with Broadwood over a poor review of *English County Songs* and wrote of her accompaniments approvingly: 'Your harmonies so far as my poor knowledge goes are not only scholarly but light and in sympathy; the reverse of the Bussell and Sheppard school.' He then went on to remark that he did not like the idea of people who had no sympathy with the songs performing them for a popular audience.

> My personal feeling is the utmost dread of popularity for the old traditional & country song. To me they are very sacred, & to hear them sung by people who have not the slightest sympathy with them would be very galling. Then would come the "<u>arrangement</u>' of them by popular music caterers, then "farewell to all their freshness".

A few years later the Folk Song Society, in which both Kidson and Broadwood were leading figures, would publish songs in its journal without accompaniments for its more limited but sympathetic readership. Kidson's later folk song collections were published with accompaniments by Alfred Moffat.

In a letter dated 17 October 1896 Kidson told Broadwood:

> I believe Mr Baring-Gould is putting my portrait in his English Minstrelsey!! I tell him he must certainly include yours & his own among folk tune collectors. In the last volume he has issued there is a particularly good & lengthy sketch of the Vauxhall & other gardens & the singers etc.

---

32 VWML, Lucy Broadwood Manuscripts, Letter of Sabine Baring-Gould to Lucy Broadwood, 4 February 1894, LEB/4/27.

Kidson's portrait did, indeed, appear in volume 7 of *English Minstrelsie*, in the 'Introductory Essay On English Folk-Music' in that volume. In this essay Baring-Gould refers to '…My friend, Mr. Frank Kidson, who collects Yorkshire folk-airs' and adds, 'I doubt if there be any man in England better acquainted with old English songs than Mr. Kidson, and I gratefully tender him my thanks for much advice and help generously rendered me.'

It is fascinating to be able to see the relationship between the two men as reflected in the correspondence with Lucy Broadwood and to look at the part she played. We do not have the words she wrote, but we can sense that she was testing the two men, perhaps even encouraging some tension between them. But the statements they made were what they felt at the time, and it is with some relief that we discover that as they got to know each other better their opinions of each other improved.

Though the first meeting between Kidson and Baring-Gould was fleeting and left only the lightest of impressions, Baring-Gould later took the opportunity to stay with Kidson in Leeds. We can infer that the two men grew to understand each other better, but Kidson's niece, Ethel, became a great admirer. She wrote:

> A great gentleman, Baring Gould, when in Yorkshire he came to visit Uncle and I and stayed a couple of nights with us. I think he had the most striking face I have ever seen. I was very young to play hostess to such a distinguished visitor. But he complemented me on my cooking and said it was a novelty to get dinner hot as at home by the time he had carved for his fourteen children it was usually cold. He must have thought me very young for when he got home he sent me a book of Fairy Tales![33]

Kidson wrote an article for the *Yorkshire Weekly Post* when he stayed with Baring-Gould at Lew House in 1911.[34] He described having dinner with the family and swapping stories about Yorkshire with Grace Baring-Gould.

> For one who has so long recognised the sterling qualities that lie in the vast library which the pen of Mr Baring-Gould has contributed to English literature during the past fifty years, there are few more gratifying joys than to sit at his hospitable board and

---

33 Ethel Kidson, *Life of Frank Kidson* (Leeds Central Library, c. 1926), unpublished memoir. The date of Baring-Gould's visit is not known.
34 Frank Kidson, 'The Rev. S. Baring-Gould at Home', *Yorkshire Weekly Post*, 16 September 1911.

to watch the twinkling humour that lights up his face, and that of Mrs Baring-Gould in response to the badinage that passes round the table.

He enjoyed 'cosy chats' with Baring-Gould in the evening and during the day they took a long walk out on Dartmoor to look at the archaeological discoveries that Baring-Gould had made.

This article is rich in its depiction of Kidson's visit and his enjoyment of the time spent in Baring-Gould's company. If there were any lingering doubts in Kidson's mind about Baring-Gould's commitment to the cause of folk song they must have been set at rest by this visit, as he wrote:

How his heart was warmed to the old Devonshire songs and their singers only those who have heard him talk on the subject can tell. If any man had sympathy with the old country labourer whose songs and traditions he has so lovingly preserved, surely Baring-Gould is the one.

Kidson and Baring-Gould had very different upbringings and had different opinions about the way in which folk song should be collected and published. They had perhaps more in common in respect of their enthusiasm for antiquarian study and, particularly, the search for the backstory of the songs that they had discovered. They worked in the places where they had grown up and were happy to maintain a degree of isolation while remaining connected to the other key workers in their fields of interest. Ultimately this isolation would lead to both men being undervalued as the revival of interest in folk song grew in the twentieth century.

Cecil Sharp

Cecil James Sharp's energetic pursuit of folk song and dance and his advocacy of it has led to his becoming regarded as the key figure in the folk music revival in the first quarter of the twentieth century. When he started to collect folk songs he talked to other collectors, including Baring-Gould, and in later years the two men worked on some projects together. There are letters, mostly written by Baring-Gould, in the Vaughan Williams Memorial Library and Plymouth Library that give us, when taken with manuscript material, a good picture of their working relationship.

Cecil Sharp was born in 1859, the eldest son of a London slate merchant who had prospered as London boomed in the late nineteenth century. He was a good scholar and won a place at Clare College,

Fig 8.4 – '… such an excellent likeness of yourself', Cecil Sharp from 100 English Folk Songs (1916) (Courtesy of Vaughan Williams Memorial Library).

Cambridge (Baring-Gould's *alma mater*), to study mathematics. In fact, much of his time at university was spent in musical activities, so it is not really surprising that he achieved only a pass degree. He left for Australia in 1882 shortly after coming down from Cambridge and took various jobs while furthering his musical interests and came eventually to rely solely on music for his living. He returned to England in 1889 and took on two part-time jobs as music master at Ludgrove School and as principal of the Hampstead Conservatoire.

While he was teaching at Ludgrove, Sharp started to take an interest in folk song, as part of his quest for material for his pupils. A result of this was *A Book of British Song for Home and School*, published in May 1902, in which he used twelve songs from Baring-Gould's published collections, with appropriate acknowledgement.[35] We can therefore be reasonably certain

35 Cecil J. Sharp, *A Book of British Song for Home and School* (London: John Murray, 1902).

that the first contact between them would have been in connection with this book, though no correspondence relating to it has been discovered to date. An illuminating remark, made in the note to the song 'Jordan' (No. 33), is that 'the song required rewriting, and this has been very cleverly done by the Rev. S. Baring-Gould'. At the time, Sharp's book came in for some criticism regarding the suitability of the material because it included songs about drinking and the pursuit of loose women. The *School Music Review* took the example of No. 19, 'Outward Bound', which had been taken from *Songs of the West* saying:

> Are these the words and ideas we wish our children to take to heart? What 'character' do they instil? Quite apart from their frank vulgarity, in which quality they compete successfully with the much-abused, beery music-hall song, are they so valuable as poetry. ... The song is in its proper place in the Rev. Baring-Gould's collection, but is wholly out of place amongst songs for 'schools and homes'.[36]

It was not until 22 August 1903 that Sharp heard his first 'live' folk singer, John England, who sang 'The Seeds of Love' in the garden of his friend Charles Marson at Hambridge in Somerset. By the end of his stay with Marson, Sharp had noted forty songs from a dozen singers. This was the start of his work as a folk song collector which was to occupy his holidays from teaching for several more years and, ultimately, to net him thousands of songs in England and the United States of America.

He visited Somerset and North Devon again in December 1903 and January 1904. He had hoped to visit Baring-Gould but the meeting did not take place, as the letter received by Sharp and dated 26 January 1904 makes clear. Baring-Gould wrote:

> It was most unfortunate that I could not see you when in Devon. But as it chanced, I was called away by telegram to an uncle who was found dead in his bed, and had to be away to see to the funeral and arrange his affairs and am only just home. If you had arranged to come here, I would have had to wire to you that I was called away. So our cook's illness after all saved this.[37]

---

36 'Folk Songs for Schools', *The School Music Review*, March 1904, pp. 185–86.
37 VWML, Cecil Sharp Manuscripts, Letter of Sabine Baring-Gould to Cecil Sharp, 26 January 1904.

It is reasonable to assume that Sharp had contacted Baring-Gould at short notice and planned to talk to him about song collecting. In the letter Baring-Gould also says:

> Thank you so much for the notice of your lecture and the leader in Morning Post. I am so grateful that at last the public is being roused to the fact that we have a body of fine traditional music. It is full late now to collect, all my old men are dead but one now.

The lecture in question is the one Sharp gave at the Hampstead Conservatoire on 26 November 1903 and the *Morning Post* leader was published the following day. Sharp has marked this passage, and quoted it in the letter that he wrote to the *Morning Post* on 2 February 1904, where he took the Folk Song Society to task for its lack of activity in recent years. It was this letter that galvanised Lucy Broadwood and other members into taking action to revitalise the society. Sharp appears to have persuaded some of his friends and colleagues to join the society at this time to support his case for increasing the emphasis on collecting and the use of folk songs in education. Baring-Gould was elected to membership on 13 October 1904, but was never active and did not contribute directly to its journal, though there are some references to him. He remained a member of the society until 1910.

In an interview with the *Morning Post*, which had been published on 18 January 1904, Sharp was asked if he had exhausted the store of songs to be found in North Devon. He replied:

> 'Exhausted! Why, I have scarcely tapped them. That part of Devonshire is a perfect mine of folk-song, and yet you must remember that it is in Devonshire that Mr Baring-Gould has done such splendid work, though he has not, I believe, attempted to work the northern part of the county. Here,' said Mr Sharp, producing three stout folio volumes, 'are Mr Baring-Gould's manuscripts which, with rare generosity, he has placed at my disposal. It shows what can be done by one man and it also shows what a slight impression one man can make on the mass of our traditional songs which every day are slipping into oblivion.'[38]

It was indeed a generous gesture on Baring-Gould's part to lend Sharp what must have been, from the description, the three volumes of his

---

38 'English Folk Songs, Song-Hunting in the West, Mr. Cecil Sharp Interviewed', *Morning Post*, 18 January 1904.

Personal Copy manuscript for several weeks. (Baring-Gould refers to the return of these volumes in a letter dated 7 July 1904). Faint pencilled notes against some of the songs confirm that Sharp made an extensive study of the manuscript. We are left with a small mystery. How did Sharp obtain the manuscript volumes? The implication of the letter of 26 January 1904 quoted above is that the two men had not met at that stage. The manuscripts were presumably sent to Sharp by post for him to study. One would have liked to see the covering letter for that loan.

Methuen, the publishers of *Songs of the West*, were keen that Baring-Gould should produce a new edition, but the death of Henry Fleetwood Sheppard in 1901 meant that a new musical editor was required. Sharp was suggested for this role and we know from a letter written to Baring-Gould by George Webster, the general manager of Methuen, that he had agreed to do this by April 1904.[39] Though, with hindsight, he was an ideal candidate, his reputation in folk music circles had not yet risen to the heights that it would in later years.

Sharp visited Baring-Gould's home at Lew Trenchard a number of times so that they could work together on the book, and there may have been other meetings when Baring-Gould was in London. While Sharp was in Lew Trenchard, Baring-Gould introduced him to some survivors among the singers from whom he had collected songs a decade earlier. Most notably, Sharp spent time with John Woodridge, whose songs he recorded in his manuscript under Woodridge's nickname of 'Ginger Jack'. He also met John and Elizabeth Dingle, who lived at Eastcott in Coryton parish, a short walk over the hill to the south of Baring-Gould's home. Baring-Gould said, in a letter to Sharp:

> There is an old man named Dingle near here. I will get him to sing to you. But we have never used his tunes, either because we had them already or because he was not sure. However I have no doubt that he has others he has not sung to us and he may sing them to you.[40]

Sharp photographed the old couple standing outside their house.

---

39 Devon Heritage Centre, Baring-Gould Papers, 5203 M, Box 33, Letter of George Webster (Methuen & Co.) to Sabine Baring-Gould, 21 April 1904.
40 VWML, Cecil Sharp Manuscripts, Letter of Sabine Baring-Gould to Cecil Sharp, 18 July 1904.

Fig. 8.5 – John and Elizabeth Dingle, Photo by Cecil Sharp (Courtesy of Vaughan Williams Memorial Library)

It is clear that, like Lucy Broadwood and Frank Kidson, Cecil Sharp enjoyed his visits to Lew Trenchard. He wrote to Charles Marson's wife, Chloe, with good wishes for the New Year of 1905 saying:

> I am always a little sad when I leave Hambridge and I was glad when I arrived here [i.e. Lew Trenchard] at 5 o'clock and found myself once more amongst friends! It has been very jolly here and we have got through a good deal of work in connection with the book. [...] I missed your choir supper on Thursday but ran into the same function here on the same night. It was very much like yours except that the supper is managed in relays and that they keep it up till about 1.30 a.m.![41]

Sharp and Baring-Gould appeared together in public on at least three occasions. The first was the annual meeting of the Devonshire Association at Princetown in 1905, where on the evening of 19 July Sharp delivered a talk on 'The Musical Value of Devonshire Folk Airs'.[42] The chairman

---

41 Taunton, Somerset Heritage Centre, Letter of Cecil Sharp to Chloe Marson, 1 January 1905, A/DFS/1/20/294.
42 Maxwell Adams and J. Brooking-Rowe, 'Proceedings at the Forty-fourth Annual Meeting of the Association, Held at Princetown, 18 July to 21 July, 1905', *Report and Transactions of the Devonshire Association for the Advancement of Science, Literature and Art*, 37 (1905), pp.23–27.

for the meeting and president-elect of the association for the coming year was Basil H. Thomson, the governor of Dartmoor Prison, and the lecture took place in the prison's recreation room. Baring-Gould made most of the arrangements for the event, including the booking of the singers who would provide the musical illustrations for Sharp's talk. The evening opened with a performance of 'A Song of the Moor'. The tune had been collected from William Nankivell at Merrivale, four miles from Princetown. Nankivell's song was 'A Lying Tale' but it had been given a new set of words by Baring-Gould. The report in the *Western Mercury* said that Baring-Gould not only prefaced each item with 'an intensely interesting introduction' but also sang 'John Barleycorn'. Their reporter noticed that the songs used to illustrate the lecture were not all to be found in the first editions of *Songs of the West*, and reported with some excitement that he had learnt from Baring-Gould that they would be included in a new and enlarged edition of the book to be published a few weeks later.[43]

The new edition of *Songs of the West* was published in October 1905 and caught the wave of interest in folk song. Sharp was able to say in a letter acknowledging receipt of a cheque for £5 13s 9d as his share of the royalty for the half year, 'It is selling fairly well, isn't it?'[44]

Even before the new edition left the printers Baring-Gould and Sharp had agreed to work together on a book of songs for use in schools – something both felt strongly about. This was to become *English Folk Songs for Schools*, published in 1906 by Curwen. The introduction expresses their views very clearly arguing, for example:

> The folk-song of one race is not the folk-song of another, any more than the warble of the blackbird is the twitter of the finch. Why, then, should we endeavour to force our children to learn the notes of Germany, France and Italy, instead of acquiring that which is their very own? Why dress a Japanese in English hat and frock coat, and force English feet into French sabots?[45]

---

43 VWML, Cecil Sharp Manuscripts, Press cuttings, 1902–05, p. 201, 'Devon Folk Airs – Mr. Baring-Gould's New Work', *Western Mercury*, 20 July 1905.
44 Plymouth Central Library, Baring-Gould Collection, Letter of Cecil Sharp to Sabine Baring-Gould, 20 January 1907.
45 Sabine Baring-Gould and Cecil J. Sharp, *English Folk Songs for Schools*, (London: J. Curwen and Sons Ltd, 1906). The 'Introduction' can be seen, from the reference to living 'forty years in country parishes', to have been written by Baring-Gould.

English Folk Songs for Schools contains 53 songs and ballads selected from the two men's collections and from other sources. It was 'made to meet the requirements of the Board of Education', and accordingly the words of some of the songs had to be modified. Sharp regretted this but felt that the end justified the means.[46] Yet they did proudly state that with the exception of three songs sent to Baring-Gould by Lady Lethbridge every one of the tunes had been 'taken down by ourselves from the mouths of the people'. The book was published in the summer of 1906 but seems to have attracted little critical notice, despite the energetic debate about the use of folk song in schools that still continued in the musical press. Nevertheless, Sharp was able to say, in a letter to Baring-Gould the following summer:

> The book has sold very well. 1700 copies of the large book and 3000 of the small ones in a little more than a year. What strikes me about the matter is that Curwen has done extremely well and has probably alread [already?] recouped himself over the initial expenditure and has a handsome profit as well. It is rather hard lines because he has done extremely little to sell the book – the force has been applied by ourselves and the Esperance Club. I should suggest that in our contemplated new book we either get very much better terms out of Curwen or go elsewhere or publish at our own expense. We will talk this over in the holidays.[47]

This letter also mentions a lecture in Plymouth that Sharp says 'will I hope do good'. This refers to the National Convention of Choirmasters, Music Teachers &c., at which Sharp spoke on the afternoon of Saturday 14 September 1907 with Baring-Gould taking the chair for the session. This was very much the target group for their book. That evening J. Spencer Curwen gave a talk on 'The Story of Tonic Sol-fa'.

Baring-Gould was wary of Curwen, following an altercation with the publisher over piracy of some of the songs from *Songs of the West* a few years earlier. The Curwen company was wedded to the use of the tonic sol-fa notation, which neither Sharp nor Baring-Gould approved of, and they had persuaded Curwen to publish the early editions of the book without it. A letter from Baring-Gould to Sharp on 9 October 1906 refers to this

---

46 Arthur Fox Strangways, and Maud Karpeles, *Cecil Sharp* (Oxford: Oxford University Press, 1933), p.55.

47 Plymouth Central Library, Baring-Gould Collection, Letter of Cecil Sharp to Baring-Gould, dated 20 July 1907. I discovered this letter inside Francis Nicolle's copy of *English Folk Songs for Schools*, which was part of his large bequest to the library.

and to his refusal to accede to a request from J. Spencer Curwen to endorse the system. He wrote, 'If Curwen insists that he will not publish a cheap ed. without tonic sol-fa as well as the old notation I suppose reluctantly we shall have to give way – but I don't like it.'[48]

In his letter of 20 July Sharp had also written, 'Could you put me up a few days before the 14th at Lew? We could then go to Plymouth together and have time to arrange something about the next book.' This was to be a second collection of songs for schools, working again with Curwen. This progressed only slowly and in November 1907 there was an exchange of letters about it between Sharp and Curwen. Sharp's main concern was about royalties on sales of *English Folk-Songs for Schools* and he demanded that the amount be doubled, threatening that he would take his business elsewhere. Curwen demonstrated the validity of Baring-Gould's concerns about him by writing: 'Your trouble comes from having to share the royalties. Why bring in Mr Baring Gould? You can easily revise the words yourself, and we feel sure that he would not mind as his disposition is so generous.' Sharp chose not to go ahead with Curwen and subsequently worked with Novello to publish a new series of songbooks for schools, though without Baring-Gould's involvement.

Among the books from Baring-Gould's library that are now in the Heritage Collections Library at the University of Exeter is a water-damaged copy of Cecil Sharp's *One Hundred English Folksongs* which is inscribed 'To S. Baring-Gould, Xmas 1916'.[49] This is one of several of Sharp's books that Baring-Gould owned that would have been gifts from the author. In a letter dated 7 January 1917 Baring-Gould wrote: 'Thank you very much for your *One Hundred English Folk Songs*, and I am so glad in it to find such an excellent likeness of yourself'. He went on to tell of six weeks' illness with bronchitis and then:

> I want you very much to consent to a great wish that I have. I have always loved Mr Sheppard's settings of the Devonshire songs in the original edition and from all sides I get entreaties of those who know and valued them that they can not get copies. There was a radiance of poetry about his arrangements. No doubt they were not archaic-musically correct. Now I want as

---

48 VWML, Cecil Sharp Manuscripts, Letter of Sabine Baring-Gould to Cecil Sharp, 18 July 1904.
49 Cecil Sharp, *One Hundred English Folk Songs* (Boston: Oliver Ditson Company, 1916). Published in Britain in 1920 in 2 volumes as English Folk Songs by Novello.

sole memorial to myself when gone to have 'Songs of the West' reproduced with those settings of Sheppard restored, leaving all the rest to you.[50]

Sharp replied the following day with a typewritten letter in which he said:

Dear Mr Baring-Gould
I can quite understand your feeling about Mr. Sheppard's settings and I should be very sorry indeed to stand between you and the realisation of your wishes. The only thing that I cannot do is to have my name associated with them in such a way as to lead others to believe that I approved of them. Would not the best way be to reprint your original edition, which has now in a sense become historic and leave the editions to make their separate appeals to the musical public.[51]

There is then a gap of three days before Baring-Gould replied:

Dear Mr Sharp
I think perhaps it will be the best way to reissue the original edition with the arrangements of Mr Sheppard and Dr Bussell. I had an application the day before yesterday from Plymouth in connection with a forthcoming musical festival, for a loan of a copy of the original arrangements for something they wished to produce and they found great difficulty in obtaining the early edition.[52]

This reissue never happened and the problem was never resolved to Baring-Gould's satisfaction.

Though there was never a serious falling-out between Sharp and Baring-Gould, this disagreement continued to trouble him. There was no further correspondence between them. This feels like a sad end to what had been a good partnership for a few years. Baring-Gould's grandson, Bickford Dickinson, writes of an occasion on which the topic cropped up in conversation when Baring-Gould was staying with his daughter Mary (Dickinson's mother) in North Devon some years later:

50 VWML, Cecil Sharp Manuscripts, Letter of Sabine Baring-Gould to Cecil Sharp, 7 January 1917.
51 VWML, Cecil Sharp Manuscripts, Letter of Cecil Sharp to Sabine Baring-Gould, 8 January 1917. Sharp mistakenly dated this letter 8 January 1916.
52 VWML, Cecil Sharp Manuscripts, Letter of Sabine Baring-Gould to Cecil Sharp, 11 January 1917.

The old man, as he then was, insisted on Mary going to the piano and playing through a number of the songs, first in the original edition and then in the Cecil Sharp edition, while he hummed the tunes and afterwards expressed himself very forcibly on what was still a sore subject.[53]

George Gardiner

Another collector of the Edwardian era with whom Baring-Gould was in contact was George Barnet Gardiner, best known for his collection of songs from Hampshire, but who consulted Baring-Gould early in his song-collecting career about some songs he had found in Cornwall. Gardiner was born in Kincardine in 1852, the fifth son of a Presbyterian minister. He studied classics at school and then at Edinburgh University before becoming the classics master for eleven years at the prestigious Edinburgh Academy. He then worked independently as a translator and writer, with a particular interest in music.

He first became aware of folk song in Scotland, and then of the European countries that he travelled to, particularly Germany. He joined the Folk Song Society when he realised that England also had folk songs and began to collect folk songs some time in 1904 with a former colleague from Edinburgh Academy, Henry Hammond. At first they tried to pick up the gleanings of Sharp's harvest in Somerset but in 1905 Gardiner decided to try his luck in Cornwall. In February of that year he visited the Launceston area and recruited a local music teacher and church organist Charles Parsonson to help him by noting the tunes. They met five singers and collected thirteen songs. Gardiner returned to Minehead, where he had been staying, and sent his collection to Baring-Gould, asking for his comments on the songs. As well as the songs that he had collected around Launceston, he included a couple of tunes sent to him by Joseph White of Nancledra, who had heard them in the early 1850s and had written them out for Gardiner.

The songs arrived while Baring-Gould was away on the French Riviera doing the research for his next book. He responded with a postcard on 12 April, saying that he had just got home and seen Gardiner's 'budget of songs'.[54] He made a few comments about the songs on the postcard and then wrote again five days later with some more detailed observations. Cecil Sharp was staying at Lew House and he also looked over the songs

---

53 Bickford Dickinson, *Sabine Baring-Gould*, p. 137.
54 London, Vaughan Williams Memorial Library, George Gardiner Manuscripts, Postcard of Sabine Baring-Gould to George B. Gardiner, 12 April 1905, GG/6/5.

and commented on them. Baring-Gould enclosed Sharp's comments with his own.[55] Sharp's comments were perhaps a little more severe than Baring-Gould's; where Baring-Gould said of the 'Little Dun Mare', for example, 'I have a different and better tune, this printed on broadside 13 verses', Sharp wrote, 'not of much interest'. Nonetheless, the comments were sufficiently positive that Gardiner sent the songs, with the notes made by Baring-Gould and Sharp, to Lucy Broadwood as soon as he received them remarking: 'I am glad to see that Mr. S. finds as many as 3 or 4 of the tunes interesting. The percentage, though small, is not quite disappointing'. Baring-Gould copied nine of the songs that Gardiner had sent him into his Personal Copy manuscript.

Gardiner's own manuscript contains some other songs from Cornwall with dates in May and June 1905 assigned to them. The tunes of those from the Launceston area were again noted by Parsonson. It is not clear if Gardiner was present on this occasion or whether his colleague had sent them to him. If Gardiner had visited the area he might have taken up Baring-Gould's invitation to visit him, but there is no record of such a visit. There is another group of songs from Helston in Gardiner's manuscript, which had been sent to him by a music professor and organist, Edward Quintrell, who had heard them from Joseph Boaden of Curry Cross Lanes, near Helston. One of these was 'Bedlam', which was published in the *Journal of the Folk Song Society*.[56] The words of the song were not sent and could not be obtained so Gardiner and Lucy Broadwood attached the text of a song from a garland in the British Museum to create 'I'll Love My Love, Because I Know My Love Loves Me'. This was later taken up by Gustav Holst who incorporated it with great success in his *Six Choral Folk Songs* Op. 36B (1916).

Gardiner did not return to Cornwall after 1905 because, at Lucy Broadwood's suggestion, he had moved his field of activity to Hampshire, which was where he found greater success as a collector, amassing nearly 1,500 songs and tunes. Illness curtailed his activities in 1909 and he returned to Scotland, where he died in 1910.

There was one occasion on which Baring-Gould and Gardiner are known to have met and that was in Alresford, Hampshire. George

---

55 VWML, George Gardiner Manuscripts, Letter of Sabine Baring-Gould to George B. Gardiner, 17 April 1905 (with enclosure of notes by Sharp), GG/6/4. This accompanies the letter of George Gardiner to Lucy Broadwood, 18 April 1905 with the same reference.

56 'I'll Love my Love, Because I Know my Love Loves Me', *Journal of the Folk-Song Society*, 2 (1905), pp.93–94.

Gardiner had collected a number of songs from Richard Hall, from Avington, and he arranged for Hall to travel over to Alresford to sing some of his songs to Baring-Gould. The story runs that he was offered a pint of beer for every song that he sang, and that he sang something like eighteen songs. This cannot, of course, be verified. Baring-Gould gave the singer a copy of *Songs of the West*, which he took to the Rectory in Avington where the rector's daughter, Chloe Osmond, played the songs from the book for him to learn. They performed some of them at local concerts, though she would not allow him to sing 'The Tythe Pig' since it was disrespectful to the clergy.[57]

Ralph Vaughan Williams

There is very little surviving that documents the contacts between Baring-Gould and Ralph Vaughan Williams and those contacts had little to do with traditional song.

Fig 8.6 – Ralph Vaughan Williams by William Rothenstein.

---

57 This anecdote comes from an excellent piece of research by Steve Jordan. Gardiner had placed Richard Hall at Itchen Abbas but Jordan discovered that he actually lived in Avington where he worked on the estate at Avington Park. The story of his meeting with Baring-Gould and his learning and performing songs from *Songs of the West* was told to Jordan by Chloe Osmond's brother. I am grateful to Steve Jordan for sharing this story in a personal communications.

Ralph Vaughan Williams had become interested in folk song through Lucy Broadwood who was a distant relative. The two had first met at a social gathering in Surrey in 1887, when he was a teenager. In 1893 he was greatly impressed by the songs in her collection *English County Songs*, particularly 'Lazarus', a tune that he returned to several times in his work as a composer. In 1902 he gave the series of talks about folk song for the Oxford University Extension Unit referred to earlier where Lucy Broadwood joined him for one of the lectures and the occasion in December of that year on which he collected folk songs from Mrs Chidell.

A year later he famously met Charles Potiphar in an Essex garden and heard the beautiful 'Bushes and Briars', the song which propelled him into regular folk song collecting. Over the next decade he collected more than 800 songs. He also lectured and wrote about folk song lucidly and more thoughtfully than many others. Vaughan Williams was a professional musician and nearly forty years younger than Baring-Gould. Despite these differences, they cooperated on a revised edition of *Church Songs*, a book that Baring-Gould and Henry Fleetwood Sheppard had published with Skeffington and Son in 1884.

Nowadays we would find it hard to distinguish between hymns and religious songs, but Baring-Gould saw the latter as being intended for singing outside the context of worship and quoted the example of the songs of Sankey and Moody and the Salvation Army, who Baring-Gould considered to have been particularly adept at crafting 'catching' songs that people enjoyed singing in the home or elsewhere. Two series of *Church Songs* were published, the first containing 22 songs and the second 28. Though Sheppard was identified as the co-editor and was responsible for the majority of the harmonies, some were harmonised by Frederick Bussell and some by the publisher, Martin Skeffington. In 1905 Baring-Gould suggested to Skeffington that he would like to issue a new edition but since Sheppard had died in 1900, it was necessary to find a new musical editor.

At that time Vaughan Williams was working on *The English Hymnal*, which included several well-known hymns and introduced several new tunes that he had taken from folk songs. *The English Hymnal* contained five of Baring-Gould's hymns and he was also acknowledged as the composer of 'Eudoxia', the tune for 'Now the Day is Over'. There is also a tune in the book called 'Lewtrenchard', associated with the hymn 'Gentle Jesus, Meek and Mild' which was said to come from a traditional tune. It was Vaughan Williams' practice to name tunes after the place where they were collected, so it seems likely that the tune is somehow associated with Baring-Gould but no one has yet been able to identify the song from which it was taken.

We can infer that the two men corresponded or met in connection with *The English Hymnal* and, as Baring-Gould cast round to find a replacement for Sheppard, he thought of Vaughan Williams. A letter to Baring-Gould from Martin Skeffington, the original publisher of *Church Songs*, dated 1907, mentions Vaughan Williams, but the burden of the letter is that Skeffington did not wish to re-publish the book and suggests that they find someone else to publish it. The new edition of the first series of *Church Songs* finally appeared in 1911, under the imprint of the Society for Promoting Christian Knowledge (SPCK), and the cover identifies Baring-Gould as the 'collector' and that the music was by Vaughan Williams, though Sheppard's name is included on the title page. It is a much-changed collection, as only five of the original 22 songs in the original 'Series 1' were carried forward into the new edition.

There is just one letter from Baring-Gould to Vaughan Williams, dated 15 October 1911, which has survived in the British Library, and in it Baring-Gould announces that he is putting together material for a second series of *Church Songs*, though he does not think SPCK will publish it. In this he was right, and Wright and Hoggard of Beverley, another publisher of religious books and parish magazines, published the second series in 1912. The main purpose of the letter, though, is to give Vaughan Williams permission to make use of one of the songs that Baring-Gould had collected. He wrote, 'By all means use the words that you want. There are more that I took down which I have not printed in *Songs of the West* but they are in Child's Ballads.' The song in question was 'How Cold the Wind Doth Blow', a version of 'The Unquiet Grave' which was included in volume 5 of the series *Folk-Songs of England*, edited by Cecil Sharp.[58] This volume comprised songs collected by W. Percy Merrick in Sussex, for which Vaughan Williams provided piano accompaniments. Merrick had only obtained a partial text, so Vaughan Williams used phrases from versions collected by Baring-Gould, Sharp and Hammond to complete the song.[59]

This is the only record that we have of Baring-Gould and Vaughan Williams having discussed folk song. It is hard to imagine that they would not have done so on other occasions, particularly given the fact that both

---

58 Cecil Sharp (ed.). *Folk-Songs of England, Book 5, Folk-Songs of Sussex collected by W. Percy Merrick with piano accompaniments by R. Vaughan Williams and Albert Robins* (London: Novello, 1912), pp. 16–21. A note to the song acknowledges Baring-Gould's contribution.

59 I am grateful to American scholar, Julian Onderdonk, who identified the song and the publication in question. (Personal communication).

were corresponding with Cecil Sharp and Lucy Broadwood – but we have no evidence that supports the suggestion.

Anne Gilchrist

It is appropriate to say a few words about Anne Geddes Gilchrist (1863–1954), another important figure in the early days of the folk song revival of the first half of the twentieth century. She was born in Manchester of Scottish parents and recalled that folk song had been very much a part of her childhood. She heard songs such as 'Four Jolly Fishermen' and 'The Rantin', Tearin', Highlan'man' from her nursemaid and Welsh folk songs from her nurse, as well as the singing of her parents. As reported earlier, she heard Frederick Bussell sing 'The Chimney Sweep' at an Oxford concert and her interest was re-awakened to such an extent that she went out and bought Baring-Gould's *Songs of the West*, which contained this song in Bussell's arrangement. Her copy of the book is in the Vaughan Williams Memorial Library and it contains a number of pencilled comments against the notes to the songs.

Fig. 8.7 – Anne Gilchrist (Courtesy of Vaughan Williams Memorial Library).

In an autobiographical article written in 1942 she says that she sent a song of her father's to Baring-Gould for comment, but thought that he had found it 'too Scotch for him' and so referred her to Frank Kidson.[60] She became good friends with Kidson and also with Lucy Broadwood, but continued to exchange ideas with Baring-Gould. A letter loose in Baring-Gould's manuscripts appears to have been written after the publication of the 1905 edition of *Songs of the West* and sets out her thoughts on some of the songs. About 'Death and the Lady', for example, she says:

> I turned with some curiosity to this, to see whether, since the first edition of Songs of the West was published, you had elucidated the meaning of 'Branchy Tree', but finding it still 'wrapt in mystery', may I offer the suggestion that it is a corruption of 'an-ces-try'? This would fit in with the statement that 'Lords, Dukes and Squires bow down to me', and the lines might perhaps be restored as: –
> 'Lords, Dukes and Squires bow down to me
> For of a high ancestry am I'.[61]

Baring-Gould wrote enthusiastically on a postcard to her on 15 January 1906: 'I am in no doubt that you have solved "The Branchy Tree". A very happy hit.'[62]

As with other favoured correspondents, he also lent her books. In 1909 she appears to have asked about the influence of the Holy Grail on folk song. He sent her a copy of François-Marie Luzel's *Contes Populaires de Basse-Bretagne* (1879) in which he has marked a song for her, though he goes on to say in his covering letter:

> I have no belief in any Grailic influence on folk song. The cycle of the Grail was an invention of the chivalry & the clergy combined, & had in it none of the elements that appeal to the common people. You know, of course, that all la Marque [Jouprée] is utterly unreliable. He was a manufacturer of ballads that he got translated for him into Breton & published as traditional. You will see what Luzel says of him – & he restrains himself.[63]

60 Anne Gilchrist, 'Let Us Remember', *English Dance and Song*, April – May 1942, pp. 62–63.
61 Devon Heritage Centre, Sabine Baring-Gould Papers, 5203M, Personal Copy MSS, 'Notes on songs sent to Baring-Gould by Anne Gilchrist', P2, 617a, (--).
62 VWML, Anne Geddes Gilchrist Papers, Postcard of Baring-Gould to Anne Gilchrsit, 15 Jan 1906, AGG/7.983.
63 VWML, Anne Gilchrist Papers, Letter of Baring-Gould to Anne Gilchrist, 28 September, 1909, AGG/4/36.

This observation prompted a bittersweet, and rather revealing, addition to his letter: 'P.S. I have touched up old ballads but then I say so.'

Anne Gilchrist's is another name that deserves to be better known. Her contribution to collecting songs and as a member of the editorial board of the *Journal of the Folk Song Society* and its successors was recognised in her lifetime by several awards. She wrote articles for the *Journal* and for other magazines as well as giving a number of public lectures. Her knowledge about folk song was a help to many of her colleagues and the collection of her manuscripts in the Vaughan Williams Memorial Library contains much of interest.

Francis Child

The last person to be described in this chapter is out of sequence chronologically and was an editor rather than a collector. Francis James Child, a professor at Harvard University, was one of the most important figures in the study of folk songs and, particularly, ballads. He was the editor of the famous *English and Scottish Popular Ballads*, the collection of 305 traditional ballads that has provided food for both thought and table for several generations of ballad scholars.[64]

Francis Child was born in Boston in 1825, the son of a sail maker. After doing well at school, he won a scholarship to Harvard where he was appointed Boylston Professor of Rhetoric and Oratory at the age of 26. As well as his teaching role he took on the task in 1853 of editing the mammoth series *British Poets*, which ran to 130 volumes. Included in the series was a set of eight books (later combined into four) in which Child ventured into ballad publication for the first time. This was *English and Scottish Ballads*, a selection from more than 100 published sources. Though he revised the book over the next two decades, Child was never fully satisfied with it, and his thinking on balladry had developed.

As a result, in 1872 he started to plan a new publication upon different principles. His stated intention was that he would not commence printing his collection until he had 'at command every valuable copy of every known ballad' – a very tall order. He sent a letter to the British publication *Notes and Queries* headed 'Wanted, Old Ballads' before traveling to Britain in his summer vacation. Here he met several people with whom he had corresponded as well as spending time in the British Museum Library looking at ballad manuscripts, before heading on to Scotland. He did not

---

64 Francis Child, *The English and Scottish Popular Ballads* (10 Volumes), Boston (MA): Houghton Mifflin Company, 1882–98. I have quoted the part numbers of the original ten-book edition, rather than those of the later five-volume edition.

Fig. 8.8 – Prof. Frances J. Child.

give much consideration to English balladry. His visit did not give him a lot of new material but it did motivate some of those he met to cooperate, sending him the material that he needed over the following years. After a decade of gathering all these 'valuable copies' the first volume of *English and Scottish Popular Ballads* appeared in 1882. The book was originally issued in ten parts (later combined into five volumes) with 305 ballads documented in multiple variants, not just from Britain but also from other European traditions. It was a great achievement and is rightly regarded as Child's masterwork. Child died in 1896 with his great project nearly complete. The final volume was almost ready for the press and he left only the bibliography to be completed by his colleague, George L. Kittredge. The last volume was published in 1898.

The correspondence between Child and Baring-Gould began in January 1880, before he started to collect folk songs. Child had pointed out an error in one of his books and Baring-Gould wrote to acknowledge his letter, claiming that it had been a mistake by the printer. A decade later on 6 June 1890, Baring-Gould wrote a lengthy letter to Child in which he said:

> Dear Sir
> I have long known your book of English & Scottish Ballads –
> and did not know till the other day, when in the Brit. Museum
> that a new & admirable edition was in progress. I have sent you
> a copy of the 3 first parts of my "Songs of the West". I have
> been engaged mainly in collecting the old melodies in Devon &
> Cornwall, but in so doing have collected the old ballads & songs as
> well. In publishing for the general public it has not been possible
> to give all the ballads, nor all such as we do give in quite their
> original form, as some have a freeness in morals that will not suit
> the pianoforte. Now I have been rather puzzled what to do with
> the originals, but now I have seen your book my difficulty ceases.
> I will send them to you.[65]

The letter went on to describe his singers briefly and to state his view that the ballad repertoire was held in common by England and Scotland, but that the balladry of Scotland was recorded better than that of England. While he had been collecting songs he had heard some ballads that had

---

65 Cambridge (MA), Harvard University, Houghton Library, Baring-Gould Manuscript, Ballads and Songs collected by the Rev. S. Baring-Gould, Chiefly in Devonshire, and sent by him to Professor F. J. Child, MS Eng 863, Letter of Sabine Baring-Gould to Francis J. Child, dated 6 June 1890.

not been found in Scotland, while the Scots had some ballads not found in England. He went on to describe some of the ballads that he had collected and offered to send over any that Child would like to have.

A month later he wrote a letter accompanying a 'budget of copies', in which he makes some illuminating comments. This is the first of seventeen letters and associated packets containing a total of 68 songs. This collection is now in the Houghton Library of Harvard University and is remarkable not just because of the songs transmitted, but also because of the information conveyed about Baring-Gould's singers and his thoughts on folk song, some of it not to be found elsewhere. Child's colleague, George L. Kittredge, assembled the collection after Child's death and attempted to place the various items in order.

In June 1890 Child was working to complete the seventh volume of his book and Baring-Gould's letters may have come as something of a shock. Not only was he sending him material that he had not seen before, but he was telling Child that he was hearing ballads that were being sung by living singers – and English singers at that!

Child had, in fact, already included one item from Baring-Gould in part 4 (1886), which was the story of 'The Golden Ball' which Baring-Gould had collected in Yorkshire and which had been included by him in an appendix to Henderson's *Folklore of the Northern Counties* (1866) as a variant of 'The Maid Freed from the Gallows' (No. 95). Child extracted the fragments of the ballad from the *cante-fable* to create a reconstruction of the ballad form. In the 'Additions and Corrections' in volume 5 he included a version of the *cante-fable* sent to Baring-Gould by Mrs Bachellor from North Cornwall. This is mentioned in the letter Baring-Gould wrote to Child on 5 June 1892, though the text is not present in the correspondence.

Baring-Gould's later contributions were first acknowledged in the 'Advertisement to Part 7', published in February 1890. Child's introduction to 'The Gypsy Laddie' (Child 200) in this volume gave a description of Baring-Gould's collected version and his treatment of it, though no song text is included. Other song texts sent to Child by Baring-Gould, such as 'Henry Martyn' (Child 250), were included in the body of this volume and in the 'Additions and Corrections' section. Part 9 also contained other texts.[66]

---

66 For a detailed analysis of Child's use of Baring-Gould's contributions see David Atkinson, 'Sabine Baring-Gould's Contribution to The English and Scottish Popular Ballads' in *Ballads into Book*, Tom Cheeseman and Sigrid Rieuwerts, eds. (Bern: Peter Lang, 1997), pp. 41–52.

In his letter to Child of 14 July 1890 Baring-Gould wrote: 'For some time I did not think much of the words we took, as I took it for granted that they were from stall copies of ballads, but after a while I began to doubt this in every case.' As a result of this belief he reconstructed a number of the texts, not always well. It has been suggested that these alterations amounted to forgery but this is, in my opinion, too harsh a judgement as there is no evidence that he intended to deceive Child. The question of the authenticity of the texts that Baring-Gould sent to Child cannot be ignored and a specific example will be examined in the next chapter.

The songs he sent Child included two rather racy songs, 'The Maid and the Box' and 'The Jolly Sportsman'. In his manuscript entry for the latter in Working Notebook 1 he had noted, 'nasty one to be rewritten'. Child was very sensitive to bawdy material and was disgusted by many of the broadside ballads he had examined. He said, of the volume of Percy's *Loose and Humorous Songs*: '…if it ever comes in your way I advise you to put up the chimney (where it will be in its element) or into the fire – where the authors no doubt are! They are just as dirty as they can be.'[67] He may have been rather surprised to receive such songs from a man of the cloth.

The English and Scottish Popular Ballads is a remarkable achievement and one can only admire the effort that went into it. One can sympathise with Child that he could not have anticipated that, as the light at the end of the tunnel appeared, Baring-Gould and other English folk song collectors would bring forward a host of newly collected ballads from a living tradition in England.

In his letter to Child of 23 August 1890 Baring-Gould asked him: 'Would you mind allowing me to buy your new edition at cost price, the published price is rather heavy, & I will help you all I can.' As a result, there is a set of the ten volumes of *The English and Scottish Popular Ballads* in Baring-Gould's personal library. These volumes remain in their paper covers, as he never had them bound. They are also uncut, except in a few places where he has checked that his versions were included.

Connections

As a pioneer of the first phase of the folk song revival Baring-Gould had extensive and significant contacts, not just with his contemporaries, but also with many of those who followed him.

These connections over two decades are of great interest and are, I believe, fully revealed here for the first time. The role played by Lucy

---

67 Mary Ellen Brown, *Child's Unfinished Masterpiece, The English and Scottish Popular Ballads* (Urbana: University of Illinois Press, 2011), p. 84.

Broadwood is similarly significant and her correspondence has been critical in revealing this high level of interconnectivity. In her case this led to her embracing the Folk Song Society and influencing the course of events through that organisation.

Several of the people described in this chapter became members of the Folk Song Society and contributed to the growing body of song published in its journal. Cecil Sharp fell out with Broadwood and the society, though he never lost momentum as a result and, posthumously, it was his camp that achieved leadership of the movement when the Folk Song Society was subsumed into Sharp's English Folk Dance Society in 1932. Baring-Gould never sought to lead a national movement. It can be seen that his connections placed him at the centre of a network and he had often, through his public writing, made the call for action. As already stated in respect of his work on folklore, his greater interests were more local. And as his life moved into its final phase, his world was getting smaller.

Plate 1 - Sophia and Sabine Baring-Gould (Merriol Almond).

Plate 2 - Detail from Baring-Gould's drawing of the mosaics in the villa he discovered at Pau in 1851 (Merriol Almond and Devon Heritage Centre).

Plate 3 - Grace Taylor in her working clothes (Merriol Almond).

Plate 4 - Sabine Baring-Gould as a curate (Merriol Almond).

Plate 5 - Grace Baring-Gould (Merriol Almond)

Plate 6 - Lew House (Author's Photo).

Plate 7 - The singer's settle, Lew House (Author's photo).

Plate 8 – Poster for 'Songs of the West' Costume Concert (Courtesy of the Bodleian Libraries, The University of Oxford, John Johnson Collection: Entertainments Folder 12 [8]).

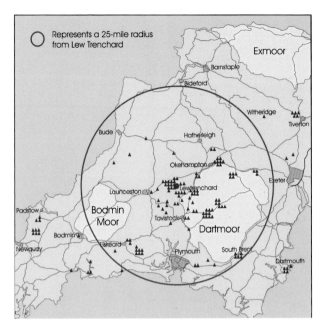

Plate 9 - Locations of Baring-Gould's Singers.
Each triangle represents one individual. (Map prepared by Roger Bristow).

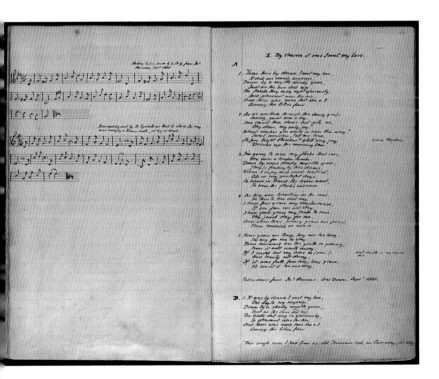

Plate 10 - Page spread from Baring-Gould's Fair Copy manuscript (Wren Music).

Plate 11 - Baring-Gould's Church, St Peter's, Lew Trenchard (Author's photo).

Plate 12 - Graves of Sabine and Grace Baring-Gould, St Peter's Church, Lew Trenchard (Author's photo).

9: The Songs of the People

When I was quite a lad, if ever I heard the women singing at their work, and the song was unfamiliar, I took them down. They were doggerel often enough, but they were poetry sometimes and, in any case, were the songs of the people, and worth preserving.[1]

What Can Be Found in the Collection? – Pride of Place – What People Sang to Baring-Gould – Bawdy Songs – Strawberry Fair – Jordan (is a Hard Road to Travel) – The Drunken Maidens – The Hostess' Daughter – I Would that the Wars were Well Over – Polly Oliver's Ramble – Pretty Dorothy and the Brown Girl – Contemporary Songs – Why Do these Songs Matter?

The songs that Baring-Gould published have, ever since they appeared in print, provoked discussion, scepticism and controversy as well as admiration for his achievement in collecting them. They have also been taken up and sung widely – a variant of one of them even reached number 3 in the pop music charts. There is still no definitive list of all the songs that Baring-Gould recorded in manuscript and we will never have a complete total of the number of songs that he heard or was sent, since we know that there are notebooks that have not come down to us. One of the tasks carried out as part of my own project has been to list and describe each of the individual entries in Baring-Gould's Personal Copy manuscript. More than 2,000 items have been identified in this, the most comprehensive of his manuscripts, and these individual items appear under more than 700 song titles. As well as songs that he collected himself or had been sent, they include some song texts from printed sources or references to songs in print. But there are a number of songs in other manuscripts that he did not transfer to the Personal Copy. Completing the analysis of the whole manuscript collection is a job for the future, and probably for someone else.

This chapter will describe the songs in the collection and then give some examples that illustrate Baring-Gould's approach to song collecting and to his treatment of the songs in the songbooks that he published. The focus will be on the words of the songs rather than the tunes, though Julia Bishop has written and insightful analysis of the music of Baring-Gould's collection which has been included as Appendix A.

---

1   Frederick Rogers, 'Priest and Scholar, An Interview with the Reverend S. Baring-Gould', *The Treasury*, May 1914, pp. 97–103.

What Can Be Found in the Collection?

One of the criticisms of the Victorian and Edwardian folk song collectors is that they were selective in what they wrote down, recording only songs that accorded with their vision of what a folk song was. This is a perennial problem and is a factor in the discussion that continues among folk song enthusiasts to this day. Defining 'folk song' is a game frequently played, often late at night, and with drink taken. The result is always unsatisfactory and, in the end, participants generally resort to a variation of 'well, I know what I mean when I talk about folk song'. Substitution of the words 'traditional' or 'vernacular' for 'folk' may ease the pain, but the issue is unlikely to be resolved any time soon as it touches on romantic visions, issues of class and a residue of beliefs based as much on feelings as on facts. And perhaps that is a satisfactory situation as long as everyone knows in his or her heart what they mean by folk song and that no one actually comes to blows.

Songs heard, either then or now, might be dismissed by folk purists as 'music hall', 'country' or (worst of all, it sometimes seems) 'art-song'.[2] Confusingly the same song can in one context be a folk song, and in another context be – well, something else, depending on who sings it, the way in which it is sung and the situation in which it is performed. Baring-Gould's criteria for writing a song down were elastic. He noted some blackface minstrel songs and a few music hall songs that other collectors would have ignored and although he did not publish them (with the exception of one that will be described below), they can be studied in his manuscripts. He was not very familiar with popular musical culture and in some of these cases he did not recognise the provenance of items that he heard as 'songs of the day'. At the other end of the spectrum, he noted some songs from his old singers that had been popular in the late eighteenth century or earlier and which some of his colleagues might have passed over. An example of this is 'Fair Cloe', which he heard from James Olver, the Launceston man who as a boy sneaked out at night to listen outside the pub window to what was being sung inside.

---

2   This antipathy travels in both directions. The composer Elizabeth Lutyens famously described the use of folk tunes by English composers as 'Cowpat Music'. Nicholas Cook in *Music, A Very Short Introduction* (Oxford: Oxford University Press, 1998), p. 42, completes his twelve line (!) summary of folk song by saying that despite their purity and their evocation of the unspoilt national character of the countryside and its inhabitants, they remain 'low art' because they 'do not spring from the individual vision of an inspired composer. The voice of the people might be heard through them, but hardly the voice of music.'

JAMES OLVER.
From a Photograph by HAYMAN, LAUNCESTON.

9.1 – James Olver from *Old Country Life*

Baring-Gould recognised the song from old song books in his collection as 'The Thorn': a poem by Robert Burns, set to music before 1800 by William Shield (1748–1829), a highly regarded composer of popular songs at the beginning of the nineteenth century. Olver (and, presumably, the man who he heard sing it) had retained the shape and sense of the song, though with several changes to the words.

Version from James Olver	As written by William Shield
From the white blossom'd snow	*From the white-blossom'd sloe*
Requested fair Cloe	*My dear Chloe requested*
A sprig her sweet breast to adorn	*A sprig her fair breast to adorn*
O maiden said I	*No by heav'n I exclaimed*
Thy request I deny	*May I perish if ever*
The sloe neath the flower hath a thorn	*I plant in that bosom a thorn*
Etc.	*Etc.*

When the digitised images of Baring-Gould's manuscripts were being prepared for online publication, part of the work was to add the songs in the collection to the Roud Folk Song Index and to assign Roud Numbers to those that had not already been given them. By that time the Roud Index database included a very large collection of songs from publications and manuscripts from the nineteenth and twentieth centuries. It was discovered that more than 40% of the songs in Baring-Gould's manuscripts had not previously been included in the Index. While not a perfect measure, it suggests that a high proportion of the songs that Baring-Gould recorded were not heard by other collectors – or, if they were, that they chose not to include them in their collections.[3]

Knowing that, it seemed sensible to establish how the content of Baring-Gould's collection compared with English folk song collections more generally. Again, it is hard to give a definitive answer to this question, but a crude measure can be made by reference to another aspect of Steve Roud's work. When compiling the *New Penguin Book of English Folk Songs*, Roud and his co-editor, Julia Bishop, sought to represent the 'core tradition of English song'.[4] To do this they compiled a list of about 300 of the songs most frequently collected from the nineteenth century onwards and selected from them 151 songs for publication; 95 songs (63%) out of the 151 songs in this list occur in Baring-Gould's collection. While this is not a statistically valid analysis the number is sufficiently high to suggest that even though Baring-Gould's collection contains a number of previously unrecognised songs it also contains a high proportion of the songs occurring in Roud's selection.

In writing about folk songs and ballads Baring-Gould often presented theories or made statements of opinion. There is no question but that he was at times wrong in what he wrote: often completely, gloriously and embarrassingly so. Sometimes he realises this, admits it and presents a new, more reasonable opinion. Sometimes the idea is quietly abandoned, possibly in the hope that no one is going to notice. And sometimes the

---

3   The Roud Folk Song Index is a digital database containing details of English-language traditional songs that have been recorded in any medium – books, journals, newspapers, manuscript collections, sound recordings, etc., designed and compiled by Steve Roud. Within the database each song is given a 'Roud Number', which enables a search that will identify all variants of that song, no matter what title it was originally given. At the time of writing more than 25,000 songs have been assigned Roud Numbers and the database holds entries for 237,000 variants.

4   Steve Roud and Julia Bishop, *The New Penguin Book of English Folk Songs* (London: Penguin Books, 2012).

statement is so founded on his personal prejudices that he blusters on. The fact that he was willing to publish his theories is to his credit. In this respect he was acting like a scientist: developing a hypothesis, putting it forward and then waiting for other experts in the field to criticise, comment and add to the theory.

Where Baring-Gould showed his greatest strengths as a researcher was in discovering the origins of songs. He was not collecting for the sake of building a collection. His interest was antiquarian, a kind of musical archaeology. Not all of the other folk song collectors came at the task from that angle but William Chappell and Anne Gilchrist had a strong interest for discovering a song's origin, as did Francis Child in his more specialised field of traditional ballads. Frank Kidson was so assiduous in his searches into the origins of songs that he earned the soubriquet 'The Musical Sherlock Holmes'.

It is hard to imagine how these dedicated researchers achieved as much as they did without the aids to research that are available today. We can only be impressed by the extent to which they managed to find early versions of songs from the printed and manuscript versions in the British Library and in old song and play books. As with his work on folklore, Baring-Gould invested in the books that would help in his quest, including several volumes of plays and ballad operas from the eighteenth century. He also had a formidable collection of street literature – broadsides, chapbooks and songsters – which he scoured for early versions of the songs he had collected. Where he succeeded he included the information (often with a transcription) in his manuscripts or in the notes to the published version of the song.

Pride of Place

Like many folk song collectors, Baring-Gould started with the idea of collecting songs that came from a geographical area, in this case his native territory of Devon and particularly the area around his home. The Personal Copy manuscript contains 708 song variants that he collected in Devon with his colleagues Frederick Bussell and Henry Fleetwood Sheppard, the great majority of them within 25 miles of his home. This was the typical distance that could be covered easily by a horse-drawn vehicle in a day. The circle on the map shown as Plate 9 marks an approximate 25-mile radius around Lew Trenchard. Each triangle represents a singer. An additional 124 Devon songs were sent to him by correspondents, mostly living in the county.

Lew Trenchard is only seven miles from the River Tamar and the Cornish border and so he also collected songs in Cornwall. The Personal

Copy contains 109 songs that were collected directly from Cornish singers, and correspondents sent him a further 44. He also made some extended visits to the county, staying overnight to spend time in places that he had been told would be rich in song – though he was sometimes disappointed. His collection remains one of the most important collections of Cornish songs 'taken from the mouths of the people' rather than from the literature.

He quickly realised that not all of the songs that he had heard were exclusive to the two counties. In an article published in December 1888 he noted: 'Some of the ballads are common property all over England, but *not* so the airs. The great bulk of these, I believe, to be of pure West of England origin.'[5] There were some locally composed songs, telling the stories of particular places and events. Examples include the song about the 'Egloshayle Ringers', said to describe men who were bell-ringers in the 1830s, and the story of 'My Ladye's Coach', based on a West Devon legend. The majority, however, were taken from the shared store of songs that were sung throughout the British Isles. There are only a few dialect songs in the collection, though there are many where Baring-Gould has recorded the local vocabulary and speech patterns in his manuscripts. He has often softened these in the published versions.

Baring-Gould, particularly in the early days of the project, valued the tunes over the words. He recognised that the words were likely to have been of 'national' origin and set to a tune locally. He knew that some had been published on broadsides, though he felt that what he was hearing was often poetically superior to the printed versions. There were some strong melodies that transferred to the region unaltered, but in a large number of cases the tune was one already in use in the locality and used to carry a new set of words. He also acknowledged that some tunes were the work of the singers themselves. Sheppard described these as 'the productions of untaught composers, singing, as it were, by inspiration'.[6]

As the songs were almost always sung unaccompanied, their vitality depended entirely on the quality, the originality and the freshness of the melody. For a song to have become so popular that it was enjoyed and passed on from one singer to another it must have had that vitality, though the later singer may have embellished and improved it in his own way. Cecil Sharp suggested that this was a demonstration of an evolutionary

---

5   Sabine Baring-Gould, 'Folk Songs and Melodies of the West', *The Western Antiquary*, 8 (1888–89), pp. 105–06.

6   Henry Fleetwood Sheppard, 'On the Melodies of Songs of the West', *Songs of the West* (1891), Part 4, p. xliv.

mechanism of oral transmission that he described as continuity, variation and selection.[7]

The evolutionary principle can as easily explain the decline of folk song as its growth. There are many instances of garbling as a result of singers mishearing or misunderstanding what they had heard. Baring-Gould gave the example of a singer who sang 'Bag of Biscuits' when he should have referred to the 'Bay of Biscay', while one of his favourite singers, James Parsons, rendered 'The Outlandish Knight' as 'The Outlandish Cat' in a version of the traditional ballad with overtones of 'Puss in Boots'.

An outlandish cat from the northern land
He said he would marry me... etc.

The quality of the singing and the ability of the singer to present the song well would also have influenced the likelihood of the song being requested again and being taken up by other singers. Not all of the old singers had Parsons' redeeming qualities as a performer and if a good song got into the hands of a poor singer then it is easy to imagine the audience forming a low opinion of it. In the worst cases the evolutionary principle could lead towards decline and extinction.

What People Sang to Baring-Gould

Looking at the content of collections such as Baring-Gould's gives us a picture of what was sung by the men and women of the day, albeit with the distorted view that arises from the selectivity on the part of the collectors described above.

We can make the assumption that each singer chose to sing a particular song because he liked it, and because he thought that those who were listening to it would also like it. When looking through a book of old songs you might come across one that seems to be devoid of any interest or musical character. 'Surely no-one sang that?' you might think. That may well be the case. The Victorian songsters are filled with songs that it is hard to imagine anyone singing. By contrast, if you are looking through songs that were collected 'from the mouths of the people' then you know that at least one person chose to sing it. This means that they found something in the song that appealed to them; either the words contained an idea that resonated with them or the tune was so special to

---

7   This principle was proposed in Sharp's, *English Folk Song, Some Conclusions* (London: Simpkin; Novello, Taunton: Barnicott and Pearce, 1907) in the chapter 'Evolution', pp. 16–31.

them that it was worth singing with nonsensical words. It might be that the song evoked personal memories that led the singer to keep it in his repertoire. And they might know that a particular type of song would be enjoyed by their audience.

The greatest proportion of the songs the people sang in this period were about love and courtship, the simple stories of boy meets girl, boy leaves girl, boy courts girl against her parents' wishes (and gains her), or the variants where the woman fails to cooperate in some amusing way. Sometimes the song is about seduction and abandonment rather than courtship, and the woman may be left bereft and often pregnant. The man usually leaves her without remorse (e.g. 'The Barley Rakings', 'O No My Love Not I', 'What Did Your Sailor Leave You?'). In several cases he cannot marry her because of the terms of his apprenticeship and must leave or, in the worst cases, murder her.

Another group of songs that were greatly loved were those about soldiers and sailors. This gave singers the opportunity to sing about shipwrecks and battles as well as popular heroes like Napoleon Bonaparte. Military or naval service could also be combined with the love story, with the woman begging him not to go, or to allow her to go with him. When that request was refused there would be a tearful exchange of tokens that, when he returned after the customary (in folk song, at least) seven years abroad, would identify him. Often the returned hero will pretend that he is someone else to test her, but she will dry up her tears after his 'little joke' and they will live happily enough ever after. Military service also creates the possibility of the loved one dressing as a man to follow her love. This was a favourite male fantasy, but there were sufficient documented instances of it happening to make it a possibility. 'Polly Oliver's Ramble', described below, is an example of this type of song.

It can come as a surprise to find that the country singer's repertoire contains so few songs that express discontent or protest. Baring-Gould wrote:

> I have spent ten years in collecting the folk songs of the West of England, and I have not come across one in which the agricultural labourer grumbles at his lot. On the contrary, their songs, the very outpouring of their hearts, are full of joy and happiness. Once, indeed, an old minstrel did say to me, "Did y' ever hear, sir, 'The Lament of the Poor Man'?" I pricked up my ears. Now at last I was about to hear some socialistic sentiment, some cry of anguish of the oppressed peasant. "No," I answered, "never — sing it

me." And then I heard it. The lament of a man afflicted with a
scolding wife. That alone made him poor, and that affliction is not
confined to the dweller in the cottage.[8]

In saying this, he echoes the findings of the majority of those who collected
songs in the countryside. In more recent times the late Bob Copper, of the
well known singing family, stated in a Radio 4 interview in 2002, 'There's
no protest in our songs. The world is a lovely place to be in. And I should
know, I've been here 88 years.'[9] In the larger collections and in the lists we
have of the songs that were sung there are only a very small number that
express any protest against 'The Establishment', though there are a few
songs that detail the hardships that were endured.

Samuel Fone did have some of these 'protest songs' in his repertoire.
One of them was 'A Country Lad Am I', in which the protagonist jeers at
the pretensions of some farmers and threatens to emigrate if things do not
improve.

> They say there's something in the wind
> Now mark you what I say,
> The farmer's men refuse to work
> For eighteen pence a day.
> If you don't mind what you're about
> They'll toddle by and bye.
> You'll have to plough the lands yourselves
> And that will ope your eye.

With assisted passages available to emigrants bound for the colonies, the
opportunities for skilled farm workers overseas looked rosy and once they
had gone, life on the farm would have had to change.

> Then Master Henry has to throw
> Aside his dog and gun.
> To hedge and ditch, no matter which,
> He will not find that fun.
> No more at the piano
> Will Emily sit and scream.
> She'll have to milk the cows herself
> And likewise skim the cream.

---

8   Sabine Baring-Gould, *An Old English Home*, p. 224.
9   'Obituary, Bob Copper', *The Telegraph*, 17 April 2004.

This song, like many of those that Sam Fone sang, was published as a broadside. Others that he may have learnt from printed sources included songs about social issues such as poverty ('In the Days When I Was Hard Up') or the economic downturn when the French Wars ended ('Hard Times in England'). In this respect he was unique amongst Baring-Gould's singers.

Bawdy Songs

In any discussion about Baring-Gould and his song collection you are going to come up, sooner or later, against the issue of bawdy songs. He wrote:

> Of course, it is only some, and they not very numerous among the popular lyrics, that are objectionable, and the singers have no thought that they are offending ears polite, when they mention in their songs and ballads matters not generally talked about, and when they call a spade 'a spade' and not 'an agricultural implement employed by gardeners'. The relation of the sexes is the basis of most poetical compositions that circulate among the peasantry.[10]

All of the collectors of English folk song have had to face this issue, although the ladies who collected were less likely to hear such songs from their singers. Baring-Gould had been deeply shocked by the robust behaviour of his public school-educated fellow students when he was at Cambridge and wrote of a song, sung at a boating supper that was so filthy that he writhed in his seat. Thirty years in the real world had ironed out his attitudes, and he knew where babies came from. As a result he was tolerant (to a point, at least) of such songs, though it is clear that he did not like them. His concern was what other people would think if they were exposed to them, and perhaps what they would think of him for being the cause of that exposure. We have already heard that he tried to protect the sensitive young bachelor Frederick Bussell from having to endure such material.

When dealing with bawdy songs, he sometimes left out lines or verses, particularly in the earlier days of his collecting project. Yet there are a number of songs that could be considered bawdy and for which he has given a full text in his manuscripts, though he never published them. We are not, of course, talking about the level of filth that might have been encountered at a boating supper (or, nowadays, in a rugby club). There

---

10 Sabine Baring-Gould, *Further Reminiscences*, p. 191.

were limits to his tolerance, but some of the songs in the manuscripts raise the eyebrows slightly, particularly when the bawdiness is associated with violence or other behaviour that would be regarded as even more unacceptable today.

A few examples will demonstrate the way in which Baring-Gould treated the songs he collected in both his manuscript record and his publications.

Strawberry Fair

A song that is frequently quoted when talking about Baring-Gould's bowdlerisation is that of 'Strawberry Fair'. The version that he published in *Songs of the West* was:

> As I was going to Strawberry fair
> Singing, singing, Buttercups and Daisies
> I met a maiden taking her ware
> Fol-de-dee
> Her eyes were blue and golden her hair
> As she went on to Strawberry Fair
> Ri-fol, ri-fol, tol-de-riddle-li-do
> Ri-fol, ri-fol, tol-d-riddle-dee. Etc.

Taught over several decades to schoolchildren through the medium of Baring-Gould and Sharp's *English Folk Songs for Schools*, this song was sufficiently well known in 1960 for a parody of it by Anthony Newley to get to number 3 in the Top Ten, and to remain in the charts for eleven weeks.

The song that Baring-Gould originally heard made use of the sexual metaphor of the key and lock, which was also employed in Riddle 44 of the *Exeter Book*, compiled sometime in the tenth century. In his note to the song in the early editions of *Songs of the West* Baring-Gould wrote, 'As this ballad is very undesirable, I have been constrained to re-write it. ... The words turn on a *double entendre* which is quite lost – and fortunately so – to half of the old fellows who sing the song.' Baring-Gould noted that the same metaphor was employed in the song 'Kit Hath Lost Her Key', printed in about 1561 and a parody of the earlier and more innocent 'Kitt Hath Lost Her Kye' [i.e. Cow]. It is important to realise that this does not mean that the song that Baring-Gould collected is more than 400 years old. A comparison of the words of the two songs shows that only the metaphor itself survives. 'Strawberry Fair' was written much later.

Baring-Gould observed that other singers knew 'Strawberry Fair', but he only recorded the version that was sung to him by John Masters of Bradstone, whom he visited in the company of Sheppard. We do not have a date for this visit but since the song appeared in the third volume of *Songs of the West* it would have been no later than the spring of 1890. The version that he included in his Fair Copy manuscript has been mentioned by a number of writers. The first verse of this is as follows:

> As I was a going to Strawberry Fair, Ritol &c.
> I met a fair maid of beauty rare, Tol di di
> I saw a fair maid go selling her ware
> As she went on to Strawberry Fair, Ritol &c.

Study of the manuscripts reveals, however, that this is a rewriting of what Baring-Gould and Sheppard actually heard. In Working Notebook 2 the following is given and described as the 'original version'.[11]

> As I was going to Strawberry fair (repeat)
> I saw a fair maid was a selling her ware
>
> O pretty fair maid come say what you sell (repeat)
> Come tell me truly my pretty damsel
>
> O I have a lock that is wanting a key (repeat)
> If you've one will fit, then come sir away
>
> Between them I reckon, when that they did meet (repeat)
> The blacksmith the key in the lock he did fit
>
> O I wish that my lock it had been but a gun (repeat)
> I'd shoot that same blacksmith – for I'm undone

What he heard from John Masters, it seems, had three-line verses and no 'Ri-tol &c.'. This demonstrates the difficulty of discovering what it was that Baring-Gould and his colleagues actually heard, particularly in the first few years of his project. Though Baring-Gould accepts the responsibility for the changes in his notes, it appears likely that Sheppard sometimes influenced him to adapt the words of a song to fit his treatment of the melody. In this case, unfortunately, we have no field notes to guide us towards the tune that was originally collected, and it must be assumed that these were among the papers burned by Sheppard's wife after his death.

---

11 Devon Heritage Centre, Baring-Gould Papers, 5203M, Box 23, Working Notebook 2, p. 165.

Jordan (Is a Hard Road to Travel)

In December 1889 Baring-Gould went to the village of Whitestone, a few miles to the west of Exeter, where he met a farm labourer, Thomas Dart, who sang four songs to him, one of which was a version of 'Jordan Is a Hard Road to Travel'.[12]

> I looked in the East, I looked in the West
> I saw John Bull a-coming according
> With four blind horses driving in the clouds
> To look at the other side of Jordan
> Pull off my old coat and roll up my sleeves
> Jordan is a hard road to travel I believe

Baring-Gould included a rewritten version of the song in *A Garland of Country Song*. The reason that he gave for this was that, in Dart's text: 'There is much variance in the words, a good deal of "gag" being inserted relative to various political events … We have recast the words, preserving its essential rollicking, defiant humour.[13] In his notes on the song he refers to a broadside ballad, though he only gives a reference to it, not the text. He goes on to suggest that the original was an African-American song or a nursery rhyme.

In 1971 Roy Palmer included 'Jordan' in his collection of songs, *Room for Company*, and Frankie Armstrong sang it on a recording associated with the book.[14] The sleeve notes for the record described it as 'curious and rare' and attributed it to Baring-Gould's collection. The song was picked up by a number of other singers in the English folk song revival and became very popular.

I asked Roy Palmer how he had arrived at his version of the song and he confirmed that he had found it in *A Garland of Country Song*. He told me that he liked the tune that Baring-Gould had taken down from Thomas Dart, but was not so keen on Baring-Gould's reworking of the text. At that time he did not have access to a manuscript copy of the song, since it was not recorded in the Plymouth 'Fair Copy'. He chose to use the first five verses of the broadside referred to by Baring-Gould.

---

12 Baring-Gould refers to Thomas Dark or Darke. Public documents, including the Calendar of Probate, identify him as Thomas Dart of Lower Kingwell, Whitestone. When he met the collector he was 66 years old.

13 Sabine Baring-Gould and Henry Fleetwood Sheppard, *A Garland of Country Song* (London: Methuen, 1894), p. 23.

14 Roy Palmer (ed.), *Room for Company* (Cambridge: Cambridge University Press, 1971), pp. 36–37 (Piano Edition). Various Artists, *Room for Company; Folk Songs Festive & Sociable*, Topic/Impact Records IMP-S 104 (LP, UK, 1972).

Further study established that Baring-Gould was correct in his suggestion that the song had arrived from America, since it came from the blackface minstrel movement that parodied the African-American style of singing. 'Jordan Is a Hard Road to Travel' was written by Daniel Decatur Emmett from Ohio, who was one of the originators of the Ethiopian minstrel genre and responsible for a number of other well-known songs including, 'Dixie', 'Old Dan Tucker and 'The Blue-Tailed Fly'. Emmett's version starts:

I jest arrived in town fo' to pass the time away,
And I settled all my bizness accordin'
But I found it so cold when I went up de street
Dat I wished I was on de oder side ob Jordan.
    So take off your coat, boys, and roll up your sleeves,
    For Jordan is a hard road to trabel,

The song was first published in America in 1853 and the original tune is completely different from that sung by Thomas Dart. Daniel Emmett and his 'Virginia Minstrels' had toured in England between May 1843 and September 1844 (before 'Jordan Is a Hard Road to Travel' was written). Though not a financial success for Emmett, this tour introduced the blackface minstrel genre to England and many of the songs by writers such as Emmett and Stephen Foster became popular as sheet music, and were taken up by English performers imitating the style of performance.[15] By 1889 these songs were in the repertoires of many rural singers.

Some of the English broadside versions of the song include a verse:

There was such a dreadful shindy and mutiny in India
Sir Colin Campbell's gone there according
And with our British boys, we will tame the black sepoys
And will drive them to the other side of Jordan

Since the Indian rebellion took place in 1857 it appears that it took little more than four years to appear in its modified form in the British broadside press and for its origin as a written song to be lost.

There is a little twist to the story. Another well-known recording of the song was that by Peter, Paul and Mary on their 1963 LP *Moving*, where the song acquired the title 'Old Coat'. You might expect that their version

---

15 Hans Nathan, *Dan Emmett and the Rise of Early Negro Minstrelsy* (Norman: University of Oklahoma Press, 1962), pp. 135–42.

would have been derived from one of the many American versions current in their country, but it was in fact a reworking using three verses (verses 1, 2, and 4) and the tune of the version Baring-Gould published in *A Garland of Country Song*. The song is credited on the LP and in sheet music as having been written by Stookey, Travers, Mezzetti and Sears and the copyright is assigned to Peter, Paul and Mary's publishing entity, Pepamar Music Inc. The shape of the song and the inclusion of about 70% of lines from Baring-Gould's published version, rather than those from Emmett or the broadsides, confirm that this was the source of the Peter, Paul and Mary song. The phrases 'Like some ragged owlet' and 'Silver spoons to some mouths, golden spoons to others' are particularly telling since they are purely Baring-Gould's invention.

The Drunken Maidens

The song of 'The Drunken Maidens' has been widely performed by folk revival singers since it was popularised by A. L. Lloyd, who recorded it in 1956.[16] Sabine Baring-Gould included it in *Songs of the West*, after hearing it sung by Edmund Fry, a thatcher from Lydford in 1890. Baring-Gould described Fry in *Old Country Life*:

> There is a Cornishman whose name I will give as Elias Keate – a pseudonym – a thatcher, a very fine, big-built, florid man, with big, sturdy sons. This man goes round to all sheep-shearings, harvest homes, fairs, etc., and sings. He has a round, rich voice, a splendid pair of bellows; but he has an infirmity, he is liable to become the worse for the liquor he freely imbibes, and to be quarrelsome over his cups. He belongs to a family of hereditary singers and drinkers. In his possession is a pewter spirit-bottle – a pint bottle that belonged to his great-grandfather in the latter part of the last century. That old fellow used to drink his pint of raw spirit every day; so did the grandfather of Elias; so did the father of Elias; so would Elias – if he had it; but so do not his sons, for they are teetotallers.[17]

Fry was still thatching in 1903 at the age of 68 when he fell from the roof of a cottage that he was working on and fractured his skull.

Baring-Gould heard only three verses of the song from Edmund Fry.

---

16 A. L. Lloyd, *English Drinking Songs*, Riverside Records, 1956, RLP 12–618. Reissued by Topic Records, 1998, TSCD496.

17 Sabine Baring-Gould, *Old Country Life*, pp. 276–77.

'Twas three drunken maidens, came from the Isle of Wight,
They drank from Monday morning, nor stayed till Saturday night.
When Saturday night did come, sirs, they would not then go out,
So the three drunken maidens they pushed the jug about.

It was woodcock and pheasant and partridge and hare,
It was all kinds of dainties, no scarcity was there.
It was four quarts of Malaga, they fairly drank it out.
So the three drunken maidens, they pushed the jug about.

Then down came the landlady, and asked for her pay.
O! a forty pound bill, sirs! the damsels drew that day.
It was ten pounds apiece, sirs! but yet they would not out
So the three drunken maidens, they pushed the jug about.

His research revealed that the earliest version of the song was that printed in *Charming Phyllis's Garland* in about 1710. When he copied this into his manuscripts he omitted verse 4 from this text as 'coarse' – quite correctly as it included a reference to male genitalia.[18] He also recorded another English version that had been published on a broadside by Croshaw of York in about 1750. This, like Fry's version, contained nothing that could be regarded as offensive, except female intoxication and the idea that young women would settle their bill by handing over items of outer clothing. In the Personal Copy entry he also identified a partial version recorded in Scotland by Kinloch and a Breton version, 'Merc'hed Caudan' in which the girls of Caudan obtain money for drinking by amours with monks, soldiers and tailors.[19]

For *Songs of the West* Baring-Gould took Fry's three verses and added a verse from the York broadside which introduces 'Bouncing Sally', to give a total of four drunken maidens. He also added the last verse from the same source but since this is slightly garbled he has rewritten it. His note to the song in early editions of his book is short and identifies Fry as his source and mentions the version in *Charming Phyllis's Garland* and the Breton version. In 1905 the note is expanded slightly to include mention of the York broadside and adds, 'The last verse has had to be modified'. Some later writers have taken this comment to mean that he had cut out something unsuitable and it may have been the prompt for A. L. Lloyd

18 The text of this version is included in the song study of 'The Drunken Maidens' on www.sbgsongs.org.
19 François-Marie Luzel, *Chansons populaires de la Basse Bretagne* (Paris: Emile Bouillon, 1890). Vol. 2, p. 142.

to substitute the word 'maidenheads' for Baring-Gould's 'characters', so giving the song a bit of spice. This change has become the new norm and is replicated in the many recordings of the song that have been produced in Lloyd's wake. It hardly seems fair that in this case Baring-Gould has been criticised for bowdlerising a song by leaving out something that was never there.

In his sleeve notes for the record Lloyd described the song as having 'spread from the far south of England to every boozing den where good singers gathered'. This is something of an overstatement since only a few other versions of the song have been found over the years. Francis Collinson heard a version in the 1940s from a Mrs Kitchen in Guildford, who sang about 'Three Irish Girls' who visited the Isle of Wight, but a version collected in Carlow, Ireland, in the late nineteenth century by John McCall is adamant that the maidens hailed from the Isle of Wight. Several Irish groups have recorded the song over the years and it is frequently described as an Irish drinking song, though their texts make it clear that it is A. L. Lloyd's version that is the source for their performances. It is in fact unlikely that the song would have achieved the popularity that it now has without Lloyd's intervention.

It was one of Baring-Gould's favourite songs and he would often sing it after dinner, while one of his daughters played the piano. As previously noted, Marianne Mason enjoyed hearing him sing this when she stayed at Lew House in 1892.

The Hostess' Daughter

If Baring-Gould could be considered innocent of violating the drunken maidens, he does not escape so lightly in the case of 'The Hostess' Daughter'. This example has been chosen because it is a good demonstration of how he changed a song for publication. As collected, 'The Hostess' Daughter' is unusual in that, unlike other songs where a man makes a young woman pregnant, the protagonist shows remorse for what he has done.

Baring-Gould heard it from John Masters in the company of Sheppard. He wrote up the words of the song in Working Notebook 2.

To London town when first I came,
Then no one knew my face or name,
And there five months I did remain,
At Smithfield at an inn.

The hostess had a daughter fair,
With raven locks of waving hair,
And eyes as coals that are aflame,
They were so glittering.

I kissed her ruddy lips, her brow.
Her face was mixed of blood and snow.
We loved each other well I trow.
We loved tenderly.

I sowed the seeds, the seeds of love,
I sowed them in a pretty grove.
And now away I must remove
From London Town must fly.

The seeds I sowed they grew apace.
I saw the tears run down her face.
I would not tarry in that place
To reap where I had sown.

And when the pretty babe is born,
'Twill lie on't mother bosom warm.
No father hold it on his arm
No father will it own.

He later used these words as the basis for rewriting the song and the page of the notebook is covered with pencilled verses, as he tried different ideas. This is something that can be seen frequently in his notebooks. In Working Notebook 3 he has written out Masters' version again, though with some minor changes. Alongside this is a second version of the song collected from James Parsons in which, after

'I kissed her lips, her chin and she
Was pleased well, & she pleased me

two lines are omitted as the couple's behaviour exceeds Baring-Gould's level of tolerance.

Then, in the Personal Copy manuscript, he included another rewrite of Masters' text, this time with eight-line verses and a tune. This version is included in Appendix B. But the song was too risqué for publication in *Songs of the West* and Baring-Gould reconstructed it, using some of the ideas that he had pencilled into Working Notebook 2. His note on the song said, 'The frankness and rudeness of the original words demanded modification before the song was fitted for the drawing room.' Happily we still have the Masters' original form of this rather wistful song in Baring-Gould's manuscripts.

It had been published on broadside, some versions being called 'London Town' and others 'The New Batchelor'. Other collectors also found it and Henry Hammond heard a version in Dorset by Ishmail Cornick of Burstock. Martin Carthy, one of the leading singers of the modern folk revival, recorded a reworked version of the song as 'I Sowed Some Seeds' using Cornick's version with additions from that collected from John Masters. His version uses some clever repetitions of the rhyme stranger-danger, which occurred in James Parsons' version, as well as the broadsides.

I Would That the Wars Were Well Over

Baring-Gould collected 'I Would That the Wars Were Well Over' from Samuel Fone in February 1893, the only instance of it having been collected from a singer in the field.

> 'Twas down in the meadows where violets are blue,
> I saw pretty Polly a-milking her cow.
> The song that she sung made all the grove ring,
> O my Billy's gone from me to serve George the King,
> And I would that the wars were well over,
> Crying, O that the wars were well over.
>
> I stepped up to her and made this reply,
> I said, Pretty Polly what makes you to cry?
> My Bill is gone from me, that I love so dear,
> And the 'Mericans will kill him, so great is my fear.
> And I would that the wars were well over,
> Crying, O that the wars were well over.
>
> I said, Pretty Polly can you fancy me?
> I'll make you as happy as happy can be.
> O no, pretty Sir, I can never love you.
> To my Billy alone I am constant and true,
> And I would that the wars were well over,
> Crying, O that the wars were well over.

It is Fone's version from which the song has entered the folk revival repertoire and is an instructive example of the way in which a song does so.

Baring-Gould chose to rewrite the song for *A Garland of Country Song*.

In the meadow one morning when pearly with dew
A fair pretty maid plucked violets blue
I heard her clear voice making all the woods ring
Oh my love is in Flanders to fight for the King
And I would that the wars were well over
O I would that the wars were all done

O violet, in-vil'ate, the oath may it prove
My lover swore to me, when in the green grove
In France and in Flanders are maidens as well
He sings of his Nell as to battle he goes
And I would that the wars were well over, etc.

I'll pluck the Red Robin so jaunty and gay
Yet I have my Robin – but he's far away
His jacket is red and his cheeks as the rose
He sings of his Nell as to battle he goes
And I would that the wars were well over, etc.

Ten thousands of blue bells now welcome the spring
Oh when will the church bells for victory ring?
And the soldiers return and all England rejoice
O then I'll be wed to the lad of my choice
And I would that the wars were well over, etc.

While this is quite a clever piece of writing, using the theme of different flowers and colours in each verse (Red Robin is a Devon name for Herb Robert) it seems unnecessary as Sam Fone's original text is more than adequate.

To my knowledge, the first to record the song for commercial release were Sam Richards and Tish Stubbs in 1977 and they then included it in their book, *The English Folksinger*.[20] They used Sam Fone's text from the Fair Copy manuscript, augmented from the eighteenth-century text, 'New Sea Song, I Wish The Wars Were All Over', which they found in George Carey's book, *A Sailor's Songbag*.[21] Carey's source was a manuscript written by the American Timothy Connor, who had been a prisoner of war in England.

---

20 Tish Stubbs sings the song on *Invitation to North America: the New World Seen through English Song*, Saydisc, 1977 – re-released in 2011 as Saydisc CDSDL280. The book reference is Sam Richards and Tish Stubbs, *The English Folksinger* (Glasgow and London: Collins, 1979), p. 92 (notes p. 119).
21 George Carey, *A Sailor's Songbag, An American Rebel in an English Prison*, 1777–1779 (Amherst: University of Massachusetts Press, 1976), pp. 74–75.

The primary source for most revival singers has not been Fone's original text, but the one re-written by Baring-Gould for his book *A Garland of Country Song*. The transmission of this text has been through the edited version that was published by Roy Palmer in *The Rambling Soldier*.[22] Roy Harris sang the song for the recording issued in association with that book. A number of other performers have since picked up the song from Palmer's book or the recording.

Another version of the song has been popularised by American singer, Tim Eriksen, who has used the seventeenth-century text published by Carey. Most recently a further new strand has been created by the Askew Sisters using Baring-Gould's revised text. It will be interesting to continue to follow the way in which the song changes in revival performances both here and in the United States.

(Fig 9.2) outlines the way in which the song has developed from the eighteenth-century street print version to some of the versions that are being sung in recent years.[23]

Polly Oliver's Ramble

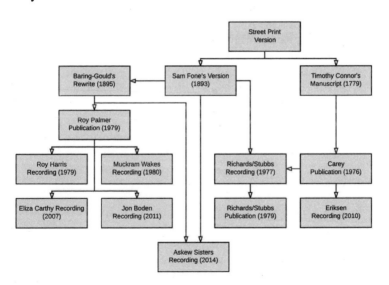

Fig. 9.2 – Relationship between versions of 'I would that the wars were well over'.

22 Roy Palmer, *The Rambling Soldier* (Harmondsworth: Penguin Books, 1979).
23 A full song study of 'I Would that the Wars Were Well Over' can be found on www.sbgsongs.org.

Several readers will have first discovered military transvestism as children in the pages of *The New National Songbook*, which was widely used in schools for many years.[24] The book contains the song 'Pretty Polly Oliver' which is about a young woman who dressed up as a soldier and headed off to London to follow her true love. Like many of the songs in the book it was rewritten by A. P. Graves, and in his version she discovered on arrival that her true love was sick and was ordered by the sergeant to nurse him back to health. When the doctor told him/her that he/she had looked after him as well as a wife would have done, she burst into tears, told the doctor her secret and, when her lover recovered, he '…took joyfully his pretty soldier nurse'.

Baring-Gould's manuscripts contain the song in its earlier guise as 'Polly Oliver's Rambles' as a result of a well-meant action by the Rector of Lifton, Rev. W. W. Martyn.

> There was an old man named Masters at Bradstone. The rector of Lifton heard that he was a song-man and that he was bed-ridden. Accordingly, to do me a kindness, he drove over and visited the apple-faced old fellow, who was in bed, but quite well enough to sing. The rector, the Rev. W. W. Martyn, was a specially modest-minded man. He could not note the music, but he could take down the words; so placing himself on a chair by the bed, he pulled out a copy-book, and pencil, and settled himself to write what Masters sang. The ballad selected by the sick man was 'Polly Oliver', and it relates how that Polly fell in love with a gay cavalier, and, so as to be with him, dressed herself as a page boy and accompanied her beloved. The denouement of the tale is what might have been anticipated. Mr. Martyn, later, gave me the manuscript. It was begun in a firm hand, but after a few verses, the writing became shaky, and the final stanzas were quite illegible.[25]

We do not have the Rev. Martyn's original mansuscript – which it would have been helpful to see. Baring-Gould wrote this anecdote shortly before his death, and it is clear that he has misremembered the circumstances in which the song was heard. In his Fair Copy manuscript, written a quarter of a century earlier, he says that the Rev. Martyn collected it from John Masters' bedridden wife. This is interesting, as we know that Grace Masters

---

24   Charles Villiers Stanford, *The National Song Book* (London: Boosey and Co., 1906).
25   Sabine Baring-Gould, *Further Reminiscences*, p. 191.

could read and had taught her husband songs from broadsides. However, about ten years earlier than that, in one of his working notebooks, Baring-Gould recorded that the Rev. Martyn had the song '…from the dictation of an old bed-ridden and half-crazy old woman at Lifton'. This is a tangle that will never be sorted out.

Rev. Martyn was not musical, so he did not give a tune for the song. Baring-Gould heard other versions over the years and one of the melodies he noted was that sung by William Kerswell at Two Bridges in January 1890. Baring-Gould looked at the history of the song when he decided to include it in his epic collection, *English Minstrelsie*. In his notes to the song in that book he followed the lead of William Chappell who reported that it had been published as 'The Maid's Resolution to Follow Her Love' in the second half of the eighteenth century, and that the existence of a parody, 'The Pretender's Army', published in 1717, shows that the song must have been earlier still. It was published on a number of broadsides in the nineteenth century and the song was collected by most of the Victorian and Edwardian collectors.

The version that Martyn noted from the old woman (whichever it was) told the same story as that in the nineteenth-century broadsides of 'Polly Oliver's Rambles', but had twelve verses while most of the extant broadsides have between seven and nine. The text appears genuine, and Baring-Gould has not rewritten it. We can be confidant that this is so because the entry in his working notebook referred to above includes a recast version, 'The Little Squire' that he created but never used. Here is the first verse.

One night as fair ~~Cecily~~ Polly was lying in bed,
A project right wondrous came into her head.
She'd go through the country, disguiséd to rove,
And so would she seek for her own dearest love.

Having tried the name Cecily in his first draft, Baring-Gould replaced it with the original Polly, possibly because he had already created another song using Cecily as the main character.

So what was it about the ballad with its 'not very delicate verses' that caused the Rev. Martyn's palpitations and led to A. P. Graves rewriting the song so completely for schoolchildren? In the ballad Martyn noted Polly has a 'wonderful fancy' to disguise herself in men's clothing and ride to London. She finds the inn where her lover is staying and orders herself a beer. When her captain comes in she goes to him and after a few drinks the

POLLY
OLIVER'S RAMBLES.

One night as polly Oliver lay musing in bed,
A comical fancy came iuto her head,
Neither father nor mother shall make me false prove
I'll list for a soldier and follow my love,

Early the next morning this fair maid arose,
She dre·t herself in a suit of men's clothes,
Coat' waistcoat, and breeches, ands word by her side
On her fathers black gelding like a dragoon did ride

She rid till she came to fair London town,
She dismounted her horse at the sign of ihe crown,
The first that came to her was a man from above,
The next that came down was Polly Olivers true love

Good evening. good evening kind captain said she
Here's a letter from your true love Polly Oliver said
        she,
He opened the letter and a guinea was found,
For you and your companions to drink her health
        round,

Supper being ended she held down her head,
And called for a candle to light her to bed,
The captain made this reply I have a bed at ease
You may lie with my countryman if you please,

To lie with a captain is a dang·rous thing,
I·m a new elisted soldier to ftght for my king,
To fight for our king by sea and by land,
Since you are my captain I'll be at your commad

Early next morning this fair maid arose,
Ano drest herself in her own suit of clothes,
And down stairs she came from her chamber above,
Saying, here is Polly Oliver your own true love.

He at first was surprised then laughed at the fun,
And then they where married and all things where
        done,
If I had laid with you the first night the fault it
        was mine,
I hope to pleas you better love, for now it is time

Jackson and Son, (late J. Russell,) Printers,
21, Moor-street, Birmir·····.

Fig. 9.3 – 'Polly Oliver's Rambles' Broadside, by Jackson, Birmingham (Courtesy of Steve Roud).

captain tells him/her that he/she looks very pretty with his/her smooth chin, curly locks and 'A voice as a flute warbles softly and thin'. Polly has by now had a couple of drinks herself and is feeling sleepy, but the landlady says there are no spare rooms. The captain offers to share his bed with him/her. She tells him that 'to lie with a captain's a dangerous thing', but then, in most broadside versions, the story loses itself in confusion as to whether she did or did not. The Martyn version is definite on the subject. She declines the captain's offer and says she will sleep by the fire with her saddle as her pillow. In the morning, in all versions, she dresses in her own clothes and goes downstairs to breakfast, to the surprise of her captain who duly marries his sweetheart

> So now she is married, and lives at her ease
> She goes where she wills, and comes when she please.
> She has left her old parents behind her to mourn,
> And give hundreds of thousands for their daughter's return

One is tempted to ask whether it was the mild eroticism or Polly's shocking independence that was the problem for the reverend gentlemen, but she was exactly the kind of young heroine whom Baring-Gould enjoyed portraying in his novels, so this is unlikely to have been his main concern.

When he published 'Polly Oliver' in volume 7 of *English Minstrelsie*, Baring-Gould quoted a significant part of the ballad as he had collected it in the notes to the song (with some minor alterations), though he omitted the three verses dealing with the sleeping arrangements, as they were 'not very delicate'. For the song itself he has capitulated to the whims of his co-editor, Henry Fleetwood Sheppard, who has provided new words to the song and arranged it to the tune given by William Chappell, which is that most familiar to us today. In Sheppard's creation Polly is married to a highwayman who is caught and 'hanged for his robberies on Old Tyburn tree'. Poor Polly pines for him 'like a linnet, bereft of her fate' and goes mad so that 'To Bedlam's dark corridors they bore her away'. There she lies, weaving posies from her straw bed and smiling vacantly as she sings a plaintive harmony to the music of her chains. What a sad contrast to the vigorous young heroine of the old ballad.

Pretty Dorothy and the Brown Girl

Baring-Gould sent several versions of the great traditional ballads from his collection to Professor Francis Child, as has already been described, and some of these were included in *English and Scottish Popular Ballads*. One of the ballads he sent was 'The Brown Girl' but in doing so he unwittingly created a source of confusion for later ballad scholars.

In an article that he wrote for *The Western Antiquary* in July 1889 Baring-Gould described a song he had heard from John Woodridge, 'Pretty Dorothy', which he initially thought was a version of 'Barbara Allen'.[26] James Parsons sang some verses of the same ballad and he recorded this in Working Notebook 2 where he called it 'Pretty Dorothy or Barbara' and gave parallel texts for both singers. The story is that of a young woman who passes over a young man for another but six months later is taken ill and calls him to her bedside to cure her. He refuses to forgive her and will not take her rings saying that he is planning to dance on her grave.[27]

Having observed that his younger singers were often literate enough to get their songs from broadsides, Baring-Gould initially assumed that Woodridge had acquired the song from a printed source, either directly or indirectly. He did not identify the broadside that might have been Woodridge's source, but Steve Gardham has recognised that the song is a variant of 'Sally and her True Love Billy' or 'The Sailor of Dover'.[28]

There was not a printed copy of this ballad among those in Baring-Gould's own collection of more than 4,000 items of street literature, or in those that were available to him in the British Museum Library. This illustrates one of the practical difficulties that Baring-Gould faced in identifying songs. There were thousands of songs and ballads to look through, and finding a particular song was like looking for a needle in a haystack. This does not, however, excuse the confusion he has caused for modern ballad researchers through the actions that followed.

He had seen the ballad of 'The Brown Girl' in *The Brown Girl's Garland* in the British Museum and recognised that the story ran along similar lines, although the gender of the protagonists was reversed.[29] The idea of the aggrieved lover dancing on the grave of the other is common to both ballads, though in the printed version it is the Brown Girl who does the dancing. He chose to rewrite Woodridge's ballad as 'The Brown Girl',

---

26 S. Baring-Gould, 'Ballads in the West', *The Western Antiquary*, 8 (1888–89), pp. v–x.

27 Devon Heritage Centre, Baring-Gould Papers, 5203 M, Box 23, Working Notebook 2, pp. 75–76.

28 Steve Gardham, '"The Brown Girl" (Child 295B): A Baring-Gould Concoction?' in *Folk Song: Tradition, Revival and Re-Creation*, ed. Ian Russell and David Atkinson (Aberdeen: Elphinstone Institute, University of Aberdeen, 2004), pp. 363–76.

29 *The Brown Girl's Garland, composed of four extraordinary new songs* (Newcastle upon Tyne?, 1765?) British Library, 11621.c.3. (10).

combining elements of 'Pretty Dorothy' with the 'Brown Girl' text from the chapbook garland. He never published this version himself, but sent Child a copy of the reworked song, along with the garland version of 'The Brown Girl' in 1890, as part of a selection of ballads copied out from his manuscripts.[30] Although he had written in the *Western Antiquary* article that 'in the mouths of younger singers the bachelor is converted into [a] sailor', he did not identify his text to Child as a reconstruction. Both Baring-Gould's reworking and the broadside version were included in *The English and Scottish Popular Ballads* as Child No. 295.

Gardham has taken the view that this was a deliberate deceit by Baring-Gould, intended to hoax the American professor. This is out of character for Baring-Gould who had invested considerable effort into his working relationship with Child and written of him with respect. It is more likely that this was simply carelessness on Baring-Gould's part in not making his assumptions clearer to Child. This is characteristic of their early correspondence and of Baring-Gould's records in those first years, before he began to document his work more carefully. He was somewhat overwhelmed by the quantity of material he was recovering and by his thoughts about it. As he re-copied 'The Brown Girl' in the same form into successive manuscripts he lost sight of what he had originally collected. Since he did not publish the song himself he never needed to review what he had done and so his reconstruction was, by default, allowed to stand.

Contemporary Songs

The singers whom Baring-Gould met enjoyed singing the old folk songs that he was seeking but they often sang popular songs of their time as well. If they performed to entertain other people they might well select a range of material, including more modern songs. The visit to South Zeal in 1894 described earlier demonstrates this.

> Evidently a grand concert was expected, and the old men rose to the occasion, and stood up in order and sang – but only modern songs – to suit the audience.[31]

---

30 The copy sent to Child is in the Baring-Gould Manuscripts, Houghton Library, MS Eng 863, pp. 73–77. This version was copied from Devon Heritage Centre, Baring-Gould Papers, 5203M, Box 17, Working Notebook 4, where this and some of the other ballads are marked 'Sent to Child'. In this notebook the rewritten ballad is identified as collected from John Woodridge but without the information about its origin as 'Pretty Dorothy or Barbara'.

31 Sabine Baring-Gould, *A Book of the West, Vol. 1 Devon* (London: Methuen, 1899), pp. 216–17.

Baring-Gould did not leave us a record of what was sung that night and in general did not record the modern songs, which he was quite frank about disliking. It has been said that he and the other folk song collectors of his time were misrepresenting the singers' repertoires by only recording what they thought of as 'folk songs'.[32] He never intended to record everything they sang and passages like that above make it clear that he was well aware that several of his folk singers performed other types of songs as well.

The inclusion of blackface minstrel songs has already been described and the example of 'Jordan' given. Baring-Gould was not always up to date with the latest musical hits and sometimes did not recognise a recently written song for what it was. An example of this is 'Little Maggie May', which Robert Hard sang on one of his early visits. Baring-Gould did not publish the song and there is a pencilled note in his manuscript: 'probably a minstrel song'. It was, in fact, a sentimental song written in 1869 by the Americans G. W. Moore and Charles Blamphin, with a chorus that appealed to the old country singers.

> My little witching Maggie
> Was singing all the day
> Oh how I love her, none can tell
> My own dear Maggie May

It has survived in the repertoire of several singers to the present day and is particularly popular in Cornwall because of its association with popular performers such as Charlie Bate and Brenda Wootton. Their source was Ralph Dunstan's *Cornish Dialect and Folk Songs*, which included a version reconstructed from a single verse which had been sent to him.[33]

Another example of a contemporary song making its way into the collection is the hymn-like 'Sailors at Sea'. Baring-Gould heard this song in October 1892 at Horndon on the edge of Dartmoor from a farmer, J. Rich, whom it has not yet proved possible to identify further. He was said to have learnt the song from another Horndon man, J. Friend, in 1867. This song, which I have included in the Appendix, asks the hearer to think of the plight of the sailors who took to sea in the 'coffin ships' operated by unscrupulous merchants. These were old, poorly maintained and frequently overloaded. Their owners cared little whether they reached port or not, as the ships and their cargoes were well insured.

---

32 See, for example, Dave Harker, *Fakesong: The manufacture of British 'folksong' 1700 to the present day* (Milton Keynes: Open University Press, 1985).

33 Ralph Dunstan, *Cornish Dialect and Folk Songs* (London: Ascherberg, Hopwood and Crew, 1932), p. 43.

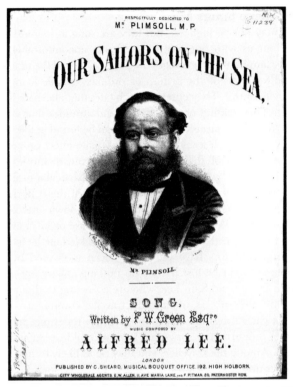

Fig. 9.4 – 'Our Sailors on the Sea' (1874) Sheet music cover.

The song is, properly, 'Our Sailors on the Sea', written in 1873 by F. W. Green with music by Alfred Lee in support of the work of Samuel Plimsoll who was at that time engaged in a campaign to improve the safety of British shipping. The original sheet music carries a portrait of Plimsoll, but the song appeared on a number of broadsides (without acknowledgement to the writer or composer). The only other collector to find it was Alfred Williams, though he failed to record where he heard it and from whom. This song is a curious survival, recalling Plimsoll's great political struggle. He was ultimately successful, though at great personal cost, and ships were made to carry the loading marks that still bear his name and which have saved many lives. Baring-Gould did not spot the connection of the song, and certainly did not spot that the date when Farmer Rich claimed to have learnt it was some years before the song was written. This is one of the few overtly political songs that Baring-Gould heard from his singers.

Why Do These Songs Matter?

Folk songs may not be high art, but they are song at its most accessible. They confront us with our past, occasionally uncomfortably, but often with an easy familiarity that bridges the years. They tell the timeless stories of love and loss, and of the actions of ordinary people living lives they endure rather control. They entertain with tales that alternate horror with amusement. They remind us of activities and attitudes that we could no longer condone. Most facets of human life can be found in folk song. They can be very direct, with a visceral and passionate effect on an audience. This is often a result of their nostalgic appeal and memories of friends and family prompted by a song associated with a particular individual who sang it or whose favourite it was. A good example of this is Baring-Gould's anecdote, given earlier, about Sam Fone breaking down after singing 'I'm a Man That's Done Wrong to My Parents' because of his memories of a man he had worked with as a navvy and the troubled life he had led.

Folk song collectors have universally been motivated by the sense that something might be lost if they do nothing. There are still people, like Gwilym Davies and Sam Lee, who are collecting traditional songs in England with some success, often in the traveller community. Versions of some of the early songs are still found, but the repertoire has changed, with a higher proportion of songs that Baring-Gould would have regarded as 'modern'. Among the travellers you may be as likely to hear American country songs nowadays, but the old songs can still be found.

The men and women who populated the 'folk scene' at the end of the twentieth century are now being followed by a new generation of young performers who are making English traditional songs their own. The enduring value of Baring-Gould's song collection for singers of all ages is to provide material, context and inspiration. Not to slavishly imitate what the singers of the past did, but to perform it in a way that communicates something that the new performer values to their audience. There is sometimes a worry that moving away from the original performance is somehow wrong. But that original singer would have taken the song and shaped it in his or her own way, even if that shaping was less dramatic than adding electric instruments. Thanks to the work of Baring-Gould and his colleagues and those who have worked to secure his collection for future generations, the unique songs that he recovered will remain available in his manuscripts for singers of the present and those who come after them to find inspiration and a springboard for their own creative artistry.

10: From the Mouths of the People

> *These old minstrels all are in the same tale, when asked to sing, 'Lord, your honour, I haven't a sung these thirty year. Volks now don't care to hear my songs. Most on 'em be gone right out o' my head'. Yet a good many come back; and I find that when I read over the first verse or two of a series of ballads in any collection, that the majority are either known to them, or suggest to them another, or a variant.*[1]

Songs of the West – Methuen – Publication History – Critical Reception – A Garland of Country Song – A Book of Nursery Songs and Rhymes – English Minstrelsie – English Folk Songs for Schools – Baring-Gould on Songs

From the very beginning of his song collecting project, Baring-Gould was determined to share the outcome of his collecting with the wider public and to promote traditional English song, particularly that of Devon and Cornwall. As an experienced and well-connected writer, publication in print was an obvious route, and Baring-Gould began almost immediately to write the articles that paved the way for the publication of his first book of folk songs, *Songs of the West*. The second strand of his campaign was less predictable. In 1890 he undertook a series of lectures and concerts

Fig. 10.1 – Songs of the West (Author's photo).

---

1   Sabine Baring-Gould, *Old Country Life*, p. 262.

based on his work. The concerts became more elaborate, with costumes and tableaux, until they became a professional, franchised theatrical production, touring throughout Britain and even to the United States. This activity will be described in the next chapter, but it is important to realise that the one was intimately linked to the other, and that the function of both was to make the general public, and the book-buying public in particular, aware of and interested in traditional English song.

Songs of the West

Baring-Gould first announced his intention to produce a book containing the songs that he had collected in a letter to the *Western Morning News* dated 7 December 1888, just eleven weeks after he made his first appeal to the readers of the same newspaper for help in recovering old songs. He wrote:

> Already I have been able to collect at four points about Dartmoor as many as ninety songs and ballads, with their traditional airs. [...] The Rev H. Fleetwood Sheppard, an accomplished musician, and I intend, if we get sufficient support in the West, to issue these West of England – Devon and Cornwall – songs, music and words, at as low a price as possible, so as to put them within the reach of the many, in the hopes of re-awakening in the men of the West a love and reverence for their own proper songs.

The same issue of the *Western Morning News* carried an advertisement for the proposed book.

Proposed To Be Published By Subscription
Songs Of The West

TRADITIONAL BALLADS AND SONGS, with their Proper Melodies, collected from the mouths of the people in Devon and Cornwall, and arranged for the voice and piano by the Rev. S. Baring-Gould and Rev. H. Fleetwood Sheppard.

To be issued in three parts at 2s. 6d. each, at intervals. Subscribers names for the complete issue, which will contain at least 75 songs, thankfully received by
Rev. S. BARING-GOULD, Lew Trenchard, N. Devon.

At this stage, it was a private, crowd-funded venture, undertaken for Baring-Gould by the London-based music publishers, Patey and Willis. They were not one of Baring-Gould's regular publishers and they were probably chosen because of their expertise in engraving and publishing music at a time when the technology was in the hands of relatively few companies. Patey and Willis were to handle sales to the book trade and to private individuals who did not subscribe.[2] They never advertised the book themselves and it was not listed in their catalogue, though a review of the first part in the *Exeter and Plymouth Gazette* on 16 February 1889 identified them as the publisher. It is remarkable that the book moved so rapidly from the advertisement in early December to being in a reviewer's hands less than six weeks later.

As the advertisement above shows, the sales by subscription were to be managed personally by Baring-Gould from his home at Lew Trenchard. In one of his song notebooks there is a dated list of subscribers for Part I.[3] The payments from the first two subscribers (Dr T. G. Vawdrey of Plymouth and Miss C. Borlase of Penzance) are listed as having been received by Baring-Gould on 7 December, the same day as the advertisement appeared. One of the most generous subscribers was Daniel Radford, whose spark originally ignited Baring-Gould's collecting project, and who signed up for twenty copies.

Baring-Gould did not advertise the book after December 1889, but relied on the 'public relations' effect of his reputation to generate a number of newspaper reports on the venture. Like any modern author or singer with a book or CD to sell, Baring-Gould was intent on making the most of any opportunity to promote his book, and the fact that he was taking responsibility for the sales gave him a strong incentive to do so. Responding to the vote of thanks after the lecture that he delivered in Tavistock on 24 January 1889 he urged the audience to subscribe to the series of three volumes of *Songs of the West*. If they signed up at the meeting, they would be entitled to buy them at the special price of two shillings and sixpence for each part, but that the price after publication would be three shillings. A modern marketing specialist would applaud his tactic of emphasising the opportunity that might be missed. At later concerts there would be a table at the back of the hall with copies of the book for sale. There is no evidence that his sales technique evolved as far as book signing, though he received a number of requests for signed photographs.

---

2   One such was Lucy Broadwood who noted in her diary that she had sent her payment to Patey and Willis on 11 May 1891. Surrey History Centre, Lucy Broadwood Papers, Diary, 6782/613, 11 May 1891. 'Sent Patey and Willis 5/-, w. to Mr Baring-Gould'.

3   Devon Heritage Centre, Baring-Gould Papers, 5203M, Box 23, Working Notebook 2, pp. 174–77.

This was by no means a certain venture. On 11 December 1888 Baring-Gould wrote to one of the subscribers, Mrs Gillard of South Brent, and told her that he would prefer to take subscriptions for each part separately since:

> If the Songs of the West be not taken up cordially so as to pay cost of production we shall not issue the whole. Very often subscriptions fall off after a first or second number. I can hardly tell yet.[4]

The list in his notebook accounts for subscriptions for 179 copies of the first part. No list of subscribers has yet been discovered for the later volumes, but we can assume that the venture was 'taken up cordially' for two reasons.

Firstly, the project was not only completed, but grew in scope, from the three volumes originally planned to four. A notice was sent to subscribers in July 1889, which read:

Songs Of The West

> The amount of original old Ballads and Songs, with their melodies, that are being collected is so great, and the quality so good, that the Editors are desirous of extending their issue to four numbers instead of three. They will be glad to hear from the Subscribers if they are content to take four instead of three numbers.

> S. Baring-Gould
> Lew Trenchard
> N. Devon
> July 23, 1889[5]

The second reason is that Methuen & Co. took over the project and carried it forward.

Methuen
Methuen & Co. was a new publisher for Baring-Gould, but was also a very new company. Algernon Methuen Marshall Stedman (1856–1924) had been

---

4 Plymouth, West Devon Record Office, Baring-Gould Papers, Letter of Sabine Baring-Gould to Mrs Gillard, Date illegible but probably December 1888, Ref 470/4.
5 Cyril Tawney gave me a copy of this slip when I visited him in Leeds in February 1999. It was loose in his own copy of *Songs of the West*.

a teacher and had written school textbooks using the pseudonym of A.M.S. Methuen.[6] He launched his own publishing company, 'Methuen & Co., ...', in June 1889 and Baring-Gould was the second author Stedman signed up. The publisher had considerable success with their first book, Edna Lyall's novel, *Derrick Vaughan, Novelist*, which went through four editions in a week. The business flourished, due in large part to Stedman's astute choice of authors. The novelist Marie Corelli became a great asset to the firm, and Stedman's decision to publish Kipling's poetry, notably *Barrack Room Ballads*, was very profitable. Baring-Gould contributed to their success with both his fiction, the volume of which was increased under Stedman's influence, and with the antiquarian compilations and travelogues that he preferred writing.

Before returning to *Songs of the West*, another book by Baring-Gould that was published in 1890, *Old Country Life*, should be mentioned.[7] This was a *bravura* production for the fledgling company since it demonstrated Methuen & Co.'s commitment to producing books to a very high standard. They employed several illustrators, including the then newly qualified Francis Bedford, later to be famous as the first illustrator of J. M. Barrie's *Peter Pan and Wendy*. The cover design, gold blocked on blue cloth over bevel-edged boards, is based on the frieze above the fireplace in the hall at Lew House. Methuen also produced a limited edition of 125 copies of the book in a larger format (though using the same printing plates), of which 100 were made available for sale in England.

There is much of interest in the book, which is one of Baring-Gould's best. Two of the chapters, 'The Village Musician' and 'The Village Bard', are relevant, the latter particularly so since Baring-Gould has written some pen portraits of the singers he had met at that time, including James Parsons, James Olver, Roger Luxton, Jonas Coaker, Robert Hard (though he is misnamed as Richard) and John Helmore. John Woodridge was not named, but is described as a 'little blacksmith'. Edmund Fry was assigned the pseudonym Elias Keate, perhaps because the description given of him included his drinking habits. This chapter was written at the time that Baring-Gould was forming his thoughts on traditional song and its origins and it predates the notes he wrote a year later for inclusion with the fourth part of *Songs of the West*. It contains a number of the ideas that were to feature in his theories about folk song in coming years.

In the issue of 2 November 1889 *The Athenaeum* carried 'Messrs. Methuen's List' which advertised:

---

6   He later changed his name to Algernon Marshall Stedman Methuen.
7   Sabine Baring-Gould, *Old Country Life* (London: Methuen, 1890).

SONGS OF THE WEST: Traditional Ballads and Songs of the
West of England (With their traditional melodies). Collected by
S. Baring Gould, M. A., and H. Fleetwood Sheppard, M. A.,
Arranged for Voice or Piano. In 4 parts (containing 25 songs in
each). 3s each. (*Parts I and II now ready*).

This was the first indication of Methuen having taken on the publication of
Songs of the West. No correspondence between Methuen and Baring-Gould
about the agreements that led to this has been discovered as yet, but some
basic details can be worked out. It appears that managing the sales of the
book was proving an inconvenience to Baring-Gould, but that Methuen
had some reservations about entering a branch of publishing in which
they had no experience and which brought new technical challenges. The
sales figures for the first two parts, however, were good enough to persuade
Stedman that it was worth the risk.

Baring-Gould had expected that Methuen would take all responsibility for
the book and would purchase the printing plates for it from Patey and Willis,
but Stedman decided that it would be a better strategy to enter a partnership
with them and retain their expertise rather than to take full ownership. As a
result, after November 1889 both names appeared as publishers on the title
page of the book and would continue to do so (though not consistently) until
1905, though Methuen's name appeared in larger letters.

Letters from Henry Fleetwood Sheppard to Baring-Gould suggest that
Methuen's working relationship with Patey and Willis did not always go
as well as they had hoped. Sheppard wrote, 'As to Methuen and money
matters they will settle themselves in time, so long as they mean to do it &
have stirred up those P & Ws with a long pole.'[8] In a letter a month later he
thanked Baring-Gould for a cheque for £6 11s and then went on to suggest
that people in business could not be trusted, though he supposed that
'business has a morality of its own, according to which people in business
act & are conscientious'. But there was some good news:

Up to date, one has about recouped one's original outlay, so that
whatever comes after may be reckoned as profit. I rather hoped
that P&W's accounts with us, sale of plates &c. wd be transferred to
Methuen & Co. & that they wd have settled all: but it seems we are
still in the hands of P&W, who, as you say, are maddening people.[9]

---

8 Devon Heritage Centre, Baring-Gould Papers, 5203M, Box 36, Letter of H.
Fleetwood Sheppard to S. Baring-Gould, 7 July 1890.
9 Devon Heritage Centre, Baring-Gould Papers, 5203M, Box 36, Letter of H.
Fleetwood Sheppard to S. Baring-Gould, 11 August 1890.

Publication History

The publication history of *Songs of the West* is a Gordian Knot that several bibliographers have tugged at over the years and I do not propose to go too far into its complexities here. It is enough to say that there are still a number of unanswered questions about the different editions and printings issued by Methuen and the formats in which they were issued. I have examined many different examples of the first version of *Songs of the West*, both those issued in parts and printed as a single volume. The difficulties of coming to definite conclusions are founded in Methuen's inconsistency in printing dates, and assigning edition numbers. I have in my collection, for example, a copy of Part 1 that has '5th Edition' on the cover and '4th Edition' on the title page.

Throughout this account the book has been referred to as *Songs of the West*. This is the title that Baring-Gould himself invariably used and which appeared on the boards and spines of each of the one-volume publications. The title page of the early published versions reads *Songs and Ballads of the West. A Collection made from the Mouths of the People*. It was never advertised under this title. The first advertisement gave, as shown above, *Songs of The West. Traditional Ballads And Songs, with their Proper Melodies*. This was changed when Methuen took over the publication to *Songs of The West. Traditional Ballads And Songs, with their Traditional Melodies*. With the 1905 revision, the title page was changed to *Songs of the West. Folk Songs of Devon and Cornwall collected from the Mouths of the People*.[10]

Some changes were made in the early years of publication, including the removal of two songs, 'Thomasine Enys' and 'On the Settle', in which Baring-Gould and Sheppard had replaced the text they had collected with their own words. The majority of the changes, though, were made to the prefaces and the notes on the songs. The 1889 edition of Part 1, for example, had a short preface and notes on the 25 songs it contained. When Part 4 was issued it had a new, revised preface and notes on all of the songs in the four parts which, for those who chose to bind the four parts together, could replace that in Part 1.[11] Purchasers of later editions of Part 1 found a new, shortened preface. With the issue of the single volume edition in 1891 the book became essentially stable until the major revision that took place in 1905 when Cecil Sharp replaced Sheppard as the musical editor. Some

---

10 Bibliographers will, rightly, seek to present the title in its proper form when appropriate. I hope that readers will welcome the simplification I have chosen.

11 The different ways in which purchasers chose to bind the four volumes has proved another source of confusion for researchers trying to understand the publishing history of *Songs of the West* – including the writer.

bibliographers refer to a '3rd edition' of the single volume version of *Songs of the West* being issued in 1895. I have a copy that bears this date on the title page but no edition number. It appears to be only a reprint with no obvious changes to the content.

Among Baring-Gould's papers are copies of a few of the later royalty statements sent to him by Methuen. These show that 77 copies of the complete version were sold in 1896, as well as 392 separate parts. By 1901 the annual sales had dropped to 57 complete copies and 191 parts. Reducing the price of the complete edition from fifteen to ten shillings did not produce the increased sales that had been hoped for. In March 1903 Methuen suggested that they should produce a new, cheaper edition of the book selling at 10s 6d. Baring-Gould's royalty would be reduced from 2s to 1s 6d. Discussion on this new edition was protracted but, in June 1905 an agreement was signed for Methuen to publish a revised edition using new technologies and in a quarter-cloth binding. This would be sold for five shillings with a royalty of nine pence per copy, which was to be shared with Sharp. The two men had actually started work on the book some months earlier and it was well advanced before the agreement was signed. This edition was launched in October 1905 and Baring-Gould's accounts for the year-end show that it had already sold 385 copies from the print run of 2,000. The 1905 version continued to sell well and was reprinted several times.

Critical Reception

The reception for *Songs of the West* was generally good, though some reviewers had reservations. The *London Daily News* described it as a 'unique and carefully got up series of traditional ballads and songs', and spoke of 'the elaborately prepared preface, which is not only entertaining, but shows the large amount of pains and labour which has been expended upon it'.[12] The review continued to say of the songs, 'Some few are extremely coarse' giving as an example, 'The Drunken Maidens'. This shows that despite some people having criticised Baring-Gould's editing others thought that he had not gone far enough. *The Lute* concluded a balanced review by remarking that 'in every respect the collection of Songs and Ballads of the West is worthy of the attention and patronage of all lovers of music'.[13]

The most frequent cause of criticism was Sheppard's arrangements, which were seen as florid and inappropriate as well

12 'Music of the Day', *London Daily News*, 11 June 1891, p. 6.
13 Review, *The Lute*, 1 April 1892, p. 200.

as being too difficult for most amateur pianists to play. A minority of reviewers suggested that Baring-Gould's editing was heavy-handed. In a review of the book published in June 1891, for example, the critic of *The Anti-Jacobin* wrote

> It is strange that Mr Baring-Gould should have taken so much trouble to collect the traditional ballads and songs of the West of England and should then have treated his material in so slovenly and uncritical a manner. [...] Had the collection been properly edited it would have been an addition of real value to what we know of English folk songs. As it is the melodies seem to have been treated with deference, and not edited, like the words out of all recognition. For so much we cannot but be grateful. And when Mr Baring-Gould tells us that the words have been altered, 'to avoid grossness or banalities', he is not to be blamed as far as the grossness is concerned. But we are not so ready to accept the re-writing of a ballad because Mr Baring-Gould has decided it is banal. Here he is in danger of going beyond the duty of an editor. He himself, however, has no scruples of conscience and does not even pay so much homage to editorial virtue as to conceal his shortcomings and misdemeanours. [...] Every page of the notes contains statements like these: 'I have ventured to add the last verse;' 'There were 10 verses in the original: I have cut them down to 7,' 'The words were of no merit.' We cannot feel at all sure that this is as it should be and it happens too, that Mr Baring-Gould is not a clever versifier.[14]

This criticism is valid, though the complaint is, perhaps, overstated. Baring-Gould answered it, to a degree, when he inserted the following into the Introduction to the 1905 edition:

> In giving these songs to the public, we have been scrupulous to publish the airs precisely as noted down, choosing among the variants those which commended themselves to us as the soundest. But we have not been so careful with regard to the words. ... Accordingly we have rewritten the songs wherever it was not possible to present them in their original form.

---

14 'West-Country Songs and Ballads', *The Anti-Jacobin Review and Magazine*, 27 June 1891, p. 529.

He provided an alphabetical index in the fourth part of *Songs of the West* in which he listed the songs with an indication of whether they had the original words, had been altered, or had new words written for them. Out of the 120 songs 71 were claimed to have the original words as collected. Further examination shows that this is not strictly true. Comparison of the published texts with the manuscript versions shows that many others have been rewritten to some degree. The majority of these changes are trivial and are the result of Baring-Gould substituting a word or two in the song, often quite appropriately. Songs were rewritten because they were 'unsuitable' or 'coarse' less often than might be expected but, as the reviewer in *The Anti-Jacobin* points out, some of the songs have been rewritten for no very good reason. While Frank Kidson's comment that 'I cannot in the least believe that a single song is there placed as it was sung to Baring Gould' is an exaggeration, a large number of the songs have undergone some degree of alteration. Yet Baring-Gould clearly believed that what he had done captured the spirit of the original.

Looking back with the knowledge of folk song that we now have and with the expectations that have arisen as a result, there is much in the book that can be criticised. While Baring-Gould's Preface is certainly one of the earliest attempts to explain the origins of folk song to the general public, some of what he wrote is now known to be fanciful and inaccurate. His notes include valuable information about the singers as well as their songs, but he could have told us more. The songs give us a rare picture of what ordinary country people were singing at the end of the nineteenth century, although Baring-Gould's selection and editing processes distort that picture somewhat. Sheppard must shoulder a large share of the blame for the book's failings, since he was solely responsible for the alterations made to some of the melodies. What is less clear is the extent to which it was he, rather than Baring-Gould, who altered the words in the published songs. That Sheppard was responsible for alterations to song texts is shown in some of Baring-Gould's notes to the songs in *Songs of the West* and the later publications.[15] Sheppard's concise essay on the music of the songs, however, is perceptive and his recognition of the significance of the modes was an important contribution to thinking about folk song.

A Garland of Country Song (1895)

In a letter to Lucy Broadwood, dated 29 January 1893, Baring-Gould wrote, 'Do you know that he [Sheppard] and I are meditating a book of

---

15 Examples of Sheppard's being on record as having altered words to songs in *Songs of the West* include 'On a May Morning Early' (No. 73), The Grey Mare' (No. 51) and 'The Barley Rakings' (No. 85).

folk songs of the English country people? We have so many that we did not use because we knew they were not special to the West'.[16] This is the first reference to the project that would result in *A Garland of Country Song* two years later.[17] Six months on, in another letter to Broadwood, he listed the songs that were planned to appear in two volumes of 25 songs each.[18] In the event, the book was issued as a single volume of fifty songs.

An advertisement for 'Messrs Methuen's New Books' in *The Athenaeum* of 6 November 1894 reports that *A Garland of Country Song* is 'nearly ready':

> In collecting West of England airs for 'Songs of the West,' the editors came across a number of songs and airs of considerable merit, which were known throughout England and could not justly be regarded as belonging to Devon and Cornwall. Some fifty of these are now given to the world.

The equivalent list in *The Athenaeum*'s issue of 24 November reports that the book '… is now available', and this is confirmed by the appearance of a review in the *Saturday Review* of 22 December 1894. I have listed these dates because of the confusion created by Baring-Gould and his publishers, where the Introduction is dated 20 April 1894 and the publication date on the title page is given as 1895. Many bibliographers have adopted the latter date, though the British Library hedges its bets by adding '[1894]' after the publisher's declared date. Only one edition of *A Garland of Country Song* was published, suggesting that the book was not as successful as *Songs of the West*. This is borne out by the royalty accounts sent to Baring-Gould by Methuen which show that just 34 copies were sold in the second half of 1895 and 23 in the whole of the following year. That the public appetite for folk song was already waning is suggested by the fact that no significant English song collections were published for a decade.[19]

---

16 VWML, Lucy Broadwood Manuscripts, Letter of Sabine Baring-Gould to Lucy Broadwood, 29 January 1893, LEB/4/6.

17 Sabine Baring-Gould, *A Garland of Country Song*, London: Methuen, 1894.

18 VWML, Lucy Broadwood Manuscripts, Letter of Sabine Baring-Gould to Lucy Broadwood, July 1893, LEB/4/26. This letter is undated, but the reference to the death of Broadwood's father places it in mid to late July 1893.

19 The Folk Song Society was formed in 1898 and published some songs in its journal, but the next published collection of English songs was that by Geoffry Hill, *Wiltshire Folk Songs and Carols* (Bournemouth: W. Mate, 1904), followed shortly by the first volume of Cecil Sharp's *Folk Songs From Somerset* in December 1904.

Sheppard composed all of the settings for the songs and also contributed occasional notes on them. Two songs in the book were recalled by him from his youth. On 'High Germany', which he had heard in Watford 'some fifty years ago', he comments, 'it struck me then, and still strikes me as an admirable specimen of the true folk song of its date, as regards both words and music'. He recalled 'All Around My Hat' from a decade earlier still and he describes it, rather condescendingly, as 'more than popular, it was the delight – the ecstasy of the London street-boy'. He reports that an old lady upbraided him for having altered the character of the song saying, 'in my childhood it was a low song to a vulgar tune, and you have treated it as a refined and delicate melody'.

Baring-Gould, in his Introduction, lamented that foreign songs were so well received by the English public and Anglicised before being used in English schools – a worry that he would address in Cecil Sharp's company a decade later. The Introduction includes some interesting descriptions of collecting from singers whom he met after publishing *Songs of the West*, such as the two Samuels – Gilbert and Fone – as well as saying more about old favourites like Sally Satterley, James Parsons and John Woodridge. In one respect he reported that he had changed his mind about the origin of folk songs, as he had come to accept that many of them were genuine products of 'the folk muse'. Though they may have started as songs or ballads composed in the city, the words had mutated to suit the culture of the countryside and they had been given tunes that were created by ordinary people, to their own local taste.

Unfortunately we have the same problems with his editing in *A Garland of Country Song* as with *Songs of the West*. He has changed some of the songs on the ground of indecency. He could also be forgiven for having reduced the number of verses in some ballads, since his audience may not have been inclined to sing them all. Where he is less justified is in the arbitrary changes that he makes to the words of songs, sometimes altering a seemingly acceptable set of lyrics for no good reason.

Baring-Gould and Sheppard aimed to provide a book of songs that would be listened to and sung by the public in preference to 'the sawny, sentimental stuff that is poured forth in floods today from the music printers'. Baring-Gould hoped that there would be a revolution in the concert halls and that the 'idealess, characterless stuff, whose only merit is in a certain skilfulness of accompaniment writing' would be swept away. 'We have imitated Italian, German, and French masters long enough. A revolt against musical vacuity is inevitable. Then the demand will come – sing us some of the songs of our own dear English Zion!'

A Book of Nursery Songs and Rhymes

The October 1894 issue of *The Bookman* reported that two new books by Baring-Gould were scheduled to be published in the coming months: *A Book of Nursery Rhymes* and *A Book of Fairy Tales*. Some newspapers picked up the report, but while the book of tales was published in time for Christmas, the plan to launch the nursery rhymes book was quietly dropped, and the book was finally issued the following year. No reason has been discovered for the delay but looking at the number of publications Baring-Gould was working on during 1894, one might conclude that he had taken on rather too much.[20] It is also possible that the fact that he had written a lengthy preface for another publisher's edition of the Grimm brothers' fairy tales, which was launched at the same time as his own book, might not have gone down well with Methuen, who had invested heavily in artwork and design for Baring-Gould's fairy tale book.[21]

Both of these books were high quality publications with 'Arts and Crafts' designs from the staff and students of the Birmingham School of Art. In the case of *A Book of Nursery Songs and Rhymes* the illustrations were by students of the school, under the supervision of Arthur Gaskin.

One of the students was Georgie Cave France, who had married Arthur Gaskin in March 1894. She provided the six different designs for the page borders surrounding the text and illustrations. She also made the drawing

Fig. 10.2 – Title page of A Book of Nursery Songs and Rhymes (Author's photo).

20 Baring-Gould had 66 new items published in 1894–95.
21 Sabine Baring-Gould, 'Preface' to [Anon], *Fairy Tales from Grimm* (London: Wells, Gardner, Darton and Co., 1894).

of 'Little Tom Tucker'. The book was printed and bound by the highly regarded specialist printers T. and A. Constable of Edinburgh (Printers to Her Majesty). It was printed on a good quality paper with gold edging to the top and rough-cut edges side and bottom, using a 'heavy type' designed to appeal to the book's young readers. This was a gift book destined for the Christmas market and the standard edition was priced at six shillings – roughly £30 at today's prices. There was also a limited edition of fifty copies on Japanese Vellum, costing thirty shillings – about £150 today.

The book is divided into three parts, the first being 77 'nursery songs'. Many of these are songs that Baring-Gould himself collected, and which can be found in his manuscripts. They include some of the nonsense songs like 'A Lying Tale', 'Tommy-a-Lynn' and 'Three Jovial Welshmen', as well as old favourites like 'The Fox' and 'The Frog He Would a Wooing Go'. He includes some well-known folk songs like 'Green Broom' as well as ballads like 'The Lover's Tasks', and 'The Prickly Bush'. He also felt it safe to include the blood libel ballad 'Little Sir William' – not a choice that an editor of a children's collection would make nowadays. The texts he has given are on the whole faithful to those in his manuscripts. He has collated verses from different versions in a few cases, filled out missing passages in others. While there are a few word changes these are not as frequent or arbitrary as those in the adult books.

The second section contains ten 'game rhymes' and the third 91 'nursery jingles'. He provides notes about most of the songs, though he does not include music. Many of them are taken from Baring-Gould's own collection but he also draws on the publications of Marianne Mason, James Orchard Halliwell, Laurie and Marbry, and others. Occasionally he makes a stab at the origins of a song, pointing out, for instance, that 'Sing a Song of Sixpence' was quoted in Beaumont and Fletcher's play *Bonduca* in 1647, indicating an earlier origin. For the rhyme 'Lucy Locket' he describes Lucy Locket and Kitty Fisher as 'well known personages in the time and about the court of Charles II', a more accurate description of their role in society being impossible in a book for Victorian children.

The ten game rhymes are provided with minimal instructions on the way in which the game is played. Only one of the games has a note in the appendix and that is 'Pretty Little Girl', which Baring-Gould tells us came from Black Torrington in North Devon. With the 'jingles', though, we are on familiar territory; the classic nursery rhymes, usually a single verse, that most of us heard when we were young, many of which we still sing to our children today.

The Introduction and the notes to the songs are written in much the same way as those for his other books of songs. The notes give references to texts, where appropriate. The singers are not named, though a brief description is sometimes given, such as 'a Devonshire nurse', or 'a white-haired tanner who died three years ago'. In the introduction he demolishes the fanciful theories of some who had written on the origin of nursery rhymes such as J. B. Ker, who postulated that they came to us from Holland and were coded tirades against the Church, by joking, 'It is quite true that we drew a king from the Netherlands – William of Orange: but there is no record of his having brought over with him a fleet filled with nurse-maids where with to inundate our English homes'.[22] He likewise dismisses the work of Henry George, who alleged, for example, that 'the man all tattered and torn' represents the Protestant Church at the time of Henry VIII.[23] He accepts, however, that some nursery songs and, especially game rhymes, have their origin in early beliefs and usages. In most cases, though, they are songs that a nurse would have sung to her little charges to amuse or to lull; the words half remembered, the story not always completed, the phrases sometimes chosen because of a good rhyme.

It is a disappointment that he did not include the melodies for the songs, at least. The tunes of the games and jingles might already have been in the memories of the nurses and governesses who were reading the book with their children, but the songs would have been less well known to them. If they had been included it would have been a very different book. As it stands, it is one of the most attractive books that Baring-Gould ever published and one of my personal favourites.

English Minstrelsie

In November 1894 Baring-Gould was approached by the Edinburgh publishers, T. C. and E. C. Jack, who invited him to contribute to a multi-volume collection of English songs similar to their recently published *Scots Minstrelsie*. That series had contained extensive notes about each of the songs. They did not believe that there could be as much to say about English songs, nor even that there would be many English songs worthy of inclusion.

---

22 John Bellenden Ker, *An Essay on the Archaeology of our popular phrase and Nursery Rhymes* (London: Longman and Co., 1837).

23 Henry George, *An Attempt to show that our Nursery Rhyme, "The House that Jack built" is an historical allegory, portraying eventful periods in England's history since the time of Harold* (London: Griffin and Farren, 1862).

> In the "Scots Minstrelsie" there appeared a series of very interesting notes dealing with each song under a separate heading, and we are anxious to have some such feature in our English collection. We suspect that the material for such treatment of English popular songs is far from being so rich and abundant as in the case of the songs of the Scots song-writers, and we are doubtful whether in many instances any definite information whatever is obtainable. Were this the case, we should suggest that this section of the work should take the form of an article on 'English Popular Song', without dealing necessarily with each individually.[24]

The suggestion that there was a deficiency of information about English song, particularly a suggestion that came from Scotland, would have caused Baring-Gould's hackles to rise. He persuaded them that this was similar to a project that he already had in mind and it was agreed that they would combine forces to produce what was to become *English Minstrelsie*, with him in the driving seat.[25]

This was another large project that Baring-Gould took on at a time when he was already busy. He co-opted both Sheppard and Bussell to work on the arrangements alongside the Edinburgh-based composer, W. H. Hopkinson. By April of the following year work on the first volume was complete, and a prospectus was sent to interested parties. The advertisement for the book started well, with the announcement that they had been given permission to dedicate the book to Queen Victoria. Described as 'A National Monument of English Song', the book was to be 'a compendium of the best English Songs that have stood the wear and tear of time, and have become rooted in the affections of the people'. It was to contain 'upwards of 300 songs' (the final total was 348) covering the broad sweep of English song. Baring-Gould's selection included 'folk' and 'old English' songs (many not previously published) as well as classical and art songs by English composers down the ages.

---

24 Devon Heritage Centre, Baring-Gould Papers, 5203 M, Box 16, Letter to Baring-Gould from T. C. & E. C. Jack (probably from Edwin Jack), 9 November 1894.

25 That this is the case is made clear in an endnote to the essay 'An Historical Sketch of English National Song' in *English Minstrelsie*, I, p. xxiv: '...for the selection of songs the Editor is responsible'.

DEDICATED BY GRACIOUS PERMISSION TO
H.M. THE QUEEN

ENGLISH MINSTRELSIE:

A National Monument of English Song.

COLLATED AND EDITED, WITH NOTES AND ILLUSTRATED

HISTORICAL INTRODUCTIONS, BY

S. BARING-GOULD, M.A.

The Airs, in both Notations, arranged by H. FLEETWOOD SHEPPARD, M.A;
F.W. BUSSELL, M.A. Mus. Bac, Oxon.; and W.H. HOPKINSON, A.R.C.O.

ENGLISH MINSTRELSIE professes to be a compendium of the best English Songs that
have stood the wear and tear of time, and have become rooted in the affections of the
people.

It will contain in all upwards of 300 Songs. The Editing of the whole Collection, and the
writing of the Introduction and Notes on the individual songs, has been entrusted to
the Rev. S. BARING-GOULD, who has been engaged for ten years in collecting the Folk
Music of the English people and in the study of Old English Printed and Engraved Music.

The Introductions by the Editor will be on the History of English Song, The English
Opera, English Folk Song, and other subjects, with illustrations of Early Musical
Instruments, Minstrels, Ballad Singers, Portraits of English Composers, and Facsimile
representations of Old Copper-plate Music, &c.

Great care has been taken to secure that Words and Music shall be arranged and
engraved in such a way as to be thoroughly legible, and easily followed both by Vocalist
and Pianist.

The Work will be issued in Eight Volumes, royal 4to, (piano size), rich cloth gilt, gilt
edges, at 10s. each (at intervals of three months or less. Vol. I ready. Orders accepted
only for the entire Work.

———

Edinburgh: T.C. & E.C. JACK,

Grange Publishing Works

Fig. 10.3 – Advertisement for English Minstrelsie, as it appeared in The
Athenaeum, June 1895 (facsimile).

Baring-Gould set out to deal with the assertion that there was insufficient
information about English song by writing detailed notes on the songs he
had selected. These were based on extensive research on their origins in the
British Museum and in his own library, for which he continued to buy the
books he needed to support these studies. He also contributed four lengthy

essays: 'An Historical Sketch of English National Song' (in volume 1), dated February 1895; 'A Sketch of the History of English Opera' (in volume 3), not dated; 'The Concert Halls, Gardens, and Singers' (volume 5), dated June 1896; and 'Introductory Essay on English Folk Song' (volume 7), not dated.

The book was to be issued in eight volumes at three-monthly intervals, at a price of ten shillings each. Orders would only be accepted for the complete set of volumes. It was produced to a high standard, with a large number of illustrations.

Volume 1	May 1895
Volume 2	September 1895
Volume 3	December 1895
Volume 4	April 1896
Volume 5	August 1896
Volume 6	December 1896
Volume 7	May 1897
Volume 8	September 1897

Fig. 10.4 - *English Minstrelsie* Publication Dates.

A criticism made of the book while in progress was that the content was not given chronologically. This had never been part of Baring-Gould's plan, but he took the opportunity to address the complaint by providing a 'chronological index' to the airs in the book in volume 8. He also included a 'General Index to Songs' (with the first lines where different to the title), an 'Index of Composers' and an 'Index to Songs and Airs incidentally mentioned in the Notes and Essays'.

Each successive volume of the book was reviewed when issued, and the reviews seem to have been generally positive. Frank Kidson responded to Lucy Broadwood when she sent him a copy of a rather negative review of the book. He felt that although there were musical faults in it and 'sundry little points which you and I don't care for', he thought that the critics 'are a little bit too much "down" on Baring-Gould'.[26] In another letter he mentioned that Baring-Gould had asked him if he could include his photograph in the book and describes the essay on the concert halls and gardens as 'particularly good'.[27]

---

26 Letter of Frank Kidson to Lucy Broadwood, dated 19 January 1897, Lucy Broadwood Papers, VWML, LEB/4/111.
27 Letter of Frank Kidson to Lucy Broadwood, dated 17 September 1896 [reference lost].

Fig. 10.5 - *English Minstrelsie* (Author's photo).

Several critics had reservations about the arrangements, which were seen to be, like those in the earlier books, too elaborate. Baring-Gould was also criticised for not dealing properly with Purcell. His notes and essays, however, were singled out for praise in several reviews, and his interest in the subject matter and his knowledge of it was favourably commented on, though one reviewer, probably with his tongue headed towards his cheek, presented his readers with a vision of Baring-Gould's work as a collector:

> Those familiar with the methods of Mr Gould know that he has somehow discovered an English peasantry far away in the dreamy West, who lean over five-barred gates and linger upon rustic bridges, crooning snatches of priceless old melodies and pouring out reams of quaint old ballad-lore uncontaminated by 'The Man That Broke the Bank at Monte Carlo' and 'Hi Tiddley hi Ti', which is all the average song-collector can hear upon a breezy moorland or in a village inn.[28]

---

28 'The Songs of the English', *St James Gazette*, 14 May 1895, p. 5.

Another reviewer, though, had a much more critical view of Baring-Gould personally. In a lengthy article published in *The Saturday Review* in August 1895, 'J.F.R.' wrote of having 'devoted a tedious afternoon to a careful study' of a volume that he had discovered in a pile of books for review.[29] This was the first part of *English Minstrelsie*, and he speaks sarcastically of his 'unlimited admiration' for the 'boundless bumptiousness' of Baring-Gould and his publishers. He talks of '…the authoritative pose charmingly combined with an entire lack of knowledge that, did Mr Baring-Gould possess it, might justify him in posing as an authority', and suggests that a 'real authority', such as Mr Dolmetsch, should be brought in as editor of the remaining volumes. J.F.R had also published a review in the *Monthly Musical Record* a month earlier in which he discovered *English Minstrelsie* 'at the base of a heap of ambitious tomes'.[30] In this article he writes that Baring-Gould makes him angry because of his style, knowledge and pretentions, though he does not employ the sarcasm displayed in *The Saturday Review*. But J.F.R. seems to be in the minority, and did not offer his views on later volumes.

The publication history of the book has proved difficult to unravel and no advertisements for it have been discovered after the first short run in 1895. Part of the reason for this was that most sales were made by 'canvassers' who visited booksellers across the country. There are no sales figures available, but in March 1896 Edwin Jack wrote to Baring-Gould admitting that sales were proving 'somewhat stiff'. He suggested that they might send a complimentary set of the books to a prominent musician such as Charles Stanford or Hubert Parry with a covering letter in which Baring-Gould should discreetly ask them for an opinion about the book which could then be quoted in advertising. It was, though, successful enough to have been issued in at least three different formats, including a luxury version in gold-blocked green cloth and a more utilitarian version with black printed card cover.

Because it is not a book composed entirely of traditional songs, *English Minstrelsie* has not received as much attention as Baring-Gould's other songbooks, though there is much in it that is of interest to the folk song enthusiast. Opening the 'Introductory Essay on English Folk Song' in volume 7 he writes that 'It is not easy for me to say more on a topic already treated by me with some fullness in my introduction to the *Songs of the West* and also to *A Garland of Country Song*'. He nonetheless included more than 9,000 words of quotations from earlier writers and descriptions of

---

29 J.F.R, 'The Rev. S. Baring-Gould, Musical Historian', *The Saturday Review*, 24 August 1895, pp. 236–37.

30 J.F.R., 'Recent Musical Literature', *The Monthly Musical Record*, 1 July 1895, pp. 148–51.

his journeys in search of song. This enabled him to say more about his most active period of song collecting, and about some of the singers he met after the publication of *Songs of the West*. The notes on the songs in *English Minstrelsie* are often more expansive than those in his earlier books and there is additional information and anecdote about a few of the songs that he had already published. He wrote about 'Old Adam' for example:

> This curious air was taken down from William Andrews, a fiddler at Sheepstor, on the edge of Dartmoor. I made two visits to the old man, one in 1890 with Mr. Sheppard, when we failed to extract much from him. I went again in 1892 with Mr. Bussell, and then his shyness was broken down, and we spent two hours with him, noting down his old airs. We might have got more, but the Rector most kindly came in and insisted on our going to tea with him. We could not refuse, and then had to hasten to catch our train to return, and as we passed, more than an hour after having left the old man, we heard him still fiddling. His memory was stored with old airs. As he told me, in ancient days when there were dances in the farm-houses, all the young folk sang as they danced, and the "burden" or refrain served to mark the turns in the dance. Unhappily, he could not recall much of the words of the ballads thus sung. As he told me, he "minded his viddle more than them zingers" consequently we could obtain the words in a fragmentary condition—rarely more than the first verse. The poor old fellow died last autumn, and there is an end to his music on earth. "Old Adam" was one of the songs of which he could recall but a scrap of words, and I have therefore been compelled to write new verses, following as far as I could the idea of the ancient song. The air is peculiar in character, and the metre unusual. One would like to know what was the dance performed to it.[31]

I have come to believe that *English Minstrelsie* is a more interesting and important book than is generally thought. There are songs in it that can genuinely be considered to be folk songs. Others fall into that group of songs that originated from the theatres and pleasure gardens of the

---

31 Note to 'Old Adam', *English Minstrelsie*, IV, p. 54. The song was included in the 1905 revision of *Songs of the West* as 'Old Adam the Poacher'. In the note to this Baring-Gould writes, 'Mr Sheppard arranged this for *English Minstrelsie*, but did not perceive that the first four lines of air have to be repeated to complete the tune; and in taking the melody from the fiddler, one could not detect at first, not knowing the words, where the tune precisely ended.'

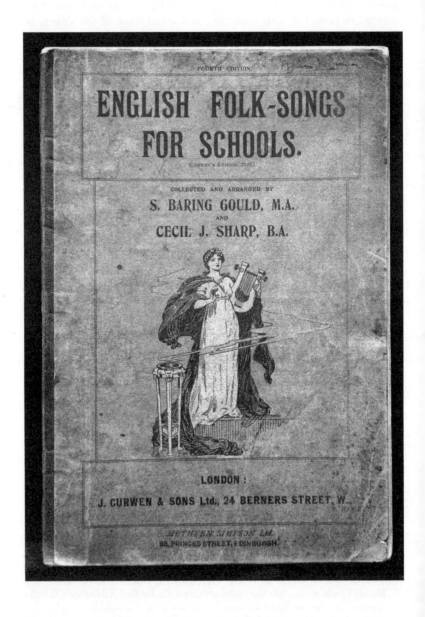

Fig. 10.6 – English Folk Songs for Schools (Author's photo).

eighteenth century which were popular in their day and were remembered by some of Baring-Gould's singers, but which were not noted down by other folk song collectors. Several of these appear in Baring-Gould's manuscripts and he sought out their origins in plays, engraved music and in street literature to provide the background to the songs. There is much to learn from this book about the songs, and about Baring-Gould's understanding of them.

English Folk Songs for Schools

Baring-Gould and Sharp's cooperation on *English Folk Songs for Schools* has already been described in Chapter 8. It should be said, though, that of all the books described in this chapter, this has proved to be one of the most influential and enduring. For much of the twentieth century, most of the schools in England used either Sharp and Baring-Gould's *English Folk Songs for Schools* or Stanford's *New National Songbook*. It was published in many different editions and formats.

Both books were designed to meet the requirements of the Board of Education, which, in its *Blue Book of Suggestions for the Consideration of Teachers* (1905) had recognised the importance and potential of national and folk songs in school music. It is hard for us to understand the depth of the controversy that there was at the time it was written over the direction that music teaching in schools should take, with battle lines drawn between two contrasting nationalistic views. Put simply, Sharp and Baring-Gould, and their camp wanted genuine English folk songs to be taught to English children and felt that that the definition of 'folk song' was being drawn too widely. Stanford's supporters, on the other hand, believed that the emphasis should be on reflecting the cultures of England, Ireland, Scotland and Wales through the songs that had been popular down the years, many of them by known composers. They also suggested that many of the orally collected folk songs were entirely unsuitable for children, dealing as they did with drink, women and loose living. They also made the point that many folk melodies have a wide range, which is unsuitable for children's voices. This debate, carried forward in the pages of newspapers and musical magazines, consumed much paper and ink but never really reached a conclusion.

English Folk Songs for Schools and *The New National Songbook* were both successful books and the teaching of music in schools benefited greatly from the process that, most importantly, had confirmed the value of teaching song in schools. Sharp could feel that he had at least succeeded in making teachers aware of English folk song and could choose to include them in their teaching. Those who were taught using Baring-Gould and Sharp's book benefited from an early introduction to the genre. There is no doubt that this had a positive effect on the course of the interest in folk song and its revival.

Baring-Gould on Songs

In a letter to Baring-Gould written in December 1897 Henry Fleetwood Sheppard set out his reflections on *Songs of the West*.[32] This appears to have been in response to a letter in which Baring-Gould was complaining about the lack of recognition that their book had received at that time. Sheppard seeks to reassure him of the value of his collection as 'a record, and that a valuable and reliable one, of what is passing and soon will have passed away'. He says that the value of *Songs of the West* will be realised 'when the time shall come for the whole question of English folksong to be scientifically, comparatively & critically examined' and that, though some have features in common with the rest of England, 'the great bulk of them fairly represent, I believe, the Celtic element in English Song – as it is nowhere else represented'.

Songs of the West was a landmark in English traditional song; the first publication from the first large-scale folk song collection made 'from the mouths of the people'. It deserves credit on that ground alone, but I can imagine the reader asking at this point, 'If *Songs of the West* is an unreliable record, why is it of any importance?' The answer is that even if it is a flawed book by modern standards it was influential in its time, not least because of Baring-Gould's status as a celebrity author, whose doings always attracted attention. Other collectors did not have that advantage and whatever the quality of their work did not attract the same level of interest among the general public, though the musical establishment may have appreciated their achievements better.

The pairing of Baring-Gould and Sharp was a powerful and effective partnership within which ideas could be shared and developed. Though the 1905 edition of *Songs of the West* retained much from the earlier versions, Cecil Sharp helped Baring-Gould to revitalise the book to meet the new taste for folk song that had emerged as a consequence of not only his work but also that of others, notably Lucy Broadwood and Frank Kidson. The 1905 edition did not just benefit from Sharp's input, however. Baring-Gould himself had done and learnt much more

---

32 Devon Heritage Centre, Baring-Gould Papers, M5203, Box 25, Letter of Henry Fleetwood Sheppard to Sabine Baring-Gould, dated 7 December 1897. Pasted into Baring-Gould's 1880 Diary-notebook.

in the fifteen years that had elapsed since he had written the first edition. Though he may have preferred Sheppard's accompaniments to Sharp's simpler settings, the latter met the needs of the new generation and it sold well. Songs from it could be heard at village concerts and many, as Baring-Gould had hoped, found their way back into the repertoire of singers in Devon and Cornwall.

There are many other publications by Baring-Gould that built on his work in *Songs of the West*. As well as his other song books, *A Garland of Country Songs, English Minstrelsie* and *English Folk Songs for Schools*, he wrote a number of magazine articles that brought the message about his work on folk song to a wider audience. As we shall see in the next chapter, he took the songs out on the road in his stage shows, raising public awareness of folk song further. After 1904 he lent his support to Cecil Sharp, who was even more skilled than Baring-Gould in publicising his work. Though the older man remained in touch with developments his influence dwindled as a new generation of song collectors took up the challenge.

The Folk Song Society had produced guidelines for folk song collection and it was clear that Baring-Gould's methods and interpretations had not always met those aspirations. When they started collecting, there were few useful precedents for Baring-Gould and Sheppard to follow. The Society was less concerned with performance of the songs and more with the accuracy of its collection and in its preservation in that pure form. Baring-Gould aimed to produce a volume that would sell to drawing room performers. This was the style in which the material was represented to the audiences who attended their concerts. The Devon antiquarian, Charles Laycock, described Sheppard's accompaniments as 'dainty little pieces of art music founded on folk-song themes'. Though he would have preferred simpler arrangements he felt that Sheppard's approach was justifiable, because they had to conform to the public taste and expectations of the time.[33]

James Reeves, writing in 1960, saw Baring-Gould as having approached folk song firstly as a West Country Briton, secondly as an amateur of music and thirdly as an historian.[34] He viewed Baring-Gould's belief that the

---

33 Charles Laycock, 'English National and Folk Music with Special Reference to the Folk Songs of Devonshire', in *Report and Transactions of the Devonshire Association*, 49 (July 1917), pp. 296–319.
34 James Reeves, 'Introduction', *The Everlasting Circle, English Traditional Verse from the Mss of S. Baring-Gould, H. E. D. Hammond and George B. Gardiner* (London: Heinemann, 1960).

words of folk songs had been corrupted by contact with broadside ballads, and his tendency to try to repair songs from printed texts as a handicap. He believed that Baring-Gould, who had above average poetical skills, had been too ready to deploy those skills in 'improving' song texts. But he also recognised that Baring-Gould was ahead of the pack, and had no good models to work from.

11: Putting Folk Song on the Stage

Next to the pulpit, I really think the stage is the best moral education of the people.[1]

The Lecture-Concerts — Mrs Mason — The Costume Concerts — The Royal Institution Lectures — On the Road Again — Frank Pemberton — Touring in North America — Red Spider, a Folk Opera — Passing the Baton, Later Ventures

Of all of the aspects of Baring-Gould's work with folk song, one of the most intriguing and original is the way in which he took it to the stage, in person and in association with experienced playwrights, singers and actors. From his early illustrated lectures he developed a format for professionally performed costume concerts that were staged regularly for two decades. One of his cherished projects was his folk-opera, *Red Spider*, based on his novel of that name and which was staged more than 100 times around Britain. Dramatists, meanwhile, fought for the rights to stage his novels, with varying degrees of success.

His experience in the Church had taught him that there was more than one way to get a message across. He recognised the effectiveness of ritual in engaging the senses of sight and sound — and even, with the help of a little incense, that of smell (though Baring-Gould did not use incense at Lew Trenchard). He understood that gorgeously coloured costumes, sumptuous music and well-decorated stage sets could transform the church service into a multimedia experience, while acknowledging the need to tailor the service to the needs and understanding of the congregation. But he had seen in venues like St Barnabas in Pimlico or in the churches of France and Italy that the spectacle created extra channels through which the message could be broadcast to the people.

In the same way, he knew that he could not spread the gospel of traditional song through print alone. These lovely old songs needed to be performed, and to have their power amplified by increasing the scope of the performance.

Baring-Gould's early theatrical experiences while he was teaching at Hurstpierpoint in his twenties have been described earlier. There is no indication in his memoirs or in other records that he took part in any further

---

1 · Devon Heritage Centre, Baring-Gould Papers, M5203, Box 25, 1880 Diary-Notebook, 3 June 1864.

theatrical ventures until he moved to Lew Trenchard. Then, as he settled into village life, we know that he sang in local concerts, though we have very few details of these events. He also created a theatre in the outbuildings near the house, where his children put on their plays and where the people of the village would come for entertainments and for feasts.

The Lecture-Concerts

Baring-Gould's early lectures on folk song included examples of the songs in arrangements for voice and piano by Henry Fleetwood Sheppard that were performed by amateur singers from the South West. The first of these lectures was on the evening of 21 January 1889 at the Royal Albert Museum in Exeter. He began his talk with a description of his quest, and of the songs that he had found, before four singers performed examples of the songs: Mrs Mason and Messrs Bennett, Davey and Easterling. Baring-Gould himself sang 'The Last of the Singers', one of his own songs set to a traditional tune, for which he was loudly applauded. The programme included fifteen songs, most of which were taken from *Songs of the West* which was about to be published.

This talk was followed by two more, in South Brent on 23 January and Tavistock on the 24th. Baring-Gould was reported as having said that any profits from these latter two concerts would be shared among his old singers and at South Brent a tea was provided for them and their wives. The old miller, John Helmore, would have heard Baring-Gould sing 'The Miller's Last Will' which had been collected from him a few weeks earlier.

The *Tavistock Gazette* covered the Tavistock lecture-concert at some length and this report gives us some useful information. The chairman for the event was Daniel Radford, who commended his friend's efforts saying that '…if Mr Baring-Gould had not taken the trouble he had, many of these old songs and ballads would have been lost entirely, and it was through that gentleman's timely intervention that they would be preserved to them and to future generations – (applause).'[2] Baring-Gould told his audience about the theory that folk song had come from the medieval minstrels who had been forbidden to perform in the reign of Henry VIII and who had settled into village life where their sons learned and passed on their ballads. He described his meetings with old singers, remarking that he had just the previous day written out the fair copy of the hundredth song that he and his colleagues had noted down, and that he believed they had heard eighty distinct melodies. Though the words of the songs were

---

2   *Tavistock Gazette*, Friday 8 February, 1889.

encountered elsewhere in England and were often printed on broadsides, many of the tunes were unique to Devon. That they were of great quality he had no doubt, and Sheppard had written to him, saying: 'I am more and more amazed every day with what you send me. What a wealth of musical imagination and ideas you have in the West of England.'

The lecture-concert raised £16 6s, of which £10 16s was given to Tavistock Cottage Hospital. The remaining £5 10s was distributed among 'the old men who helped Mr Baring-Gould by their contribution of old songs and ballads'.

Mrs Mason

The performers were different for each of the three lecture-concerts and only one person, the soprano, Mrs Nannie Mason, performed at all three. She was an important member of Baring-Gould's company during its first two years when it developed from a simple lecture with sung illustrations to a staged performance with costumes and *tableaux vivants*. Several letters that Baring-Gould wrote to Mrs Mason between May 1889 and July 1890 have survived among his papers.[3] These give us some idea of how he went about designing and producing these early shows, as well as some useful gossip about other members of the cast.

Mrs Mason was born Nannie Mitchell in 1854 to Samuel and Elizabeth Mitchell. Her father was a copper mine agent, then living at Collacombe Down, near Lamerton, Devon, where there were a number of mines. He then moved to another mine, Wheal Maria, a little further to the south and west, and in the 1871 census Nannie was living there and working as a music teacher. She was then seventeen years old. She married a bank cashier, John Herring Mason, and they had two children, a son John Walter, and a daughter Josephine Honoria Charlotte, who was fifteen years younger. They lived initially in Tavistock, but John's career with the bank took him to Plymouth and later to Ashburton.

Nannie Mason combined her job as a music teacher with regular engagements, throughout the South West, singing popular classical pieces and sacred songs in concerts as well as performing as a soloist in choral works. A review of her performance at that first lecture-concert in Exeter in January 1889 singled her out for praise, remarking that she was 'decidedly a singer of ability whom we should like to see more often on an Exeter platform'. Her reputation grew from 1890 onwards, helped, no doubt, by her association with Baring-Gould.

---

3   Devon Heritage Centre, Correspondence: Reverend Sabine Baring-Gould to Mrs Mason, 3316 M/F1 – F23.

Her son became a professional musician, following in his mother's footsteps. Then, in 1912 a new soprano, Mlle Fifine de la Cote, started to appear on stages throughout the South West and rapidly gained a reputation exceeding that of Mrs Mason. She was advertised as having performed at the Albert Hall and other leading venues, and was said to have a magnificent soprano voice of great range and power, with perfect enunciation. She was reported to come from Tavistock and she frequently appeared in concert with members of the Herring Mason family. In 1914 she was the soloist for Mrs Herring Mason's Operatic Society in Ashburton, performing Gilbert and Sullivan's *The Sorcerer* before a large and appreciative audience. Both Mr and Mrs Mason were listed as her accompanist at different times and Walter Mason appeared on the same bill, playing the violin. An article in the *West Briton* in October 1912 confirmed my growing suspicion that 'Mlle de la Cote' was in fact Josephine Herring Mason then aged seventeen She went on to have a long career and in the 1920s she performed a number of times on BBC Radio. A programme broadcast from Plymouth in 1925 included 'Green Broom' and 'Sweet Nightingale', both from the Baring-Gould collection. Walter went on to lead his own ensemble – Mr Walter Herring Mason's Light Orchestra, which sometimes accompanied his sister. This was a very musical family.

The Costume Concerts

After the first three lectures there was a quiet period until August 1889, when the Devonshire Association held its annual meeting in Tavistock. Baring-Gould had been elected a vice-president of the association for the year and was involved in the organisation of the meeting. On the evening of 1 August there was a *Conversazione* at Tavistock Town Hall, where the proceedings were 'enlivened with vocal and instrumental music, which was highly appreciated, including a collection of *Songs of the West*, conducted by Rev S. Baring-Gould'.[4] We do not have as much detail on this concert as some of the others, though a letter from Baring-Gould on 7 June to Mrs Mason reveals some of the difficulties he had experienced in putting a team of performers together. He asks her if she knows of a harpist, as he wants to have a harp accompaniment for 'Childe the Hunter'. He is also looking for a violinist to accompany 'Lullaby'.[5] But they were already

---

4   'Report of the Council', *Transactions of the Devonshire Association*, 12 (July 1890), p. 18.
5   Devon Heritage Centre, Letter of Sabine Baring-Gould to Mrs Mason, 7 June 1889, 3316 M/F2.

discussing a series of concerts that Baring-Gould called the 'Grand Tour'. This was being planned for September and October 1889 and, originally fifteen concerts throughout Devon and Cornwall were planned.

The Rev. J. BARING-GOULD, M.A.

WILL DURING THE AUTUMN DELIVER A SERIES OF

CONCERT ✳ LECTURES

ON

The SONGS and BALLADS of DEVON and CORNWALL (with their traditional melodies), illustrated MUSICALLY and by a Series of

✳ ✳ ✳ Tableaux ✳ Vivants, ✳ ✳ ✳

With appropriate Scenery and Costumes, by

Mrs. MASON, *Tavistock*.
Miss BOGGIS, *Tavistock*.
Miss SHEPPARD, *Thurnscoe*.
Mr. FERGUSON, *Magdalen College, Oxford*.

Mr. W. BICKFORD, *Tavistock*.
Mr. F. W. BUSSELL, *Fellow, Brazennose College, Oxford*.
Mr. H. WOOD, *Thurnscoe*.
Mr. J. H. TREHANE, *Plymouth*.

Miss BUSSELL, *Lew Trenchard*, will preside at the Piano.
Mr. F. LESLIE MORETON, *Plymouth*, General Manager.

Copies of Parts I. & II. of *Songs of the West*, at 3/- each, can be obtained in the Hall.

P.T.O.

Fig. 11.1 – 'Songs of the West' invitation card 1890 (Courtesy of Plymouth City Council Library Services).

Baring-Gould's concept for the show had now advanced considerably. It was to be more of a spectacle, as described in a newspaper report:

> The concert and tableaux vivants are interspersed with historical and entertaining comments illustrating the old songs and ballads of the West of England, collected by the Rev. S. Baring-Gould, M. A., with special accessories and lime-light effects. [...] The method adopted is that each tableaux shall represent a certain period from Elizabeth downwards. The songs, duets, quartettes, &c., selected are of the period represented, while the realism is completed and set off by the faithful costumes adopted.[6]

6 'Costume Concert at Exeter', *Western Times*, 26 November 1889, p. 5.

Some of the letters to Mrs Mason describe preparations for this series of concerts. At this stage, Baring-Gould himself was designing every aspect of the show: content, costumes, scenery and dramatic effects. He described, for example, the costume he wanted her to wear for the first scene, 'A Garden by Moonlight', in which she and Mary Sheppard (Sheppard's daughter) would be on stage together:

> The first scene is by moonlight, a ray thrown on the performer.
> I thought for you a flowing white dress with a black mantle and
> black girdle; as Miss S. will be in white with blue girdle, and flowing
> hair and a crown of roses on her head, holding a garland of yew.[7]

The period of the costumes worn for each scene changed to reflect the era depicted, and the situation described. Baring-Gould asked the female singers to arrange their own costumes, suggesting to Mrs Mason that she should obtain a 'Charles II dress with blue as the prevailing colour' and a costume for a 'village girl, with a scarlet skirt'.

Throughout the summer Baring-Gould sent her a number of letters about the preparations for the concert, including a series of draft programmes. These demonstrate some of the delicate negotiations that Baring-Gould had to indulge in as he sought to make changes without upsetting any of his key performers. Mrs Mason was one of those star performers and another was Arthur Ferguson who had been the leading bass with the Magdalen College choir, and had performed at the Leeds Music Festival. Ferguson was to become a regular with the 'Songs of the West' Company for several years. The other men involved in the tour included Messrs Trehane, Wood and Bickford. Apart from these there were several friends and family who performed including Baring-Gould's daughter, Joan, Sheppard and his daughter Mary, and Frederick Bussell, whose sister Mary was the accompanist, as she had been for all the previous lecture-concerts other than the first.

On 24 August Baring-Gould wrote to Mason with the final version of the programme:[8]

---

7   Devon Heritage Centre, Letter of Sabine Baring-Gould to Mrs Mason, undated, 3316M/F12.
8   Devon Heritage Centre, Letter of Sabine Baring-Gould to Mrs Mason, undated, Letter 3316M/F4, Programme /F16.

Scene 1 – A Garden by Moonlight
1	Flowers and Weeds	Mrs Mason
2	Green Cockade	Miss Sheppard
3	My Ladye's Coach	Mr Ferguson
4	Sweet Nightingale	Miss Sheppard and Mrs Mason

Scene 2 – The Hall, Tetcott
5	Arscott of Tetcott	Mr Ferguson
6	Why Should We	Mr Bickford
7	Parson Hogg	Mr Ferguson
8	Blue Muslin	Mr Moreton and Mrs Mason
9	Widdicombe Fair	Mr Bickford

Scene 3 – The Garden by Daylight
10	Imprisoned Lady	Quartet
11	A Hearty Good Fellow	Mr Bickford
12	By Chance it Was	Mrs Mason
13	The Rout is Out	Miss Sheppard

Scene 4 – Cottage interior
14	On the Settle	Mrs. Mason, assisted by Mr Moreton
15	Chimney Sweep	Mr Ferguson.
16	Cicely Sweet	Mr Sheppard & Miss Sheppard
17	The Orchestra	Mr Bickford

Scene 5 – Village Green
18	A Sweet Pretty Maiden	Miss Sheppard
19	Cottage Thatched With Straw	Mr Ferguson
20	The Bonny Blue Handkerchief	Miss Sheppard
21	'Twas on a Sunday Morning	Mrs Mason
22	The Mallard	Mr Bickford and Miss Sheppard

Scene 6 – Cottage Interior, Night Scene
| 23 | Lullabye | Mrs Mason |

Baring-Gould had tried to select songs that were appropriate to the period depicted in the scene. They were taken from *Songs of the West*, though the availability of the songs for the show depended on Sheppard having completed the musical arrangements. There were some cases where a song that had been promised arrived only just in time.

Baring-Gould did not plan to sing in these costume concerts, since his role was to give the lectures that filled the gaps between the scenes, talking about the collection, the songs, and their history. There was a basic script and, when he was not able to be there in person the stage manager, Leslie Moreton, would read the script on his behalf.

Moreton had been born in Plymouth where his father had the contract for transferring prisoners between Millbay station and the prison at Princetown. He had achieved a good position with the Great Western Railway, but gave up the railways to follow his dream of a career in the theatre. He had some success with writing pantomimes and various short pieces for Devon theatres. He had been brought into the production team because he had access to theatrical materials and props, including a portable proscenium arch, behind which the stage could be set. He also had experience of the sort of show Baring-Gould was planning, since he had previously designed a series of shows based on *tableaux vivants*, with which he had toured in the South West.

One of the difficulties that Baring-Gould faced was finding singers who could commit to such a long series of concerts. Because he had problems with male singers in particular, Moreton was persuaded to perform as well as act as manager.

The Grand Tour began with two concerts (matinee and evening) at the Assembly Rooms in Plymouth on 17 September 1889. It continued for four weeks, with concerts on four evenings each week. They visited Truro, Redruth, Penzance, Plymouth (again) Tavistock, Kingsbridge, Dartmouth, Newton Abbot, Ashburton, Torquay, Teignmouth, Sidmouth, Exmouth, Exeter and finally Totnes on 10 October. With two performances each day in the larger towns this meant twenty concerts in all. This was quite a punishing schedule and a big commitment for the mainly amateur performers.

The newspaper reviews were positive and audiences seem to have been large and enthusiastic. The review of the concert at the Plymouth Mechanics Institute, for example, reported that the hall was

> Filled to overflowing in every part by an audience, many of whom belong to a social class not often seen in that building, and the

number who sought but could not gain admission would have well-nigh filled another hall of equal size.[9]

The 'Grand Tour' was so successful that a second tour was planned immediately and on 19 October 1889 Moreton placed an advertisement in the theatrical magazine, *The Era*, for performers:

> WANTED: Principal soprano, mezzo, contralto, tenor and pianist for second costume concert tour on ballads of West of England, commencing Nov. 7th. Four weeks guaranteed. Attractive appearance indispensible. Lowest terms, references, photos (stamps for return).[10]

This was very short notice, and some of the singers could not take part, including Bussell and Sheppard. It must have been something of a relief to Baring-Gould that Mrs Mason and Arthur Ferguson were able to continue as a members of the company. Christine Ward, who had come from the D'Oyly Carte company, joined the company for the one season, as did the Exeter based tenor, David Culley.

The second tour started in St Austell on 12 November and ended on 28 November, after visiting Falmouth, Helston, Cambourne, Saltash, Plymouth, Launceston, Plympton, Paignton, Torquay, Exmouth, Exeter and Barnstaple; another sixteen performances. Reviews were again favourable. To give some idea of how the performances were viewed, let the following extract from the report of the Helston concert on 15 November stand as an example:

> The costume concert and tableaux illustrating the songs of Cornwall and Devon, which were given at the Godolphin Hall, Helston, on Friday night, were a great success. There was a large attendance – a fair sprinkling of the elite of the neighbourhood and most of the leading tradespeople of the town. Mrs Mason was the prima donna; Miss C. Ward, another capital singer suffering from the effects of a bad cold. Mr Bickford was in good form and captivated his audience with his charming rendering of Widdicombe fair. Encores were so frequent that eleven o'clock was nearly reached before the audience dispersed.[11]

---

9   'Old Songs of the West', *Western Morning News*, 25 September 1889, p. 5.
10 Advertisement, *The Era*, 19 October 1889, p. 18.
11 'Helston', *The Cornishman*, 21 November 1889, p. 5.

As 1889 drew to a close it was clear that the shows were working well, though sales of the book were rather slower than had been hoped. With the prospect of the third volume coming in the spring of 1890, plans were laid for a new round of concerts. Baring-Gould decided that he would not take part in the shows as frequently as he had in 1889. He would save himself for a few particularly important occasions and let Moreton deliver the lectures. The concert party toured Somerset at Easter 1890. Baring-Gould had expressed some doubts about this tour outside Devon and Cornwall in a letter to Mrs Mason, but the published reviews suggest that he need not have worried.

Baring-Gould was travelling in Europe until the end of April and the concerts carried on without him. There was one especially important engagement for the company at Torquay on 5 May, when they performed before Princess Louise who was visiting the borough. Reports of the concert record that on this occasion Sheppard gave the readings and there is no mention that Baring-Gould was present. He had only been back in the country for five days and it may have been thought that his presence could not have been counted on. *The Western Times* described the concert as 'a success from start to finish'. The *Exeter Flying Post* was more sanguine, concluding, 'Considering the fact that only one full rehearsal was possible, the concert was excellent.'

The Royal Institution Lectures

Baring-Gould was, though, more concerned about the series of lectures on 'Ballad Music of the West of England' that were to take place at the Royal Institution in London in May and June. He had first written to Mrs Mason about these events on 5 February 1890 while he was in London, having been taken ill with influenza while on his way to Italy and France to do some research for his books. He told her that he wanted to illustrate the lecture with songs, writing, 'I fancy I have material enough, but to give the ballads proper effect it needs someone like you who can enter into them with zest.' A month later he wrote from Italy, asking her to persuade her brother to obtain a copy of Francis Mori's ''Twas on a Sunday morning' so that she could learn it, as he wanted to use it alongside the version that he had collected from Robert Hard. His intention was to demonstrate the differences between the tune composed by Mori in 1853 and the version he had collected from the tradition in 1888, which he thought was superior.

The first of these lectures took place on 30 May 1890, and was followed by two more on 7 and 14 June. They seem to have been well received. The

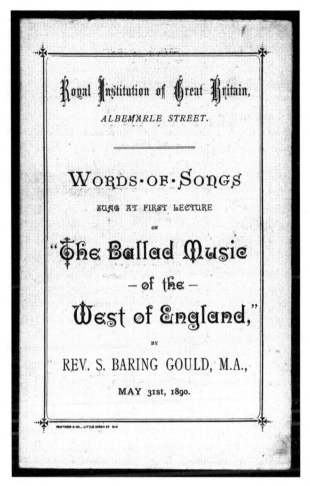

Fig. 11.2 – Programme for Royal Institution lecture, 31 May 1890 (Courtesy of Wren Music).

review of the first lecture from the *Glasgow Herald* gives us a description of Baring-Gould himself, as well as the event:

> A refreshing breath of the west countrie found its way into the greenhouse atmosphere of the Royal Institution and the vicinity of Bond Street yesterday afternoon in connection with the first of three lectures on the ballad music of West England by the

Rev S. Baring-Gould with musical illustrations. The author of "John Herring" and "Mehalah," who is a tall, spare man with light blue eyes, straight fair hair, prominent aquiline nose, and close shaven face, began his lecture by tracing the common origin of English and Scottish ballads, claiming the latter not to be essentially Scottish, but the property of an English-speaking people. Examples of various classes of ballads, preceded by a brief sketch of their history and development, were tastefully sung by two ladies and two gentlemen.[12]

Baring-Gould wrote to Mrs Mason two days after the first lecture to inform her that the head of music at the Royal Institution, Dr McKenzie, had been particularly impressed with her singing of 'Cold Blows the Wind', and that several others had spoken of it as 'vastly striking'. He said that he had discovered that there were several 'musical stars' in the audience, and that he had been asked whether she was available for engagements – to which he had replied she was.

Early in his first lecture Baring-Gould had launched into one of his favourite themes, the expropriation of English ballads by the Scots, claiming, 'The Scottish ballads so called were not of Scottish but of English origin. They owed their Scottish colouring to transference across the Tweed, and to alterations made by Scottish Collectors.' It is likely that this notion had arisen from his reading of William Chappell's *Popular Music of the Olden Time*, where a number of examples of such borrowing are given.[13] Baring-Gould took Chappell's ideas on board and then added a number of his own. Though he had a genuine desire to provide well-researched facts about these songs, I am sure that Baring-Gould was delighted to have a tilt at the Scots, for whom he had acquired a dislike in his early years. He returned to his theme several times during the lecture, and Sheppard, in a letter written a few months later, chided him for his self-indulgence in making these comments, referring to an adverse report on his talk in *The Scotsman* and suggesting that he had done himself no favours north of the border.[14]

Baring-Gould also repeated his belief that folk songs had descended to the current generation of 'song-men' from the old minstrels who were

12 *Glasgow Herald*, 2 June 1890, p. 7.
13 William Chappell, *Popular Music of the Olden Time* (London: Chappell and Co., 1859).
14 Devon Heritage Centre, Baring-Gould Papers, Letter of Henry Fleetwood Sheppard to Sabine Baring-Gould, 7 July 1890, 5203 M, Box 36.

put down by the Vagabonds Act of 1597 and settled with their songs in rural districts. This idea, too, is one that was probably sparked by his reading of Chappell, much of whose information about the minstrels was derived from Thomas Percy's *Reliques of Ancient English Poetry*.[15] Percy's account of the ancient minstrels was disputed but Chappell believed that the facts he chose to present were correct. Surprisingly, it appears that Baring-Gould did not consult Percy early on, perhaps because the *Reliques* deals solely with texts rather than tunes. He first referred to them in *English Minstrelsie*.

In his second lecture Baring-Gould talked more about the songs themselves. He traced the development of the broadside trade and its influence on what was sung in the nineteenth century. His third lecture started with reminiscences of some of the singers from whom he had heard the songs before reverting to the idea that the best songs came originally from the minstrels. He finished the lecture with the example mentioned above of ''Twas on a Sunday Morning' contrasting the version collected from Robert Hard with the song as it had been written by Francis Mori.

On the Road Again

The costume concerts resumed in August 1890, travelling throughout the South West until December. Part 3 of *Songs of the West* was now published and Baring-Gould revised the show to include songs from all three parts, presented in six new scenes. Reports of the concerts were again favourable and there were instances of people being turned away from performances in Cornwall, where it was particularly popular. The venues included Princetown, where the company set up their show in Dartmoor Prison to entertain the officers and their families. In a newspaper article in 1930 Moreton recalled that they had the help of a number of the prisoners in transporting the scenery and props, who were allowed to stay and watch the rehearsals – which they did with keen interest.[16]

There was one London concert, at Terry's Theatre on 13 November. In an undated letter Baring-Gould expressed some misgivings to Mrs Mason before this event.[17] While assuring her that he was pleased she was going to take part, he wrote: 'I see little Mr. Moreton is very sanguine over that [The Terry's Theatre concert]. I only wish there were to be more matinees, as people are slow to hear of a thing, as I found out with my lectures.' The

---

15 Thomas Percy, *Reliques of Ancient English Poetry* (London: Dodsley, 1775).
16 F. Leslie Moreton, 'Recollections of Princetown', *Western Morning News*, 28 August 1930, p. 6.
17 Devon Heritage Centre, Letter of Sabine Baring-Gould to Mrs Mason, 3316M/F14, No date but late summer 1890.

mildly disparaging comment about 'little Mr. Moreton' is the first hint that Baring-Gould is not completely happy with that gentleman. He added to this by confiding that 'I heard the new professionals at Prince Town, well – I won't say all I thought, but I should not care to hear them a second time'. But the letter also contained some disappointing news, which make clearer why Baring-Gould was unhappy with Moreton.

On 6 July Baring-Gould had written to Mrs Mason, telling her that he had been made an offer for an eight-month tour of the United States in 1891–2.[18] He had asked Moreton to do the negotiations, but had given him some conditions. There should be a royalty on each performance, which he and Sheppard would share, though he said that his share was 'to be distributed among my old fellows'. Secondly, he would nominate a clergyman to act as lecturer and to look after the interests of the artistes while they were on tour. Finally, he insisted that Mrs Mason, Miss Sheppard and Miss Bussell should be offered the chance to take part before any other artistes were engaged. In a postscript to the letter about Terry's Theatre he reported:

> The American tour is not to be of amateurs. Mr. Behenna said the only one of the compy. that would go down in Yankee land was F.L.M.!!! [F. Leslie Moreton] under these circumstances it was obvious that broad comedy rather than quality of voice was regarded, and neither Mr. S nor I cared that a highly talented class of amateurs should go and not meet with proper recognition in U.S.A. Let Behenna choose such professionals as will suit the American taste. Mr. Moreton will dull them.

S. Cornelius Behenna was the manager of the Redpath Lyceum Bureau, and travelled to Europe several times a year to find and book acts for the Lyceum circuit in the US. The Lyceum Movement had grown up in the years before the Civil War to improve society by providing the public with classes, concerts, debates and drama, and continued into the early years of the twentieth century. There were various different 'circuits' and providing the speakers and performers for them occupied several agencies like Redpath. An eight-month tour would not have been unusual. Behenna may have been concerned about the ability of amateur performers to stay the course, but one is left wondering about Moreton's capabilities (and motivation) as a negotiator. He had failed in his plan to replace the

---

18 Devon Heritage Centre, Letter of Sabine Baring-Gould to Mrs Mason, 3316M/F10, 6 July 1890.

amateurs in the second tour with more professionals. Baring-Gould, we know from the same letter, was clearly unhappy with the professionals recruited for the third tour. Now Moreton was set to be the only person from the original show who was likely to go on the tour to the US.

In the event the tour did not go ahead, and we do not know whether this was Baring-Gould's choice, or whether terms were not agreed. But Baring-Gould's trust in Moreton had been diminished by the episode. Schemes were being drawn up for a further tour, but there is no record of any shows having taken place in 1891 or 1892. Moreton made plans of his own and in January 1891 commenced a tour of the pantomime *Sinbad the Sailor* throughout the South West. The publicity did not fail to point out his connection to the 'Songs of the West' concerts and boasted that some of the company had been on those tours (though no names, apart from that of Moreton himself, are recognisable from the reviews of the pantomime). No doubt Baring-Gould would have felt that pantomime was more Moreton's *metier* than folk song. But he was already working on a big, new project – an opera based on his novel, *Red Spider*, which would be another showcase for folk song, and which I will come back to shortly.

As professional singers replaced the amateurs in the concerts, Mrs Mason dropped out of the picture. Her career as a singer in religious and light music in the South West continued to flourish. The other singers dispersed to follow their own careers and most of them were not involved with Baring-Gould's concerts again.

There is one person, however, who has had few mentions and yet was the most constant of participants in the series of lectures and concerts. Frederick Bussell's sister, Mary, had been the accompanist for all but one of the shows, and it was she who brought into the picture the man who picked up the torch and ran with it.

Frank Pemberton

We do not know where Mary Bussell met Frank Pemberton but by January 1893 they knew each other well enough that he was staying in her brother's house in Exbourne, where she was living with her mother. There is a newspaper report of a village concert at Exbourne in January 1893 at which Mary Bussell and Frank Pemberton performed together. The Bussells had moved to Exbourne a few months earlier, when Frederick Bussell bought the manor house in the village and with it the manorial and ecclesiastical rights. Until then they had been living at the house that they rented from Baring-Gould at Lew Trenchard. Baring-Gould would have been in regular contact with the Bussells, particularly when Frederick

MR. FRANK PEMBERTON.
...Tenor and Director...

Fig. 11.3 – Frank Pemberton (Courtesy of Redpath Chautauqua Collection, University of Iowa Libraries, Iowa City, Iowa).

Bussell was there during university vacations. It is highly likely that if Pemberton had visited the Bussells at Lew Trenchard he would have met Baring-Gould.

Frank Pemberton was a tenor whose real name was Edmund Badger and he sang frequently under this name as well. It seems that he reserved 'Badger' for performances of religious and classical music and 'Frank Pemberton' for light music. He had been born in Derby in 1860, the son of Benjamin Badger, a builder, and his wife Elizabeth. He was the youngest of their four children and his brothers were both in the building trade. He had trained as a teacher but began to make a name for himself as a singer. As Edmund Badger he performed in concerts of sacred music, initially as an amateur but later as a member of the Birmingham Town Hall Concerts, and then of a London company. Reviews of his performances were good, describing him, for example, as having 'a voice satisfactory alike in purity of tone and accurate intonation'. Meanwhile, his alter ego, Frank Pemberton, was simultaneously working as an actor and as a manager for various theatre companies.

Badger/Pemberton's *curriculum vitae* clearly impressed Baring-Gould, who invited him to become the director and manager for a new series of 'Songs of the West' costume concerts in 1893, a role in which he continued until 1910. Edmund Badger married Mary Bussell in April 1894 in a ceremony held by special licence in Exbourne parish church, at which Baring-Gould officiated and whose daughter, Vera, was the bridesmaid. Edmund had been living in London, but the newly wed Mr and Mrs Badger now settled into village life in Exbourne. Mary was a popular figure and took the lead in organising parties and Christmas presents for the children of the village. They left Devon frequently to take part in performances of 'Songs of the West' and for other engagements around the country. When Frederick Bussell sold his properties in Exbourne, in 1898, the Badgers moved to Notting Hill in London.

The new season of concerts began in September 1893. It is clear that while Baring-Gould had retained an interest (and was probably getting a royalty on each performance) this had become Pemberton's show. The advertisements state that the programme was selected from the collection made by Baring-Gould, but it is Frank Pemberton's name that appears in the larger letters. This was still a costume concert, with a brief history of Baring-Gould's collection between the scenes, which had been reduced from six to four. The 1893 cast included Frank Pemberton and Miss Gage Goodfellow and Arthur Ferguson, both of whom had sung during the 1890 season. Miss Hannah Thorley was new to the show, as was Leslie Walker.

The accompanist was named as Miss Bussell, though she was now Mrs Badger (her name was given as Mrs Pemberton in some later programmes). Baring-Gould was not expected to attend and deliver the readings, which in 1893 were given by Leslie Walker, though he did go along to see at least one of the performances. We do not know which of them he attended, since the programmes were produced to suit a number of concerts, but we do know his opinions of it, since the programme is one of those in his 'Day Book' and he has written at the top of it: 'Unsatisfactory company. Miss

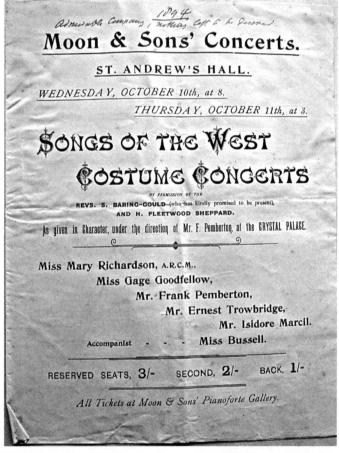

Fig. 11.4 'Songs of the West' Concert Programme, 1894 (Courtesy of Dr Merriol Almond and Devon Heritage Centre).

Thorley is not much good, Leslie Walker decidedly vulgar'.[19] The group remained unchanged for a second tour in October and November. This included their first concert at the Crystal Palace, a venue they appeared at regularly in later years.

The same group of singers continued into 1894, with a short break at the New Year, but for the summer season, which commenced at the Crystal Palace on 2 May, Hannah Thorley and Leslie Walker were replaced by Mary Richardson, Isidore Marcil and Ernest Trowbridge, the last named being responsible for delivering the lectures. Baring-Gould's note on his copy of the new season's programme states simply: 'Admirable company, nothing left to be desired.'

A few days later they were all at the Royal Institution for another lecture by Baring-Gould, where they sang the example songs for him, though this time no costumes were worn. The *Exeter and Plymouth Gazette* reported the event, claiming that there was an audience of over 800, of whom, it estimated, more than two-thirds were women. One of those women was Lucy Broadwood who had been given tickets by Baring-Gould. She recorded in her diary:

> In evening went to hear Rev S. Baring-Gould, by his invitation, lecture on 'Traditional Song' at The Royal Institution. Bad singing – was irritated afresh by Rev. Fleetwood Sheppard's accompaniments.[20]

Clearly the memory of the concert she had attended with Baring-Gould in Launceston the previous autumn had not yet left her. *The Times* was more generous: 'Though one felt that a smock frock and a village inn were necessary to bring out the full flavour of some of the airs, yet they were very charming and greatly delighted the large audience that heard them.'

1894 was the busiest year for the company so far, with at least 36 shows for which I have found newspaper advertisements or reviews.[21] The show was now well established at the Crystal Palace and was performed there regularly throughout 1894. But this was the zenith of its popularity.

---

19 Devon Heritage Centre, Baring-Gould Papers, 5203M, Commonplace Book, p. 28.
20 Surrey History Centre, Lucy Broadwood's Diary 6782/25, 11 May 1894.
21 A similar count for previous years has given me thirty shows in 1889, 29 in 1890 and, following the change to Pemberton's management, 25 in 1893. These numbers are certainly an underestimate, and are still growing as I come across more instances.

Though 'Songs of the West' and related shows continued to be performed until at least 1910, advertisements, reviews and reports can be found less frequently. I have not yet discovered any reports of Pemberton's attempt to mount a show based on *English Minstrelsie*. He told Baring-Gould about this in a letter shortly after the first performance in North Finchley on 12 December 1897 of which he said, 'It went very well indeed'. Three further performances were scheduled for 1898 in New Cross, Streatham and Ramsgate.[22]

As well as 'Songs of the West' Frank Pemberton was busy in both of his incarnations. As Edmund Badger he continued to perform as a soloist in choral concerts while as Frank Pemberton he found new opportunities for creating groups and concert parties, many of them involving the singers who worked with him on the 'Songs of the West' concerts. In 1895, for example, he was 'proprietor and manager', promoting the 'Grand English Opera Company', which offered performances of Balfe's *The Bohemian Girl* and Mascagni's *Cavalleria rusticana*. In the same year he found time to help his brother-in-law Frederick Bussell who provided the incidental music for a production of *The Merchant of Venice* by the Oxford University Dramatic Society. Bussell's music was highly praised in the reviews. Pemberton sang two songs, but while *The Era* praised the 'two capital songs' performed by Pemberton and *The Oxford Journal* considered them to have been rendered 'in faultless style', the *Pall Mall Gazette* reported that 'Mr Pemberton, the vocalist, sang a Neapolitan song from a gondola; and he sang it flat'.

Touring in North America

The concert party continued to perform throughout England and Scotland in the second half of the decade. The production was now fully under Pemberton's control and Baring-Gould rarely appeared in the role of lecturer after 1896. The repertoire still featured 'Songs of the West' from Baring-Gould's collection, but Pemberton began to broaden the scope, often billing a concert as 'English Minstrelsie' as a way of introducing parlour songs into the programme, though every concert still included those folk songs, like 'Widdicombe Fair', that audiences had come to love.

The main reason for Baring-Gould's disengagement from the concerts was that he was heavily engaged, as will be described shortly, in preparing his folk opera, 'Red Spider'. The principal role in this had been awarded to the soprano Lucy Carr Shaw, the sister of George Bernard Shaw. She

---

22 Devon Heritage Centre, Baring-Gould Papers, 5203M, Box 26, Letter of Edmund Badger to Sabine Baring-Gould, 13 December 1897.

became good friends with Frank Pemberton and, after the opera closed, she joined the company performing the 'Songs of the West' costume concerts in the early part of 1899. She and Pemberton then became involved in Albert Chevalier's performances at the Queen's Hall for a three-month run from April to June. She stayed on with Pemberton for a further further series of costume concerts which toured in the South West during the summer.

An increasing number of the concerts had been given in an educational context rather than as a pure entertainment. The venues for these were the literary, scientific and philosophical institutions where the audience would have been primarily middle-class, but Pemberton was also offered engagements at working men's institutes. It is perhaps because he was able to point to this success that Pemberton succeeded, where Moreton had failed, in securing a tour for the show in the United States and Canada. For this, the concert party called themselves The London Glee Singers. The company included Lucy Carr Shaw, Miss Emlen Jones, Robert Hyatt and Isidore Marcil. Mary Pemberton travelled as the accompanist for the party.

In the USA the show went out on the Lyceum circuit, as had been the plan nine years earlier. A programme for the show has survived in the archives at the University of Iowa that identifies the promoter as Fred Pelham of the Central Lyceum Bureau in Chicago. The programme was called 'English Folk-Songs' and was described as a 'Character and Costume Concert'. The title 'Songs of the West' was not used as it would not have had the same meaning in the US – the audience might have been expecting cowboy songs. The programme did, however, identify Baring-Gould, Sheppard and Bussell as having given their permission for the songs to be used. The format was similar to that used at home, with four scenes: 'Old England' (seventeenth century), 'Romantic England' (eighteenth century), 'By the Seashore' (sea songs) and 'On the Village Green' (songs of rural life), with appropriate costumes for each. The programme included some composed songs, such as Dibdin's 'Tom Bowling' and two songs by Sir Henry Bishop that might more appropriately be considered parlour songs but which would have been enjoyed by the audiences. Mary Pemberton was given an opportunity to demonstrate her virtuosity at the end of the third part with a piano solo, 'The Patrol', by A. H. West. The majority of the songs, though, were from Baring-Gould's collection. America was thus introduced to 'Widdicombe Fair', 'Sweet Nightingale', 'Richard of Taunton Deane' and other traditional Devon songs.

Fig. 11.5 – Concert Programme for 'London Glee Singers' tour of USA, 1899 (Courtesy of Redpath Chautauqua Collection, University of Iowa Libraries, Iowa City, Iowa).

Their tour opened in Toronto at the end of October 1899, but most of the next two months was spent in the US. There is not a complete list of the places they visited, but they included Chicago, Whitewater (Wisconsin), Beatrice (Nebraska), Rock Island (Illinois) and Genesco (New York) among others. The reviews of the concerts were generally good. The *Toronto Globe* said of their concert that: 'One cannot speak too highly of the vocalists. The pure and sympathetic voices, and the refined singing of the ladies was well supported by the fine voices and admirable vocalization of the gentlemen.' The *Rock Island Argus* reported that the concert was 'highly enjoyed' by a 'large and appreciative audience'. The *St Paul Globe* made a number of positive comments about the show while commenting, rather more ambiguously, that 'the performance pleased to some degree and appealed to portions of the audience'.

The latest concert for which I have found a record is that which took place in Genesco on 29 January 1900 and it is likely that the party returned to the UK shortly afterwards.

There is a mystery concerning the involvement of Lucy Carr Shaw in this tour. At the concert given in Dartmouth on 18 September the reviewer in the local paper wrote:

'The only regrettable feature was the indisposition of Miss Carr Shaw, from whom great things were expected in consequence of the reputation that had preceded her. Mr Pemberton announced that she had caught a severe cold and it was very evident that she was labouring under great disadvantages while taking her concerto parts. She was unable to sing the songs allotted to her in the programme and, in one instance, an extra song was substituted by Mr Hyatt.'[23]

Then, on 5 October, *The Stage* reported that:
Miss Carr Shaw, who should have sailed on by SS. Pavonia on the 3rd inst., for a twenty-six weeks' concert tour in the United States and Canada, has at the last moment been obliged to relinquish the engagement owing to serious lung trouble, which may incapacitate her for work for some time.[24]

The programme for the tour included Lucy Carr Shaw's name and a notice in *The Stage* for 7 December reported that Mr Pemberton was being '… well supported by Miss Carr Shaw, and the other cast members'. The review of the concert in St Paul, Minnesota on 26 December mentioned Carr Shaw by name as 'an attractive soprano, who dressed her part well'.[25] In a letter to Janey Drysdale she says that she was disappointed at not getting to

---

23 'Songs of the West and English Minstrelsie', *Dartmouth & South Hams Chronicle*, 22 September 1899, p. 2.
24 *The Stage* – Thursday 05 October 1899, p. 18.
25 *St. Paul Globe*, Sunday, Dec 24, 1899, p. 2.

America for her 24 week tour, suggesting that she had other engagements planned around the concerts with The London Glee Singers.[26] But did she make a late visit to join the company for part of the tour?

Pemberton continued to put on the 'Songs of the West' concerts in the years that followed. A proposal to take the show to Australia came to nothing. One particularly interesting event was in February 1907, when 'Frank Pemberton's London Costume Concert Party' put on a performance of well-known West Country songs at the Colston Hall in Bristol as part of the Cooperative Trades Unionist Festival. The speaker during the interval was Ramsay MacDonald, who talked about the principles of trade unionism and the Cooperative movement. After the concert ended there was dancing to the Amalgamated Musician's Union Band.

In October 1910 Frank Pemberton ('of Songs of the West and Operatic fame') put on a show by his 'Operatic and Costume Concert Party' at Wells (Somerset) Town Hall.[27] Into a mixed programme of condensed versions of popular operas and items from the 'enormously popular Al Fresco season at Minehead' he opportunistically added 'Folk Songs from Somerset, recently collected by Mr Cecil Sharp'. These were also featured in the last concert for which I have found a record, which took place a month later in Reigate, Surrey, on 28 November. The advertisement that appeared in the *Surrey Mirror* spoke of 'Mr. Frank Pemberton's Celebrated Costume Concert Party in their unique entertainment of Folk Songs from Somerset and *Songs of the West*', with Somerset now being given prominence in the billing.[28]

After sixteen years of very successful performances based on Baring-Gould's work the steam had finally run out and adding Cecil Sharp to the mixture failed to raise the pressure sufficiently. There are no further records of Pemberton putting on shows based on *Songs of the West* or on folk song (though there were a few more shows put on by others which used the costume concert format, as we shall see). In the remaining years before the outbreak of the First World War Pemberton remained active. In 1911 he took on the job of touring manager for a production of *The Arcadians* mounted by a company assembled by his old 'Songs of the West'

---

26 Letter of Lucy Carr Shaw to Janey Drysdale, dated 31 Dec and included in Henry G. Farmer, *Bernard Shaw's Sister and her Friends, A New Angle on G. B. S.* (Leiden: E. J. Brill, 1959), pp. 129–31. Farmer dates this to 1901 but I believe it to be 1899, since Alys Rees (another of Pemberton's crew) is mentioned as being in rehearsal for 'Dorothy' in which she toured in February 1900.

27 Advertisement, *Wells Journal*, 20 October 1910, p. 4.

28 Advertisement, *Surrey Mirror*, 18 November 1910, p. 1.

colleague, Leslie Moreton, and which toured the country for the next three years. When not involved in these productions he sought longer-term engagements at seaside resorts, such as the series he ran at Burnham, Somerset, in the summer of 1911. His own performances became more infrequent, an exception being his involvement in comic operas put on by a small company at Redgrave and Botesdale in Norfolk, initially to raise funds to build a church hall in Botesdale.

On 11 January 1915 Edmund Badger recorded his first day as head master at the Woughton and Simpson Council School in the school log. Before his arrival in Simpson (now subsumed into Milton Keynes) he had been teaching for short periods at Steppingly and Dunstable in Bedfordshire. Perhaps the travel involved in theatrical management and performance was proving too much for him in his fifties and he returned to the profession in which he originally qualified. He settled to life in a village school, and the school logbook reveals the minutiae of that life, dealing with fireguards and furniture as well as disciplining wayward schoolboys and coping with sickness among pupils and staff. Mary Badger sometimes took on voluntary work to fill gaps, teaching sewing or cookery, for example. Her brother, Frederick Bussell, visited the school and made several gifts to it. Music was still important and he instituted regular school concerts. At a 'Tea and Entertainment' held at the school on 15 December 1921 there were a number of musical items and Badger, 'acceding to many requests ... gave his inimitable version of the old Devonshire folk song, Widdicombe Fair'.[29]

Throughout 1921, though, Badger had been having health problems, described as 'septic anaemia' and had taken time off as a result. In February 1922 he returned to Norfolk to play the role of Aladdin (as Frank Pemberton) in the church hall at Botesdale that he had helped raise funds for in 1913. On 10 March he was certified as unfit for school duties and ordered to rest for three weeks. He died in the schoolhouse on 18 April, aged 62. Mary Badger returned to London, where she died in Hackney in 1938 at the age of 82.

Red Spider, a folk opera

Another stage project particularly dear to Baring-Gould's heart occupied much of his time between 1890 and 1898: the creation of a light opera based on his 1887 novel *Red Spider*. The book is set in the Devon countryside and tells of a dispute over inheritance between Hillary Nanspian and

---

29 *North Bucks Times*, 17 December 1921. For this reference and for other information about Badger's time in Simpson I am indebted to local historian Peter Barnes.

Taverner Langford, the smouldering embers of which were ignited by the killing of a money spider. In Devon, as in some other parts of England, this was one of the red-coloured varieties and so also the nickname given to the young heroine of the story, Honor Luxmore, because she habitually wore a scarlet cloak and red stockings. Her marriage would prove the key to resolving the dispute, but her first duty was to look after her younger siblings and manage her widowed and delusional father. There is a wonderfully drawn villain in the form of Taverner Langford's housekeeper, Mrs Veale. The story is located in the area around Bratton Clovelly, to the north of Lew Trenchard, where Baring-Gould spent part of his childhood and he gives a convincing portrayal of village life in Devon in the mid-nineteenth century as well as introducing some local folklore. It was a very successful book, and a good choice for the plot of an opera. Baring-Gould's original idea was a simple one. He would use his novel, some folk airs and some additional narrative to create a libretto, which Henry Fleetwood Sheppard would set to music.

Baring-Gould had been approached by Aimée Beringer, the wife of the musician and composer, Oscar Beringer, who wanted his permission to dramatise his novel *Mehalah*. She had been encouraged to write operatic *libretti* by her husband's friend, Sir George Grove (the founding editor of *Grove's Dictionary of Music*) but had turned towards playwriting as well as writing novels and short stories. She produced a number of her own plays, which enabled her to claim experience as a theatrical manager and impresario. She was, as can be gauged from her letters to Baring-Gould, a forceful personality who was also active in the cause of women's rights.[30]

Baring-Gould was impressed by her stagecraft and by her experience as a librettist and in 1890 invited her to assist with the project to turn *Red Spider* into a light opera. While Baring-Gould was keen on this arrangement, there is a sense from the outset that the other partner in the venture, Sheppard was not. There were a number of letters written by Sheppard to Baring-Gould in 1890 in which he made various proposals for songs that he felt fitted situations in the opera. His letter of 7 July 1890 opens with the phrase, 'It grieves me to be considered obstructive...' and he goes on to explain that he is not happy that songs he was working on for the operetta were being diverted into the 'Songs of the West' concerts.

By August 1892 Sheppard was very unhappy indeed and felt unable

---

30 Many of Aimée Beringer's letters survive in Baring-Gould's papers in the Devon Heritage Centre, 5203M, Box 26.

to carry on, as he was finding it difficult to work with Aimée Beringer and her constant changes in plan, particularly since he was in Yorkshire, Beringer in Hampshire and Baring-Gould in Devon. He was also feeling the limitations of his musicianship and wrote: 'I cannot face putting myself in a position which would be not only false but ridiculous – or at least ludicrous. An old country parson verging on 70, unknown in the musical world is hardly the man to raise expectations or create sympathy.'[31] He referred back to a meeting in Taunton two years earlier where all the interested parties had come together and where, because he was able to play his music over and explain his thinking, he felt that they all understood what he was trying to achieve. He lists the songs he has produced for the opera and reports that in six cases the words were his own, and that he felt that Mrs Beringer would not retain them. Though he leaves the possibility of continuing open, it is clear that this was the point at which he withdrew from the project. He wrote: 'But when I look at the music which I have done or partly done for R. S. [*Red Spider*] I am dismayed to think what labour in vain it has been. Mrs. O. B. in her selection of new incidents & situations, would probably have no place for it.'

The work on *Red Spider* had been mentioned briefly by a number of newspapers over the years, and there was a report in January 1893 that Mrs Beringer and Baring-Gould had completed the libretto.[32] They now needed to find a composer to replace Sheppard. Another newspaper report suggested that Mrs Beringer's husband had written the music for the opera. Hubert Parry was approached and in the spring of 1895 Baring-Gould told his daughter, Mary, that Mrs Beringer was trying to engage Engelbert Humperdinck to compose the score.[33] Shortly afterwards, however, an agreement was reached with the Scottish composer Learmont Drysdale to work with Baring-Gould and provide the music. After a long session at Lew Trenchard in which the old libretto was literally torn apart, a new version was created using the scraps. A typescript copy of a draft bearing the names of Baring-Gould and Drysdale is in the manuscript collection at the Devon Heritage Centre, dated 10 September 1895. Mrs Beringer is not mentioned.

---

31 Devon Heritage Centre, Baring-Gould Papers, 5203M, Box 32, Letter of Henry Fleetwood Sheppard to Sabine Baring-Gould, 9 August 1892.
32 There is a script for a two-act opera in the collection of papers about *Red Spider* in Devon Heritage Centre, 5203 M, Box 16. This carries the names of Baring-Gould and Mrs Beringer and is dated 12 December 1893.
33 Devon Heritage Centre, Baring-Gould Papers, 7444M, Letter of Mary Dickinson to Sabine Baring-Gould (her father), undated, but March or April 1895.

There was still a long way to go before the opera could be staged and a particular problem was raising the money needed to put the show on. Appeals to various sources, including the D'Oyly Carte Opera Company, were not successful and in the end Baring-Gould and Drysdale had to put up most of the money themselves to form the 'Red Spider Syndicate'. It was agreed that 55 percent of the profits would go to Drysdale and 45 percent to Baring-Gould. Edmund Badger was taken on as manager for the production.

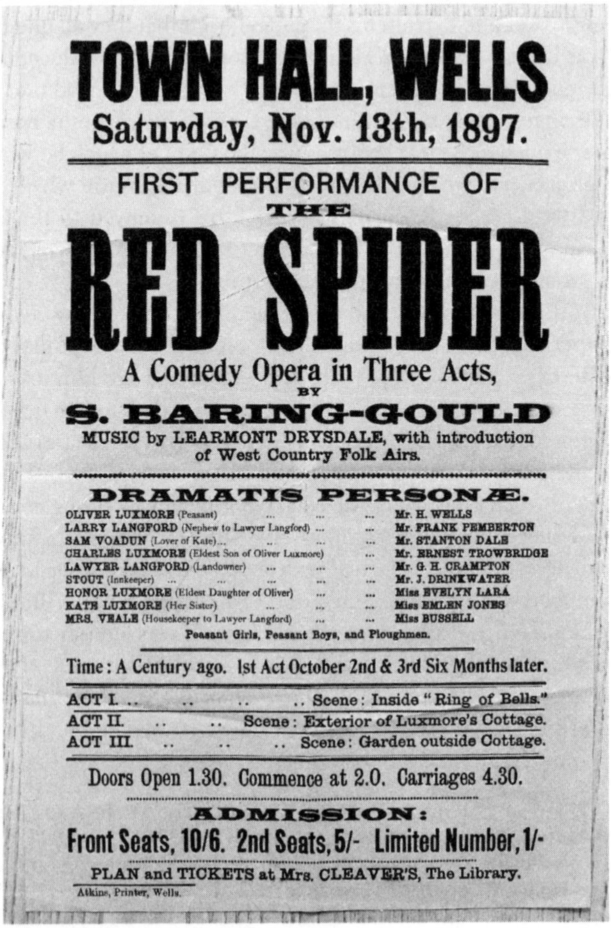
TOWN HALL, WELLS
Saturday, Nov. 13th, 1897.
FIRST PERFORMANCE OF
THE
RED SPIDER
A Comedy Opera in Three Acts,
BY
S. BARING-GOULD
MUSIC by LEARMONT DRYSDALE, with introduction of West Country Folk Airs.

DRAMATIS PERSONÆ.

OLIVER LUXMORE (Peasant)	Mr. H. WELLS
LARRY LANGFORD (Nephew to Lawyer Langford)	Mr. FRANK PEMBERTON
SAM VOADUN (Lover of Kate)...	Mr. STANTON DALE
CHARLES LUXMORE (Eldest Son of Oliver Luxmore) ...	Mr. ERNEST TROWBRIDGE
LAWYER LANGFORD (Landowner)	Mr. G. H. CRAMPTON
STOUT (Innkeeper)	Mr. J. DRINKWATER
HONOR LUXMORE (Eldest Daughter of Oliver)	Miss EVELYN LARA
KATE LUXMORE (Her Sister)	Miss EMLEN JONES
MRS. VEALE (Housekeeper to Lawyer Langford)	Miss BUSSELL

Peasant Girls, Peasant Boys, and Ploughmen.

Time: A Century ago. 1st Act October 2nd & 3rd Six Months later.

ACT I. .. .. Scene: Inside "Ring of Bells."
ACT II. .. .. Scene: Exterior of Luxmore's Cottage.
ACT III. .. .. .. Scene: Garden outside Cottage.

Doors Open 1.30. Commence at 2.0. Carriages 4.30.

ADMISSION:
Front Seats, 10/6. 2nd Seats, 5/- Limited Number, 1/-
PLAN and TICKETS at Mrs. CLEAVER'S, The Library.
Atkins, Printer, Wells.

Fig. 11.6 – 'Red Spider' Poster for 1897 private performance. (Courtesy of Dr Merriol Almond and Devon Heritage Centre).

There is some mystery about the first performance of *Red Spider*. There is a poster among Baring-Gould's papers (Fig. 11.6) for a performance of the opera at the Town Hall, Wells, on 13 November 1897. This followed the opening concert of a new season of the *Songs of the West* costume concert at the same venue the previous night. The cast for the opera identified on the poster were all members of the *Songs of the West* concert party. While the concert was advertised in the *Wells Journal* a week beforehand and reviewed a few days later, the opera was neither advertised nor reviewed.[34] In a letter dated 13 December 1897 Edmund Badger told Baring-Gould that he had sent a copy of the libretto to the Lord Chamberlain's Office and expected to receive a licence once it had been read. There was a receipt (dated 10 December) attached for two guineas from the Examiner of all Theatrical Entertainments in respect of a licence for a performance at the Town Hall, Wells. This suggests that the performance at Wells might not have gone ahead because a licence had not been obtained before the proposed November date. This might explain a comment made by Sheppard in his letter to Baring-Gould dated 13 December 1897 in which he says:

> So glad to hear that the Red Spider is once more spinning her web: may no rash hand of chambermaid – I mean of chamberlain interfere with its due completion and production. If he finds evil suggestion in that drama he must be a nice man of eminently nasty ideas.[35]

Work resumed on the opera in earnest in 1898. The production called for a very large company, numbering more than fifty performers. Edmund Badger's *alter ego* Frank Pemberton took on the lead role of Larry Langford and Lucy Carr Shaw took on the principal female role of Honor Luxmore. The other leading singers included some alumni of the 'Songs of the West' costume concerts, but for the majority this was their first experience of singing West Country folk songs. Baring-Gould had hoped to attend the rehearsals to make sure that the artists were singing and speaking with good Devonshire accents. Unfortunately, he was too ill to attend at the critical time and so sent his daughter Mary in his place.

---

34 'Songs of the West' (review), *Wells Journal*, 18 November 1897, p. 4.
35 Devon Heritage Centre, Baring-Gould Papers, Letter of Henry Fleetwood Sheppard to Sabine Baring-Gould, 13 December 1897, in Baring-Gould's 1880 Notebook-Diary, 5203 M, Box 25.

Fig. 11.7 – Lucy Carr Shaw and Frank Pemberton in costume for 'Red Spider' (Courtesy of the National Trust, G. B. Shaw Collection)

On 23 July 1898 *The Era* announced that Pemberton had succeeded in organising a twenty-week run for the opera, and the first public performance of *Red Spider* took place on 25 July 1898 at Great Yarmouth. Two weeks before the premiere Baring-Gould wrote to Lucy Broadwood saying

> Dear Miss Broadwood
>
> I wonder whether you would care to come to one of the final (but not dress) rehearsals of my opera Red Spider. It is to be produced at Lowestoft on 25 July and to travel the provinces. I come up on Wednesday for rehearsals. I believe there will be no dress rehearsal in town, but you will hear the music. Several of our folk airs are introduced.
> 1. Blue Kerchief
> 2. Oxen Ploughing
> 3. Why shd. [should] We Be Dullards Sad?
> 4. Lemonday
> 5. Flowers in the Valley
> 6. An unpublished melody for "Matthew, Mark, Luke and John"
> I fear the music is very modern, but it is good of its kind.[36]

---

36 Surrey History Centre, Lucy Broadwood Correspondence and Papers, Letter of Sabine Baring-Gould to Lucy Broadwood, 10 July 1898, 2185/LEB/1/296.

Much of the music was Drysdale's own composition rather than from the tradition, and not all of the words were those originally collected. The statement on the 1895 script had been changed in pencil: 'In this opera the composer has made use of some of the more characteristic of the old West Country folk airs'.

The reception for the opera was generally good, unsurprisingly so when it reached Devon. At the performance in Plymouth both Baring-Gould and Drysdale, who had conducted the orchestra himself, were called for a standing ovation and short speeches at the conclusion of the performance. The only disappointment while they were in Devon was that when members of the Red Spider Company took on the Wonford House cricket team they were soundly beaten, scoring only 66 runs, while Wonford passed that total for only two wickets, finally reaching 206 for four wickets. Pemberton batted last and scored four runs.

Praise for the show was not universal; the *Bury and Norwich Post*, while recognising Baring-Gould's strengths as a writer, commented: 'If the truth must be told, Mr Gould's lyrics sail pretty close to the wind of that mediocrity abhorred of the gods; still they serve as a useful peg on which Mr Drysdale hangs some excellent music...'[37] When the opera moved to Scotland in October the critics became even less kind about Baring-Gould's libretto, while admiring Drysdale's music. The critic of the *Edinburgh Evening News*, for example, wrote:

> Mr S Baring-Gould is a novelist of considerable power and a man of great attainments, but does not understand the art of writing a libretto. What 'Red Spider' is all about, no one could possibly conceive from the operetta version, the lyrics are 'bosh', and the connecting dialogue unintelligible, with the redeeming feature that their bathos is frequently funny. All this is the more regrettable, inasmuch as Mr. Learmont Drysdale has wedded to this farrago of nonsense music which, under happier auspices, would have proved of some enduring reputation, and certainly added largely to the composer's claims as a musician.[38]

But the adverse reviews were only a part of the problem. The show was losing money and no new bookings were coming in. Lucy Carr Shaw reported, in a letter to Janey Drysdale in October 1898 that Pemberton and Drysdale

---

37 'Eothen', 'The Red Spider at Lowestoft', *Bury and Norwich Post*, 9 August 1898, p. 6.
38 *Edinburgh Evening News*, 18 October 1898, p. 2.

had never been able to 'hit it off since the very beginning' and that they each came to her to tell of their problems with the other.[39] After some lively disagreements about who was to blame an advertisement appeared in *The Era* announcing that Pemberton would be 'at liberty in December'. He was replaced at the beginning of November by a new manager, Ernest Gerard, and a new singer, Faithful Pearce – so increasing the costs for the company further. Drysdale conducted the hundredth performance of the opera in Dundee on 18 November before a disappointingly small audience. He was called onto the stage and presented with an engraved silver cigarette case by the cast. Ernest Gerard struck a valedictory note in his speech, wishing that Drysdale's next opera might reach a thousand performances rather than a hundred. The next few days saw more advertisements by members of the cast such as Alys Rees, who announced on 26 November that her last performance in *Red Spider* after eighteen weeks would be that evening. The opera closed in Coatbridge and has never been produced since.

Passing the Baton, Later Ventures

Baring-Gould's feelings about this are not recorded anywhere, but he never undertook another full-scale stage production, though Frank Pemberton carried on the franchise for several more years. There were also other former members of the 'Songs of the West' company who had absorbed sufficient interest in folk songs to create performances based on them. Ernest Trowbridge (cast member 1894–95) presented concerts in Devon based on *Songs of the West*. Gage Goodfellow (cast member 1890–94) put together her own ensemble to perform the songs Baring-Gould had collected. Particularly interesting was the work of Arthur Ferguson (cast member 1889–94) who developed his enthusiasm for folk song to the point where he became a collector and arranger of folk songs. His census entry in 1911 describes him as 'Lecturer in Folk-Lore and Singer', and he founded the 'Folk Song Quartet' as a vehicle for his interest. He corresponded with Lucy Broadwood and sent her songs he had collected in various parts of England, though none were published. In February 1899 he gave a lecture at the Royal Institution, 'Jack in the Green and his Ancestry', for which Lucy Broadwood sang some of the examples for him.

A later venture that Baring-Gould took an interest in was a show put on by A. J. Coles, better known as 'Jan Stewer', the author of a number of Devonshire dialect books. This was *Revel Day* variously described as a 'musical play' and an 'operetta'. It included twenty songs from Baring-

---

39 Letter of Lucy Carr Shaw to Janey Drysdale, 5 Oct 1898, quoted in Henry G. Farmer, *Bernard Shaw's Sister*, p. 108.

Gould's collection and was performed in period dress much like Baring-Gould's costume concerts. The play was put on several times, mostly in and around Newton Abbot, where Coles lived. Baring-Gould attended a performance at the Town Hall, Bovey Tracey, in May 1908 and then again at the Alexandra Hall in Newton Abbot the following month. He gave a short talk on the second occasion, announcing that 'it was the greatest pleasure for him to hear again this operetta, which was so clever' and complimenting Coles on his production. He went on to talk about the songs and the way in which he had collected them. This was a return to the spirit of the shows that he had first put on nearly twenty years earlier.

I have identified advertisements and reports in national and local newspapers for more than 180 separate stage performances using folk songs from *Songs of the West*. There were certainly more. Baring-Gould's sustained effort to put traditional song from Devon and Cornwall into the public eye is remarkable, but there is little or no mention of it in the histories of the Victorian and Edwardian revival of interest in English folk song. His popularity as an author certainly helped in attracting audiences who were curious to see the man whose books they had read, or of whom they had heard. Those audiences would have heard some eminently singable songs, which they might have wanted to learn. Some might have bought *Songs of the West* or *A Garland of Country Song* from a table at the back of the hall so that they could play the tunes on the piano when they got home and learn the songs. Some of these people created a sub-species of 'Songs of the West' costume concerts, put on in village halls by local performers for whom it offered an alternative to the usual village concert fare – and one that gave them the opportunity to sing songs from their own county rather than the product of London-based publishers of popular song.

Baring-Gould published very little about his theatrical ventures, and our main source of information about them is contemporary newspaper advertisements, notices and reviews. In talking about his early lectures on folk song in *Further Reminiscences* he admitted:

> We always had good attendance, but I do not think the results were what we anticipated. Mr Sheppard and I especially aimed at stimulating the interest of those capable of continuing our work. But the collection of these songs with their melodies demands time, money and musical capacity. This last especially we could not reckon on. Musicians by profession were not interested.[40]

---

40 Sabine Baring-Gould, *Further Reminiscences*, p. 213.

It is true that there have never been large numbers of trained professional musicians who have taken an interest in folk song. That is so even today. Nonetheless, these shows must have been seen by thousands of people and it would be surprising if they had played no part in paving the way for the Edwardian folk song collectors. They would also have played a small but significant part in conditioning the general public (or at least a section of them) to be receptive when Sharp, Vaughan Williams and others of a new generation of folk song collectors began to explore and publish the treasures of English traditional song.

12: A Precious Legacy

Our object was not to furnish a volume for consultation by the musical antiquary alone, but to resuscitate, and to popularise the traditional music of the English people. As, however, to the antiquary everything is important, exactly as obtained, uncleansed from rust and unpolished, I have deposited a copy of the songs and ballads with their music exactly as taken down, for reference, in the Municipal Free Library, Plymouth.[1]

The Plymouth Manuscripts – Seekers After Truth – Francis Nicolle – The Baring-Gould Family Library – The Personal Copy – The Boxes in the Basement – Other Manuscripts – Street Literature – Other Musical Items –Entering the Digital Age – An Opportunity for Exploration

Having written so much about Baring-Gould and his folk song manuscript collection it would be as well to describe that collection as it stands today. An archivist would not, in fact, describe it as 'a collection' since it is not one entity in a single location. In the present context it makes sense to look at it as a whole and to describe the separate elements within it, the various documents in which he recorded the songs that he and his colleagues collected, as well as those that were sent to him. The original manuscripts, notebooks and other papers are mostly located in Devon, which is entirely appropriate. For those not blessed by living in that county, digital versions of most of the manuscripts that relate to his work on song can now be viewed in the online collection of Baring-Gould's manuscripts that forms part of the Vaughan Williams Memorial Library's Digital Collection, described later in this chapter. The various manuscripts described in this chapter with their current locations and references in the VWML Digital Database (where included) are listed in Appendix C.

The Plymouth Manuscripts

Anticipating criticism of his editorial choices, Baring-Gould had committed himself in December 1888 to making two fair copies of the songs in the original form that he collected them, and placing one with Plymouth Library and the other with the Devon and Exeter Institution. While the latter never received a copy of his collection, Baring-Gould delivered a large volume containing 202 songs to Plymouth in October 1900. This is the manuscript that has become known as the 'Fair Copy'.[2]

---

1 Sabine Baring-Gould, 'Introduction', *Songs of the West* (1905), p. xi.
2 Plymouth, Central Library, Baring-Gould Collection, Fair Copy Folk Song Manuscript.

On the front pastedown of this volume two items have been stuck in. The first is a postcard dated 19 September 1900 and written by Baring-Gould to the librarian, W. H. K. Wright, in which he says:

> I have not forgotten about the Vol of 'Songs'. I go on slowly transcribing, but it is a long business. More than half the first volume is copied out and 130 songs with all their variants of tune or words. I go abroad for the winter and shall take the books with me and go on copying.

Less than a month later, on 12 October, the manuscript volume arrived at the Library with the following enclosure:

> Dear Mr Wright
> I have worked hard and have succeeded in finishing one volume of songs – 202 copied out, and I present it to the mun. [Municipal] library.

The manuscript that Baring-Gould gave to the library in 1900 contains the words and tunes (with their variants) of most of the songs that he had published in *Songs of the West* and *A Garland of Country Song* as well as a few unpublished items. This large volume is set out with the song texts on the right hand (recto) page and the melodies on the left hand (verso) page, all in Baring-Gould's hand (see example in Plate 10). The notation is written in black ink on hand drawn staves in red ink. For each song he gives the variants of the words and of the tunes that he collected or was sent, often with a version copied from a printed source. The songs are numbered, the earlier ones using the same numbers as in *Songs of the West*.[3] The inclusion of the variants means that the 202 headings in the volume comprise 900 individual items. Most of these have a note identifying the source, and sometimes adding further information. In a few cases there is a printed version of a song that has been pasted in. Baring-Gould has also compiled an index to the volume.

The title page carries a note:

> I give these as near as possible, but singers sometimes vary the words, & the airs slightly, when singing at intervals of time. Also where there have been four or five versions of the same, slightly varying, I have not always noted all the differences. This in my

---

3   It will not surprise the reader to know that the numbering has gone astray in some places.

opinion, when I first started collecting, in 1888, was not necessary, as I was under the impression that they were all taken from Broadsides.

Later, I came to a different opinion; & I now hold that in a good many cases the traditional forms are earlier & sometimes more correct than the broadsides, which were taken down in many cases from oral recitation in London, or Manchester, or other large towns, where correct forms were less likely to be preserved than in Country villages.

S. Baring-Gould
Jan 27, 1892.

The date given in this note suggests that Baring-Gould began to compile this volume early in 1892, though he did not complete it until 1900. It should be said that his handwriting, though still difficult to read in places, is better in this manuscript than in most of the others. Baring-Gould's postcard refers to 'the first volume' and his letter to 'one volume of songs'. It can be inferred from this that there was to be a further volume. There is no evidence that this was ever worked on.

On St Valentine's Day 1914 he wrote another letter to William Wright at Plymouth Library.

Dear Mr Wright
I shall be in Plymouth some day next week, & will bring in 14 music books containing the taking down, mostly in pencil, of the Folk airs in Devon & Cornwall by the late Rev. H. Fl. Sheppard & Dr Bussell. These were taken down direct from the old singers, & will serve as the best guarantee for the genuineness of the tunes I published. Unhappily two more volumes are missing, One of Mr Sheppard's was destroyed at his death and one with the taking down by Dr. Bussell was not very distinct and I sent it him at Oxford to ink in, & he never returned it. I wrote thrice to him, but he failed to answer me, and didn't return the book.

There is also a letter to Baring-Gould from Bussell, apologising for not having sent on one of the notebooks:

My Dear Mr. Baring-Gould
I am so sorry, have only just come back from a long time abroad; & no letters were forwarded during the time. I am so vexed; you must

have tho't is all is lost! The MS Book is no doubt quite safe and at my house in Mundham, which is to be vacated at Michlemas [sic]. The tenant just in throes of departure. My housekeeper will I know put it away safely. If you cld wait till then I will send it most carefully back as I appreciate the value of the early impressions.

Both of these letters are preserved with the set of manuscript music notebooks that has become known as the 'Rough Copy'.[4] There is still a little confusion about this group of manuscript books. It is known that Plymouth Library only ever had thirteen notebooks, but it is believed that Bussell did return the stray volume, so it is not clear why there is no 'volume 12' in the set. Understanding the set has been confused further as a decision was taken by the library at some point to rebind all the thirteen volumes into one. When this was done the covers of the original notebooks were removed and were not kept. In the 1990s the manuscript was examined by a book conservator who recommended that it should be rebound again in the original thirteen separate volumes. This work was started but was not completed, and manuscript is currently archived unbound.

The Rough Copy manuscript contains 1,224 items, the majority of them the notation of songs by Bussell in the field, with some additional notes added later by Baring-Gould. Several of these are not found anywhere else in Baring-Gould's manuscripts and so we do not have the words that went with the tunes. Other parts of the manuscript contain drafts of arrangements by Sheppard and Bussell for performance or publication. The information given about the songs is limited. The singers are named in many cases and some dates of collection are given. Where this information is incomplete it is sometimes possible to identify the song by reference to another manuscript. Each volume has a typescript index prepared by Plymouth Library staff. The song titles assigned at the time of collection are not always the ones used later on. A brief description of the content of each volume is given in Appendix C.

These are the hardest of Baring-Gould's manuscripts to work with and few people have studied them in detail. Though frustrating, they are at times a delight, as you come across little gems of information about a singer, or a joke, usually by the ever-exuberant Bussell. There is also some value in looking at the order in which the songs are noted down, as this can often help to understand the journeys made by Baring-Gould and his colleagues in search of song. In these manuscripts we are usually

---

4   Plymouth, Central Library, Baring-Gould Collection, Rough Copy Folk Song Manuscript (13 volumes).

Fig. 12.1 – Example page from Rough Copy Vol 1 – Songs collected in Fowey, 20 Aug 1894 (Courtesy of Wren Music)

looking at the tunes in their raw state, before any changes were made for publication, sometimes before they were barred, and with the mistakes that the imperfect process of collection before the advent of recording devices ensured.

Seekers After Truth

Baring-Gould is the only English folk song collector who made his folk song manuscripts available to the general public in his lifetime in this way. Until the discovery of further manuscript material in the 1990s his reputation as a collector was established on the basis of his published work and, to some extent, by study of the Fair Copy and the Rough Copy. The number of people who actually consulted the manuscripts in Plymouth between 1900 and 1998 seems to have been small.[5] The first person to examine and write about them was Charles Laycock who gave a talk on folk song to the Devonshire Association at its annual meeting in 1917.[6] Laycock was a London solicitor who returned frequently to his home in

---

5   1998 was the year in which Baring-Gould's manuscripts became available at several libraries in microform as a result of the Baring-Gould Heritage Project.

6   Charles Laycock, 'English National and Folk Music with Special Reference to the Folk Songs of Devonshire', *Report and Transactions of the Devonshire Association*, 49 (1917), pp. 296–319.

Moretonhampstead where he adopted the habits of an old Devonshire countryman. His large collection of artefacts associated with Devonshire rural life can now be seen in the Torquay Museum.

He was a skilled musician and composed some songs, as well as studying the collections of Baring-Gould and Sharp. In his Barnstaple talk he said that when he first heard a selection of Baring-Gould's songs performed in concert by a travelling party of musicians (probably Pemberton's *Songs of the West* crew in the 1890s) he thought, 'Surely a Dartmoor peasant never sang a song in that language.' He recognised no trace of dialect and the language and diction were not the vernacular speech of Devonshire people. He also knew several of the songs from childhood and these were not like those he remembered. They had, as we know, been tidied up for performance on the concert platform and in the drawing room.

In 1916 he visited Plymouth Library and spent some time looking at Baring-Gould's Fair Copy. He wrote: 'There I found, as I anticipated, the language which I should have expected a Dartmoor singer to have used.' He understood that past generations had been happy to sing about things that his own generation would not tolerate, except in 'low music hall songs'. What he regretted particularly was the replacement of archaic or dialect words with their literary equivalent. He gave the example of 'The Barley Rakings' (No. 85 in *Songs of the West*). This was almost completely rewritten by Baring-Gould, as it deals with unmarried pregnancy and abandonment. Laycock is more concerned, though, with the replacement of the archaic word 'style' which occurs in the line 'They had a mind to style and play'. In the published work this was given as 'With sighs their last farewell to say'. Baring-Gould, in his note to the song mentioned this word, observing that it derived from the Anglo-Saxon *styllan*, to leap or dance. Laycock's view was that such an interesting survival should have been retained.

Though not in the song, the word, with a short explanation was retained in Baring-Gould's notes, and in his manuscripts. He cared greatly about language and dialect but in practice needed to make choices as to what was appropriate for his audience. In his novels and in other books where the speech of country-folk is quoted he tried to reproduce what he had heard – whether in Yorkshire or Devon. He may not always have succeeded well enough to please everyone, but he did need to carry his readers with him, and successful representation of dialect from whatever part of the country is a difficult matter that has been known to cause more than a few arguments. Not all of the people towards whom *Songs of the West* was directed at that time would have understood the archaic and dialect words, or wished to sing them. By the time that Laycock was writing there was much more interest in dialect and there might have been a case, as he goes on to suggest, for reissuing *Songs of the West* with more representative language. But we do have Baring-Gould's manuscripts in which this language can be read, as well as his prose elsewhere.

The next person to study the manuscripts in depth was the poet and anthologist James Reeves, who made a selection of the songs from the Fair Copy for his book, *The Everlasting Circle* (1960).[7] He excuses himself for not having presented the songs with their music, as that was not his interest or speciality, but he writes at length about Baring-Gould, and about what he discovered in the manuscript. He had previously published a similar book based on Cecil Sharp's collection, *The Idiom of the People*.[8] Reeves found Baring-Gould's collection disappointing compared with that of Sharp, the Hammond Brothers or George Gardiner, since he believed that Baring-Gould should have found more than was included in the Fair Copy. He was right to expect more, but could not know that he was only examining a selection of the songs that Baring-Gould had collected. If he had had the opportunity to study the full collection he might have reached a different conclusion.

There were also a number of folk song researchers who 'visited' the manuscripts by post. In 1932, for example, Maud Karpeles wrote asking about the manuscripts and was sent a copy of the indices of the various volumes. Roy Palmer requested copies of several songs that interested him in 1967, and the folk song collector Peter Kennedy had a complete photocopy of the manuscripts made for reference.

One of the most assiduous students of the manuscript collection and of Baring-Gould's life was Cyril Tawney who, after he left the Royal Navy and became a full time folk-singer, was living in Plymouth. He wanted to know more about Baring-Gould and his songs and spent much of his spare time in the library, looking through the manuscripts. He read several of his books and also travelled out to many of the villages where Baring-Gould collected to get a feel for the place and an idea of the sort of people he might have met. He spent hours searching for good songs, copying them out in longhand. Because he lived near the library he was able to visit frequently to look in detail at the Rough Copy manuscripts, which most of the visitors who journeyed from a distance did not have time to do.

---

7   James Reeves, The Everlasting Circle, *English Traditional Verse from the Mss of S. Baring-Gould, H. E. D. Hammond and George B. Gardiner* (London: Heinemann, 1960).

8   James Reeves, *The Idiom of the People, English Traditional Verse from the Mss of Cecil Sharp* (London: Heinemann, 1958).

In 1969 Tawney was scheduled to record an album with fellow singer Louis Killen for the record producer, Bill Leader, in Plymouth. Killen was taken ill and unable to travel so Leader, keen not to waste an opportunity, asked Tawney if there were any projects that he was working on that could be recorded. Tawney had been studying the 'big ballads' in the Baring-Gould collection with a view to a future recording and after a couple of days' hard work the two men headed off to Plymouth Library. They borrowed a room where Cyril recorded ten of the Child Ballads that had been collected in the South West.[9] He recorded several more songs taken from Baring-Gould's collection in the coming years, including an LP of 'songs of seduction' from the original song manuscripts.[10] He also wrote some magazine articles about Baring-Gould. In the early 1970s, for example, he published two articles responding to a spate of criticism of folk song collectors in general, and Baring-Gould in particular, for their bowdlerisation of folk songs, pointing out that in their time they had few options and that Baring-Gould was not significantly worse in respect of his editing of folk song than Sharp and other collectors.[11]

In 1974 David and Charles published *Folk Songs of the West Country*, a collection of fifty songs taken directly from the Fair Copy manuscript.[12] The editor was Gordon Hitchcock, who had formerly worked for the music publishers, J. Curwen and Sons and who had edited a number of folk song compilations. A letter dated 30 April 1971, written by Hitchcock to Plymouth Library, explains that when Curwen closed their business at the end of 1970 he had taken over responsibility for their Baring-Gould copyrights and was hoping to exploit them before the term of the copyright ran out in 1974 (fifty years after Baring-Gould's death). A note with the letter sets out the position as Bill Best Harris, Plymouth's chief librarian at the time, saw it. He recognised that the library did not necessarily own the copyright of the songs, even though the manuscripts were its property. Curwen's claim to copyright was doubtful and said to be a result of a trust set up in the 1920s, but no record of this had survived. While it is feasible that Curwen might claim copyright in the print of *English Folk Songs for Schools* it is hard to see how they could have justified any ownership of other

---

9   Cyril Tawney, *The Outlandish Knight*, Polydor 236577.
10 Cyril Tawney, *Down among the Barley Straw*, Trailer LER 2095.
11 Cyril Tawney, 'Collectors of folk songs: Baring-Gould defended', *Western Morning News*, 10 September 1971. Cyril Tawney, 'Censor or sensible', Folk Review, April 1972, pp. 7–8.
12 Gordon Hitchcock, *Folk Songs of the West Country* (Newton Abbot: David and Charles, 1974).

material. One can only wonder what Baring-Gould himself would have made of such a claim, given the past difficulties he had endured in dealing with Curwen which were described in Chapter 8.

In the event, Hitchcock's book was published with no copyright claimed other than on the book itself, and with appropriate acknowledgement to Plymouth Library. Hitchcock worked from the Fair Copy manuscript and one must have a little sympathy for him working on what was probably a limited number of visits with a manuscript that is, even in the neat version, hard to read. It is not surprising that there are some errors in names of singers and of places. In his short Foreword he states that he has corrected inaccuracies and completed missing lines. He also reduced the length of some ballads, and made several word changes.

Hitchcock's book was severely criticised by Cyril Tawney in a full-length article in *Folk Review*.[13] He acknowledged the need for a new edition of Baring-Gould's songs and was disappointed that this was not the book that he had hoped for. He felt that the book had missed the opportunity to present alternative versions of some of the well-known songs like 'Widdicombe Fair' or 'Strawberry Fair'. The notes were mostly Baring-Gould's words, with no additional information or corrections where something was known to be wrong. And, beyond giving guitar chords rather than a piano accompaniment, it made little effort to appeal to the new generation of singers. It was, as Baring-Gould's original had been, designed to sit on the piano in the drawing room. The book was not a great success and was rapidly remaindered.

Francis Nicolle

In 1955 the Plymouth Library's collection of Baring-Gould's books and manuscripts was significantly increased by a bequest from a London clergyman. Francis George Stainforth Nicolle was born in Jersey in 1871 where his father was in the wine trade. He gained his degree at Pembroke College, Oxford, and was ordained deacon in 1895 at the same ceremony in Exeter as his good friend, Arthur Baring-Gould, Sabine's half-brother. In his unpublished memoir Arthur says of Nicolle that he:

> …as a boy, from reading his books, had created for himself a sort of hero-worship of my half-brother. […] He had taken a Curacy at Plymouth, and I went to be Sabine's Curate at Lew Trenchard. I was able to introduce him to Sabine, and his admiration for

---

13 Cyril Tawney, 'Oh Well, Back to the Drawing-Room', *Folk Review*, September 1974, pp. 14–15.

him greatly increased. Thereafter he set himself to collect all the books written by Sabine, and continued his collection till every known work stood in his bookshelves. [...] It involved searching the second-hand bookshops all over the Kingdom, travelling to all points of the compass. He has in his collection more of Sabine's books than has the British Museum.[14]

Nicolle was a committed Anglo-Catholic and a member of the Society of the Holy Cross, an organisation whose master was Rev C. R. Chase, the Vicar of All-Saints, Plymouth, where Nicolle was curate from 1895 to 1899. He worked in several London parishes (with a brief break in Penzance) before becoming Vicar of St Thomas, Bethnal Green in 1925. The church was damaged by bombing during the Second World War and demolished in 1951. Nicolle retired to St Leonards-on-Sea where he died in October 1955 at the age of 84.

As Arthur Baring-Gould reported, he made a large collection of Sabine Baring-Gould's books. Remarkably, after his hero's death, he helped Sabine's son, Edward, by purchasing many of the books and magazine articles a second time for the Baring-Gould family archive.

When Nicolle left his entire collection to Plymouth Library the *Western Morning News* reported that it consisted of more than 400 books, pamphlets and magazine articles.[15] The smaller items are gathered into folders, neatly labelled in Nicolle's hand. He was working in an age before photocopiers, and where he could not obtain a copy of a printed article he copied it out by hand. Plymouth Library already had a good collection of Baring-Gould's books, but Nicolle's bequest was said, in the article, to have increased it by 75%.

There were two manuscript items in Nicolle's bequest. One is a collection of Baring-Gould's own verse in fair copy and which includes some of the songs that he substituted for traditional songs that he felt unable to use in *Songs of the West*. This is now known as Composition Notebook 1. The more interesting item is another notebook, now known as Working Notebook 1, which is the oldest song manuscript in the Baring-Gould collection. He started to use it early in the project to record the songs he had received and collected. It was, in effect, the first fair copy of his collection, but he soon outgrew it and it became a field notebook, a place for working out versions for publication and finally for all sorts of rough notes, sometimes filling spaces left earlier in the book. The first songs

---

14 Arthur Baring-Gould, unpublished memoir (in private ownership).
15 'Baring-Gould Treasury in Plymouth', *Western Morning News*, 16 November 1955.

in the book are those sent to him by friends and helpful strangers. These are interspersed with songs connected to the South West from books, including Bell's *Ballads and Songs of the Peasantry*. Some of the original letters were stuck into the book, while others were left loose, including some written to Baring-Gould's grandfather at the beginning of the century.

The first item in the book is dated 15 September 1888 and records the version of 'Widdicombe Fair' sent to Baring-Gould by William Collier. The last entry for which a date can be confidently assigned is a list of the songs that were proposed to be sung at the three lecture-concerts that he gave in Exeter, South Brent and Tavistock at the end of January 1889. This suggests that Baring-Gould filled this book in the first four months of the project but that he went back to it to add other notes and reworking later. It is unlikely, though, that this was the only notebook he was using at the time. There are several songs that were collected in the winter of 1888–89 that are not in this manuscript and have not been found in rough notes elsewhere.

'Jolly Fellows that Follow the Plough', on pages 26–27, is the first item in the book that was noted from a singer, in this case Robert Hard whom Baring-Gould visited at South Brent in the autumn of 1888. This may be Baring-Gould's note of the song made in the field. The eight verses are written in pencil on the right-hand page and have been copied out in ink on the facing page with some alterations. Alongside Hard's rough text there

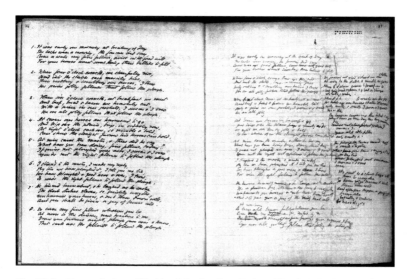

Fig. 12.2 – Example from Working Notebook 1, Robert Hard's Jolly Fellows That Follow the Plough' (Courtesy of Wren Music).

are some additional verses, noted a few months later from James Olver of Launceston. It is Olver's version that Baring-Gould chose to transcribe into his later manuscripts, with the note that Hard sang a similar version. The song had been listed as one of those contemplated for inclusion in Part 2 of *Songs of the West* but it was never published.

We do not know how Nicolle obtained these two notebooks, but they are not the only items that have escaped to the outside world since 1924. Local gossip says that after Baring-Gould's death some cartloads of paper were taken to the quarry to be burnt. The locals would poke around and some interesting items found their way into their cottages and then, perhaps, to collectors like Nicolle. Whatever happened, we owe a huge debt of gratitude to Francis Nicolle for the effort he put into assembling his collection, and for bequeathing it to Plymouth Library.

Several generations of librarians have ensured that despite war damage to Plymouth Library and the confusion of local government reorganisation the Baring-Gould song manuscripts and Nicolle's collection have been looked after. The originals of the Fair Copy, the Rough Copy and the two notebooks have now been transferred to the Plymouth and West Devon Archive for safekeeping, since they can be studied in paper or electronic copies. The large collection of books that Nicolle gave to the library is available for reference in the library and makes Plymouth one of the best locations for the study of Baring-Gould's work by the general public.

Librarians are not usually passive jailers of books. Past librarians at Plymouth have looked at the Baring-Gould collection and thought, 'is that all there is?' The story is told that one of them was so sure that there was more to be found that he went out to Lew Trenchard and peered in through the windows, looking for a secret store of forgotten manuscripts. He did not discover any – but that was because he was looking in the wrong place.

The Baring-Gould Family Library

Baring-Gould's forebears had started the collection of books that made up the library at Lew House. Some have the bookplate of his grandfather, William, and a few more that of his father. These were the books that you would expect to find in the house of a well-educated gentleman, including many classical texts and the almost inevitable books on country pursuits. There were also some books and music added to the collection by Baring-Gould's children and grandchildren.

When Baring-Gould died, his son, Edward, was faced with the task of sorting out his father's effects: his papers, his books, his house and, of course, the Lew Trenchard estate. Edward and his wife, Marian, lived in

Lew House from 1919 though, in practice, Edward spent much of his time in London. After Marion died in 1931 he rarely visited the house, which was let with the contents. It was opened as a hotel in 1949 and has been operated as such since, with only a brief hiatus in 1981, when it was opened to the public (unsuccessfully). The house and its contents remain the property of the family. Given this chequered history it is something of a surprise that many of the paintings and several items of furniture from Baring-Gould's time are still there. Crucially, much of his library has survived; even though more than 2,000 books that were not directly connected to Baring-Gould were sold as a single lot in 1937. They fetched £8.

In the 1970s it was recognised that because of problems with water damage and a lack of space the Baring-Gould book collection was at risk. At the same time Sir Richard Acland left Killerton House, near Exeter, which had been given to the National Trust some years earlier, taking his books with him and leaving the shelves in the library there empty. This presented the opportunity for an elegant solution to the difficulties for both houses. It was also assumed that Killerton would be a more secure location than Lew House, where there was the potential for books and other material to be 'lost' while the house was being operated as a hotel.

Bill Best Harris, who had recently retired from the post of Plymouth City Librarian, made a selection of over 3,000 volumes from the most valuable and interesting books from Lew House. This included a number of Baring-Gould's own copies of books that he had written, as well as the historical collection made by the family in the years before his time and, to a smaller extent, afterwards. It also included many of the books that he had bought for his research on all his areas of interest, including several shelves of books about folk song. Best Harris' selection also took into account the visual qualities of the books with the aim of making the library at Killerton look attractive to visitors. The books were, though, wired into the shelves and could not be studied by visitors without special arrangements being made.

I had visited the house and seen (and admired) the books, but had not suspected that there were untold riches to be uncovered. After the day in 1992, described earlier, when I first saw the three volumes of manuscript songs, I became determined to find out more about them. I wrote to Merriol Almond, Baring-Gould's great-granddaughter, to obtain her permission to examine the contents of the Killerton Library, and then to the National Trust to secure their co-operation. At that time it was only possible to get access on the days when the house was closed to the public or during the winter closure. Visits had to fit with my job and required that I should use leave days and then pack as much into the day as possible in order to work through the manuscripts and to list and understand their contents. Because the house was closed and mostly unheated during the winter, that work was sometimes undertaken wearing overcoat and gloves. The results of my study of the manuscripts and of the content of the library threw a powerful new light on Baring-Gould's work as a song collector.

The Personal Copy

The most important of the song manuscripts discovered at Killerton is what is now known as the 'Personal Copy' manuscript. This is the set of three large, vellum-bound volumes, first seen on the evening in March 1992 and mentioned in the Introduction. Though set out in the same fashion as the Fair Copy, it was immediately obvious that this was a much larger piece of work. These volumes were Baring-Gould's primary reference; the books that several journalists had described, and which had been lent to Cecil Sharp. Lucy Broadwood referred in a letter to the *Morning Post* on 2 February 1904 to 'the three great manuscript folios of the Rev. S. Baring-Gould, in which his collected tunes and words are given in their unaltered form', which she had seen in Lew House when she visited in 1893. It is surprising that the knowledge of their existence faded so completely and that they remained neglected for nearly seventy years after Baring-Gould's death.

It is probable that the Personal Copy was the source from which Baring-Gould prepared the Fair Copy given to Plymouth Library, but further analysis is needed to establish the exact sequence of events, as there are some differences in the notes between the two manuscripts. The song 'The Golden Vanity' does not appear in the Personal Copy, though it is in the Fair Copy and published in *Songs of the West*. In this case we do have an explanation. 'The Golden Vanity' is No. 64 in the book and in the Fair Copy. In the Personal Copy Baring-Gould has jumped from No. 63 to No. 65, omitting 'The Golden Vanity'.

There are a few errors in the numbering of the pages in the Personal Copy and Baring-Gould stopped giving the songs Roman numerals after number DLXVIII (568). He indexed all the volumes and only a few pages escaped his lists. The last dated entry in the Personal Copy manuscript is the penultimate song, which is a version of 'The Hundred Haymakers' that had been collected by Priscilla Wyatt-Edgell from a man at Cowley Bridge and is dated 13 August 1920.

The first volume of the Personal Copy contains most of the songs used in *Songs of the West* and the second volume those in *A Garland of Country*

Song. Once he had made a record of the songs that he had published, Baring-Gould continued adding any new songs that he found to this manuscript. He also seems to have gone back to copy out songs that he had not published or included elsewhere in the manuscript. This means that volume 3, in particular, contains a large number of songs that he never published or used, many of which are unique to Baring-Gould's collection. There are some very interesting songs to be found here, and it is a paradise for singers seeking unusual material for their repertoire.

The Boxes in the Basement

I mentioned in my Introduction that after I had made a few visits to Killerton House to study the Personal Copy, the house manager, Denise Melhuish, told me about 36 boxes of other Baring-Gould material in the basement. I looked at several of these and it became clear that the contents were of great interest. I had also by this time had an opportunity to get a general sense of what was on the library shelves and it was clear that the 'Killerton Hoard', as it became known, was of importance far beyond my own interest in folk song and would be valued by researchers with wider interests in Baring-Gould's life and work.

I reported my discoveries back to Merriol Almond and it was decided that the boxes should be transferred to the Devon Record Office (now the Devon Heritage Centre) in Exeter, which was done in August 1994. Once they had been transferred a provisional list of the contents was then drawn up with the items listed as received in the boxes brought from Killerton.[16] When the Record Office was moved from the centre of Exeter to its present location, some boxes were divided into two because of their weight. This part of the collection has still not been fully catalogued at the time of writing and it is planned that when this is finally done the contents will be re-ordered to group important items together. The contents are a mixture of material including damaged books and incomplete volumes, as well as correspondence, photographs, printers' proofs and manuscript material. One of the most important items discovered was the Diary-Notebook by Baring-Gould that covers the period 1880–99. The document is neither consistent nor complete and disappointing in that it contains no record of his folk song collecting. There is, though, much else that is of interest, and this is a valuable document of that period (referred to several times already), much of which is not covered in his autobiography.

---

16 The Devon Heritage Centre reference number for the Baring-Gould Papers is 5203M. The provisional list of contents of the boxes can be consulted in the Centre.

There were a number of other items in the boxes relevant to the folk song collection, including three more 'Working Notebooks'. These are, like the Plymouth Working Notebook, records of song texts with only a very few tunes. Each of them also contains reworking of some of the texts for publication as well as other notes and lists. I have described these notebooks in more detail in Appendix C.

I believe that Working Notebook 2 followed the Plymouth Working Notebook, since the first entry is a list of songs being considered for the third part of *Songs of the West*. Working Notebook 3 is the first in which he started to collect together all the different variants of the songs that he had heard under one title and it contains some songs copied from the two previous notebooks. Working Notebook 4 seems to have started as a repository for ballads, though the second half contains copies of songs collected on tours such as that to Dartmoor and Chagford in September 1890. It was probably started in 1889, and there are a number of items marked as having been 'sent to Child' and which do appear in the collection of letters to the professor. There are, though, items in it as late as 1894, so I think that it likely that it was used at the same time as other notebooks.

Baring-Gould copied the majority of the song variants from these notebooks into the Personal Copy. There are, though, a few variants to be found only in the notebooks. There are also some important and interesting differences to be found between some of the song texts in the notebooks when compared to those in the Personal Copy.

Other items found in the boxes also included three more composition notebooks, one of which dates back to his time in Cambridge, and a second that has the label of a Cambridge stationer. These comprise mainly hymns and religious poetry. The third (Composition Notebook 4) was started in 1898 but he has also copied in verses that he had composed in earlier years. There are some sets of verses that were inspired by the folk songs he had collected such as 'The Mole Catcher', 'The Cottage on the Hill' and 'The Flowery Land of Canaan'.

Other Manuscripts

Apart from the material found in the Killerton basement boxes, there are some other manuscripts that should be mentioned, many of which have only come to light in recent years. These include two notebooks that Baring-Gould used as a journal, one when he was in his teens, and the other in the 1860s.[17] The latter was referred to in Chapter 3 as being the place where he wrote up the first folk song that he collected when he was a curate in Horbury. This notebook was rediscovered in 1969 among a bundle of papers at Lew House.

In the Personal Copy, Baring-Gould includes nine songs that he took from a manuscript nursery rhyme book compiled by his aunt, Emily Baring-Gould, in about 1868. This compilation was made for the four-year-old Sabine and his sister Margaret. The original notebook was rediscovered at the same time as the 1862 Diary Notebook and is a charming piece of work. She has written out 31 songs, with accompaniments that are probably her own work, though there are a few songs written by known composers. Images of this notebook have been included in VWML Digital Collection.

There is another small collection of six music books that had belonged to the Baring-Gould family, which was bought at auction by Devon Library Services in the 1970s. They include four manuscript books, one of which contains mostly sacred music, but a few spare pages have been used to note a set of tunes heard at Lamerton from John Rickards and William Rice in 1889. They include 'Duke William', 'Adam and Woman', 'Now the Corn is All Ripe', 'The Fox Hunt', 'General Wolfe', 'William and Mary His Bride', Jolly Joe the Collier's Son' and others. These are in the Plymouth and West Devon Record Office and have not yet been digitised.

Street Literature

Though it is not manuscript material as such, it is important to describe the collection of printed popular literature that Baring-Gould made including broadsides, chapbooks, songsters and other street literature.[18] When he started to collect folk songs, Baring-Gould had a low opinion of the song texts given in broadsides or other forms of cheap printed literature, believing that they were a poor reflection of the original form of the ballad. Later he came to realise that broadsides were, for many of his singers, an important source of song words, whether they read them or heard them from someone who could read. He began to visit the British Museum Library and examine its volumes of broadsides such

---

17 Both of these have been transcribed by Ron Wawman and his transcriptions can be downloaded from his website where they are called 'The Adolescent Notebook', and 'Sabine's Diary Notebook, 1862 to 1868' respectively. <http://www.nevercompletelysubmerged.co.uk/index.htm> [Accessed 26 Jan 2017]

18 For a fuller description of this collection see Martin Graebe, 'I'd have you to buy it and learn it: Sabine Baring-Gould, his Fellow Collectors, and Street Literature' in David Atkinson and Steve Roud (eds), *Street Ballads in Nineteenth-Century Britain, Ireland, and North America* (Farnham: Ashgate, 2014), pp. 173–94.

as the Crampton and Roxburghe collections as well as a host of other volumes such as the wonderfully named 'Swimming Lady's Garland' and 'The Mountains of Hair's Garland'.[19] In July 1889 Baring-Gould wrote an article for the *Western Antiquary* called 'Ballads in the West,' in which he describes broadside ballads.[20] By the summer of 1890 he was able to report to Child that he had searched all the volumes of broadsides in the British Museum.[21] As a result of these studies he began to refer to printed sources more frequently in his published notes and in his manuscripts.

He had also started to collect broadsides himself. In fact, he must have built his collection very rapidly since we know from another letter to Child that he already had 1,700 ballads by the end of August 1890.[22] His collection, at its peak, contained more than 4,000 printed items. The most important part of this collection are the ten volumes into which he (or perhaps one of his children) pasted 2,766 broadsides – many of them having two or more songs per sheet. Most of these volumes are indexed in Baring-Gould's hand. He gave this collection to the British Museum, which also acquired some other volumes that had belonged to him and which he appears to have sold at auction.

Several volumes of street print remained in the Baring-Gould family library and most of these are now in the Devon Heritage Centre at Exeter. They were photographed for the microfiche issue of 1998 and will, in time, be added to the VWML digital collection. Unlike the broadside volumes mentioned above, they had hardly been used, as the bindings were still very tight and many items were uncut.[23] This group of material included seven volumes titled 'Broadsides' and three titled 'Chapbooks', though the content of all is an eclectic mixture of songsters, children's books and 'penny dreadfuls'. One large volume is titled 'Broadsides' and contains a number of large format broadsides (some of which are hand coloured), songsters, political posters and other ephemera. This is an outstanding collection and it was a great sadness when this 'went missing' for several years. Happily, it was rediscovered in 2014, and though it is in need of

---

19 'The Swimming Lady's Garland, containing several excellent new songs, etc', Publ. Newcastle 1765(?), 'The Mountains of Hair's Garland beautified with several excellent new songs', Newcastle, 1790.
20 Sabine Baring-Gould, *Western Antiquary*, 8 (1888–89), pp. v–xi.
21 Cambridge (MA), Houghton Library, Harvard University, Baring-Gould Manuscript, FMS Eng 863, Letter of 14 July 1890, Appendix item 4.
22 Houghton Library, Baring-Gould Manuscript, FMS Eng 863, Letter of 23 August 1890, Appendix item 5.
23 The Baring-Gould Heritage Project team took the decision to cut the pages to allow the content to be photographed.

conservation work it is hoped that this volume can be digitised so that a wider audience can see this remarkable selection.

As well as these volumes, which were shelved with the other folk song material in the library at Killerton House, two other bound collections of chapbooks have been found. A small volume titled 'The Blackbird' contains six Scottish chapbooks printed in the 1820s. More recently, another small volume titled 'Irish Ballads' has been discovered. This has yet to be examined in detail but is also a collection of chapbooks from the 1820s, this time printed in various Irish towns.

Other Musical Items

Even after 3,000 volumes had been moved to Killerton House, nearly 2,000 books remained on the shelves in Sabine Baring-Gould's former library at Lew House. They were for many years regarded as the poor relations of those at Killerton and they remained vulnerable to the predation and carelessness of hotel guests. A few years ago I spent some time looking through them and found that there were several interesting and valuable books. After I shared my findings with Merriol Almond, she asked retired librarians, Ian and Jill Maxted, to compile a complete list of the books in Lew House and to re-organise them. As a result, the most valuable are now safely enclosed in glass-fronted shelves. The Maxteds have prepared a listing of all the books in the Baring-Gould family library at Lew Trenchard and also those formerly housed at Killerton and which are now in the Heritage Collections of Exeter University Library.[24]

Among them are a few of the more up-market songsters from the seventeenth and eighteenth centuries, some of which had belonged to his grandfather. These include, for example, *Calliope or The Musical Miscellany* (1788), *The Bullfinch* (c. 1775) and *A New Whim of the Day or Musical Olio* (c. 1790) among others.

A concealed cupboard at Lew House contained other musical treasures, including a number of the volumes of Cecil Sharp's folk song and dance tunes, given to Baring-Gould by the author, as well as other sheet music. The shelves also hold books of folk songs and children's songs from France and Germany as well as a number of anthologies of songs sent to Baring-Gould by editors who had used songs from his collection, such as Sydney Nicholson's *British Songs for British Boys* (1903).

---

24 The list of the books in Baring-Gould's library has been prepared by Ian and Jill Maxted and can be found on Ian Maxted's website *Exeter Working Papers in Book History* – <http://bookhistory.blogspot.co.uk/2012/01/baring-gould-library.html> (Accessed 21 January 2017).

Other interesting music books on the shelves at Killerton included several that were gifts from fellow song collectors. He also had a beautifully bound (but, it appears, little used) set of the *Journal of the Folk Song Society*.

Entering the Digital Age

Not long after the Killerton manuscripts were discovered it was realised that this nationally important collection should be made available to folk song researchers throughout the world. In 1995 a number of individuals and institutions joined together in the Baring-Gould Heritage Project, with the intention of publishing the folk song manuscripts and other unique material from the Baring-Gould collection. The project brought together Paul Wilson and Marilyn Tucker of Wren Music, Dr Merriol Almond, Baring-Gould's great granddaughter, and Ian Maxted, then County Local Studies Librarian responsible for heritage collections throughout the county of Devon. I acted as project manager.

Wren Music obtained funding to photograph all the song manuscripts that had been identified at that time, together with the volumes of popular literature (broadsides, chap-books, etc.) and to publish them as a microfiche edition. Digital imaging was considered, but the expert advice received at the time was that the technology was not yet sufficiently developed. The final collection consisting of 209 fiches was launched together with indices prepared by Ian Maxted and me in November 1998. Sets of the fiches were given to the principal libraries in Devon, to the Vaughan Williams Memorial Library in London and to the Lamont Library at Harvard University.

The Devon Tradition Project, which commenced in the summer of 2009, was the successor to the Baring-Gould Heritage Project and was led, once again, by Wren Music. As part of this project the Baring-Gould song manuscripts were re-photographed as high-resolution digital images in full colour, to maximise the visibility of some of the faint pencilled writing that could not be seen on the microfiches. Some items that were not included in the earlier project were photographed for the first time. The project team, with the support of the English Folk Dance and Song Society (EFDSS), catalogued the manuscripts to enable a database of the images to be placed online with the manuscripts of six other collectors on the Vaughan Williams Memorial Library's digital collection. This work was completed in February 2011. The VWML Digital Collection has subsequently been extended as a result of the 'Full English' project to include further manuscript collections.

The successful completion of these projects has made the Baring-Gould folk song manuscripts available to all who wish to look at them free of charge, anywhere in the world where internet access allows them to do so.[25] The database is fully searchable, and in addition to the digital images of the manuscripts, transcriptions of the songs and the music are being added by volunteers. Given the quality of Sabine Baring-Gould's handwriting, this is a welcome addition to the website.

An Opportunity for Exploration

Before 1992 we relied upon Baring-Gould's published collections of songs and on other books and articles together with the Plymouth manuscript collection to understand his folk song collection and how he went about it. The evidence was not always accurate and it was quite obviously incomplete. Neither did it look to be, at face value, a very large collection. Collectors like Cecil Sharp had left much more manuscript material to work with and, particularly in Sharp's case, for later writers to analyse, annotate and publish. Baring-Gould had fewer champions. Since the discovery of the Killerton Hoard it can be seen that Baring-Gould's collection of 853 songs collected directly from singers (as well as another 238 received from informants) was more substantial than had previously been understood.[26]

Even this large quantity of manuscript material does not fully represent all that Baring-Gould collected. There are some songs for which tunes can be found in the Rough Copy manuscript for which no words can be found in the collection. It may be that these were deliberately omitted. There is, for example, a tune for 'Lock Hospital', which was probably a tune for a version of 'The Unfortunate Rake', which deals with death from venereal disease. I can imagine that Baring-Gould might have balked at writing this out. A bigger question is about other field notebooks that are not in the collections. While most, if not all, of Bussell's field notebooks have survived, we know that Sheppard's papers were destroyed by his family after his death. The biggest question, though, is about Baring-Gould's own field notes. Most of the surviving 'notebooks' in Baring-Gould's hand began life, as I have explained above, as fair copies, though they were later used for some rough work and in some cases for noting down songs. We know that other rough notebooks of song texts must have existed, from which

---

25 The VWML Digital Database can be accessed on the VWML website, <http:// vwml.org/vwml-projects/vwml-the-full-english> (Accessed 26 January 2017).
26 Of other collectors of song in England, Sharp heard 3,022 songs (mainly in Somerset). George Gardiner collected 1,452, and Henry Hammond 925. Vaughan Williams collected about 800 songs, Clive Carey 580, Percy Grainger 400, Lucy Broadwood 311 and Janet Blunt 223 songs. These numbers are all estimates and I am grateful to Steve Roud for giving them to me (personal communication).

Baring-Gould transcribed his fair copies. While it is unlikely that further manuscripts will turn up, the possibility cannot be ruled out completely.

This is a remarkable set of manuscripts. It forms a part of a previously hidden treasure that, while not in the league of 'The King under the Car Park', has dramatically transformed our knowledge of this unique man. The finding of the 'Killerton Hoard' was the first step in a process of discovery, since it focused attention on the possibility that there was more manuscript material to be uncovered. The result has been that researchers have found a considerable quantity of 'new' material about Baring-Gould's life and work, much of which had been hidden in plain sight. While many of the manuscripts have now been looked at and some significant pieces transcribed and published, there is still a good deal of largely untouched material to be studied so that we can better understand the enigma that is Sabine Baring-Gould. His personal collection of books, for example, which is now kept in the Heritage Collections of the Library at Exeter University, offers numerous possibilities for looking more deeply into the work of this extraordinary writer who found challenges and delight in so many aspects of the Victorian world.

His collection of folk song manuscripts is large and complicated. There are, as this book has demonstrated, many questions about the detail of this area of his work. A few of these have been answered, and many more will be with further study and analysis. And, as with all studies of this kind, there are some questions that can never be answered. What we have is an exciting opportunity to explore a large collection of songs made, mostly, in Devon. Though a visit is to be recommended, the folk song enthusiast does not have to travel to Devon to explore Baring-Gould's song collection. The Vaughan Williams Memorial Library Database has made it available for anyone, anywhere in the world to browse or to search for particular songs, people or places.

The creation of this collection occupied a large part of Sabine Baring-Gould's long life and his intention was that it should provide a record of what used to be sung in the part of the world that he loved best. With all of its admitted imperfections this collection is a glorious celebration of that heritage.

13: Shadows of the Evening (1894–1924)

Now the day is over
Night is drawing nigh
Shadows of the evening
Steal across the sky.[1]

A Premature Obituary – Destruction of his 'Later Reminiscences' – Folk Song – Life at Lew Trenchard – Village Entertainments – Grace – Kindness to his Employees – What Was He Like? – Recognition and Memory – The Closing Years – Squab Pie

A Premature Obituary

On 5 June 1906 Sabine Baring-Gould was reported to have died on board a ship in Port Elizabeth, in South Africa. It was a mistake on the part of the news agency, Reuters, since it was his cousin, Edward Sabine Baring-Gould, who had died. He did not respond as amusingly as Mark Twain when faced with the premature report of his death, as his telegram to the news agency read simply, 'The news of my death is false. I have not been in Africa.' The following day the *Hull Daily Mail* chose to correct the error under the rather odd heading 'Rev S. Baring-Gould alleges that he is not dead'. They reprinted their article reporting his death, above which they added, 'Although the Rev. gentleman is today one day nearer the dissolution which lies before the best of us than he was yesterday, we can assure our readers that this morning's statement is slightly wide of the real facts of the case.'[2]

Like a handful of other public figures whose deaths have been reported prematurely he was granted the opportunity to read his own obituaries. He chose not to do so and packed them in an envelope that was put away with his will. He did, though, read and enjoy the letters received from friends and strangers. He wrote: 'I find that I have more friends than I knew of, and old friends drew closer so that this little error has softened my heart, and made me thankful that I have a wider circle of such as feel kindly towards me than the little ring of my own family.'[3]

---

1 Sabine Baring-Gould, 'Now the day is over', *Church Times*, 16 February 1867. Written for the children of Horbury in 1865.
2 'Rev. S. Baring-Gould alleges that he is not dead', *Hull Daily Mail*, 5 June 1906, p. 3.
3 'Open Diapason', *Musical Opinion and Music Trade Review*, July 1906, p. 734.

Baring-Gould was then 72 years old, and this *memento mori* came at a time when he was finding that many of his friends were succumbing to illness and old age. He was still in good health, apart from the respiratory problems that had dogged him all his life, and which were getting harder to deal with. His doctor recommended that he smoked a type of herbal tobacco called Pinoza, impregnated with pine oil to disinfect and sooth the throat and lungs.[4] He smoked this in a pipe or as cigarettes, but his favourite medicine was a good dose of Dartmoor air, and he could still out-walk many younger men. There was no decline in his intellect and he continued to write prolifically on a wide range of subjects. He had stopped writing novels and, as a result, he was losing a large part of his readership.

Destruction of his *Later Reminiscences*

We will never be able to read the final volume of his trilogy of reminiscences, which covered the last thirty years of his life, 1894 to 1924. Though he completed a draft of the book before his death, he gave an instruction to his son, Edward, that he was only to allow it to be published if he thought it right to do so, since there were some hard things said about some of Baring-Gould's contemporaries in the Church. After his father's death, Edward put about the story that he had searched diligently for the manuscript but had not been able to find it. He said that one of the maids had told him that while cleaning his room a few days before he died she had found a large quantity of ash from burnt papers, which he believed to have been the missing draft. We now know from family sources that it was Edward himself who burnt the manuscript, having judged it to be, as his father had feared, too controversial to publish.[5]

Given that this was, in many respects, a very active period of his life, there could have been much to learn from this volume had it appeared, but judging by the first two volumes it is unlikely that we would have learnt much more

---

4   Though it is highly unlikely that any modern medical practitioner would recommend smoking as a treatment for bronchitis, it is worth pointing out that Cecil Sharp was similarly prescribed a herbal tobacco for his asthma. Lucy Broadwood's diary (6782/9, June 1894–November 1895) records that she had her throat burned with electricity three times and that her doctor gave her cocaine for her nose.

5   Ronald Wawman, 'The Last Thirty Years of The Life of Sabine Baring-Gould as revealed by Correspondence with Others, Part III, Sabine's Last Thirty Years, An Overview': <http://www.nevercompletelysubmerged.co.uk/another-diary/sabines-last-years-overview.pdf> (Accessed 16 January 2017). Wawman writes: 'In recent years, when discussing Sabine's last years, Merriol Almond informed the author that Edward's daughter, Adele, had witnessed her father burning the manuscript. Edward's explanation at the time was that he thought the contents would be offensive to the church hierarchy'.

about his inner feelings and private beliefs. His half-brother, Arthur Baring-Gould, described his *Reminiscences* as entertaining, but added, 'Everything is there except himself'.[6] His 1880 diary is a little more personal and gives us a few extra glimpses into his mind, but it ends in 1899 and is in any case fragmentary. Fortunately there are other sources of information available in the form of magazine interviews and personal letters, as well as accounts by members of the family. These include the memoirs of his daughter, Joan Priestly, and his half-brother, Arthur Baring-Gould, as well as people who had worked for him or had known him through other connections. We also have a torrent of articles about him in the press including several by journalists who turned up 'on spec' at Lew Trenchard seeking an interview.

Dr Ronald Wawman has looked at the available evidence carefully and has offered his interpretation of Baring-Gould's final years in his book and in a number of talks and articles. In this final chapter I will cover some key points of his last thirty years, acknowledging Wawman's work but adding to it from my own perspective and with additions from my own research.

Folk Song

His work with folk song continued for much of this period though the pace of collecting new songs in the field slowed after 1894, and came to a near standstill by 1897. In January of 1898 Frank Kidson wrote to Lucy Broadwood saying:

> I had a letter from Mr Baring Gould a couple of days ago saying he had put away with a sorrowful heart all his Mss tunes as nearly all his old singers were dead. He promises to send me them to go carefully over.[7]

Baring-Gould never actually sent Kidson his manuscripts and he continued to work with them, copying songs that he had not already included (and, occasionally, duplicating some he already had) into the third volume of his 'Personal Copy' manuscript of songs.

He decided to let his large collection of broadside ballads go, and he gave them to the Department of Printed Books at the British Museum in 1898. They are now one of the most important of the British Library's collections of nineteenth-century street literature. This was a very generous gift as he could have chosen to sell them and raised some cash

---

6   Arthur Baring-Gould, Unpublished Memoir, (private collection).
7   VWML, Lucy Ethelred Broadwood Manuscripts, Letter of Frank Kidson to Lucy Broadwood, 9 January 1898, LEB/4/95.

to help meet the losses that he encountered that year as a result of the failure of the opera, *Red Spider*. With the additional problem of reduced farm incomes from the estate, his financial situation became so desperate that he sold most of his horses, dismissed several servants and took Grace and the younger children to Dinan in October 1900, hoping to live more cheaply.[8] They stayed in Brittany for fourteen months, enabling him to study the archaeology and local history of the area and gather material for a few more books and articles. He also drafted three novels while in Dinan, which together with the savings made by running a smaller establishment enabled him to face his bank manager with equanimity.

Cecil Sharp arrived on the scene in 1903 and Baring-Gould re-discovered his passion for folk song, though he never went out collecting songs in the cottages and pubs as he had in the past. The publication of the new edition of *Songs of the West* and of *English Folk Songs for Schools* created some fresh interest among the general public. He spoke at a number of public meetings, and sometimes shared the platform with Sharp.

Though Sharp had persuaded him to join the Folk Song Society in 1904 there is no record of Baring-Gould having attended any of the society's meetings in London or of making any significant contribution to its activities apart from correspondence with fellow collectors. Neither were there any further publications until, in 1923, he included a chapter describing the project in *Further Reminiscences*.

His pride in his folk song collection was maintained to the end of his life, though he admitted that he could have done better. In a lecture 'The Folk Music of Devon and Cornwall', given at the Annual Conference of The Incorporated Society of Musicians in Plymouth on 5 January 1899, he remarked, 'When we began, the Phonograph had not been invented; had it been, a vast amount of trouble would have been spared.' It would be some years before his fellow song collectors started to experiment with using the phonograph and decades before Peter Kennedy and his colleagues at the BBC perfected the use of electrical recording machines to record birds and folk songs. Almost inevitably, there are those who say that the phonograph and its successors have 'harmed' folk song – but then, there are those who have said that printing has had an adverse effect on traditional music.[9]

---

8 This partly explains the rush to get the Fair Copy finished and delivered to Plymouth Library. He planned to be away for a long time and would not have wanted to take all the folk song manuscripts with him.

9 See, for example, Josiah P. Combs, *Folk Songs of the Southern United States* (Austin: University of Texas Press, 1967).

Life at Lew Trenchard

Frank Kidson painted a charming picture of family life at Lew House in the article that he wrote for the *Yorkshire Weekly Post* in 1911.

> There are few more gratifying joys than to sit at his hospitable board and to watch the twinkling humour that lights up his face, and that of Mrs Baring-Gould in response to the badinage that passes round the table. With a Yorkshire visitor it is, of course, a foregone conclusion that the young people of the family should air the modicum of dialect of that county which they possess, while Mrs Baring-Gould, a Yorkshire lady, and the visitor smile indulgently at the effort and recall other half forgotten words and modes of expression. It is pleasant to have cosy evening chats with the novelist and antiquary. By the old chimney of grey Devonshire granite, in a halo of tobacco smoke, we interchange ideas of literature, politics, of current incidents, and I hear many romantic stories of the doings of the Goulds, the Sabines, and the Barings. Of himself and of his writings it is more difficult to make him talk, for his modesty is as great as his talents.[10]

It is quite likely that Kidson would have heard some folk songs while he was staying at Lew House, as singing in the evening after dinner was a regular part of family life. Baring-Gould's daughter, Joan, described how they would adjourn to the ballroom, where there was a grand piano, and the family would join in as he sang songs from *Songs of the West*, accompanied by his daughter Vera (Veronica). Joan adds:

> He had a good voice and he impressed us (his children) greatly and we would implore him to sing another and another and we would join in the chorus. We loved 'Madam will you talk, Madam will you walk with me' and 'Tom Pearce, Tom Pearce – lend me your grey mare.[11]

Other writers describe him as having a fine baritone voice.

---

10 Frank Kidson. 'The Rev. S. Baring-Gould at Home', *Yorkshire Weekly Post*, 16 September 1911.
11 Devon Heritage Centre, Baring-Gould papers, 7444M, Joan Priestley Memoir Notes.

Village Entertainments

Outside the gates of Lew House and opposite St Peter's Church there is a group of buildings that include a dilapidated barn. Though it is not now safe to enter the building, I was shown inside it several years ago. You could then see that it had been fitted out as a very basic theatre. This was done so that the Baring-Gould children would have somewhere to go on wet days to enjoy creating plays or other games, away from the ears of the adults. It was also the place where the villagers came at the invitation of their squire for feasts and for entertainments, and it remained in use until the late 1940s, apart from a break when it was used to house American soldiers preparing for D-Day.[12] In the 1970s, when an audit of the estate was being made, a brown paper parcel was discovered in the theatre containing two smocks and some bell-pads, clearly Morris-men's costume. At the time the finder, Mary Martin, took the parcel away with her (with permission). In 2013 she rediscovered it and returned it to Lew House. It proved the catalyst for an investigation, and confirmation that Baring-Gould had instigated the formation of a country dance and Morris troupe in the village.[13]

It had been known that Baring-Gould had encouraged his daughters to teach country dancing in the years before war broke out though little was written about the venture. Baring-Gould was enthusiastic about dancing, particularly the old country dances, as can be judged from the chapter he wrote on the subject in *Old Country Life* in 1890.[14] As previously described, William Ford was brought from Cowley to Lew House in 1907 to teach some country dances to a team of villagers. This was in preparation for an 'entertainment' that Baring-Gould staged at Lew House on 19 June that year. The event had been organised to raise funds towards the building of a parish room and it included displays of traditional dancing and song. A group assembled by Gage Goodfellow (who had worked with the 'Songs of the West' company in the 1890s) was to provide the singing, the programme for which was similar to the programmes of the earlier costume concerts. A dance display was presented by the Lew Trenchard Morris Dancers and after tea there were old English country dances on the lawn.

---

12 Personal communication, Arthur Perkin, Lew Mill, 30 April 2014.
13 For more on this see Martin Graebe, 'Dancing with Sabine Baring-Gould', *Folk Music Journal*, 10 (2015), pp. 637–43.
14 Sabine Baring-Gould, 'Country Dances' (Chapter 7), *Old Country Life*, pp. 174–97.

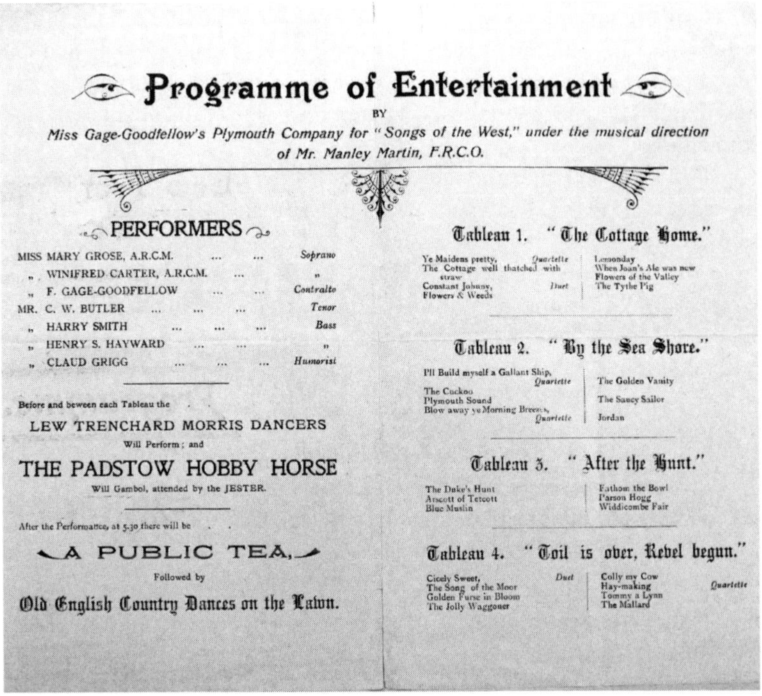

Programme of Entertainment
BY
Miss Gage-Goodfellow's Plymouth Company for "Songs of the West," under the musical direction of Mr. Manley Martin, F.R.C.O.

PERFORMERS

MISS MARY GROSE, A.R.C.M.	Soprano
„ WINIFRED CARTER, A.R.C.M. ...	„
„ F. GAGE-GOODFELLOW	Contralto
MR. C. W. BUTLER	Tenor
„ HARRY SMITH	Bass
„ HENRY S. HAYWARD	„
„ CLAUD GRIGG	Humorist

Before and beween each Tableau the

LEW TRENCHARD MORRIS DANCERS

Will Perform; and

THE PADSTOW HOBBY HORSE

Will Gambol, attended by the JESTER.

After the Performance, at 5.30 there will be

A PUBLIC TEA,

Followed by

Old English Country Dances on the Lawn.

Tableau 1. "The Cottage Home."

Ye Maidens pretty, *Quartette*
The Cottage well thatched with straw
Constant Johnny, *Duet*
Flowers & Weeds
Lemonday
When Joan's Ale was new
Flowers of the Valley
The Tythe Pig

Tableau 2. "By the Sea Shore."

I'll Build myself a Gallant Ship, *Quartette*
The Cuckoo
Plymouth Sound
Blow away ye Morning Breezes, *Quartette*
The Golden Vanity
The Saucy Sailor
Jordan

Tableau 3. "After the Hunt."

The Duke's Hunt
Arscott of Tetcott
Blue Muslin
Fathom the Bowl
Parson Hogg
Widdicombe Fair

Tableau 4. "Toil is over, Revel begun."

Cicely Sweet, *Duet*
The Song of the Moor
Golden Furse in Bloom
The Jolly Waggoner
Colly my Cow
Hay-making *Quartette*
Tommy a Lynn
The Mallard

Fig. 13.1 – Programme for Lew Trenchard 'Entertainment', 19 June 1907 (Courtesy of Plymouth City Council Library Services).

The dancers appeared again at other local charitable events in 1907 and then, in 1912, the team was brought together again for a fete at Lew Trenchard in support of the Three Towns Church Extension Fund which brought people in from Plymouth and Exeter by special trains. The newspaper report of this event identifies those who took part. They were nearly all employed on the Baring-Gould estate and included his coachman, Charlie Dustan, and Charles Davy, carpenter and bell ringer.[15] The pianist was Cicely Baring-Gould.

Additional training was necessary for this event and it was provided by Maud and Helen Karpeles, who spent several days at Lew Trenchard at Baring-Gould's request during April 1912. They stayed at the Castle Inn in Lydford and were picked up every evening by Baring-Gould's pony

15 *Western Times*, 26 July 1912, p. 2.

and trap and taken to Lew House, where they had dinner with the family before meeting with the dancers. Maud Karpeles recalled in her memoir that Baring-Gould took them out for walks on the moor during the day and that 'his discourses on the local antiquities were both enlightening and stimulating'.[16]

Two summers later the dancers of Lew Trenchard were swept into the chaos of war. All of the men returned safely, but Baring-Gould himself had been changed in those years by the loss of other men from the parish and particularly by the death of his wife, Grace. Cicely Baring-Gould had married in 1916, the last of his daughters to do so. In 1918 Baring-Gould wrote to his wife's niece Hannah Taylor, after she had told him that they were reviving country dances in Wakefield, where she lived, to say that:

> I am so glad to hear that you have begun Country Dances. We have had them here, also Morris Dances for a good many years, till this war put an end to them by carrying away our young men. I have never collected any special dances here, but we practised some that were traditional.[17]

Grace

Grace Taylor, the teenage mill girl whom Baring-Gould had courted and won in Yorkshire, had grown to be a very capable manager of the family and of the household. She had also learned to manage a more than usually wayward husband with considerable success. It is said that she still longed for the moors of her native Yorkshire and that she sometimes missed the company of adult women, but her great delight was in her family. She had given birth to fifteen babies, fourteen of whom had grown to adulthood: five boys and nine girls. Her last child, Grace, was born in 1891 when she was 41 years old and she became a grandmother two years later when her eldest daughter, Mary, bore her first child.

Mary had been the first to leave the nest and the Baring-Goulds could congratulate themselves for having married all their daughters to suitable men. The boys found that when they were considered old enough a boot was applied firmly to their backsides, and that they were

---

16 London: Vaughan Williams Memorial Library, Maud Karpeles papers, Maud Karpeles, *Manuscript memoir*, MK/7/185.
17 Oxford, Oxford University, Bodleian Library Special Collections, Letter of Baring-Gould to Hannah Taylor, 19 March 1918, MS Eng Lett d 298.

given little choice in the matter. Baring-Gould was determined that each of them would make their way in the world on their own merits, and this did not include a university education. With the exception of Henry, who died in Borneo, they succeeded in establishing themselves in America or the Empire and there are now Baring-Goulds scattered around the globe.

A wonderful group photograph was taken in 1908 when the Tavistock Cycling Club visited Lew Trenchard – an annual event when the cyclists made their way en masse to St Peter's Church for the morning service before they were entertained to lunch in Lew House. The photograph shows the cyclists on the steps outside the house with some of the servants. Sabine and Grace Baring-Gould are in the centre of the front row among the better-dressed people (who have clearly not cycled there). Neither of them is looking at the camera.

Fig. 13.2 – Tavistock Cycling Club at Lewtrenchard, 1908 (Courtesy of Dr Merriol Almond).

By this time Grace Baring-Gould was already suffering from rheumatoid arthritis, a disease that was to cause her much distress as it worsened. Her husband tried to ensure that she kept active and she travelled abroad with him for several more years. It seemed that she enjoyed walking more when abroad than when she was at home, and when they stayed in Munich in 1908 he told Mary, 'Mamma has also developed walking powers and does her two hours easily'.

But by 1913 she was no longer able to travel to France with him. By July 1914 she was described as 'crippled' and a course of the waters at Bath did not give her any relief. The illness progressed until she became completely bedridden and required two nurses to ensure that help was on hand 24 hours a day.

There have been some suggestions that Baring-Gould was insensitive to Grace's illness. Cicely Briggs, one of his granddaughters, reported that her mother (also Cicely) had looked after Grace during the final stages of her illness, and felt that her father had not taken sufficient care of her.[18] This view is countered by Mrs S. Mathias of Plymouth in a letter to the *Western Morning News* dated 22 August 1961 in which she shared her memories of living in the Baring-Gould household. She was a trained nurse who had been engaged to look after Grace Baring-Gould when her illness became severe. She said that Grace bore her suffering with patience and consideration for those attending her, though she was in great pain which was in those days relieved by oven heated sand-bags. She added:

> Nor could any husband have shown more devotion. A magical smile from the patient always greeted the entry of Mr Baring-Gould to the flower-adorned sick-room. On one occasion I remember him describing her as the 'queen among the flowers'. She was indeed a lovely lady, and one would have needed to go a very long way to find a kindlier and more considerate gentleman than the Rev. Baring-Gould.

Grace died on 8 April 1916, with her husband and five of her daughters by her side. In the midst of his grief, Baring-Gould set himself to writing letters to those who needed to know. One of those letters was addressed to Mrs Elizabeth Ramsden, who was his son Julian's, mother-in-law:[19]

---

18 Cicely Briggs, *The Mana of Lew* (Pulborough: Praxis Books, 1993), pp. 30–31.
19 Letter of Sabine Baring-Gould to Mrs Elizabeth Ramsden, 9 April 1916. (Author's collection).

Lew Trenchard

N. Devon

9 Apl. 1916

Dear Mrs Ramsden

My dear wife passed away this evening at
8.15, most peacefully. Indeed we hardly knew when
the last breath was drawn as I gave her the last kiss and
commended her pure soul to the hands of her merciful
creator. What should we do without Christian faith
and hope? It can not be long before we meet again.
The funeral is to be on Wednesday next at 11 a.m. Her
daughters Mary, Vera, Joan & Daisy, & Cicely were with
her to the last.

I remain

Yours sincerely

S. Baring-Gould

The traveller, Rebecca Penfold, told a touching story about Grace's burial
to Peter Kennedy when he filmed an interview with her in 1973.[20] The
extension to the graveyard by St Peter's Church had only one burial in it,

20 Peter Kennedy, *Sweet Primeroses* (video), Folktrax FF2006, recorded 1973, issued
    1985.

a young gipsy boy, William Penfold, who was Rebecca's cousin. He had lain there alone for two years and her story was that Grace asked to be buried near him so that he would not be lonely. The extension is now quite full, and there are a number of others keeping him, and Grace, company, including Sabine himself.

Kindness to his Employees

Some photos and a letter purchased by the author in 2011 give some insight into the relationship between Baring-Gould and the people who worked for him. The letter is dated 11 May 1915 was sent to George Gibbons, a soldier stationed in France. It reads as follows:

> Lew Trenchard
> N. Devon
> 11 May 1915
>
>
> Dear George
>
> I wrote to you a long time ago about Lilian, but you did not get my letter. I write now again. I am so glad to hear from her that you are well. She is quite wrapt up in you, and you may be sure that you have a precious little soul in her, whom you must regard with all reverence and respect. She tells me whenever she gets a letter from you, but I can see it from her face when she has heard from you, it is just like the sunshine bursting from the clouds, she is so full of brightness and joy. She is a good, dear little soul, and you may be sure you have made a happy choice in her. You may trust that I remember you in my prayers every day.
> I remain
>
> Yours truly
> S. Baring-Gould.[21]

The letter came with a hand-coloured photograph of George Gibbons in his dress uniform, taken before he left for war. Lilian's great nephew, who had inherited the letter from his mother, told me a little more about them. She was a parlour maid at Lew House and George was said to have been a batman for an officer at General French's headquarters in France. They

---

21 Letter of Sabine Baring-Gould to George Gibbons, 11 May 1915. (Author's collection).

were married after the war and lived near Bere Alston, where George worked as a chauffeur, though they do not seem to have had children. It was said that they had just one book in the house – a copy of Baring-Gould's novel, *Red Spider*.

The letter goes beyond what we might have expected of the stereotypical relationship between a country gentleman and his domestic staff, but it is just one of the examples of the kindness shown to their workers by Sabine and Grace Baring-Gould. There can be no doubt that this was the case as it is supported by the number of stories that I have heard from people who had relatives who had been in contact with Baring-Gould.

A few years ago I heard of Bill Tucker from Tavistock, then aged 97. He used to collect Baring-Gould from the station every Monday when he came into Tavistock to do his banking and other business. He would invariably get a tip of threepence with the advice 'You be a good boy!'

More recently I was told about Lilian Newcombe who, at the age of fourteen, was a housemaid at Lew House. Baring-Gould would often collect her from the bus in his dog-cart and chat to her cheerily all the way to the house. She was too shy ever to talk back – not a problem, my informant told me, that his grandmother had later in her life.

In 2009 I heard from Mrs Marion Yeo, from Cornwall who told me about a brooch in the form of a true love knot that had belonged to her grandmother, Annie Long, and which is now a family heirloom worn by successive generations of the women in the family on their wedding day. The story associated with it is that Annie was a maid at Lew House in the 1890s and that the brooch was a gift to her from Sabine and Grace Baring-Gould in November 1897 when she left to get married to William Roberts, the blacksmith who later made the wrought iron entrance gates to Lew House. When she died in September 1923 Baring-Gould wrote a letter of sympathy to the family.

In several cases, the relationship with former servants continued for some time after they had left Lew House. Joan Bellen, from Buckland Monachorum, told Joy Lakeman about her parents, who had met when both were in service with the Baring-Goulds in the 1890s.[22] Her father, Tom Kellaway, had been a footman, and her mother, Lily Salter, was nurse to the Baring-Gould's two youngest children, John and Grace. Though Lily left the family's service when she married, she used to go back from time to time to do some sewing for them, as her mother had done before

---

22 Joy Lakeman, *Them Days, From the Memories of Joan Bellan* (Padstow: Tabb House, 1982).

her. Joan recalled that they received a goose from the Baring-Goulds every year for Christmas after she left Baring-Gould's employment.

That this was not unusual is confirmed by a copy of a postcard of Lew House that was sent to me by Tony Rudall. Baring-Gould wrote it on 22 December 1909 to Tony's grandmother, Sarah, saying, 'A goose has been sent to you by train to Loddiswell Station today, 21 Dec. Wishing you a very happy Xtmas and a merry new year. Yours truly, S. Baring-Gould.' Sarah had been housekeeper at Lew until she married George Rudall and moved with him when he became a gamekeeper at Loddiswell, in South Devon.

Fig. 13.3 – Baring-Gould with the Lew Trenchard bell ringers, c. 1909 (Courtesy of Tony Rudall).

George Rudall had worked on the Lew Trenchard Estate – probably as gamekeeper – but was also one of the bell ringers at St Peter's Church. Tony Rudall also sent a copy of a photograph of the bell ringers, in which his grandfather is second from the right. Baring-Gould is standing in the centre with his hands on the shoulders of two men, believed to be his son, Julian, on his left, and Charles Davy, who sent the photograph to Mrs Rudall. Davy was a carpenter on the Lew Trenchard estate and served as churchwarden at St Peter's for 45 years.

In the remodelling of Lew House Baring-Gould was his own architect and encouraged local craftsmen to learn the skills required to build and furnish the house. The blacksmith, William Roberts, for example, made the gates to the house. The estate mason, Arthur White, had suffered a breakdown after an illness and became unable to work. Baring-Gould persuaded him to try his hand at plasterwork and they worked together on the moulds for the ceiling of the new ballroom. White's illness receded as he became fascinated by the task and he became a skilled worker, whose plasterwork in the ballroom and the gallery at Lew House can still be admired.

An example of Baring-Gould's consideration for his workmen was given by his daughter Joan Priestley who, in her manuscript notes, described how bells were attached to the breastplate of the cob that pulled his dog-cart so that their jingle would warn his men of his approach and they could be hard at work when he arrived.[23] This was confirmed by Charles Davy who was interviewed for the *Tavistock Times* in 1951 and who said, 'Why? Just to give the men warning he was coming and he did not wish to find them idling about. He thought it was best so'.[24]

This could be seen as the sort of paternalistic behaviour that would be expected of the squire in Victorian times. The relationship relies on the idea of social station being accepted by the parties as fixed but, when managed well, this behaviour wins the loyalty of employees and parishioners.[25] Baring-Gould was very successful in this respect and went beyond what was expected of him. He appears from these anecdotes to have genuinely cared about and for 'his' people. We have already heard that he believed that his singers loved him; Charles Davy, in his newspaper article, concludes, 'everybody loved him'.

What Was He Like?

In Baring-Gould's own copy of his novel *Arminell* is an agency cutting from *The Star* printed in 1889. The article includes a description of him as:

> A tall, spare man, midway between 50 and 60, with fine, clear-cut features and straight, dark hair, which he wears rather long behind. He is clean-shaven, has kindly grey eyes, and speaks in decisive emphatic tones. If you happen to catch him when he is in the vein he will give you the impression of being a brilliant talker.[26]

---

23 Devon History Centre, Baring-Gould Papers, 7444M, Joan Priestley's Memoir Notes.
24 'With Rev. S. Baring-Gould at Lewtrenchard House', *Tavistock Times*, 25 May 1951, p. 7.
25 The fact that Baring-Gould married a mill-girl shows that his own approach to class could be flexible and his novels incorporate some progressive ideas.
26 [No title], *The Star*, 13 April 1889.

Maud Karpeles described him as 'a kindly and courteous person, and I remember him with his buckled shoes as a figure that might have stepped straight out of the mid-Victorian era'.[27] When outdoors he would wear his wide brimmed round hat. His daughter, Joan Priestley, said of him in her memoir that:

> He was enthusiastic, full of zeal, humble, original with a great sense of humour. He could be sarcastic, scathing and contemptuous of people with small minds and good opinions of themselves or snobs. He had strong convictions and he stood by what he thought was right in his own light. He was sensitive, easily hurt. He had unbounded interests on almost any subject.

As a parent he was frequently absent and at other times a hands-off father. This was an era when the young children of the landed and middle classes were in the charge of their nurse, the older ones in the hands of their governess. Sabine was not as strict a disciplinarian as the children's feared governess, Miss Biggs, and his carpet slipper, theoretically reserved for more grievous sins, was preferred to the more practised hand of the tyrant.

One of the best-known anecdotes about Baring-Gould is his failure to recognise a little girl at a children's party as one of his own. William Purcell gives a version of the story on the opening page of his biography of Baring-Gould, written in 1957:

> One Christmas, when there was a party at Lew Trenchard a child in a party dress of the early 'eighties was seen descending the great stairs into the hall. Her host advanced upon her. He bent over her; stooped from his great height in his black clothes, a smile on his formidable falcon-face. 'And whose little girl are you, my dear?' The child burst into tears. 'I'm yours, Daddy', she sobbed.[28]

The anecdote has often been repeated, and formed the subject for a poem by Charles Causley, who lived just over the Cornish border.[29]

---

27 London: Vaughan Williams Memorial Library, Maud Karpeles Papers, 'Autobiography', MK/7/185.
28 William Purcell, *Onward Christian Soldier* (London: Longmans, 1957), p. 1.
29 Charles Causley, 'The Reverend Sabine Baring-Gould', *Collected Poems for Children* (London: Macmillan, 1996), p. 26.

Some years ago I purchased a copy of Baring-Gould's *Old Country Life* in Exeter and found in it a cutting from the *Western Morning News* of 13 September 1961. Gordon Monk had recently repeated the story in a little history of Lew Trenchard and the Baring-Gould family and the writer wished to verify the story, with a correction.[30] It was his daughter, Joan, who wrote:

'I'm yours, papa'

Sir, — With regard to your review
of Mr Gordon Monk's book Lew
Trenchard it would be interesting
to record that I happened to be the
little girl whom my father, the Rev.
Sabine Baring-Gould, did not readily
recognise at the children's party.
However, my reply to his inquiry
happened to be: "I'm yours, papa."
In my young days the style "Daddy"
was never used.
(Mrs) JOAN PRIESTLEY.
(Née Baring-Gould.)

It has since been said, in Baring-Gould's defence that at the time when the incident took place the main staircase of the house had not been rebuilt into the lovely light space it is today and that, for a man whose sight had been damaged by reading in the dark cabin of a ship bound home from Iceland, the mistake was understandable – and forgiven.

There are a number of aspects of his life that are outside the scope of this book. One of the aspects is his politics. Baring-Gould was, like his father, a liberal and a devotee of Gladstone. Occasionally his writing would veer towards political statement. His dislike for the actions of Disraeli's Tory government in the Balkan Crisis of 1876 led him to write two very critical poems, as mentioned in Chapter 2. In some of his novels he set up situations where tensions arise from social and political differences. These plots led, though, to resolution, rather than revolution.

He did commit himself to causes, sometimes quietly and without publicity, as with the campaign to raise funds to support the writer William

---

30 S. Gordon Monk, Lew House, *Lew Trenchard Church and Baring-Gould* (Plymouth, 1961).

Crossing in old age and poverty. He was also one of those who campaigned for a Civil List pension for Cecil Sharp in 1911, when his fellow collector was under financial pressure. In other cases he used his *entrée* to the press to support a cause such as the relief of the Breton fishermen following the disastrous failure of the sardine fishery in 1903, for which his appeal raised £700.

Baring-Gould combined in his life many different 'jobs', several of them simultaneously. The two most important are joined together in the description of 'Squarson' that is often applied to him: squire and parson. Each of these was a demanding role in itself. He inherited the estate in 1871, just as a short period of agricultural prosperity was coming to an end. From then on it was mostly downhill and a struggle competing with cheap imported produce and the inefficiency of traditional farming methods.[31] Managing the estate required time and effort, and while he relied on its income he had made a commitment to its improvement. This included new cottages and other works for the estate, not to mention the major improvements that he made to Lew House.

To deal with his life as a clergyman is also beyond the scope of this book and a difficult matter to cover succinctly. He had committed himself to the improvement of the religious life of the people of Lew Trenchard parish and he took his duties seriously, visiting his parishioners regularly and taking little gifts of bulbs or flowers with him. His sermons were mercifully short, typically eight minutes, and when a visiting preacher strayed beyond that limit it was not unknown for Baring-Gould to tap his watch pointedly. He published many books on religious matters but he never achieved high office in the Church.

In June 1922 Lew Trenchard parish was joined with that of Thrushelton and a part of Marystow. This meant a significant increase in work for Baring-Gould, and in a letter to Evelyn Healey dated 1 Aug 1922 he described his new parish as having

> ...doubled in population and three times in extent, and with two churches to serve, through the annexation of the adjoining parish of Thrushelton, a sadly dead end unwanted parish where no resident parson, no squire and no Sunday school. Many of the parishioners are absolute heathens, so you may imagine that there

---

31 For more on agricultural economics and practice in late nineteenth-century Devon see Anthony Gibson, 'Farming in Sabine Baring-Gould's Time', *Transactions of the Sabine Baring-Gould Appreciation Society*, 14 (2014), pp. 4–13.

is much spade-work to be done, and I am so cold, and winter coming on that I shall not be able to do all I could wish.[32]

He also sought to make an impact at a regional (and, sometimes, national) level through his writing. He had little respect for some of his senior colleagues, whose conservative viewpoint he did not share, and he made this clear in some of the things he wrote. He had no interest in attending church meetings in Exeter, let alone in London. He had begun to ruffle ecclesiastical feathers with *The Origin and Development of Religious Belief* in 1869 and had continued the feather ruffling with *Lives of the Saints* (1872–77). All too recognisable pen-portraits in later books caused more ecclesiastical muttering, but in his two highly readable accounts of Church history, *The Church Revival* (1914) and *The Evangelical Revival* (1920), he set out to derange the plumage further with such statements as:

> ...The upper class – the nobility, the gentry, the plutocrats – they are pretty well left to stew in their own fat, to ride their polo ponies, play bridge, race over the country on Sundays in their motors, and eat and drink of the best. It is with the shopkeeper and the operative that the church will do best. The future of England – of the Empire – is in the hands of the working man.[33]

He recognised from the outset that the book was going to be controversial, having originally intended to publish it after his death. At the age of eighty, he may have felt that he had little to lose. Interestingly he quotes the essay 'Organised Labour' by the socialist Vicar of Thaxted, Conrad Noel.[34] Though he certainly would not have endorsed all of Noel's views, it is illuminating that he chose to read and refer to him.

This was just one of the many occasions on which he confronted the establishment of the Anglican Church. He even went so far as to publish his letters to the Bishop of Exeter on topics with which he disagreed in the form of pamphlets, which cannot have endeared him to his superior. And yet, at a local level, he was able to rein in his

---

32 Ronald Wawman, 'The Last Thirty Years of The Life of Sabine Baring-Gould as revealed by Correspondence with Others, Part II, Letters to Evelyn Healey, 1917 to 1923'. Online publication, <http://www.nevercompletelysubmerged.co.uk/another-diary/evelyn-healey-letters02.pdf> (Accessed 20 Jan 2017.)
33 Sabine Baring-Gould, *The Church Revival*, pp. 348–49.
34 Conrad Noel, 'Organised Labour: The Working Classes', in W. K. Lowther Clarke, *Facing the Facts, or an Englishman's Religion*, London: Nisbet, 1911.

passion for the benefit of his parishioners, appreciating that he would not succeed if he tried too hard to push his own ways of worship onto them.

Recognition and Memory

The topic of recognition for Baring-Gould during his lifetime will not take long to deal with. Given that he made his beliefs about the Anglican hierarchy so clear in his writing it should not be a surprise that he was never given any recognition by his Church and was never, for example, invited to preach at Exeter Cathedral. He might have been expected to receive at least a token appointment to a minor canonry, but it was not to be. Neither did he receive any official recognition from any government, beyond Gladstone's helping hand, which was more a personal gesture than an official one.[35]

He was elected president of the Royal Institution of Cornwall in 1897 and in 1902 was awarded the Henwood Gold Medal by the Institution for his two presidential addresses on 'The Early History of Cornwall' and 'The Celtic Saints'. Less predictably, given that he did no archaeology there, he was elected an honorary fellow of the Society of Antiquaries of Scotland. Then, in 1918, he travelled to Cambridge to receive an honorary fellowship of his *alma mater*, Clare College, an honour that particularly pleased him.

It is hard to find any way in which he upset the Folk Song Society (and its successors) and yet its recognition of his achievements as a folk song collector was limited. It could be said that since he was not a member of the Folk Song Society at the time of his death there should be no expectation that the Society's journal should carry an obituary for him – especially as both Sir Charles Stanford and Cecil Sharp had died a few months later. It would be churlish to point out that two-thirds of the page beneath Sharp's obituary was blank and a few words could have been fitted in. The 1948 issue of the *Journal of the English Folk Dance and Song Society* celebrated the fiftieth anniversary of the formation of the Folk Song Society and a short preface by Ralph Vaughan Williams named Baring-Gould with Lucy Broadwood and Kidson as 'the strong men before Agamemnon without whose spade-work it is doubtful if Cecil Sharp would have had the incentive to initiate his great campaign'.

---

35 For a more detailed and knowledgeable insight into the treatment of Baring-Gould by the Anglican Church I recommend reading the closing chapter of Harold Kirk-Smith, *Now the Day is Over* (Boston: Richard Kay, 1997).

That issue included a photograph of Baring-Gould, but no supporting editorial material. Rather perplexingly, the usually reliable Margaret Dean-Smith refers to an article in this issue about Baring-Gould's collecting expeditions, incorporating parts of an article by John Betjeman, but there is no such article in that volume, or elsewhere.[36]

Nowadays the name of Sabine Baring-Gould is not one that springs immediately to mind for most of the population of Britain. If asked about him, it is usually enough to mention 'Onward, Christian Soldiers', before going on to explain further. This usually works but as the nation moves away from the Church and as the Church moves away from the hymns of earlier times there are likely to be continued blank looks, particularly among the young. The hymn itself was under attack even in Baring-Gould's time by people who misunderstood its metaphor or who objected to the idea of the cross being carried in procession. While the suggested substitution of the words 'With the cross of Jesus left behind the door' was a leg-pull on an American journalist by Baring-Gould's son, the writer himself recorded that the Bishop of Exeter asked him to change the words to '"with our Lord and Master going on before" or some such twaddle'. In 1981 the columns of the *Daily Telegraph* recorded another attempt to get the hymn taken out of the approved repertoire. The position is not helped by the enthusiastic adoption of the hymn by military chaplains who fail to see the irony of their choice. It is not much sung in churches nowadays.

In recent times Sabine Baring-Gould has frequently been portrayed as an eccentric. It is an interesting and surprisingly apt word if you can escape the pejorative sense in which it is usually meant. Among a selection of different ways in which the word can be used the *Oxford English Dictionary* allows that it can mean 'deviating from usual methods, odd, whimsical'. That is certainly true of Baring-Gould's ways of living and working. Another sense of the word is 'has its axis, its point of support, etc., otherwise than centrally placed'. Again, one cannot argue with this since Baring-Gould's point of support was at Lew Trenchard, where everything that mattered to him was located. As an author he cared little for London's literary lunches and he certainly had no interest in discussions on folk song in London drawing rooms. Not wishing to drag this out too far, I will take one more of the dictionary's phrases, 'Not agreeing, having little in common' and suggest that this is quite untrue. Hundreds of thousands of people found in the more than 60,000 pages he wrote in his lifetime something that they felt in common with this remarkable man.

---

36 Margaret Dean-Smith, *A Guide to English Folk Song Collections* (Liverpool: University Press of Liverpool, in association with EFDSS, 1954), p. 28.

The Closing Years

The year of 1916 marked a watershed in Baring-Gould's life. He had lost his life-partner of 48 years and, as his half-brother Arthur said,

> Her death nearly broke his heart. He would slip out at night silently alone to say prayers over her grave. His boyishness left him after her death and never returned. [...] I think she did really understand him, and when she died, he was a very forlorn and forsaken man, and it was a true inscription that he had written on her tombstone, "the half of my life".[37]

The death of Grace had been bad enough in itself but it took place against the background of a war in which the young men of the village, including his own children, had been fighting. Two of his sons were wounded. Edward, his heir, had a lucky escape with a bullet that passed through his throat without causing serious damage. His youngest son, John, was more seriously injured when his aircraft was shot down and he spent five months in hospital. Other lads from the village gave their lives. In a letter to Mrs Ramsden, dated 2 November 1917, Baring-Gould writes, 'We have lost a fourth out of the parish in the war, Bickle, whose wife and five sons live at the sawmill'.[38] In 1920 he stood on a damp day in May for the unveiling of the village war memorial at the point in the village where the boundaries of the parishes of Lew Trenchard, Thrushelton and Marystow meet. He knew most of them, but eight of the young men were his own people, sons of those who worked for him like his coachman's son, Paschal Dustan, two sons of village carpenter Arthur White, the schoolmaster's son Ronald Dawe, and – closest to him perhaps – Frank Carver, the son of his step-sister, Leila.

When the war ended Baring-Gould was 84 years old. In 1919 he handed over management of the estate and the house to his son, Edward and his wife Marian, who moved in to live with him. In a letter dated 1 January 1920 to Evelyn Healey, who had become a pen friend, he wrote:

---

37 Arthur Baring-Gould, Unpublished memoir, (private collection).
38 Letter of Sabine Baring-Gould to Mrs Elizabeth Ramsden, 2 Nov 1917, (private collection).

I am passing over the care of the house and household to my eldest son and daughter-in-law. I was no longer able to manage my affairs; and was being robbed by my servants.[39]

Family tradition asserts that there was a concern that he had been drinking too much and that rather than stealing his spirits, the servants had been watering them down to protect him. Though Edward was nominally in charge of his father's welfare he was frequently away on business and much of the burden fell on his American wife, Marian. This led to some misunderstandings and unhappiness, summed up in a letter to an old friend, Charles Head, dated 16 February 1923:

It was my 89th birthday on Jan 28th, and my entry into my 90th year. I spent the day in bed to which I have been confined for 3 weeks. I am only now emancipated from it, and I got out yesterday and the day before for a short time. I have given up my house and household to my eldest son and his American wife, or rather they have been taken from me, as they supposed me too old and infirm to be able to manage for myself. The change is not altogether to my liking, but I have to submit to it. American ways of thought and habits are so foreign and distasteful to me. I should dearly like to see you here, but I dare not ask leave for any friends to come to me, as all sorts of objections would be raised. I do not suppose that my time here can be much prolonged, and I shall not be sorry to go to my great Master and Lord and meet again the dear ones I have lost.[40]

In the past his main health problem had been the bronchitis which plagued him every winter, but which had not stopped him from travelling out over the moor or further afield as his fancy took him. Now other problems set in and in July 1918 he wrote to Evelyn Healey that he was now 'so crippled with rheumatism, superadded to old age, that I cannot get about'. He goes on to say that he dreads the prospect of winter and confinement to his

39 The letters written by Baring-Gould to Evelyn Healey form Part II of Ronald Wawman, 'Sabine's Last Thirty Years (etc.) on his website: <http://www.nevercompletelysubmerged.co.uk/another-diary/evelyn-healey-letters02.pdf> (Accessed 26 January 2017.)
40 This letter is included by Ron Wawman in his essay 'Sabine's Last Thirty Years: An Overview', Part III of 'The Last Thirty Years of the Life of Sabine Baring-Gould as revealed by the Correspondence with Others' on his website: <http://www.nevercompletelysubmerged.co.uk/another-diary/sabines-last-years-overview.pdf> (Accessed 26 January 2017.)

room. His letters to Miss Healey document his decline over the following years. He became unable to eat meat and subsisted on a diet of milk, eggs and rice for much of the time. In 1921 he told her that he had not set foot on Dartmoor since 1913, but that he had managed to make a short walk over the down near the Dartmoor Inn, close to Lydford. In May 1923 he wrote that he had to give up preaching altogether, as his voice was failing. Then at the end of November he wrote on a postcard to her, 'Am breaking up. Confined to my bed'.

He took to his bed for the last time in December 1923 and his final weeks were spent downstairs in the room that is now the bar of the Lewtrenchard Manor Hotel. Early in the morning of 2 January 1924 he passed away. The Death Certificate gave the cause as 'Senile Decay'.

His funeral was a grand affair. The head of the procession, comprising two bishops, a host of clergymen and the family mourners, covered the distance from the house to the church before the last mourners had left it. The coffin was carried by twelve of the tenants of the Baring-Gould estate past the schoolchildren of the village who lined the path to the church. The church could only hold 100 people, so a large number of people gathered outside. Arthur Baring-Gould and Gilbert Arundell, Baring-Gould's curate, led the first part of the service. His hymn, 'Now the Day Is Over', was sung before the coffin was carried the short distance to the open grave, lined with moss and lilies, before, to the strains of another of his hymns, 'On the Resurrection Morning', he was laid to rest next to the woman he had loved.

Squab Pie

Sabine Baring-Gould ended his volume of *Further Reminiscences* with a chapter called 'Squab Pie', naming it after a traditional West-English dish containing a mixture of mutton, veal, bacon, apple, onion, pepper, salt and a pilchard, all then dowsed with Devonshire cream and overlaid with pastry. I shall follow his lead, drawing together a few last observations to complete my story.

This book has been written by one who is enthusiastic about Baring-Gould's collection of folk songs and whose achievements in that direction he admires – though, as has often been admitted, with some reservations. Since I anticipate that many of my readers will come from the same direction I must appeal to them to recognise that Sabine Baring-Gould's achievements extended far beyond his work on folk song and that he should also be remembered as a churchman, an archaeologist, an antiquarian and a man of letters whose love of the county of his birth, and particularly of his small corner of it, has endeared him to so many.

Baring-Gould lived under four sovereigns and wrote Coronation souvenir books for two of them. He recalled that as a child he rode in a sedan chair, and witnessed the horse make way for the railway and the motorcar, though he never travelled in an aeroplane. He watched the growth of the British Empire, though he never went to see it as he was more interested in Europe, which was transformed in his lifetime as new countries and alliances were formed and then broken by war and envy. He saw the growth of the English cities as industry created the wealth that flowed to an enlarged middle class and the jobs that required an immigrant labour force – at that time mainly from Ireland.

His own beloved corner of Devon was not untouched by change. Agricultural depression and epidemics had hit farming hard, affecting his workers as well as his income. He saw much of the growth of industry on Dartmoor and its surroundings flourish and then fade, leaving nature to re-clothe the hummocks and dips left behind. Then, near the end of his life, the Great War devastated a generation of the brightest and best of Britain's sons and transformed the lives of its daughters. The plot is familiar to anyone who has read or watched popular dramas about the lives of the British gentry and the people who worked for them. The great estates were broken up. The jobs they provided for servants, gardeners and labourers largely disappeared.

One of Baring-Gould's characteristics was that he had some mental flexibility and could change his mind if the evidence showed that his hypothesis was wrong. In respect of folk song his mind changed on several topics over the years. Having initially neglected the words of songs in favour of tunes he came to believe that the words were also important and deserved as good treatment as the tunes. Part of his reason for not having valued the words was his initial assumption that most traditional songs were derived from broadsides and other printed sources. He came to understand that this was not always the case and that many of the songs were older than the broadsides and better in many respects than the printed versions. He also realised that some, particularly the younger singers like John Woodridge and Sam Fone, had learnt their songs from broadsides and he recognised that not only could singers fit broadside words to tunes that they knew, but that some could compose tunes themselves. He also realised that some singers were capable of creating songs from scratch – to record a local event, for example. This flexibility of understanding on Baring-Gould's part was not a characteristic that other folk song collectors and theorists of the time demonstrated.

Like all the collectors of folk songs, Sabine Baring-Gould was motivated by the idea that if he did not gather them up they would be lost. Collections like his, as well as those of Mason, Barrett, Kidson, Broadwood, Sharp, Gardiner, Vaughan Williams and all the others who worked to save them, have ensured that this important part of our musical culture will never be lost. He believed this to be so vital that he ranked the preservation of our peculiarly English musical heritage, and specifically that of Devonshire, above everything else that he had accomplished in his long, industrious and fruitful life.

Appendix A – The Music in the Baring-Gould Collection

Julia Bishop

The recovery of our West-country melodies has been the principal achievement of my life[1]

Baring-Gould came to realise early on in his collecting that the melodies of the songs were 'in many instances more precious than the words',[2] making it important to document and publish them accurately. This was in contrast to the words which he often amended or rewrote for publication. His justification was that 'the words in their original form can be found elsewhere, not so the airs.'[3]

His early research led him to believe that the melodies of West Country songs were often distinct from those that had been collected in other parts of the country. Some had long histories, being variants of tunes that could be found in Elizabethan sources. Others appeared to be 'archaic'. His findings supported his belief that the singers were the last generation of 'song-men' – local specialists in singing tradition who were directly descended from village minstrels and whose repertoire had been passed down orally within their family from Elizabethan, if not medieval, times. The old melodies that they sang were now scorned by younger singers and other local singers. Once the song-men passed on, their melodies would be lost, 'for the present generation will have nothing to say to these songs, especially such as are in minor keys, and supplant them with the vulgarest Music Hall performances.'[4]

Taken together, the publications and archival collection contain hundreds of music notations. They are complemented by writings about the history and characteristics of the tunes, including 'such as are in minor keys', and the occasional comment reported from singers themselves. Understanding how these musical documents were produced and what they contain enables us to evaluate the work of Baring-Gould and his musical associates, and what it can tell us about traditional singing, singers and song in late-nineteenth-century Devon and Cornwall.

---

1 Sabine Baring-Gould, *Further Reminiscences*, p. 184.
2 Sabine Baring-Gould, Preface, *Songs of the West*, Part I (1889), p. x.
3 Sabine Baring-Gould, Introduction, *A Garland of Country Song*, p. x.
4 Sabine Baring-Gould, Preface, *Songs of the West*, Part I (1889), p. x.

Collecting the music

In the late 1880s, when Baring-Gould began his West Country folk song collecting enterprise, Thomas Edison, Alexander Graham Bell and Emile Berliner were each striving in the United States to perfect sound recording technology. Their inventions were never to have an impact on Baring-Gould's activities and it was not until the early years of the twentieth century that folk song collectors in Britain began to employ the phonograph. Even then, it did not become standard issue, despite Percy Grainger's enthusiasm for it.

The alternative was to notate the music of folk songs by ear directly onto paper. This could be done while the singer was performing, or sometime afterwards. The first of these techniques required a considerable degree of musical skill and so was generally the province of more accomplished musicians with formal musical training. The latter was available for those, like Baring-Gould, who needed to check the pitches against a piano or other instrument.[5]

As Baring-Gould found, this limited collecting to certain times and places, or meant having to rely on one's memory of the tune until an instrument was available to aid in its notation. Even then the process could be a laborious one if a high level of accuracy was to be gained. The tunes did not always follow the conventions of major and minor keys, and when Baring-Gould checked his notations with singers, he discovered some were highly discerning as to melodic accuracy. In particular, he describes how James Parsons:

> Sits in a settle by my hall fire, turns up his eyes, crosses his hands on his breast, and sings. Then I sing after him, and he is most particular that I should have all the turns right. 'You mun give thickey [that] a bit stronger,' he says – and by stronger he means take a tone or semitone higher. He will not allow the smallest deviation from what he has to impart.
>
> 'It's just no use at all,' says he, 'my singing to you if you won't follow correct. Thickey turn came out of your head, not mine!' Then I must go back again till I have got the tune exact. 'I be maister, and you be scholar,' he says, 'and a scholar mun larn what he be taught; and larn it right.'[6]

---

5   Sabine Baring-Gould, Preface, *Songs of the West*, Part IV (1891), p. xii. Baring-Gould wrote: 'I am unable myself to note a melody if I have not an instrument, and most of these airs must be gleaned in the cottages, often miles away from any piano'.

6   Sabine Baring-Gould, 'Among the Western Song Men', *English Illustrated Magazine*, 9 (1892), p. 477.

Baring-Gould was also aware that while the piano helped in terms of capturing the pitches, there was also the question of notating the rhythm accurately. This required a good knowledge of music theory in order to translate sound into written notation. The task was made harder by the fact that singers sang unaccompanied and so had no need to sing strictly in time. According to Baring-Gould, singers were guided by the sense of the words and 'entirely ignore time', and he often found it hard to perceive whether a tune was 'in common or in triple measure'.[7]

To preserve the tunes and get them noted down accurately, Baring-Gould was spurred to obtain assistance from two musical acquaintances, Frederick Bussell and Henry Fleetwood Sheppard. Both were experienced musicians, able to notate folk songs directly from singers. They could also arrange them for publication and, in Fleetwood Sheppard's case, provide analytical and historical observations on the melodies. Bussell's family connections to the area gave him more opportunities to go on collecting trips and his transcriptions are the more numerous. Around a third (over 300 songs) of the notations are attributed to him in the 'Personal Copy'. Fleetwood Sheppard lived in Yorkshire so the possibilities for collecting in the West Country were accordingly more limited.[8] Only around 16 percent (139 songs) of the 'Personal Copy' transcriptions are ascribed to him. On the other hand, Fleetwood Sheppard played a much greater part in publications drawn from the collection, where his notations and arrangements predominate.

As Baring-Gould describes in colourful detail, he and his collaborators found themselves writing down the songs in all kinds of circumstances, including on moorland and in pubs, and while the singer performed domestic tasks. As their experience grew, so it influenced their methods. They learnt, for example, 'never to take down too much at one sitting'[9] because singers could become influenced by others' tunes, confusing their usual melodies:

7   Sabine Baring-Gould, 'An Historical Sketch of English National Song', *English Minstrelsie*, VII, p. x, and p. xi.
8   In the appendix to Part IV of the first edition of Songs of the West, Baring-Gould notes that 'Those [melodies] noted down by Mr. Sheppard are so described in the text. Living in Yorkshire, he has not been able to make more than one or two visits to the South-West in the year song-hunting, and these songs have to be taken down when the opportunity offers' (p.xii). This sentence was omitted in the 1-vol. first edition.
9   Sabine Baring-Gould, Introduction, *Songs of the West* (1905), p. x.

When a party of singers are together, or when one man sings a
succession of ballads, the memory becomes troubled; the first two
or three melodies are given correctly, but after that, the airs become
deflected and influenced by the airs last sung. At Two Bridges one
old singer, G. Kerswell, after giving us "The Bell-ringer," sang us
half-a dozen other ballads, but the melody of the bells went through
them all so as to render them worthless. On another occasion, we
took down four or five airs all beginning alike, because one singer
impressed this beginning on the minds of the others. At another
time, when this impression was worn off, they would sing truly
enough, and then the beginnings would be different.[10]

Since some singers had not performed for some time, and also similarities
between tunes can cause singers to 'cross' from one to the other, the
situation described is not altogether surprising. Baring-Gould, Bussell and
Fleetwood Sheppard therefore tried to collect the same song from different
singers, and sometimes obtained a second version from the same singer, to
arrive at what they viewed as 'the most correct form'.[11]

Making sense of the notations
Handwritten tune notations in the Baring-Gould collection are found in the
thirteen 'Rough Copy' notebooks, the 'Baring-Gould Working Notebook 1',
the 'Fair Copy', the 'Personal Copy' and in the interleaved music manuscript
pages of Baring-Gould's annotated copy of *Songs of the West*.[12]

The Rough Copy notebooks appear disorderly but it is possible to
identify notations by Baring-Gould, Bussell and Fleetwood Sheppard, as
well as others. They are generally unattributed to collector, though, so there
is much work to be done identifying whose is whose, based on handwriting,
the attributed copies in the Fair and Personal Copies, and the publications.
This method has been used to identify the examples given below which, it
is hoped, will act as a starting point.

An example of Baring-Gould's transcription is "Twas There By
Chance' (later published as 'By Chance It Was') which he obtained from
James Parsons in 1888. A pencil notation in the Rough Copy may be his
initial transcription of this song, or among his earliest attempts to notate
it (Fig. A.1).

---

10 Sabine Baring-Gould, Preface, *Songs of the West*, Part IV (1891), p. xii.
11 Sabine Baring-Gould, Preface, *Songs of the West*, Part IV (1891), p. ix.
12 For more information about the different documents that make up the
collection, see Chapter 12 and Appendix C.

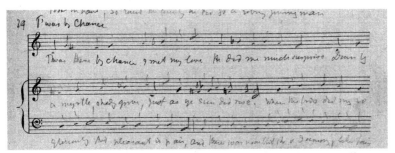

Fig. A.1 – ''Twas There By Chance' (Parsons), Rough Copy, Vol. 5, p. 41.[13]

One wonders if this was the result of Baring-Gould's 'singing after' Parsons (i.e. being able to sing the song back to him), and notating the tune using the piano. It gives the pitches of the notes, although these are not always aligned with the words. The pitches have been overwritten and amended in the second line, perhaps representing one of the places where Parsons corrected Baring-Gould's 'turn'. However, this change sounds anomalous, even in terms of modal tonality which will be described below, begging the question as to whether Baring-Gould notated it accurately. The rhythm is noted in rough terms only, crotchets and minims apparently suggesting shorter and longer notes respectively, but without reference to a particular time signature or regular barring.

Another notation of the song, apparently in Baring-Gould's hand, is also found in the Rough Copy (Fig. A.2). This is more formalised, with a key signature, time signature and barlines. The E flat in the key signature and 6/8 time signature are emendations, possibly by Baring-Gould, perhaps based on the advice of one or other of his colleagues. The key signature makes the high E at the end of line 3 into E flat. It is not clear if this was an intentional change, or the unnoticed result of regularising the key signature to B flat and E flat. A similar ambiguity is whether the F natural has been retained (in line 2). The formal musical rule is that the sharp sign with the first F in this bar makes the second F into an F sharp as well. Did Baring-Gould intend this change or had he forgotten the musical rule?

The rhythmic notation is also inconsistent in this example. Despite the time signature of 6/8, it is notated in 4/4, with occasional bars suggesting 3/4 time. This bears out the earlier observation that Baring-Gould found notating rhythm a challenge, from the point of view of what the singer sang and the conventions of western music notation.

---

13 VWML Digital Database permanent URL: https://www.vwml.org/record/ SBG/3/8/41B.

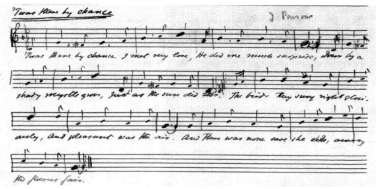

Fig. A.2 – ''Twas There By Chance' (Parsons), Rough Copy, Vol. 9, p. 54.[14]

A good many of the notations in the Rough Copy notebooks appear to have been made by Bussell. His notations sometimes contain details of melodic and rhythmic variation written on a second stave beneath his main notation. He then seems to have selected and inked over the notes and rhythms to form what is presumably a typical or basic version of the tune, as in this transcription of 'Hard Times in England', sung by Samuel Fone (Fig. A.3)

Fig. A.3 – 'Hard Times in England' (Fone), Rough Copy Vol. 3, p. 27.[15]

---

14 VWML Digital Database permanent URL: https://www.vwml.org/record/ SBG/3/12/54C. A repeat sign has also been introduced for the second half of the tune. This tallies with the words as transcribed in the Working Notebook 1, but is not found in the Fair or Personal Copy or the published version.

15 VWML Digital Database permanent URL: www.vwml.org/record/ SBG/3/6/27B.

Regrettably, it seems that most of Fleetwood Sheppard's initial transcriptions have been lost. A few examples in his hand survive in the Rough Copy notebooks. These are neatly written and may be copies he made of his initial transcriptions, such as this notation of 'The Spotted Cow' sung by J. Helmore (Fig. A.4).

Fig. A.4 – 'The Spotted Cow' (Helmore), Rough Copy, Vol. 8, p. 11.[16]

It is noticeable that there are a few places in the final phrase of the song where the placing of the noteheads makes the pitches rather unclear. In bar 10, for example, is the third note an A or a G? Comparing it with the A at the start of the bar, and the G two bars earlier, it seems reasonably certain that it should be a G, but this ambiguity affected Baring-Gould's copies of the tune, as we will see below.

An intriguing detail is that the rhythm of the words is also notated in prosodic feet — ∪. This feature is found in a number of the transcriptions in the Rough Copy notebooks and the Baring-Gould Working Notebook 1. One wonders if Baring-Gould drew on this method to capture the rhythm and to convey it to his musical colleagues when he sent them his transcriptions for help with barring.

Baring-Gould as a copyist

The Fair and Personal Copies were made by Baring-Gould. These bring together all the tune variants collected (or sent) for each song, with the relevant sets of words. For many songs, Baring-Gould also copied out tune variants he had unearthed from published sources, such as Chappell's *Popular Music of Olden Time* (1855–56) and little-known ballad operas and early songbooks, as well as other nineteenth-century folk song collections. These aided comparison of his West Country melodies with those from other times and places.

---

16 VWML Digital Database permanent URL: www.vwml.org/record/SBG/3/11/11A.

Given how difficult many Rough Copy transcriptions are to read, and his own uncertainties, it is likely that Baring-Gould sometimes had trouble making out the notation when writing it out. In 'Hard Times in England' as reproduced in his Personal Copy, there are certainly signs of confusion and corrections towards the end of the first line (Fig. A.5).

Fig. A.5 'Hard Times in England' (Fone), Personal Copy Vol. 3, p. 161.[17]

Small discrepancies have also crept into the notation during the copying process. In this case, the fourth bar of line 2 in Baring-Gould's copy is a rhythmically miscopied rendering of the same bar in Bussell's notation (where it is the first bar of line 3).

In 'The Spotted Cow', a number of pitches in the Personal Copy (Fig. A.6) differ from Fleetwood Sheppard's notation. This can be seen in bar 1 (second note) and bar 3 (all except last note). Baring-Gould has also interpreted the uncertain pitch in Fleetwood Sheppard's notation (described above) as an A rather than a G.

Fig. A.6 – 'The Spotted Cow' (Helmore), Personal Copy Vol. 1, p. 158.[18]

A possible reason for these differences is that Baring-Gould himself had taken down the following melody for this song from James Parsons the previous year (Fig. A.7). The pitches in this are virtually identical with those in Baring-Gould's copy of Helmore's melody.[19] Perhaps Baring-Gould's

---

17 VWML Digital Database permanent URL: www.vwml.org/record/
    SBG/1/3/224.
18 VWML Digital Database permanent URL: www.vwml.org/record/
    SBG/1/1/346.
19 The only difference is in bar 1 of the Parsons melody (which is the same as that in the Fleetwood Sheppard notation from Helmore).

earlier encounter with the melody influenced his copying of Fleetwood Sheppard's notation, leading him to introduce changes in some of the pitches.[20]

Fig. A.7 – 'The Spotted Cow' (Parsons), Personal Copy Vol. 1, p. 158.[21]

In the tune noted by Baring-Gould himself for ''Twas There By Chance' (Fig. A.8), the 4/4-style $\quarternote . \eighthnote$ rhythms have become more prevalent in the Personal Copy, despite the time signature of 6/8, and he notes that 'the time to which Parsons sang it difficult for me to fix'. The F sharp-F natural pitch in line 2 is still ambiguous, and the E flat near the end is retained.[22]

Fig. A.8 – ''Twas There By Chance' (Parsons), Personal Copy Vol 1, p. 1.[23]

---

20 When Fleetwood Sheppard came to arrange the song for publication he seems to have relied on Baring-Gould's copies rather than his own notation for the published melody. In *Songs of the West*, Part III (1890), the published tune is attributed to several singers, including Helmore and Parsons. See no. 74 'The Spotted Cow', pp. 44–45. The note on the song first appeared in Part IV (1891), p. xxxiv.

21 VWML Digital Database permanent URL: www.vwml.org/record/ SBG/1/1/346.

22 In the published version, Fleetwood Sheppard regularises the rhythm to conform to 6/8, retains the high E flat and amends the anomalous F natural to an E. As printed, this would be interpreted as an E flat due to the key signature and appears to be a misprint since the piano accompaniment at this point clearly contains E natural, not E flat. In the revised edition, this note has been changed to an E natural.

23 VWML Digital Database permanent URL: www.vwml.org/record/ SBG/1/1/1.

Baring-Gould acknowledged that 'to the antiquary everything is important exactly as obtained, uncleansed from rust and unpolished', and so promised that he and Fleetwood Sheppard would 'deposit a couple of copies of the songs and ballads, with their music exactly as taken down, one in the library of the Exeter, the other in that of the Plymouth Institution, for reference'.[24] At a time before mechanical reproduction of documents, let alone electronic or digital reproduction, the task of copying out by hand the words and music notations of hundreds of songs must have been an extremely laborious one. This was particularly the case for Baring-Gould who was not as proficient in music as his collaborators. As much as he intended the copies to be 'exactly as taken down', there was also no avoiding the fact that the process involved interpreting handwritten transcriptions produced at speed from a live performance, and in many cases originated by his colleagues rather than himself.

It is no wonder, then, that small anomalies and inconsistencies crop up quite frequently in the Personal and Fair Copy notations. Yet, without these copies, the music of the collection would be considerably harder to access, identify and understand, and in many instances it simply would not have survived at all. In fact, the examples above show that the original or earlier notations are not necessarily the most accurate, and each iteration drew on previous interpretations and sometimes required further judgements to be made. Below we will see how, in turn, some of these affected the way in which the key or 'mode' of specific tunes was perceived.

Folk song and the 'church modes'

Transcription by ear and copying were not the only hurdles that had to be negotiated. The debate as to how best to harmonise the traditional music of various countries and present it to the public had been raging for some time before Baring-Gould and his associates began collecting English folk songs. Edward Rimbault noted in his *Musical Illustrations of Bishop Percy's Reliques of Ancient English Poetry* (1850) that the melodies required simple and unpretending harmonisation without 'wanton alterations of the melody to suit some particular form of harmony' and without neglecting 'the mode or scale in which the respective airs are composed'.[25]

This controversy was related to fact that the tunes contained notes which sounded 'odd' or 'curious' to ears accustomed to art and popular musics of the day. In England, these were initially referred to as instances

---

24 Sabine Baring-Gould, Preface, *Songs of the West*, Part IV, 1891, p. ix.
25 Edward Rimbault, *Musical Illustrations of Bishop Percy's Reliques of Ancient English Poetry* (London: Cramer, Beale and Co., 1850), p. x.

of the 'old minor' key[26] and during the course of the nineteenth and early twentieth centuries came to be explained in terms of the 'church modes'.

Mode theory had a long and complex history, having been developed in medieval times to explain the unaccompanied plainchant of the Catholic church. It continued to evolve and alter in the hands of generations of theorists, and in relation to the rise of polyphony. Because church music was the dominant form of composition, modal music was thought to have dominated until around 1600 or so when, with the rise of a more harmonic conception of music, there was a shift to what we now think of as the standard major and minor sound of western music.

Those interested in folk song focused on the church modes (also known as the ecclesiastical or Gregorian modes) as an alternative set of scales which explained the unconventional notes sometimes found in traditional tunes. As such, they did not imply the harmonic relationships and progressions that composed melodies did, making the process of arranging folk tunes hotly contested. The modes comprised different patterns of steps and half-steps between notes, each being known by a Greek name. At the time that Baring-Gould, Fleetwood Sheppard and Bussell were collecting, English folk songs were only loosely and intermittently discussed in these terms. By the early twentieth century, though, with the development of the Folk-Song Society and the accumulation of collected examples, they became a prized characteristic. Cecil Sharp wrote extensively about them in his book, *English Folk Song: Some Conclusions*, published in 1907. He considered that around one-third of the tunes he had collected were modal, being in the Mixolydian, Dorian and Aeolian modes, while roughly two-thirds were major.[27]

In the early editions of *Songs of the West*, Baring-Gould and Fleetwood Sheppard were very cautious about the inclusion of songs with modal tunes because they felt that the public were not ready for them. This was despite the fact that they themselves particularly valued modal tunes as evidence of age and possible origins in medieval minstrelsy.[28] By the time of the revised edition of *Songs of the West*, this time with Sharp as its musical editor, public taste was changing and 'musicians have multiplied who can

---

26 William Sandys, *Christmas Carols Ancient and Modern* (London: Richard Beckley, 1833), p. 187. For an account of the development of mode theory among English folk song collectors, see Julia Bishop, 'Our History 3: Tuning a Song (Collecting the Music)' in Steve Roud, *Folk Song in England* (London: Faber & Faber, 2017), pp. 185–216.

27 Cecil Sharp, *English Folk Song: Some Conclusions*, p. 55. The major scale is also called the Ionian mode, but in general the folk song collectors tended to call it the major scale.

28 Sabine Baring-Gould, Preface, *Songs of the West*, Part IV, 1891, p. xii.

value these early melodies'.[29] Despite this, relatively few songs with modal tunes were added to the revised edition.

History and character of West Country melodies

Given the caution that Baring-Gould and Fleetwood Sheppard felt in even including modal tunes in *Songs of the West*, it was a bold move to feature an essay by Fleetwood Sheppard in which he highlights the prevalence of the church modes in folk songs. Entitled 'On the Melodies of Songs of the West', it also discusses the songs' history and characteristics at some length.

Fleetwood Sheppard believed that folk tunes originated among those who sang them. In this he differed from Baring-Gould who thought it 'more likely [that] they have taken known melodies and altered them according to their own provincial musical ideas'.[30] This and other differences of opinion show the importance of distinguishing between the views held by each man.[31]

Fleetwood Sheppard was more cautious than Baring-Gould about dating tunes but he confidently asserts that tunes in the church modes sound archaic and are as old as the Wars of the Roses (mid-fifteenth century), if not older. The modes he finds in West Country songs are the Dorian, Phrygian and Mixolydian. Those attributed to the Phrygian mode do not stand up to scrutiny. As printed in *Songs of the West* they conform to the Aeolian mode. English folk songs only came to be attributed to the Aeolian mode in the early twentieth century, however.[32]

Despite the Mixolydian mode being the most common of the modes employed in West Country tunes, Fleetwood Sheppard did not include Mixolydian tune arrangements in *Songs of the West*.[33] Bussell composed one for 'Nancy'[34] (which has a Mixolydian tune as he collected it) but, according to Baring-Gould's published notes, 'Mr Sheppard, who did not take down the tune, considers this form to be due to the way in which the men sang the air, and he has restored it to what he conceives to be the

---

29 Sabine Baring-Gould, Preface, *Songs of the West* (1905), p. v.
30 Sabine Baring-Gould, Preface, *Songs of the West*, Part IV (1891), p. x.
31 Baring-Gould later changed his view, saying that he had 'doubted their being genuine productions of the folk muse. Mr. Sheppard differed from me, and further consideration and research induce me to modify my view'. Sabine Baring-Gould, *Garland of Country Song*, p. ix.
32 Julia Bishop, 'Our History 3: Tuning a Song (Collecting the Music)', p. 206.
33 He quotes two examples in the essay. These are untitled, but identifiable as 'The Cruel Ship's Carpenter', and 'Botany Bay'.
34 'Nancy', Rough Copy Vol 5, p. 28.

correct form'.[35] This involved altering one of the notes by a semitone.[36] One senses another area of disagreement between the three.

Nevertheless, Fleetwood Sheppard's essay is the first to discuss modal scales in English folk song at any length, and the first containing detailed observations of English tunes in relation to the church modes. It was omitted from the revised edition of *Songs of the West*, though, and its significance has been overlooked in later considerations of folk song scholarship.

A final contribution by Fleetwood Sheppard and Baring-Gould is their observations on singers and the modes. Fleetwood Sheppard highlights that the flattened seventh (found in several modes, including the Mixolydian and Dorian) 'finds favour everywhere with rural singers', and is a deliberate choice by them. Baring-Gould also reports singers as being aware of modal sound in their songs:

'I reckon that's the beautifullest tune as ever were sung anywhere' says my master [James Parsons] of some specially archaic air. And I notice that he appreciates the old minor tunes much more than those in majors.[37]

Similarly:

One man I know sings nothing that is not in an old church mode – a hypo-Dorian or mixolydian [sic] melody suits him down to the ground. He cannot abide a tune of the modern sort. But it is not so with all. They have had to accommodate themselves to the altered taste of the times, and they sing songs of all dates.[38]

This awareness of an older style of singing, with its modal sound, and the move away from it that appears to be taking place at the time, is something that it would be good to know much more about.

The Piano Arrangements

The standard way of popularising any music in the nineteenth century was to publish it in a piano arrangement, and this is precisely what Baring-Gould and his associates did. They were among the first to do so in relation to English folk songs collected from living singers. The Rough Copy

---

35 Sabine Baring-Gould, Preface, *Songs of the West*, Part IV (1891), p. xxvii.
36 In exact terms, Fleetwood Sheppard has sharpened the lower seventh pitches in the tune.
37 Sabine Baring-Gould, 'Among the Western Song Men', *English Illustrated Magazine*, 9 (1892), p. 477.
38 Sabine Baring-Gould, Introduction, *A Garland of Country Song*, p. ix

notebooks contain scattered drafts of piano arrangements,[39] although not all of them reached publication.[40] Fleetwood Sheppard took the lead as the music editor and arranger for the first editions of *Songs of the West*, and for *A Garland of Country Song* and *English Minstrelsie*.

Of the 110 items in *Songs of the West*, Fleetwood Sheppard supplied arrangements to 85 songs and Bussell just 26.[41] The imbalance is due to the fact that Fleetwood Sheppard preferred only to arrange songs he had collected himself so that he could 'catch its special character, and so render it justly', as Baring-Gould later put it.[42] Fleetwood Sheppard's approach seems to have been influenced by the German *Lied*, or art-song, in which the composer strove to capture the emotional essence of a song in the accompaniment. The style of Fleetwood Sheppard's accompaniments shows the influence of Schubert in particular, such as in the running semiquavers of 'By Chance It Was', word-painting (the hunting horn effect in the introduction to 'The Hunting of Arscott of Tetcott'), and the chromatic chords which he sometimes introduced to add colour to the harmonisations. The piano parts are quite florid in some instances, with a fondness for arpeggio figurations, and it seems safe to assume that Fleetwood Sheppard was himself a pianist of some ability.

Fleetwood Sheppard justified his intentions in this way:

> It has not been thought necessary, because these songs were sung by simple folk, to make the accompaniments as simple as possible. Some require to be, and have been so treated; some seem to demand a more elaborate arrangement...when there is no story to tell, or when it has to be told in three verses, and becomes tedious after four, more prominence may well be given to the music. Songs so widely differing ...surely require very different treatment to bring out the poetical character in the melody, and to impart some interest to the accompaniment.[43]

---

39 For example, 'An Evening so Clear' Rough Copy, Vol. 9, p. 55 (published as No. 41 in the first edition of *Songs of the West*), which is arranged by Bussell but contains a handwritten editorial comment by Fleetwood Sheppard.

40 Some of Fleetwood Sheppard's arrangements in the Rough Copy were intended for the concert series Baring-Gould put on in the 1890s.

41 There were two songs ('Lullaby' and 'The Bell Ringing') for which they each supplied an accompaniment, while 'Hal-an-Tow or The Helston Furry Dance' has been arranged by J. Mathews.

42 Sabine Baring-Gould, Introduction, *Songs of the West* (1905), p. xi.

43 H. Fleetwood Sheppard, 'On the Melodies of Songs of the West', *Songs of the West*, Part IV (1891), p. xlviii.

Bringing out 'the poetical character' included casting songs in a variety of formats. Solo voice and piano settings are the most numerous but there are several choral arrangements (e.g. 'As Johnny Walked Out', 'Ye Maidens Pretty'), duets (e.g. Fleetwood Sheppard's arrangement of 'Sweet Nightingale'), a trio ('The Dilly Song'), and arrangements involving solo, duet and choral elements (e.g. 'The Mallard').[44]

Other musical elements of the arrangement sometimes appear to have been suggested by consideration of all the tune variants for a particular song, both collected and printed. An example is 'Cold Blows the Wind' in which Fleetwood Sheppard sets the initial part of the song in a minor key version of the tune and changes this to major for the two final stanzas. The only minor key variants of the tune in the Personal and Fair Copies are published ones. It is noted in *Songs of the West* that 'the original tune taken down from [Mr. H.] Westaway by Mr. Sheppard was in the major and it was felt advisable to have two verses in that key', so two stanzas of text were duly written by Baring-Gould and added. These have an optimistic tone, presumably to match the commonly perceived 'happy' feel of the major tune. It seems that Harry Westaway felt no such tension between his major key tune and the tragic tone of his words to the song.

In Fleetwood Sheppard's setting of 'By Chance It Was' (based on James Parsons' tune, see Figs. A.1, A.2, and A.8), the short piano coda to the song ends on the upper fifth (D) of the scale rather than the more usual first note (G) (Fig. A.9)

---

44 Bussell's arrangements include one for voice, piano and solo violin ('Lullaby') and another for voices and chorus ('The Sailor's Farewell') in the manner of an operetta.

Fig. A.9 – Fleetwood Sheppard's arrangement of 'By Chance It Was'

A variant tune for this song, sent in by Tyndall (Fig. A.10), which finishes on D may well have been the source of Fleetwood Sheppard's inspiration for this:

Fig. A.10 – 'It Was By Chance' (Tyndall), Personal Copy Vol. 1, p. 1.[45]

Ultimately, one suspects that the nature of Fleetwood Sheppard's arrangements reflects his own aesthetics (a love of Schubert *Lieder*?), and provided an opportunity for him to exercise his own creativity. He was no doubt sincere in his belief that, in order to preserve the melodies, he needed to present them 'in a form acceptable to the musical public, and in which they may hold their own in the great competition for public favour',[46] but his perception of public acceptability may well have been coloured by his own tastes.

In the event, Fleetwood Sheppard's accompaniments did not meet with universal approval. As far as the public was concerned, some were indeed found to be technically too demanding for amateur musicians. For many of those involved in collecting and popularising folk song in the late nineteenth and early twentieth centuries, the arrangements were out of keeping with the nature of folk song. As the later comments of Charles H. Laycock, a Devonian collector, put it:

> Many of his settings are very beautiful indeed as musical productions, but they are emphatically not in keeping with the spirit of folk-song. They are, rather, dainty little pieces of art-music founded upon folk-song themes. For the essence of folk-song is simplicity, and few, if any of Mr. Sheppard's settings could be called simple while many of them are so elaborate that it requires the technique of a skilled pianist to perform them.[47]

When *Songs of the West* was re-published in 1905, Fleetwood Sheppard had died, and much water had flowed under the folk song collecting

45 VWML Digital Database permanent URL: www.vwml.org/record/SBG/1/1/2.
46 H. Fleetwood Sheppard, 'On the Melodies of Songs of the West', *Songs of the West*, Part IV (1891) p. xlviii.
47 Charles Laycock, 'English National and Folk Music with Special Reference to the Folk Songs of Devonshire', in *Report and Transactions of the Devonshire Association* (Barnstaple, July 1917), Vol XLIX, pp. 296–319.

bridge. Cecil Sharp took charge of the music editing for a revised edition, and supplied new arrangements, as well as substituting some of the earlier songs. The duets and quartets have been discarded, and the settings simplified. Laycock's comments comparing the two editions show just how much the ground had shifted and a folk song aesthetic had been established:

> To the lover of florid art music, the airs as harmonized by the Rev. Fleetwood Sheppard in the older edition [of *Songs of the West*] will no doubt appeal more strongly than the simpler and more rugged style of accompaniment adopted by Mr. Cecil Sharp in the 1905 edition. But to the true lover of folk-song, there can be no doubt as to the superiority in musical value of the later edition.[48]

In our own times, it is Sharp's arrangements that sound dated and reminiscent of 'art music'. Many of today's arrangements are influenced by popular and world music styles, and no more preserve the supposed simplicity of folk song than Sheppard's did, so it is perhaps unfair to find fault with him on this from our contemporary vantage point.

Another criticism levelled at Fleetwood Sheppard by Laycock is his lack of 'respect' for modal tonality in *Songs of the West*. This takes two forms. Firstly, in the harmonisations used in his accompaniments, it is claimed that he has 'in practically every case totally destroyed the modal character of the folk-tunes, making them conform, as far as possible to the modern major or minor tonalities'.[49] Secondly, Laycock claims that 'in a few cases, I fear Mr. Sheppard was guilty of making slight alterations, modifications if you like, in the actual melody itself, such as sharpening the seventh in Mixolydian and Æolian airs, and flattening the 6th in addition to sharpening the seventh in Dorian ones.'[50] These have been 'corrected' by Sharp in the revised edition.[51]

On the first point, it is quite true that the accompaniments are chromatic rather than modal and do contain notes which were not part of the tune.[52] Laycock terms it 'bad musicianship to insert chromatic notes in the harmonized accompaniment of a modal melody, which cannot

---

48 Charles Laycock, 'English National and Folk Music' pp. 310–11.
49 Charles Laycock, 'English National and Folk Music' p. 311.
50 Charles Laycock, 'English National and Folk Music' p. 311.
51 Charles Laycock, 'English National and Folk Music' p. 311.
52 Sharp advocated using only the notes of the mode as represented in the tune. See his *English Folk-Song: Some Conclusions*, pp. 47–48.

possibly occur in the melody itself. It produces a hybrid, which is neither major, minor, nor modal'.[53] Scrutiny of Sharp's accompaniments in *Songs of the West*, however, reveals that he too introduces notes that are not part of the tune.[54]

On the second point, we have seen how selectively Fleetwood Sheppard and Baring-Gould included modal tunes in *Songs of the West*, so there should have been little need for alteration in the way that Laycock claims. This is contradicted by the aforementioned example of 'Nancy', however, which supports Laycock's criticism.

On the other hand, closer investigation of the two examples cited by Laycock himself in this regard does not further his case. He claims that 'Jan's Courtship' is 'a fine Æolian air, which in the older edition is made to conform to the modern minor mode by means of a sharpened seventh or leading-note'.[55] It is true that Fleetwood Sheppard's accompaniment does introduce raised sevenths liberally and Sharp's does not. But either is justifiable in this case given that the seventh note of the scale is not present in the melody. It cannot be defined as Aeolian, therefore, because all seven notes of the scale or mode are required to identify it.

The other example mentioned by Laycock is Fleetwood Sheppard's setting of 'The Mallard'. This setting is one of the more dramatized ones, arranged for two vocalists and 4-part choir. In the 1905 revised edition of *Songs of the West* (where it is entitled 'A Country Dance'), Baring-Gould notes:

> This tune is in the Dorian mode. As sung by J. Masters, the E was sharpened in the 3rd bar but flattened on the repetition of the same phrase in the penultimate bar. Mr Sheppard, when arranging the song, flattened the E throughout. It must be one thing or the other. Flattened throughout, it makes a charming melody but the last flattened E was probably due to the singer's memory failing him in the latter part of the air, but serving him at the beginning of the tune. Mr Sharp has accordingly retained the E natural throughout.[56]

---

53 Charles Laycock, 'English National and Folk Music' p. 313.
54 See, for example, the major third introduced by Sharp in the final chord of 'The Trees They Are so High' (an effect known in art music as a *tierce de Picardie*), and the introduction of the flattened sixth into the accompaniment of 'Old Wichet' whose tune contains no sixth.
55 Charles Laycock, 'English National and Folk Music' p. 312.
56 Sabine Baring-Gould, 'Notes on the Songs', *Songs of the West* (1905), p. 23.

Laycock adds that Fleetwood Sheppard has added a sharpened seventh to the accompaniment as well, thereby making the arrangement conform to the conventional minor key – 'so treated it made a very pleasing air, but it was not the true folk-melody'.[57]

A closer look at the melody shows that it lacks the seventh note of the scale, so it cannot be identified as being Dorian. As to the variable sixth note, the different copies of the tune as sung by Masters do not agree as to the frequency and placing of this detail (Figs A.11 and A.12).

Fig. A.11 'The Mallard' (Masters), Fair Copy, p. 204[58]

Fig. A.12 'The Mallard' (Masters), Personal Copy, Vol. 1, p. 168[59]

We do not have Fleetwood Sheppard's initial notation of the melody from Masters but a sketch for his arrangement of the tune in the Rough Copy gives the melody differently again (Fig. A.13).

57 Charles Laycock, 'English National and Folk Music' p. 312.
58 VWML Digital Database permanent URL: www.vwml.org/record/SBG/3/1/401.
59 VWML Digital Database permanent URL: www.vwml.org/record/SBG/1/1/383.

Fig. A.13 The Mallard (Masters), Rough Copy, Vol, 9, p. 17[60]

---

60 VWML Digital Database permanent URL: www.vwml.org/record/ SBG/3/12/17.

There is clearly more to be unravelled here but the portrayal of Fleetwood Sheppard wantonly destroying the modal character of the melodies seems overstated and oversimplified.

In conclusion, it is clear that there is a wealth of information about folk song melodies in the Baring-Gould collection. This account has done no more than lift the lid on its interest and also the issues it raises when we investigate what it can tell us about traditional singing, singers and song in late-nineteenth-century Devon and Cornwall.

The roles of all those involved in compiling the music for the collection are also fascinating and deserve more in-depth study. Each had their individual approach to the music and to the contemporary debate about its history and characteristics. In particular, Fleetwood Sheppard has tended to be judged more by his arrangements than by his analytical observations on folk tunes, and deserves more attention as a precursor to later understandings of folk music developed by Sharp and others in the Folk-Song Society.

Sheffield
April 2017

Julia Bishop holds research posts at the University of Aberdeen and University of Sheffield, where she studies both traditional music and children's play. She co-edited, with Steve Roud, the *New Penguin Book of English of Folk Songs* (2012), and is chief editor of the James Madison Carpenter Folk Song and Drama Collection critical edition (forthcoming).

Appendix B – A selection of songs from the Baring-Gould Manuscripts

To produce a book about a collection of songs without giving some examples of them would be rather strange. This small selection from Baring-Gould's folk song manuscripts has been chosen to show the different types of song that can be found in the collection. Some have already been mentioned in the text and their full versions are given here with their music. They have been edited for singing but the changes made are few. The original manuscripts can be viewed in the Vaughan Williams Memorial Library Digital Database (www.vwml.org) should you wish to see them.

The Songs

Among the Green Hay (Frances Adams)
Benjamin Bowlabags (John Hale Parlby)
The Carpenter's Wife (Joseph Paddon)
The Complaining Maid (William Houghton)
A Country Lad Am I (Samuel Fone)
A Cup of Poison (Thomas Cayzer)
The Hostess' Daughter (John Masters)
In the Winter of Life (Charles Arscott)
The Little Girl Down the Row (Samuel Fone)
The Pack of Cards (John Dingle)
Sailors at Sea (J. Rich)
The Setting of the Sun (Samuel Fone)

Notes on the Songs:

Among the Green Hay – P2, 371 (330), Roud 855.
This was one of twelve songs sent to Baring-Gould by Frances Adams, a music teacher who lived in Plymouth. She was born in 1821 and remembered a number of songs from her mother, grandmother and her nurse. Lucy Broadwood had a similar song but without the amusing misspelling in the final verse. Baring-Gould recognised that the song was in Henry Fielding's musical play *The Virgin Unmasked*, from 1786.

Benjamin Bowlabags – P3, 247 (542), Roud 1514.
Along with the miller and the weaver, tailors were often seen as untrustworthy in rural society. That they were allowed access to the house to take measurements (and, perhaps, liberties!) and then had to be trusted to make the maximum use of the cloth that the customer had provided and not divert it to his own use, was a cause for suspicion. This children's song highlights their perceived cowardice. In other versions the tailor cannot manage to wage war against a mouse and so tackles a flea.

The Carpenter's Wife – P2, 159 (196), Roud 14.
We wanted to include one of the 'big ballads' that Baring-Gould collected. This is a fine version of a ballad classic, sometimes known as 'The Daemon Lover' (Child 243), which has often been found in Britain and the USA. Though the supernatural elements are subdued in this case, the tale is still gripping.

The Complaining Maid – P2, 206 (222), Roud 1546.
Baring-Gould and Bussell met the self-confessed smuggler, William Houghton in Charlestown in August 1894. They were in the company of Richard Hansford Worth, who noted the tune for Baring-Gould. This song and its kinship with the Devon song 'Twas on One April Morning' is discussed in Chapter 7.

A Country Lad Am I – P2, 417 (371), Roud 23130.
This piece of gentle mockery at the expense of the farmer was collected from Sam Fone in March 1893. It comes from the second half of the Nineteenth Century when farming was in recession in England at a time when there were many opportunities for young people to seek their fortunes in the Americas or Australia.

A Cup of Poison – P1, 144 (66), Roud 218.
Otherwise known as 'Oxford City' or 'Poison in a Glass of Wine', this
tale of jealousy and murder-suicide was found by several collectors
in both England and the USA until modern times. It was printed on
broadsides from around 1820. Thomas Cayzer heard this version sung
in a pub at Postbridge in 1849 and sent it to Baring-Gould 40 years
later.

The Hostess' Daughter – P1, 150 (70), Roud 914.
Collected from John Masters of Bradstone, this wistful song is told from
the point of view of the man who deserts his pregnant sweetheart. The
reason why he is compelled to leave her is not spelled out but it is likely that
he was an apprentice, forbidden under the terms of his indenture from
marrying. This song is discussed in more detail in Chapter 9.

In the Winter of Life – P3, 137 (475), Roud 12609.
Baring-Gould heard this unusual song from Charles Arscott of South
Zeal when he stayed in the village in August 1894. Arscott refused to
allow the words to be taken down, but did not object to the melody
being noted. Baring-Gould wrote out the words as he remembered
them in his manuscript book, but was able to correct them when he
visited again in March 1896 and Arscott allowed him to note the words.
Peter Kennedy recorded it from Bill Westaway at nearby Belstone in
1950. Sharp heard a version in Rose Ash, North Devon in January
1904.

The Little Girl Down the Row – P2, 419 (367), Roud 6907.
Baring-Gould heard this sung by Will Huggins of Lydford, soon after
he started collecting songs. At that time he was more interested in the
tunes than the words and did not record Will Huggins' text, and he used
the tune for his own song 'The Last of the Singers', which is in *Songs
of the West*. Several years later he heard Sam Fone sing it to a different
tune, which he noted. Fone could not remember the third verse so a
version collected from William Nichols of Whitchurch has been used to
complete the text.

The Pack of Cards – P3, 82 (441), Roud 232.
This charming and mildly erotic metaphor was found by a number of
the Victorian and Edwardian collectors and, in more recent times, from
travelers among whom the card game 'All Fours' is still played. Baring-
Gould and Bussell heard this sung by John Dingle in April 1894. Dingle

also sang it for Cecil Sharp when he was staying at Lew Trenchard in August 1904, giving us an opportunity to compare the work of the two collectors, separated by a decade. Sharp's notation is recorded as number 283 in his tune book.

Sailors at Sea – P2, 305 (284), Roud 21410.
Taken down from J. Rich a farmer from Horndon, near Mary Tavy, who said he learned it from a labourer, J. Friend. This is an orally collected variant of 'Our Sailors on the Sea', written in 1874 by Frank Green and Alfred Lee supporting Samuel Plimsoll in his campaign against overloaded 'coffin ships' which resulted in the Merchant Shipping Act of 1876 and the compulsory marking of loading lines on ships. A good example of Baring-Gould including songs that fell outside the contemporary view of what constituted 'folk music' in his collection.

The Setting of the Sun – P3, 30 (409), Roud 166.
This is another ballad with several titles ('The Shooting of his Dear', 'Molly Bawn', 'Polly Vaughan', etc.), which occurs widely in Britain, Ireland and the Americas. This version, with its fine tune, was collected from Sam Fone. It cuts the story to the essentials and then, unusually, includes a chorus.

AMONG THE GREEN HAY

Sent to Baring-Gould by Frances Adams, Mutley, Plymouth

As I was a-walking one morning in May
'Twas down in the meadow among the green hay
My true love he met me the very same day
'Twas down in the meadow among the green hay.

'My father is worth five hundred a year
And I am his daughter and his only dear
Not a farthing of fortune he'll give me I fear
If I marry Y O U my dear.'

'O as for your fortune my dear I don't mind
I'll make you a husband both loving and kind
Put your hand into mine, Miss, if you are inclined
And Cupid shall U S in harmony bind.'

So then to the church they hastened away
And home to her father the very same day
Saying, 'Honoured father, I tell unto thee
I am M A R R I E D.'

So then the old man he began for to stare
'What, married, my daughter, my love and my care.'
Saying, 'If it be so – then I have a new son
And to him I say W E L C U M.'

367

Benjamin Bowlabags

Sent to Baring-Gould by the Rev John Hale Parlby, 26 December 1896

Would you know how the war began?
Benjamin Bowlabags
Would you know how the war began?
Cast threads away
Would you know how the war began?
Nine tailors make a man
And so the proud tailor went prancing away.

With his needle he made a spear
And ran the mouse through the ear.

With his bodkin he made a gun
And shot the mouse as he run.

With his scissors he dug a pit
And shoved the mouse into it.

With his thimble he made a bell
And tolled the mouse's funeral knell.

The Carpenter's Wife

Sung by Joseph Paddon, Holcombe Burnell, December 1889

Well met well met my own true love Long time am I seek - ing of thee I

am late - ly come from the salt, salt sea And all for the sake sweet love of thee.

'Well met, well met my own true love
Long time am I seeking of thee
I am lately come from the salt, salt sea
And all for the sake, sweet love, of thee.'

'I might have had a king's daughter
She fain would have married me
But I nought did hold for her crown of
  gold
And all for the sake, sweet love, of thee.

'If you might have had a king's daughter
I think you were much to blame
I would not it were for a hundred pound
That my husband should know the
  same.'

'For my husband he is a carpenter
A carpenter good is he
By him I have gotten a little son
Or else, sweet love, I would go with
  thee.'

'But if I should leave my husband dear
And my fair sweet boy also
O what have you got far, far away
That along with thee I should go.'

'I have seven ships that sail the seas
It was one brought me to land
I have mariners many to wait on thee
To do sweet love at thy command.'

'A pair of slippers, love, thou shalt have,
They're made of beaten gold
And they be a lined with coney skin
To keep thy feet from the cold.'

'A gilded boat thou shalt also have
And the oars be gilded also
And the mariners they shall pipe and sing
As through the salt waves we row.'

They had not a rowed a bowshot off
A bowshot off upon the main
But over her shoulder she looked back
And said, 'I would I were home again.'

They had not rowed a bowshot off
A bowshot from the land
But over her shoulder she looked and
  said
'Set me back upon the yellow sand.'

'For I have a child in my little chamber
And I think I hear him loudly cry
And I would not, I would not my babe
  should wake
And his mother should not be standing
  by.'

The captain he smiled and he stroked
  his arms
And he said, 'This may not lady be
Behind is the shore and the sea before
And thou must go, sweet love with me.'

She had not been long upon the sea
Not long upon the deep, the deep,
Before that she was wringing her hands
And loud did wail and loudly weep.

'O why do you wail and wherefore weep
And wring your hands,' said he
'Do you weep for my gold that is in the
   hold
Or do you weep for my fee.'

'I do not weep for your gold,' she said
'Nor yet do I weep for your fee
But by the mast-head is my baby dead
And I weep for my dead baby.'

She had not been upon the seas
The days they were three or four
But never a word she spoke nor stirred
And she looked towards the shore.

She had not been upon the seas
But six days of the week
Before that she lay as cold as the clay
And never a word could speak.

They had not a sailed upon the seas
Of weeks but three and four
But down to the bottom the ship did
   swim
And never was heard of more.

And when the tidings to England came
That the carpenter's wife was drowned
The carpenter rent his hair and wept
And then as dead he swooned.

A curse be on all sea captains
That lead such a godless life
They will ruin a good ship carpenter
And his little son and his wife.

THE COMPLAINING MAID

Sung by William Houghton, Charlestown, 20 August 1894

'Twas on a summer morning
Just as the sun was rising
There did I hear a maiden complain
She crying was, 'O Nancy
Love it is a fancy
Sweethearts and lovers are torments of pain.'

'Down in yonder bower
There does grow a flower
Do you remember vows you made there?
Go to, false pretender
Do not you remember
When you my innocent heart did ensnare?'

'Young men are deceivers
Young women believers
Young men are false and seldom prove true
They're roving and ranging
Their minds always changing
And seeking for some object that's new.'

'O had I my own heart in keeping
O had I my poor heart again
Close in my bosom
I'd treasure it sleeping
Never to wake to such exquisite pain.'

A Country Lad Am I

Sung by Samuel Fone, Mary Tavy, March 1893.

Come far-mer lads and lass-es all and list-en un-to me There's fun a-like for great and small with

me you must a-gree Why should the far-mer hang his head when he ought to wear a smile We'll

sing and shout the har-vest bread that feeds Great Bri-tain's isle Then it's all a mong the farm-ers the

har-vest home we'll cry I can plough and sow and reap and mow for a coun-try lad am I.

Come farmer lads and lasses all and listen unto me
There's fun alike for great and small with me you must agree
Why should the farmer hang his head when he ought to wear a smile
We'll sing and shout the harvest bread that feeds Great Britain's isle.
  Then it's all among the farmers the harvest home we'll cry
  I can plough and sow and reap and mow for a country lad am I.

They say there's something in the wind now mark you what I say
The farmer's men refuse to work for eighteen pence a day
If you don't mind what you're about they'll toddle by and bye
You'll have to plough the lands yourselves and that will ope your eye.
  Then it's all among the farmers, etc.

Now farmers keep your spirits up before it gets too late
The young folk they will marry soon and then will emigrate
If you don't raise their wages soon they mean to do the grand
In a great big ship they'll emigrate out to a foreign land.
  Then it's all among the farmers, etc.

Then Master Henry has to throw aside his dog and gun
To hedge and ditch no matter which he will not find that fun
No more at the piano will Emily sit and scream
She'll have to milk the cows herself and likewise skim the cream.
  Then it's all among the farmers, etc.

Look at the price of everything the farm produces now
With mutton and beef don't soil your teeth but just look on the cow
And bear in mind if farmers grind they'll soon be left alone
With help from the State to emigrate each man will farm his own.
  Then it's all among the farmers, etc.

A CUP OF POISON

Heard at Postbridge by Thomas S. Cayzer in 1849 and sent to Baring-Gould

As I walked out one Midsummer morning
To view the fields and take the air
'Twas there I met two lovers discoursing
He vowed and declared he loved her dear.

'O Nancy, Nancy, why do you slight me
Why do you stand so far away
I'll work for you both late and early
If you'll consent my bride to be.'

It was to a dance this couple departed
Up to a landlady's they did go
But when they were there her true love came after
And soon he did prove her overthrow.

For when he saw her dance with the other
Some jealous thoughts came into his mind
All for to destroy his own dear jewel
He gave to her a glass of wine.

She took it kindly, but soon did alter
'O carry me home, my dear,' said she
'That glass of wine that you gave unto me
Has made me ill as ill can be.'

As they were walking home together
These few words he to her did say
'Twas of strong poison I gave unto thee
And soon 'twill take thy life away.'

'I drank of the same, my own dear jewel
I'm sure I am as ill as thee
O in each other's arms we'll die together.'
So – all young men, don't jealous be.

The Hostess' Daughter

Sung by John Masters, Bradstone

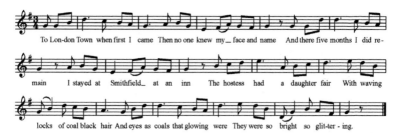

To Lon-don Town when first I came Then no one knew my— face and name   And there five months I did remain   I stayed at   Smithfield—   at an inn   The hostess had   a daughter fair   With waving
locks   of coal black hair And eyes as coals that glowing were   They were so   bright   so glit-ter - ing.

To London Town when first I came
Then no one knew my face and name
And there five months I did remain
I stayed at Smithfield at an inn
The hostess had a daughter fair
With waving locks of coal black hair
And eyes as coals that glowing were
They were so bright, so glittering.

I kissed her rosy cheeks and brow
Her face was mingled blood and snow
We loved each other well I know
We loved each other tenderly
I sowed the silly seeds of love
I sowed them in a garden grove
And now away I must remove
From London Town away must fly.

The seeds of love they grew apace
The tears were ever on her face
I would not tarry in that place
To reap the harvest I had sown
Now when the pretty babe is born
'Twill lie within her bosom warm
But ne'er be danced upon the arm
Of father for that babe has none.

IN THE WINTER OF LIFE

Sung by Charles Arscott, South Zeal, 9 Aug 1894 and 20 March 1896

I should like for to have in the winter of life   A neat lit-tle cot-tage for me and my_ wife With a bar-rel of ale and a snug lit-tle fire_ And food that's suf - fic-ient is all my des - ire For_ I'm grow-ing old and my locks they are grey   No more shall I dance with the young and the_ gay For_ time hath de - ter-mined the_ truth to un - fold_ I've a mark on my fore-head to show I am old.

I should like for to have in the winter of life
A neat little cottage for me and my wife
With a barrel of ale and a snug little fire
And food that's sufficient is all my desire.
For I'm growing old and my locks they are grey
No more shall I dance with the young and the gay
For time hath determined the truth to unfold
I've a mark on my forehead to show I am old.

And some wounded old soldier I'll have with me dwell
With his cook, and to hear the strange stories he'll tell
How he conquered his foes and the victory was gained
And how he returned and how he got lamed.
For I'm growing old, etc.

If the friend comes to see me in my little cot
I bid him partake of the luck of my pot
No ale shall be wanting while with me he doth stay
But the bailiff I always send empty away.
For I'm growing old, etc.

The very next moment I'm panting for breath
Then close by my elbow see grasping old Death
I'll ask not the time for one moment to stay
He's the great king of Terrors and we must obey.
For I'm growing old, etc.

The Little Girl Down The Row

Sung by Samuel Fone, Mary Tavy, March 1893

Come all you ladies and lasses and listen awhile to my lay
I will tell you a comical story that happened the other May Day
It's of a young tailor I'm telling and he was apprentice, I know
And this 'prentice he used to go courting the little girl down in the Row
O that sweet little girl down the Row.

One day while the tailor was working, the thought come straight into his head
Says he, 'I'll go down to my sweetheart and ask her this morning to wed.'
'O what will your master be saying,' she asked, 'If to church we both go
When he knows that you're going to be married, to the little girl down in the Row
O that sweet little girl down the Row.'

She answered at first with denial but afterwards she did come round
Saying, 'If I consent for to marry they'll spread it all over the town.'
Then the wedding day it was appointed and all things got ready in haste
And away to the church he did go with the little girl down in the Row
O that sweet little girl down the Row.

But when that he came to the church door, just thinking that married he'd be
Round the corner came the young tailor's master saying, 'Prentice boy come along with me'
He catched him right hold by the collar without any word, any blow
And he walked him right back into Limbo from the little girl down in the Row
O that sweet little girl down the Row.

Now come all you ladies and lasses and listen awhile unto me
Don't talk and let too many know it whenever your wedding's to be
For fear lest when going to church, Miss, along with your sweetheart and beau
You find yourself left in the lurch, Miss, like the little girl down in the Row
O that sweet little girl down the Row.

THE PACK OF CARDS

Sung by John Dingle, Coryton, 3 April 1894 and 12 August 1904

As noted from John Dingle by Frederick Bussell, 3 April 1894

As I walked out on a morning for pleasure
It chanced to be on a bright sunny day
I spied a fair girl a taking her leisure
I said, 'Wherefore ramble so early this way.'
Then she smiled and said, 'I'm going to fair Gloster
To that pleasant city wherein I was born.'

I said, 'Pretty maiden and shall I go with you
Along the green lane for your sweet company.'
She said, 'O young man, 'tis a lane all may go through
You may go on before or come along with me.'
And she sang as she walked, 'I am going to Gloster
To that pleasant city this midsummer morn.'

We travelled for two or three miles on together
Then under the green bracken branches did stray
All under the branches in the sweet summer weather
Then weary with walking we sat down to play
And she sang, ''Tis a fair road that leadeth to Gloster
To that pleasant city wherein I was born.'

I pulled out a pack of cards then on our ramble
As we sat in the shadows among the green fern
She said, 'O young man, I'm not given to gamble.'
I answered, 'No reason why you should not learn.'
And she sang, 'We do tarry on the road to fair Gloster
To that pleasant city this midsummer morn.'

The game that we played was the game of all fours
We laughed and we thought it was capital fun
The game that we played was the game of all fours
I shuffled the pack and took three to her one
Then she said, 'O young man this is no going to Gloster
To that pleasant city wherein I was born.'

I said it was my deal, she said she'd defeat me
I dealt myself neither a Trump nor a Jack
She threw out the ace and the deuce and so beat me
Which are thought the best cards to be had in the pack
Then she said, 'Let us up and be going to Gloster
To that pleasant city this midsummer morn.'

She played the ace and she took my Jack from me
She had the high, low and the Jack and the game
Then she said, 'O young man, you have not overcome me
Cry done – or else play the game over again.'
But she said, 'Let us up and be going to Gloucester
To that pleasant city wherein I was born.'

I took up my pack and I bade her good morrow
She beat me with high and low, Jack and the game
She laughed and said, 'Young man, depart all in sorrow
Cry done – or else play the game over again.'
And she tripped away singing, 'I go to fair Gloucester
To that pleasant city this midsummer morn.'

As noted from John Dingle by Cecil Sharp, 14 August 1904

SAILORS AT SEA

Sung by J. Rich, Horndon, Devon, 4 Oct 1892

At anchor when we're lying in
   Our beds secure and warm
We often hear the moaning wind
   That tells the coming storm
      Then midst the raging of the sea
      We, Father, humbly ask of thee
      Extend thy mighty power and save
      Poor sailors on the sea.

The sailor little dreams when he
   Sets out upon the wave
The worn out ship in which he sails
   Will bear him to his grave
      Then midst the raging of the sea
      We, Father, humbly ask of Thee
      Extend thy mighty power and save
      Poor sailors on the sea.

Such things we often hear of, and
   The wealthy merchant thrives
But what about the precious freight
   These precious human lives
      Poor honest Jack, from such a fate
      Protected may he be
      And let each do his best to help
      Poor sailors on the sea.

The Setting Of The Sun

Sung by Samuel Fone, Mary Tavy, 12 July 1893

Come all you young fellows that carry a gun
Beware of late shooting when daylight is done
For it's little you reckon what hazards you run
I shot my own love at the setting of the sun.
In a shower of rain as my darling did run
All under the bushes a shower to shun
Her apron 'bout her neck I took her for a swan
I shot the only maid I loved at the setting of the sun.

I'll fly from my country I nowhere find rest
I shot my own true love as a bird on her nest
Oh curse that old gunsmith that made that old gun
I shot my own true love at the setting of the sun.
In a shower, etc.

O it's son, dearest son, don't you run away
Don't leave your own country until the trial day
Don't leave your own country till the trial is done
For shooting your own love at the setting of the sun.
In a shower, etc.

On a night to her uncle the fair maid appeared
Saying, 'Uncle, dear uncle, of me be not afeard
With my apron 'bout my neck in the rain I did run
He shot me as a swan at the setting of the sun.
In a shower, etc.

Appendix C – The Baring-Gould Song Manuscripts

The Fair Copies

These are the principle public documents of the Baring-Gould collection, in which the songs are set out with their words and music, with a selection of the variants that Baring-Gould collected and with versions from print that are related to them. Where the manuscript is among the documents included in the Vaughan Williams Memorial Library Digital Database (The Full English) a reference is given.

The Personal Copy
(3 Volumes)
*Devon Heritage Centre
Ref 7960
(VWML Ref.
SBG/1/1 to 3)*

This set of three large, vellum-bound volumes was the set of books in which Baring-Gould recorded most of the songs that he collected. These were the volumes examined by Cecil Sharp and Lucy Broadwood and which Baring-Gould showed to many of the journalists that interviewed him. The volumes are all set out with the song texts on the right hand page and the melodies on the left hand page, all in Baring-Gould's hand. For each song he gives the variants of the words and of the tunes that he collected or was sent, often with a version copied from a printed source. Some songs required several pages to set out all the variants, suggesting that he was copying from other notebooks and had a good idea of the space required. In many cases he has added entries later, and this has meant cramming extra entries into a page or, less usually, starting a new entry in a later volume. The songs are numbered, the earlier ones using the same numbers as in *Songs of the West*. Most of his published songs are in Volume 1, with some from *Garland of Country Song* spilling over into Volume 2. In the later part of Volume 2 and in Volume 3 he has entered songs as they were collected and also added songs from earlier times not already entered. Each volume has an index, which is carried forward to very near the end of the third volume. Though the frequency of entries decreases with time, the last dated entry in the manuscript is 13 August 1920, showing that he was still maintaining his interest in the collection three years before his death.

The Fair Copy
Plymouth Central Library [Kept in the Plymouth and West Devon Record Office] (VWML Ref. SBG/3/1

This large manuscript volume, given to Plymouth Library in 1900, contains the variants of the majority of songs that Baring-Gould collected that were included in *Songs of the West* and *A Garland of Country Song* as well as a few unpublished items. Most of the entries were transcribed from the Personal Copy manuscript, though there are a few variants that are not in that volume, and it has the same layout. The volume contains 900 individual items, under 202 titles. In a few cases there is a printed version of a song that has been pasted in. Baring-Gould has compiled an index to the volume. A note in the front confirms that Baring-Gould started writing the book in 1892. Letters to W. H. K. Wright, the Plymouth Librarian, show that he was still working on this manuscript in September 1900, with 130 songs copied out. He finished what he described as 'the first volume' less than a month later. If a second volume was intended, it was never compiled.

The Rough Copy

This set of notebooks contains the field notes of many of the songs, together with some of the work carried out by Baring-Gould and his colleagues on arrangements for performance and publication.

The Rough Copy
(14 Volumes)
*Plymouth Central
Library [Kept in the
Plymouth and West
Devon Record Office]
(VWML Ref.
SBG/3/4 to 16)*

Baring-Gould gave this set of 13 manuscript music books to Plymouth Library in July 1914. They contain a mixture of field notes, copies of tunes, and musical arrangements by Baring-Gould, Bussell, and Fleetwood Sheppard. The majority of field notations are by Bussell. The majority of Fleetwood Sheppard's papers were destroyed when he died and only scraps of his work survive. The separate notebooks were at one time bound together but are currently disbound, pending possible re-binding as separate volumes again. Baring-Gould writes of 14 volumes but, I am assured, only 13 were ever given to the library and there has never been a Volume 12. The contents of the volumes are as follows.

Volume 1 – Songs noted by Bussell in: South Zeal, Charlestown, Fowey, Plympton and Lewtrenchard (August to December 1894).

Volume 2 – Starts with a mixture of material, some in Baring-Gould's hand, then Bussell's notation of session at the Saracen's Head January 1890. Ends with a mixture of material, several from John Woodridge but many unidentified.

Volume 3 – Songs collected in Menheniot, several from Sam Fone, various other singers.

Volume 4 – Tour to Merrivale Bridge, Scobbetor, Chagford and Culleyhole September/October 1890. Several songs from James Olver.

Volume 5 – Arrangements by Fleetwood Sheppard and copies by Baring-Gould. A few field notes of songs.

Volume 6 – Songs from Sam Fone, 23 December 1892 and 28 March 1893, interspersed with songs from Stoke Fleming, January 1893. Tunes from William Andrew, July 1893. Songs from John Dingle, 5 April 1894.

Volume 7 – This notebook appears to have been started by Fleetwood Sheppard in October 1888 for his first visit to South Brent. It has subsequently become a place for working out arrangements and has been overwritten in places by Baring-Gould and Bussell with notation and with other arrangements.

Volume 8 – This is not, actually, a notebook but a collection of loose sheets bound together. Mostly Bussell's work with items from South Brent, Exbourne, a sheet from Fleetwood Sheppard and a version of 'Undaunted Mary' in an unknown hand, dated 10 Apil 1902. Contains songs from Harry Westaway including 'The TRUE Uncle Tom Cobbleigh' from much earlier.

Volume 9 – Another collection of odd sheets. Includes songs from the visit to Stoke Fleming in January 1893. Also some from Lydford and other places, together with some arrangements.

Volume 10 – Also a collection of separate sheets, this opens with the songs noted by Bussell at The Falcon, Mawgan in Pydar in July 1893. There is a set of songs from James Parsons. A set of tunes copied by Baring-Gould from books in the British Museum is followed by some songs sent to him from North Devon by Mrs Clarke. A set of songs from Matthew Baker and others has been arranged by Bussell. There are several sent in by informants, Baring-Gould's notation of the Padstow songs, and a number of tunes copied out neatly.

Volume 11 – Contains arrangements by Bussell and Fleetwood Sheppard, Baring-Gould's notation of songs from Robert Hard on 8 September 1892 and from James Parsons.

Volume 13 – This is another mixture of original notation (eg, by Baring-Gould from James Parsons), Bussell's arrangements of songs he has collected, and other collected songs. Includes 'Jovial Reckless Boy'.

Volume 14 – Baring-Gould's copies of tunes (188 of them) from Playford's English Dancing Master, tunes from William Andrew's tune book and some tunes copied from other Mss. A few collected songs.

The Working Notebooks

These four notebooks were used for various purposes by Baring-Gould, firstly as fair copies, but also as field notebooks, work on compositions, programme notes for concerts, and lists of various kinds.

Working Notebook 1
Plymouth Central Library [Kept in the Plymouth and West Devon Record Office] (VWML Ref. SBG/3/2)

This is certainly the earliest of the surviving notebooks. It formed part of the collection of Baring-Gouldiana belonging to Francis Nicolle, which was bequeathed by him to Plymouth Library. The first item in the notebook, the version of 'Widdicombe Fair' sent by William Collier, is dated 15 September 1888. The last item that can be dated with confidence is the list of song examples to be sung at the lecture-concerts that Baring-Gould gave in January 1889. The notebook contains items that have been copied in from correspondence as well as songs noted during some of the early song collecting sessions. Towards the end there is a lot of rough working on songs and on lists. There are a number of letters either stuck in or inserted loosely in the notebook. There are a few pieces of music amongst these additional items, but there is no music in the main body of the text.

Working Notebook 2
Devon Heritage Centre
Ref 5203 M, Box 23
(VWML Ref.
SBG/2/1)

This notebook is, I believe, the next in the sequence of notebooks. The first entry is a pair of lists of projected contents for Part 3 of *Songs of the West*, neither of which is quite correct. The book continues with entries of single collected songs from some of Baring-Gould's early singers (Parsons, Hard, Helmore, Woodridge etc.) This was probably to be a fair copy, but at a later stage Baring-Gould has back-filled many of the verso pages. The penultimate item in the book ('Johnny and Molly' from Roger Luxton) was collected in 1889. Later in the notebook Baring-Gould has started to give some additional versions of the songs on the verso pages. The book also contains a list of the subscribers to Part 1 of *Songs of the West*, which was started on 7 December 1888. There is also a list of the songs published in Parts 1 and a projected list for Part 2 (which corresponds to that published in early editions of Part 1). He has also compiled an index to the notebook by song number and page number, in which he has marked the songs destined for publication. The numbers used do not represent those used in *Songs of the West* and in other manuscripts.

Working Notebook 3
Devon Heritage Centre
Ref 5203 M, Box 36
(VWML Ref.
SBG/2/2)

Working Notebook 3 was the first in which he set out, from the start, to bring all the variants of the songs together as a group. There is still no music. The songs are in the sequence that was used in the first two volumes of *Songs of the West*, with a few small differences that reflect changes in plan. These are often related to songs that are a little bit racier than the general run and I cannot help but wonder if Fleetwood Sheppard vetoed them. After 52 ('The Wreck Off Scilly') the sequence no longer represents that used in *Songs of the West*. The index at the end of the book lists 152 songs, though there are another 8 songs that have not been added to the index. This was, I believe, intended as a fair copy and the standard of writing is quite good throughout. Though there are a few penciled notes and bits of rough working this remains a neat book. It is not possible to date the notebook with any accuracy, since the items are not in date order. The inclusion, towards the end, of items from the visit to Stoke Fleming in January 1893 suggests that this notebook was still in use at that time. There are some letters and song texts from informants and a programme for Baring-Gould's lecture to the Royal Institution in May 1890. The last item in the notebook is a quotation from the letters of Dorothy Osborne with which Baring-Gould introduced the 1905 edition of *Songs of the West* – 'In the common that lay hard by the house, where a great many young wenches keep sheep or cows, and sit in the shade singing ballads'.

Working Notebook 4
Devon Heritage Centre
Ref 5203 M, Box 17
(VWML Ref.
SBG/2/3)

It is not immediately clear what Baring-Gould intended when he started this notebook though it is not, I think, a coincidence that the majority of the items included are ballads, rather than songs. The first 24 items are numbered and it is among these that 13 are marked as having been sent to Francis Child. The songs near the beginning of the book are from the earlier years and a number are dated 1887 though we know that this is not possible. In the second half of the book there are three sets of songs. The first is the group of songs taken down during his tour of Dartmoor and Chagford with Bussell in September 1890. Then there is a set from William Nichols of Whitchurch, dated 29 May 1891. The third group is from John Peake, Liskeard from 27–28 May 1891. Elsewhere Baring-Gould has used the notebook to record some of his own compositions and re-workings. These are undated, though 'Kitty Alone' was used in his novel of that name in 1894 and then published in *A Garland of Country Songs* a few months later. It seems possible that Baring-Gould used this notebook seriously as early as 1890 and then, at intervals, until 1894.

Other Song Notebooks

Baring-
Gould – Child
Correspondence
Harvard University,
Houghton Library
Ref. MS Eng 863
(VWML Digital
Collection lists items but
no images included)

The proper title of this document is 'Baring-Gould Manuscript. Ballads and Songs collected by the Rev. S. Baring-Gould, chiefly in Devonshire, and sent by him to Professor F. J. Child'. It contains the letters and sheets of words (no tunes) which Baring-Gould sent to Francis Child between 1890 and 1893. There is also one unrelated letter written by Baring-Gould to Child in 1880 about an error in one of his books.

As well as a number of song texts the letters contain interesting information about Baring-Gould's thoughts on balladry and on his song collection. Images of the manuscript can be viewed on the Harvard University Library website: <http://tinyurl.com/B-G-Mss-Harvard-Library> [Accessed 26 January 2017].

Emily Baring-
Gould's Nursery
Rhyme Notebook
Devon Heritage Centre
Ref 7834
(VWML Ref.
SBG/2/4)

This charming little book was compiled by Sabine Baring-Gould's aunt Emily in about 1835, when he was a child. It may have been a gift for him. It contains a number of early Victorian nursery rhymes, many of them illustrated by her with drawings in ink and watercolour. She was a competent amateur artist who later specialized in botanical watercolours. Baring-Gould copied some of these nursery rhymes into his Personal Copy manuscript.

The notebook has been recently rebound. The original boards have been retained in a pocket in the new binding.

The 'Additional Notebooks'
Plymouth and West Devon Record Office
(Not in VWML Digital Collection)

Devon Library Services purchased this set of six books at a sale in the 1970s. Two carry the bookplate of Sabine's son, Edward S. Baring-Gould's, and one that of his father, Edward. They include four manuscript music notebooks. The route by which these came to be sold is not known, but they clearly came from the Baring-Gould family collection. The first of these is significant in the present connection.

• 'Manuscript Music Book' (10' x 6', grey-green cloth)

Contains hymns and other sacred music with accompaniments (Mozart, Handel, etc.).

In spare pages in the middle, there is a section of tunes in pencil, including 'Duke William', 'Adam and Woman', 'Now the Corn is All Ripe', 'The Fox Hunt', 'General Wolfe', 'William and Mary his Bride', Jolly Joe the Collier's Son', and others.

In the back are a number of psalm tunes.

• Manuscript music book (10' x 6', Marbled paper). Plate 'Mr E. Baring-Gould'. Inscription 'Teignmouth Sept 1829'. Contains 35 parlour songs including 'Meet me by Moonlight' (1827), 'Oft in the Stilly Night' (c. 1815), 'The Soldier's Tear' (1833), and suchlike.

• Manuscript music book ('The Illustrated Manuscript Book')

In a forward direction the book contains sol-fa notation. In the backward direction it contains a number of songs such as 'Arouse ye sleepers', 'See the Stars', etc which are harder to identify and date.

• 'Music Book' 28 pp.

Inside front cover inscribed 'trebles 1st and 2nd, Probably SB-G's hand. Two hymns by him.

The Annotated Publications

These copies of Baring-Gould's two main song publications, *Songs of the West* and *A Garland of Country Song* have been bound with extra leaves so that Baring-Gould could make notes alongside his published texts. This is an approach that he adopted when he was translating Icelandic sagas, where he has placed his translation and notes opposite the original printed text.

Songs of the West, Annotated Copy (2 Volumes) *(VWML Ref. SBG/1/4 to 7)*	This is a set of the four parts of the first edition of *Songs of the West* which has been bound as two volumes with printed music manuscript paper interleaved between the printed song pages. A number of tunes have been written onto these pages and they appear to be copied from the Personal Copy manuscript.
	This document is useful as a way of comparing tunes printed with what was collected, which was probably Baring-Gould's intention.
A Garland of Country Song, Annotated Copy *(VWML Ref. SBG/1/8)*	Unlike the document above, this volume has 16 lined pages bound behind the book block. In this case Baring-Gould has written out the titles of each of the fifty songs in the book, three to a page. He has not made much use of the book but he has made notes about 17 of the songs.

The Composition Notebooks

These are the notebooks used by Baring-Gould for his own compositions. I have included them for the sake of completeness and because some of these are the song texts that he substituted for the original versions of folk songs that he chose not to use for various reasons. The majority of the texts are for hymns, other songs or verses, some of which were published in magazines.

Composition Notebook 1
Plymouth Central Library [Kept in the Plymouth and West Devon Record Office] (VWML Ref SBG/3/3)

Contains 33 songs or poems written by Baring-Gould. The writing is neat with no crossings out or re-work, so this is probably a fair copy, rather than his draft working. A number of them are texts of songs published by him in *Songs of the West.* The book starts with entries from 1898 and there are others from as late as 1905. The earliest is the last in the book, 'The Marionette Dancer' which is dated 1867.

Composition Notebook 2
Devon Heritage Centre, 5203 M, Box 23 (Not in VWML digital Collection)

This notebook opens with a draft of 'The History of the Crusades'. The second section is titled 'Hymns of Catholick Love' and is a collection of religious poetry and hymns. The texts are undated but several of the early items in the book have, under Baring-Gould's initials, 'Camb.', suggesting that they were written while he was at Cambridge University in the 1850s. One of the hymns is an early draft of 'On the Resurrection Morning', which is thought to have been written at the time of his mother's death. This draft is different in several significant respects from the final version. The last entry but one in the notebook is a record of the Annual Lady Day Vestry Meeting at which details of a new road to be built through the parish was discussed. The final item in the book is an anonymous portrait.

Composition
Notebook 3
Devon Heritage Centre,
5203 M, Box 23
(Not in VWML digital
Collection)

This notebook contains hymns and religious songs written by Baring-Gould, some with music – probably Baring-Gould's compositions. Some of the songs/hymns are familiar from the other books in this group. This, though, appears to be a book in which he drafted the songs. They are written in purple ink with the music on penciled staves. There is a lot of crossing out and rewriting.

Composition
Notebook 4
Devon Heritage Centre,
5203 M, Box 23
(Not in VWML digital
Collection)

Label on spine 'Original Songs'. This is similar in content to Composition Notebook 1 with about 30 items, though it will take some work to establish the exact number as not all have titles. Includes a draft of 'Hail the Sign' which was published in the *Church Times* in 1866. Again, there are a number of differences from the final version.

Appendix D – Baring-Gould's Singers

This appendix lists the 189 singers who have been identified as having contributed songs to the Baring-Gould song collection. They include each of the singers named in the various manuscripts as having sung to Baring-Gould and his colleagues, or identified by those who sent songs by post. There are about 30 other singers who are not identified by name and so could not be included. I have erred on the side of caution when it was not clear that the named person was actually the singer.

Ackford, J: (Unknown), Thrushelton, Devon

Aggett, William: Ag labourer, Chagford, Devon

Agus, William: Sailor (RN Rtd), Horrabridge, Devon

Andrew, William: Farmer, Sheepstor, Devon

Arscott, Charles: Carpenter, South Zeal, Devon

Baker, Matthew: Ag labourer, Lew Down, Devon

Beare, William: Carpenter, Torquay, Devon

Bennett, John: Ag labourer, Chagford, Devon

Bennet, J: (Unknown), Plympton, Devon

Bennet, Thomas: Labourer, South Petherwin, Cornwall

Benney, John: Butcher, Menheniot, Cornwall

Bickle, Ann: Charwoman, Thrushelton, Devon

Bickle, Henry: Tailor, Bridestowe, Devon

Bickle, Richard: (Unknown), Two Bridges, Devon

Bickle, William: (Unknown), Lydford, Devon

Bickle, Samuel: (Unknown), Cheesewring, Cornwall

Bird, William: (Unknown), Okehampton, Devon

Blamey, Mary: Housewife, Upton Pyne, Devon

Bowden, William: Ag labourer, Washfield, Devon

Broad, Richard: Ag labourer, St Keyne, Cornwall

Bunsell, Mr: Bootmaker, Devonport, Devon

Burgoyne, Elizabeth: Housewife, Stoke Fleming, Devon

Burnard, Robert: Factory owner, Plymouth, Devon

Bussell, Frederick: University lecturer, Oxford

Bussell, Mary: Own means, Lew Trenchard, Devon

Cann, Lucy: Housewife, Trusham, Devon

Cann, William: Ag labourer, South Tawton, Devon

Cheriton, Peter: Boot and shoemaker, Oakford, Devon

Chilcote, Betsy: Housewife, Stoke Fleming, Devon

Chowen, John: Surveyor, Bridestowe, Devon

Cleave, Moses: Ag labourer, Huckaby Bridge, Devon

Cleave, Richard: Innkeeper, Huckaby Bridge, Devon

Coaker, Jonas: Retired farmer, Postbridge, Devon

Cole, George: Quarryman, Rundlestone, Devon

Collings, Giles: Quarryman, Lanreath, Cornwall

Collins, John: (Unknown), Fowey, Cornwall

Dacy, Ernest: (Unknown), Lew Down, Devon

Dart, Thomas: Ag labourer, Whitstone, Devon

Davis, J: Licensed victualler, South Brent, Devon

Davis, John: (Unknown), Liskeard, Cornwall

Davy, Henry: Carpenter, Lew Trenchard, Devon

Dearing, William: Coachman, South Zeal, Devon

Dickinson, Harvey: Landowner, Dunsland, Devon

Dingle, Elizabeth: Housewife, Coryton, Devon

Dingle, John: Ag labourer, Coryton, Devon

Dodd, Richard: Coachman, Cornwood, Devon

Doidge, Elizabeth: Maidservant, Calstock, Cornwall

Doidge, George: Ag labourer, Chillaton, Devon

Doidge, J: (Unknown), (Unknown)

Down, James: Blacksmith, Broadwood Widger, Devon

Duke, Emmanuel: Labourer, Thrushelton, Devon

Dustan, Charles: Coachman, Lew Trenchard, Devon

Dyer, Joseph: Ag labourer, Mawgan in Pydar, Cornwall

Dyer, Charles: Dock labourer, Golant, Cornwall

Easterbrook, F: Carpenter/Builder, Holne, Devon

Ellis, James: Farmer, Lamerton, Devon

Fewins, William (Lucky): Labourer, South Zeal, Devon

Fletcher, Mary: Housewife, Lifton, Devon

Fone, Samuel: Mason, Mary Tavy, Devon

Ford, Matthew: Cobbler, Menheniot, Cornwall

Ford, William: Parish Clerk, Holne, Devon

Free, W: (Unknown) Lydford, Devon

Friend, William: Quarryman, Lydford, Devon

Fry, Edmund: Thatcher, Lydford, Devon

Gilbert, Mary: Innkeeper, Mawgan in Pydar, Cornwall

Gilbert, Sam: Innkeeper, Mawgan in Pydar, Cornwall

Glanville, James: Mason, South Zeal, Devon

Glover, (?): (Unknown), Postbridge, Devon

Gregory, Richard: Water Bailiff, Postbridge, Devon

Grimes, William: Innkeeper, Menheniot, Cornwall

Grimes, Ann: Housewife, Menheniot, Cornwall

Haloran, A: Schoolmaster, Kingsbridge, Devon

Hamley, Elizabeth: Farmer's daughter, Lew Trenchard, Devon

Hamley, Lousia: Farmer's daughter, Lew Trenchard, Devon

Hamley, Margaret: Housewife, Lew Trenchard, Devon

Hannaford, Roger: Ag labourer, Widecombe, Devon

Hard, Robert: General labourer, South Brent, Devon

Harris, G: (Unknown), (Unknown)

Hawken, Henry: Own means, Michaelstow, Cornwall

Helmore, John: Miller, South Brent, Devon

Hext, James: Ag labourer, Postbridge, Devon

Hext, John: Shepherd, Postbridge, Devon

Hext, William: (unknown), Two Bridges, Devon

Hingston, Arthur: Farmer, Chillington, Devon

Hingston, T: (Unknown), South Brent, Devon

Hockaday, Sam: Copper miner, Lamerton, Devon

Hockin, J: Ag labourer, Menheniot, Cornwall

Horn, John: Innkeeper, Lydford, Devon

Horn, Richard: Miller, Lew Trenchard, Devon

Horne, William: General labourer, Plympton, Devon

Hoskins, J: General labourer, South Brent, Devon

Houghton, William: Farmer, Charlestown, Cornwall

Huggins, Roger: Mason, Lydford, Devon

Huggins, William: Mason, Lydford, Devon

Hurrell, George: Organist, Chagford, Devon

Isaacs, Peter: Itinerant harness repairer, South Hams, Devon

James, S: (Unknown), Mawgan in Pydar, Cornwall

Jeffrey, Jane: Housewife, Dunterton, Devon

Jerred, Thomas: Ag labourer, Chagford, Devon

Kerswell, William: Farmer, Two Bridges, Devon

Knapman, Mary: Housewife, Kingsweare, Devon

Kneebone, Jane: Housewife, N Petherwin, Cornwall

Laundry, Adam: Wood ranger, Launceston, Cornwall

Langdon, Henry: Carpenter, St Ervan, Cornwall

Langworthy, Mary: Housewife, Stoke Fleming, Devon

Libby, John: Coachman, Tredethy, Cornwall

Lillicrap, J: (Unknown), Shaugh Prior, Devon

Lobb, Ellen: Housewife, Penrose, St Ervan, Cornwall

Lobb, Samuel: Carpenter, Mawgan in Pydar, Cornwall

Lugg, William: Dairyman, Launceston, Cornwall

Lukin, J: (Unknown), (Unknown)

Luxton, Roger: Labourer, Halwell, Devon

Martin, John: Shoemaker, Milton Abbot, Devon

Masters, John: Ag labourer, Bradstone, Devon

Matthews, T: Farmer, South Brent, Devon

Monk, Harry: Butcher, Tavistock, Devon

Morris, Thomas: Mason, Fowey, Cornwall

Mortimore, James: Farmer, Two Bridges, Devon

Mortimore, Richard: Mason, Princetown, Devon

Moyse, John: Farmer, Menheniot, Cornwall

Mutton, William: Farmer, Menheniot, Cornwall

Nankivell, Jane: Housewife, Merrivale, Devon

Nankivell, William: Quarryman, Merrivale, Devon

Nichols, William: Sawyer, Whitchurch, Devon

Old, John: Ag labourer, St Eval, Cornwall

Olver, James: Tanner, Launceston, Cornwall

Paddon, Joseph: Ag Labourer, Holcombe Burnell, Devon

Paddon, Robert: Labourer, Holcombe Burnell, Devon

Painter, Anne: Dressmaker, East Looe, Cornwall

Paynter, Samuel: Maltster, St Ervan, Cornwall

Palmer, J: (Unknown), (Unknown)

Parsons, James: Hedger, Lew Down, Devon

Pascoe, Anthony: Sailor (RN Rtd), Liskeard, Cornwall

Pascoe, J, (Unknown): Two Bridges, Devon

Peake, John: Tanner, Liskeard, Cornwall

Peake, Marianne: Housewife, Liskeard, Cornwall

Pearse, T. F.: (Unknown), Woodovis, Tavistock, Devon

Pengelly, John: Coachman, Lew Down, Devon

Penhallick: (Unknown), (Unknown)

Pepperell, William: Labourer, Kingswear, Devon

Perry, William: Ag Merchant, Lew Down, Devon

Persey, George: Innkeeper, Merrivale, Devon

Pike, William: Farmer, Exbourne, Devon

Pote, Thomas: Sexton, Washfield, Devon

Potter, John: Farmer, Postbridge, Devon

Quarm, Anne: Housewife, Stoke Fleming, Devon

Radford, Daniel: Landowner, Tavistock, Devon

Radford, George: Labourer, Washfield, Devon

Radmore, John: Ag labourer, South Zeal, Devon

Rich, John: Farmer, Horndon, Devon

Rice, William: Ag labourer, Lamerton, Devon

Rickard, John: Farmer/Own means, Lamerton, Devon

Rickard, (?): (Unknown), Launceston, Cornwall

Roberts, Anne: Housewife, Widecombe, Devon

Roe, J: Carpenter, (Unknown)

Rook, James: Mason, Merrivale, Devon

Roseveare, William: Farmer, Quethiock, Cornwall

Sandry, Peter: Farmer, St Ervan, Cornwall

Satterley, Sarah: Nurse, Huckaby Bridge, Devon

Setters, William: Labourer, Two Bridges, Devon

Simons, Henry: Boot and Shoemaker, Fowey, Cornwall

Smith, Henry: Farmer, Two Bridges, Devon

Sprague, William: (Unknown), Stoke Canon, Devon

Stevens, Elizabeth: Charwoman, Stowford, Devon

Stoneman, John: Ag labourer, Chagford, Devon

Sukey, Mary: Charwoman, Lifton, Devon

Symonds, G. D.: Clergyman, (Unknown),

Cornwall

Symons, Philip: Farmer, Jacobstow, Cornwall

Taylor, George: Gas works labourer, Ivybridge, Devon

Taylor, John: (Unknown), Postbridge, Devon

Thorn, Thomas: General labourer, Witheridge, Devon

Tolcher, Anne: Housewife, Wotton Hole, Devon

Townsend, James: Carpenter, Holne, Devon

Treise, Mary: Housewife, Menheniot, Cornwall

Voysey, John: Ag labourer, Lew Down, Devon

Wadge, Henry: Gamekeeper, Lewannick, Cornwall

Watts, John: Quarryman, Thrushelton, Devon

Webb, John: Mine captain, Postbridge, Devon

Westaway, Harry: Farmer, Belstone, Devon

Westaway, Samuel: Bootmaker, South Zeal, Devon

Westlake, J: (Unknown), Plympton, Devon

Westlake Ward, Thomas: Wheelwright, Exbourne, Devon

White, Joseph: (Unknown), Launceston, Cornwall

White, (?): Housewife, Merrivale, Devon

Whitfield, Henry: Brushmaker, Plymouth, Devon

Williams, Louisa: Nurse, Tamar Valley, Devon

Williams, Thomas: (Unknown), Mawgan, Cornwall

Woodridge, John: Labourer, Thrushelton, Devon

Woolridge, John: Labourer, Broadwoodwidger, Devon

Location:

Of the 183 singers whose location is known, 136 (74%) come from Devon and 46 (25%) from Cornwall.

The occupations in this list are summarised in the following table:

Agricultural Labourer	22
Farmer	19
Housewife, Widow	20
General Labourer	16
Carpenter	8
Mason	7
Innkeeper, Licensed victualler	7
Boot/shoe maker, Cobbler,	6
Quarryman	5
Coachman	5
Church: Vicar, Organist, Parish Clerk, Sexton	4
Farm worker: Shepherd, Hedger, Dairyman	3
Gamekeeper, Water Bailiff, Wood Ranger	3
Charwoman	3
Skilled Rural: Blacksmith, Sawyer	2
Farmer's Daughter	2
Miller	2
Miner, Mine Captain	2
Nurse	2
Sailor (RN retired)	2
Tanner	2
Butcher	2
Landowner	2
Living on own means	2
Agricultural Merchant	1
Thatcher	1

Wheelwright	1
Dressmaker	1
Harness Maker	1
Brush maker	1
Tailor	1
Maltster	1
Maidservant	1
Factory Owner	1
Surveyor	1
Schoolmaster	1
University Don	1
Occupation not known	28
Total Number of singers	189

Of the 161 singers whose occupations are known 44 (28%) were farmers, farm labourers or farm workers.

29 (19%) were women, most of whom worked in the home.

Appendix E – Bibliography

Books:

The following books are mentioned in the book or have been consulted during its preparation.

(Anon), *Sir Algernon Methuen, Baronet: A Memoir* (London: Methuen, 1925).

Arthur, Dave, *Bert, The Life and Times of A. L. Lloyd* (London: Pluto Press, in association with EFDSS, 2012).

Ashton, John, *A Century of Ballads* (London: Elliott Stock, 1887).

Ashton, John, *Modern Street Ballads* (London: Chatto and Windus, 1888).

Atkinson, David, 'Sabine Baring-Gould's Contribution to The English and Scottish Popular Ballads' in Cheeseman, Tom and Sigrid Rieuwerts, *Ballads into Books* (Bern: Peter Lang, 1997), pp. 41–52.

Atkinson, David, *The English Traditional Ballad: Theory, Method, and Practice* (Aldershot, Ashgate, 2002).

Baring-Gould, Sabine, *The Path of the Just: Tales of Holy Men and Children* (London: J. Masters, 1854).

Baring-Gould, Sabine, *Iceland, Its Scenes and Sagas* (London: Smith, Elder & Co., 1863).

Baring-Gould, Sabine, *The Book of Werewolves* (London: Smith, Elder & Co., 1865).

Baring-Gould, Sabine, *Through Flood and Flame*, 3 vols (London: Bentley, 1868).

Baring-Gould, Sabine, *Silver Store collected from Medieval, Christian and Jewish Mines* (London: Longmans, 1868).

Baring-Gould, Sabine, *Curiosities of Olden Times* (London: Hayes, 1869).

Baring-Gould, Sabine, *The Origin and Development of Religious Belief* (London: Rivingtons, 1869–70), 2 vols.

Baring-Gould, Sabine, *Lives of the Saints*, 15 vols (London: John Hodges, 1872 – 1877).

Baring-Gould, Sabine, *Yorkshire Oddities, Incidents and Strange Events* (London: John Hodges, 1874).

Baring-Gould, Sabine, 'Introduction' to Richard Chope, *Carols for use in Church* (London: William Clowes and Sons, 1875) pp. iii–xv.

Baring-Gould, Sabine, *Germany, Past and Present* (London: C. Kegan Paul, 1879).

Baring-Gould, Sabine, *Mehalah, A Story of the Salt Marshes* (London: Smith, Elder and Co., 1880).

Baring-Gould, Sabine, Henry Fleetwood Sheppard, Henry, *Church Songs, Series 1 and 2* (London, W Skeffington and Son, 1884).

Baring-Gould, Sabine, and Henry Fleetwood Sheppard, *Songs of the West*, 4 parts:
Part 1, London: Patey and Willis, 1889.
Part 2, London: Patey and Willis, 1889.

Part 3, London: Methuen, Patey and Willis, 1890.

Part 4, London: Methuen, Patey and Willis, 1891.

Baring-Gould, Sabine, and Henry Fleetwood Sheppard, *Songs of the West*, single volume (London: Methuen, Patey and Willis, 1891).

Baring-Gould, Sabine, and Cecil J. Sharp, *Songs of the West* (London Methuen and Co, 1905).

Baring-Gould, Sabine, *Old Country Life* (London: Methuen, 1889).

Baring-Gould, Sabine, *The Pennycomequicks* (London: Spencer Blackett and Hallam, 1889).

Baring-Gould, Sabine, *Grettir the Outlaw* (London: Blackie and Son, 1890).

Baring-Gould, Sabine, *Arminell: a Social Romance* (London: Methuen, 1890).

Baring-Gould, Sabine, *In the Roar of the Sea: a Tale of the Cornish Coast* (London: Methuen, 1892).

Baring-Gould, Sabine, *Mrs Curgenven of Curgenven* (London: Methuen, 1893).

Baring-Gould, Sabine, *A Book of Nursery Songs and Rhymes* (London: Methuen, 1894).

Baring-Gould, Sabine, and Henry Fleetwood Sheppard, *A Garland of Country Song* (London: Methuen, 1895).

Baring-Gould, Sabine, *A Book of Fairy Tales* (London: Methuen, 1895).

Baring-Gould, Sabine, 'Preface' in (Anon), *Fairy Tales from Grimm* (London: Wells, Gardner, Darton, 1894).

Baring-Gould, Sabine, *The Icelander's Sword, or, The Story of Oraefa-Dal* (London: Methuen, 1894).

Baring-Gould, Sabine, 'Colour in Composition', in (Anon), *On the Art of Writing Fiction* (London: Wells Gardner Darton & Co., 1894).

Baring-Gould, Sabine, Henry Fleetwood Sheppard, Frederick Bussell, and W. H. Hopkinson, *English Minstrelsie*, 8 vols (Edinburgh: T. C. and E. C. Jack, 1895 – 97).

Baring-Gould, Sabine, *An Old English Home* (London: Methuen, 1898).

Baring-Gould, Sabine, *A Book of the West, vol. 1, Devon* (London: Methuen, 1899).

Baring-Gould, Sabine, *A Book of the West, vol. 2, Cornwall* (London: Methuen, 1899).

Baring-Gould, Sabine, *A Book of Dartmoor* (London: Methuen, 1900).

Baring-Gould, Sabine, *A Book of Folklore* (London: Collins, 1905).

Baring Gould, Sabine, and Cecil J. Sharp, *English Folk Songs for Schools* (London: Curwen, 1906).

Baring-Gould, Sabine, *Devonshire Characters and Strange Events* (London: John Lane, 1908).

Baring-Gould, Sabine, *The Church Revival* (London: Methuen, 1914).

Baring-Gould, Sabine, *Early Reminiscences, 1834 – 1864* (London: John Lane The Bodley Head, 1923).

Baring-Gould, Sabine, *Further Reminiscences, 1864 – 1894* (London: John Lane The Bodley Head, 1925).

Barrett, William A., *English Folk Songs* (London: Novello, 1891).

Bell, Robert, *Early Ballads Illustrative of History, Traditions and Customs, also Ballads and Songs of the Peasantry of England* (London: George Bell and Sons, 1877).

Bonham, Valerie, *A Joyous Service: The Clewer Sisters and Their Work* (Cuddesdon: CSJB Books, 2012).

Bradley, Ian, *The Daily Telegraph Book of Carols* (London: Continuum, 2006).

Breeze, George, Niky Rathbone, and Glennys Wild, *Arthur and Georgie Gaskin* (Birmingham: Birmingham Museums and Art Gallery, 1981), [Exhibition Catalogue].

Briggs, Cicely, *The Mana of Lew* (Pulborough: Praxis Books, 1993).

Bristow, Roger, *The Works of Sabine Baring-Gould: A Bibliography* (Sidmouth: Roger Bristow, 2016).

Broadwood, Lucy and John A. Fuller Maitland, *English County Songs* (London: Leadenhall Press, 1893).

Broadwood, Lucy, *English Traditional Songs and Carols* (London: Boosey and Co., 1908).

Bronson, Bertrand Harris, *The Traditional Tunes of the Child Ballads*, 4 vols (Princeton: Princeton University Press, 1959–72).

Brown, Mary Ellen, *Child's Unfinished Masterpiece: The English and Scottish Popular Ballads* (Urbana: University of Illinois Press, 2011).

Browne, J. Ross, *The Land of Thor* (New York: Harper & Brother, 1867).

Buchan, John, *Memory Hold-the-Door* (London, Hodder and Stoughton, 1940).

Bussell, Frederick, *Christian Theology and Social Progress: The Bampton Lectures for 1905* (London: Methuen & Co., 1907).

Bussell, Frederick, *A New Government for the British Empire* (London: Longmans, Green and Co., 1912).

Carey, George, *A Sailor's Songbag: An American Rebel in an English Prison, 1777–1779* (Amherst: University of Massachusetts Press, 1976).

Canton, James, *Out of Essex: Re-imagining a Literary Landscape* (Oxford: Signal Books, 2013).

Causley, Charles, *Collected Poems for Children* (London: Macmillan, 1996).

Chappell, William, *Popular Music of the Olden Time* (London: Chappell and Co., 1859).

Child, Francis J., *The English and Scottish Popular Ballads*. 10 vols (Boston: Houghton Mifflin Company, 1882 – 98).

Child, Francis J., Mark F. Heiman, Laura Saxton Heiman (Eds.), *The English and Scottish Popular Ballads, Corrected Second Edition* (Minnesota: Loomis House Press, 2002).

Coleman, Hilary and Sally Burley, *Shout Kernow: Celebrating Cornwall's Pub Songs* (London: Francis Boutle, 2015).

Combs, Josiah P., *Folk Songs of the Southern United States* (Austin: University of Texas Press, 1967).

Cook, Nicholas, *Music: A Very Short Introduction* (Oxford: Oxford University Press, 2011).

Cox, Gordon, *A History of Music Education in England 1872 – 1928* (Aldershot, Scolar Press, 1993).

De Val, Dorothy, *In Search of Song: The Life and Times of Lucy Broadwood* (Farnham: Ashgate, 2011).

Dean-Smith, Margaret, *A Guide to English Folk Song Collections* (Liverpool: University Press of Liverpool (in association with EFDSS), 1954).

Dickinson, Bickford H. C., *Sabine Baring-Gould: Squarson, Writer and Folklorist 1834 – 1924* (Newton Abbot: David and Charles, 1970).

Dorson, Richard, *The British Folklorists: A History* (London: Routledge and Kegan Paul, 1968).

Duffy, Maureen, *A Thousand Capricious Chances: A History of the Methuen List 1889 – 1989* (London: Methuen, 1989).

Dunstan, Ralph, *The Cornish Song Book: Lyver Canow Kernewek* (London: Reid Bros., 1929).

Dunstan, Ralph, *Cornish Dialect and Folk Songs* (London: Reid Bros., 1932).

Farmer, Henry George, *Bernard Shaw's Sister and her Friends, A New Angle on G. B. S.* (Leiden: E. J. Brill, 1959).

Fleetwood Sheppard, Henry, *Three English Rustic Songs for Harvest Homes* (London: Novello, Ewer & Co, 1877).

Fox Strangways, Arthur, and Maud Karpeles, *Cecil Sharp* (Oxford: Oxford University Press, 1933), also Karpeles only, 1955 and 1967.

Games, Stephen (Ed.), *Trains and Buttered Toast* (London: John Murray, 2006).

George, Henry, *An Attempt to show that our Nursery Rhyme, "The House that Jack built" is an historical allegory, portraying eventful periods in England's history since the time of Harold* (London: Griffin and Farren, 1862).

Gibson, Anthony, *With Magic in my Eyes: West Country Literary Landscapes* (Bath: Fairfield Books, 2011).

Graebe, Martin, 'Sabine Baring-Gould and his old Singing Men', in *Folk Song: Tradition, Revival and Re-Creation*, ed. Ian Russell, and David Atkinson (Aberdeen: Elphinstone Institute, University of Aberdeen, 2004), pp. 175–94.

Graebe, Martin, 'I'd have you to buy it and learn it': Sabine Baring-Gould, his Fellow Collectors, and Street Literature', in *Street Ballads in Nineteenth-Century Britain, Ireland, and North America*, ed. Atkinson, David and Steve Roud, (Farnham: Ashgate, 2014), pp. 173–94.

Gregory, E. David, *Victorian Songhunters* (Lanham, MD: Scarecrow Press, 2006).

Gregory, E. David, *The Late Victorian Song Revival* (Lanham, MD: Scarecrow Press, 2010).

Gundry, Inglis, *Canow Kernow: Songs and Dances from Cornwall* (N.P.: Federation of Old Cornwall Societies, 1966)

Hahn, Jacob von, *Griechische und Albanescische Märchen* (Leipzig: Wilhelm Engelmann, 1864).

Halliwell, James Orchard, *Popular Rhymes and Nursery Tales* (London: John Russell Smith, 1849).

Harker, Dave, *Fakesong: The manufacture of British 'folksong' 1700 to the present day* (Milton Keynes: Open University Press, 1985).

Henderson, William, *Notes on the Folk-Lore of the Northern Counties of England and the Borders. With an Appendix on Household Stories by S. Baring-Gould* (London: Longmans, Green and Co., 1866), and second edition (London: W. Satchell, Peyton and Co., for the Folk-Lore Society, 1879).

Herbert, Trevor (Ed.), *The British Brass Band: A Musical and Social History* (Oxford, Oxford University Press, 2000).

Hill, Geoffry, *Wiltshire Folk Songs and Carols* (Bournemouth: W. Mate, 1904).

Kennedy, Peter, *Folk Songs of Britain and Ireland* (London: Oak Publications, 1975).

Ker, John Bellenden, *An Essay on the Archaeology of Our Popular Phrases and Nursery Rhymes* (London: Longman and Co., 1837).

Kidson, Frank, *Old English Country Dances Gathered from Scarce Printed Collections and from Manuscripts* (London: William Reeves, 1890).

Kidson, Frank, *Traditional Tunes: A Collection of Ballad Airs* (Oxford: Chas. Taphouse, 1891).

Kilgarriff, Michael, *Sing Us One of the Old Songs: A Guide to Popular Song 1860 – 1920* (Oxford: Oxford University Press, 1998).

King, Peter, *Hurstpierpoint College 1849 – 1995: The School by the Downs* (Chichester: Phillimore, 1997).

Kirk-Smith, Harold, *Now the Day Is Over: The life and Times of Sabine Baring-Gould 1834 – 1924* (Boston: Richard Kay, 1997).

Lakeman, Joy, *Them Days: From the memories of Joan Bellan* (Padstow: Tabb House, 1982).

Lister, Keith, *Half My Life* (Horbury: Charnwood Publications, 2002).

Lloyd, A. L., *The Singing Englishman* (London: Workers Music Association, 1944).

Lloyd, A. L., *Folk Song in England* (London, Lawrence and Wishart, 1967).

Luzel, François-Marie, *Chansons de la Basse Bretagne* (Paris: Emile Bouillon, 1890).

Marsden, Philip, *Rising Ground: A Search for the Spirit of Place* (London: Granta Books, 2014).

Monk, S. Gordon, *Lew House, Lew Trenchard Church and Baring-Gould*, (Plymouth: (The Author), 1961).

Nathan, Hans, *Dan Emmett and the Rise of Early Negro Minstrelsy* (Norman; University of Oklahoma Press, 1962).

Palmer, Roy (ed.), *Room for Company* (Cambridge: University Press, 1971).

Palmer, Roy (ed.), *The Rambling Soldier* (Harmondsworth: Penguin Books, 1979).

Pearsall, Ronald, *Victorian Popular Music* (Newton Abbot: David and Charles, 1973).

Purcell, William, *Onward Christian Soldier: A Life of Sabine Baring-Gould: Parson, Squire, Novelist, Antiquary, 1834 – 1924* (London, Longmans, Green and Co., 1957).

Rebecca Tope, *Sabine Baring-Gould, The Man Who Told a Thousand Stories* (Walterstone: Praxis Books, 2017).

Reeves, James, *The Idiom of the People: English Traditional Verse from the Mss of Cecil Sharp* (London: Heinemann, 1958).

Reeves, James, *The Everlasting Circle: English Traditional Verse from the Mss of S. Baring-Gould, H. E. D. Hammond and George B. Gardiner* (London: Heinemann, 1960).

Reynardson, Herbert Birch, and Lucy Broadwood, *Sussex Songs: Popular Songs of Sussex* (London: Lucas & Weber, 1890).

Rice, Jo and Tim, Paul Gambaccini, and Mike Read, *The Guinness Book of Hit Singles* (GRRR Books Ltd. and Guinness Superlatives Ltd., 1983), Fourth edition.

Richards, Sam, and Tish Stubbs, *The English Folksinger* (Glasgow and London: Collins, 1979).

Rimbault, Edward, *Musical Illustrations of Bishop Percy's Reliques of Ancient English Poetry* (London: Cramer, Beale and Co., 1850).

Rothenstein, William, *Oxford Characters: Twenty-Four Lithographs* (London: John Lane, 1896).

Roud, Steve and Julia Bishop (Eds), *The New Penguin Book of Folk Songs* (London: Penguin, 2012).

Sandys, William, *Christmas Carols Ancient and Modern* (London: Richard Beckley, 1833)

Sharp, Cecil J., *A Book of British Song for Home and School* (London: John Murray, 1902).

Sharp, Cecil J. and Charles Marson, *Folk Songs from Somerset* 5 vols (London, Simpkin, Schott; Taunton: Barnicott and Pearce, 1904–1909).

Sharp, Cecil J., *English Folk Song: Some Conclusions* (London: Simpkin; Novello, Taunton: Barnicott and Pearce, 1907).

Sharp, Cecil J., *The Country Dance Book* (London: Novello, 1909).

'S. E.' ('Sister Emma', Emma Waring), *Peeps into an old Playground* (Lyme Regis: Dunster, 1865).

Stanford, Charles Villiers, *The National Song Book* (London: Boosey and Co., 1906).

Sutcliffe, David, *The Keys of Heaven: The Life of Revd Charles Marson, Socialist Priest and Folk Song Collector* (Nottingham: The Russell Press, 2010).

Thomas, J. E., *Sabine Baring-Gould, The Life and Work of a Complete Victorian* (Stroud: Fonthill Media, 2015).

Trezize, Simon, *The West Country as a Literary Invention: Putting Fiction in its place* (Exeter: University of Exeter Press, 2000).

Vaughan Williams, Ralph, and A. L. Lloyd, *The Penguin Book of English Folk Songs* (Harmondsworth: Penguin Books, 1959).

Vaughan Williams, Ralph, and A. L. Lloyd, Malcolm Douglas (Eds.), *Classic English Folk Songs*, London: EFDSS, 2nd Edition, 2009.

Wardroper, John, *Lovers, Rakes and Rogues: A new garner of love-songs and merry verses, 1580 to 1830* (London: Shelfmark Books, 1995).

Wawman, Ronald, *Never Completely Submerged: The story of the Squarson of Lewtrenchard as revealed by 'The Diary of Sabine Baring-Gould'* (Guildford: Grosvenor House, 2009).

Wawn, Andrew, *The Vikings and the Victorians: Inventing the North in Nineteenth Century Britain* (Woodbridge: D.S. Brewer, 2000).

Wawn, Andrew, 'The Grimms, The Kirk-Grims, and Sabine Baring-Gould' in Andrew Wawn (Ed.), *Constructing Nations, Reconstructing Myth: Essays in honour of T. A. Shippay* (Turnhout: Brepols, 2007).

Weeks, Barbara, *The Book of Lydford* (Tiverton: Halsgrove, 2004).

Wilgus, D. K., *Anglo-American Folksong Scholarship Since 1898* (New Brunswick, Rutgers University Press, 1959).

Wilson, John Marius, *Imperial Gazetteer of England and Wales* (Edinburgh: A Fullarton and Co., 1870)

Wyatt-Edgell, Arthur, *A Collection of Soldiers' Songs with Music* (Exeter: Eland, 1871).

Journals, Magazines, and Newspapers

Articles from the following journals and magazines have been identified in references in the book.

The Anti-Jocobin Review
Archaeologia
Bradford Observer
Bury and Norwich Post
Church Times
Chambers's Journal
The Cornishman
Edinburgh Evening News
English Dance and Song
E.F.D.S. News (1921 – 36)
English Illustrated Magazine
The Era
Exeter Flying Post
Folk Music Journal (1965 – 2016)
Folk Review
Glasglow Herald
Grey River Argus
Hull Daily Mail
Illustrated London News
Journal of Material Culture
Journal of the English Folk Dance and Song Society (1932 – 64)
Journal of the Folk Song Society (1898 – 1931)
Leeds Mercury
London Daily News
The Lute
Methodist Recorder
Mexborough and Swinton Times
The Monthly Musical Record
Morning Post
Musical Opinion and Music Trade Review
Musical Times
North Bucks Times
Notes and Queries
The Queen
Ralph Vaughan Williams Society Journal
Sabine Baring-Gould Appreciation Society Newsletter

The Saturday Review	*Transactions of the Sabine Baring-Gould*
School Music Review	*Appreciation Society*
Sheffield and Rotherham Independent	*Treasury, The*
St James Gazette	*Wells Journal*
St Paul Globe	*Western Antiquary*
The Stage	*Western Mercury*
Surrey Mirror	*Western Morning News*
Tavistock Gazette	*Western Times*
Telegraph, The	*Yorkshire Weekly Post*
Transactions of the Devonshire Association	

Manuscript collections:

The following manuscript collections have been consulted and are referred to in the book:

Cambridge (MA), Houghton Library, Harvard University, Baring-Gould Manuscripts.

Exeter, Devon Heritage Centre, Sabine Baring-Gould Papers.

London, Vaughan Williams Memorial Library, Manuscripts of Lucy Etheldred Broadwood, Anne Gilchrist, George Gardiner, Cecil Sharp, and Ralph Vaughan Williams.

London, British Library, Ralph Vaughan Williams Manuscript Collection.

Nottingham, Nottinghamshire Archives, Marianne Mason Manuscript Collection

Plymouth, Plymouth Central Library, Baring-Gould Collection.

Woking, Surrey History Centre, Lucy Broadwood Correspondence and Papers.

Thanks

The number of people who have given help, encouragement, and information to me over the years is enormous and if I have left anyone out I sincerely apologise. My errors and wrong conclusions are not their responsibility.

Particular thanks for help in creating this book are due to:

Merriol Almond, for encouragement and support from the very beginning.

David Atkinson, for preparing the index to the book and for information and advice given during the project.

Julia Bishop, for her erudite study of the music of Baring-Gould's collection and other excellent advice.

Roger Bristow, whose bibliography of Baring-Gould has been an essential tool and for the map of the distribution of the singers.

James Ferguson, of Signal Books, for making it happen.

Vic Gammon, for reading the draft of the book and making many helpful comments.

Christine Molan, for the cover illustration.

Graham Naylor of Plymouth Library, for his enthusiastic help in digging out the unexpected from their collection.

Steve Roud, for the foreword and for much appreciated advice.

Ron Wawman, for his outstanding work on Baring-Gould's diaries and letters.

Paul Wilson and Marilyn Tucker for sharing the path and to Wren Music for the use of the digital images of the manuscripts.

Lewtrenchard Manor Hotel (Sue, James, and Duncan Murray and their staff) for practical help and providing a comfortable and peaceful refuge when needed.

Other people who have helped me on my way include:

Ollie Angus Douglas, Peter Barnes, Valerie Bonham, Elaine Bradtke, Tom Brown, Suzi Clayton, John Dyer, Matthew Edwards, Christine Faunch, Pat Fone, John Francmanis, Debbie Friese, Steve Gardham, Tom Greeves, Nick Groom, Moira Harris, Mike Heaney, Elizabeth Henderson, Steve Jordan, Toni Kemeny, Arthur Knevett, Keith Lister, Brendan Lynn, Ian Maxted, Denise

Melhuish, Graham Morley, Caroline Oates, Mike O'Connor, Julian Onderdonk, John Paddon, Joanne Parker, Joan Passey, Jackie and Bob Patten, Sigrid Rieuwerts, Bill Rothon, Tony Rudall, David Shacklock, Laura Smyth, Malcolm Taylor, Debby Thacker, Nick Wall, Charles Walters, Andrew Wawn, Peta Webb, Barbara Weeks, Philip Weller.

This is a project that has taken many years to complete and some of the people who helped me greatly have passed on. I cannot thank them in this book (though I did so in their lifetimes) but I must acknowledge their contribution and record my appreciation for their help and inspiration.

Christopher Bearman	Dorothy Hodges
Ray Cowell	Peter Kennedy
Malcolm Douglas	Roy Palmer
David Eckersley	Cyril Tawney

Libraries and Archives visited

My work on Baring-Gould's song collection has taken me to some wonderful libraries and archives, all of them staffed by clever, helpful people. They are:

Birmingham Museums and Art Gallery, The British Library, Brasenose College Archive, Devon Heritage Centre, Exeter University Library (Heritage Collections), Houghton Library (Harvard University), John Rylands Library, The Library of Congress, Museum of English Rural Life, National Library of Wales, Nottinghamshire Archives, Plymouth and West Devon Records Office, Plymouth City Library, Royal Institution of Cornwall (Courtney Library), Somerset Heritage Centre, Surrey History Centre, Vaughan Williams Memorial Library, The Wellcome Institute, The West Country Studies Library.

And –

I could not have completed this book without the constant, loving support of my wife, Shan Graebe. She has read the text several times and tempered my more intemperate comments as well as correcting some of my many errors. She also provided the musical examples. Baring-Gould brought us together in the first place – for which I am profoundly grateful. Thank you, Shan, with all my heart.

Index